Imperialism, Neoliberalism and Social Struggles in Latin America

Studies in Critical Social Sciences

Series Editor

DAVID FASENFEST
College of Urban, Labor and Metropolitan Affairs
Wayne State University

VOLUME 7

Imperialism, Neoliberalism and Social Struggles in Latin America

Edited by

Richard A. Dello Buono and José Bell Lara

BRILL

LEIDEN • BOSTON
2007

Cover design: Wim Goedhart

Photos: We would like to acknowledge the following photographers for their permission to reproduce the photos included in this book. Our thanks to Andrés Lofiego of La Tripa Collective in Buenos Aires who provided a shot from his outstanding collection on worker's self-managed factories in Argentina. More are on display at http://www. argentina.indymedia.org/news/2004/11/238810.php Hector Planes of the World Data Service in Havana provided us with various first hand shots from Cuba. We also thank Prensa Latina for offering a portion of their photo bank up for public use. The photo of Andre Gunder Frank is printed with permission and formerly appeared on Frank's web site.

This book is printed on acid-free paper.

Library of Congress Cataloging-in-Publication Data

LC Control No.: 2006049205

ISSN   1573-4234
ISBN-13: 978 90 04 15365 3
ISBN-10: 90 04 15365 9

© Copyright 2007 by Koninklijke Brill NV, Leiden, The Netherlands.
Koninklijke Brill NV incorporates the imprints Brill Academic Publishers, Martinus Nijhoff Publishers and VSP.

PRINTED IN THE NETHERLANDS

DEDICATED TO THE "CUBAN FIVE"

Gerardo Hernández
Ramón Labañino
Antonio Guerrero
Fernando González
René González

AND THE HEMISPHERIC MOVEMENT DETERMINED TO FREE THEM
FROM AN UNJUST IMPRISONMENT IN THE U.S.

Contents

Acknowledgments

Working across diverse academic, political and cultural realities presented special challenges for the production of this collection. The editors would like to thank the *Studies in Critical Social Sciences* series editor David Fasenfest for his assistance, encouragement and many helpful suggestions. We also wish to thank Eugenio Espinoza for his help in translating Emir Sader's work from the Portuguese original. A. Kathryn Stout graciously helped with the indexing and proofing of the text. Finally, we thank the entire professional staff at Brill for their fine craftsmanship.

Preface

Imperialism, Neoliberalism and Social Struggles in Latin America is a book about the present realities and future prospects for the Americas that every observer of the region is sure to welcome. This is so as much for the topics selected for reflection as for its academic rigour and exercise of critical and emancipatory thought. The articles compiled by Richard A. Dello Buono and José Bell Lara articulate a complementary logic of conceptual approaches and empirical experiences, organised into separate sections on Neoliberal Crises, Leftist Development Strategies and the Contradictions of Domination and Resistance.

The search for real alternatives to neoliberal thought and practise requires that serious efforts be made to deconstruct the "natural," "inevitable" and "unchangeable" camouflage of this hegemonic discourse and to challenge at its foundations its role in legitimating an insidious social order. In this sense, the book incorporates solid arguments for demonstrating the failures of neoliberal and dependent capitalism around the region at the same time that it helps reveal its theoretical and practical exhaustion as it continues to operate in the interests of transnational capital and its allies.

The historical patterns of exploitation and domination, the cumulative results of the application of reforms associated with the Washington Consensus, and the deepening crisis of the traditional political parties and democratic governability all require an objective analysis of the social actors and changing configuration of the popular yearning for change found across the continent. Readers of this book will be encouraged to ponder the diversity and complexities of social resistance, of popular struggles and ongoing political processes, and of the search for alternatives to the social, economic, political and cultural model of neoliberalism.

Reading this book produces timely reflections. Resistance cannot be reduced simply to protest as a set of social group actions that temporarily break norms in order to express its demands or pressure the state for action at various levels. Nor should it be solely identified with a defensive digging in at the local or sectoral level where it can subsequently be worn down over time or spend itself out in partial solutions. If it wants to *be*, resistance must combine tactical quotas and strategies with a vision that contemplates the possibility of offensive action as a means of expressing itself politically.

From a radical perspective in the tradition of José Martí, something synonymous with going to the root of the matter, the central core of resistance must ultimately be based in the liberation of human beings from all forms of oppression, domination and alienation. In Marx's words, it means to struggle to "overturn all the conditions under which the human being is despised, abandoned, diminished, enslaved."

Following this same logic, another ongoing debate comes under consideration in this book, namely, the relationship between the political and the social. On not just a few occasions, the concern for maintaining the identities and indispensable autonomy of social movements leads them down the path of non-involvement with the very political processes they are contributing to opening. Similarly, they fail to seek out the alliances necessary to join forces in order to bring about structural changes. It is absolutely essential to comprehend the endogenous relationship between the political and the social. It was also Marx who pointed out in the final lines of the *Poverty of Philosophy*, "Do not say that social movement excludes political movement. There is never a political movement which is not at the same time social. It is only in an order of things in which there are no more classes and class antagonisms that social evolutions will cease to be political revolutions."

Coming from that conceptual point of view and given the real tension between resistance and emancipation, it's worth asking: Can the various discourses of resistance be considered real expressions of emancipation? What are the limits and prospects for emancipation within the whole range of new social movements and popular struggles?

In identifying the responses to this question as to whether it is possible or not to think and act in terms of an alternative, the book considered different projects of leftist social transformation in the region that ranged from the search of a solution to the problems of development to testing formulas for confronting the problems of poverty, marginality and inequality. Brazil, Uruguay, Venezuela and Cuba are among the national experiences that are included. Clearly, this is a highly complex and multifaceted problem as well as a timely and opportune one.

A balance of the advances and setbacks on the part of the region's centre-left governments essentially concludes that these forces tended to end up siding with continuity of the system in its neoliberal form albeit with social reforms. In these cases, there is no break with the neoclassical economic model much less proposing any form of socialism as a societal paradigm. To the contrary, such efforts project the ideal of a "more balanced and humane capitalism" that combines neoliberal economic rationality and programmes with an attenuation of the social debt in their countries. They support an open regionalism of integration and Latin American cooperation from a more pragmatic perspective rather than on account of any shared ideological commitment.

The fight against poverty and inequality from a neoliberal, "free market" discourse and the second generation reforms of public policies envisioned by the centre-left governments can result, without doubt, in certain specific benefits for its peoples, including for the most excluded elements. The reforms and changes carried out within these limits, however, do not constitute any alternative to Latin American neoliberalism. The real confrontation of the economic crisis and its impact on the social debt of the peoples of this region must inevitably move to reject the structural reforms imposed by the Washington Consensus that have scorched Latin American and Caribbean economies and societies, leading them to the present state of affairs.

If the fight against poverty and social inequality were to remain definitively outside of any prospects for confronting the classist policies of capital, it would remain doomed as another failed attempt at reformism. So long as the larger objective and subjective conditions remain fundamentally unchanged, there is a historical need for any emerging alternative to neoliberalism to swim directly against the current of big capital dynamics, of the desires and interests of the powerful and imperial neighbour to the north. On the other hand, radical reforms if they want to *be* must assume in consecutive or simultaneous order, the anti-imperialist defence of independence and sovereignty and the paradigmatic objective of socialism, given that capitalism in whatever form it is found has demonstrated its incapacity to resolve the serious problems that plaque humanity.

In sum, the book *Imperialism, Neoliberalism and Social Struggles in Latin America* offers a solid critique of the worldview and epochal common sense fabricated by neoliberal hegemonic thought, analysing the crisis of the model while and at the same time providing a collective voice from within academia for the refounding of the Americas. Cuban socialism, the Bolivarian Revolution of Venezuela and the triumph of Evo Morales in Bolivia mark a step forward in this process of change.

Dr. Adalberto Ronda Varona
Director, Centre for Studies of the Americas (CEA)
Havana, Cuba

Cuban Emergency Aid arrives to Guatemala in 2005 following flood disaster

Richard A. Dello Buono and José Bell Lara
NeoLiberalism and Resistance in Latin America

The changes in the capitalist world system during
the last two decades of the Twentieth Century not
only transformed the post-WW II international order
but also fuelled a process of systemic re-structuration,
giving rise to what today is referred to as globalisation. This complex process deepened the structurally
conditioned dependency of the underdeveloped
countries, particularly in Latin America, where external debt became converted into the articulating element of a consolidated mechanism of dependency.
More sophisticated than earlier forms of neo-colonial
domination, this evolving historical formation annuls
any real possibility of development. It compels nations
to engage in the act of compliance with "legitimate"
commitments associated with servicing a debt that
has no apparent relationship with a nation's established development goals.

The impossibility of repaying the foreign debt and
the recurrent crises resulting from meeting debt
service payments have produced processes of renegotiation that are in essence political-economic interventions. They are carried out through international
financial institutions such that the economic policies
of the indebted countries can be dictated to and
thereby moulded into the purest possible forms

of neoliberalism. In short, the external debt has constituted the preferred agent for the implantation of neoliberal policies across the whole of Latin America.[1]

But it must be understood that this was not entirely a process imposed from abroad. There were powerful "national" interests in Latin America that helped give rise to these debts and their stakeholders have figured prominently among its principal beneficiaries. These are the transnational fractions of the local bourgeoisie, i.e., groups organically linked to the economic reorientation towards export driven expansion. Along with financial groups, high-level bureaucrats tied to international agencies, and other fractions, they constitute a consolidated elite of collaborators with the agents of globalised capital.

Of course, this did not all occur solely on an economic terrain. Rather, it was parallel to a political and ideological offensive that presented the neoliberal model as the "only possible alternative," while dictatorships and authoritarian governments were busily repressing and orchestrating the disarticulation of the popular movement.

At the global level, the triumph of neoliberalism coincided with the dismantling of the model of socialism that had existed in Eastern Europe and the Soviet Union. Both processes had a devastating effect upon the Left. Having lost an important ideological point of political reference, the popular forces fell into a kind of coma. This was particularly acute among those wedded to an ideology that the Soviet model constituted the one and only model of socialism. Indeed, the collapse of Soviet socialism became presented as the conclusive evidence of the non-viability of a socialist alternative. The epigones of capital did not tire of proclaiming the end of socialism and in this sense it was no coincidence that the pages penned by an obscure functionary of the US State Department entitled *The End of History* became transformed into an international best seller.

The objective of this type of message was to win hearts and minds over to the idea that there existed no alternative to capitalism. Meanwhile, successive

---

[1] The most paradoxical aspect of this, as Osvaldo Martínez points out, is that Latin America over the 1995–2004 period made debt service payments of US$1.554 trillion and at the close of 2004 still owed US$723 billion. Over a ten year period, the region paid more than double of what it owes.

waves of structural adjustment programmes swept across the continent, consolidating the reign of neoliberalism. During its glory years, legislation was continually promulgated to promote and protect the rights of capital, providing for its concentration. In collusion with transnational capital, it managed to weaken the popular classes through policies that systematically made work more precarious, increased unemployment, underemployment and invariably impoverished large sectors of the population, including a significant portion of the middle classes.

The state apparatus became largely reformulated, in reality, a counter-reform that led to the privatisation of public enterprises, the elimination of agencies and administrative organisms, the commoditisation of basic social services and the implementation of regressive taxation reforms. All such policies were justified under the pretext of providing greater facilities for capital in order to attract new investments.

As a whole, this process can be comprehended as an internalisation of neoliberalism into the structures of our societies, or perhaps more graphically, a kind of straightjacket that restrains society and compels it to operate within specific structural limits. This application of the neoliberal programme engendered long term effects, not only because it has orchestrated a correlation of forces more favourable to capital, but also because its application has induced structural changes, reshaping the social class composition of the entire continent.

If indeed the spectrum of the exploited has grown quantitatively, it has also experienced qualitative changes. These include the reduction of the industrial working class, an extraordinary growth of the informal sector, downward social mobility resulting from the impoverishment of broad sectors of the middle class, the decline of the public sector and state employment, an increasingly precarious structure of employment, and a substantial loss of purchasing power on the part of wage workers. The number of female head of households has grown and broad sectors of young people and students are living in frustrating situations with an uncertain future. Meanwhile, the advance of agribusiness in the countryside has aggravated the problem of land distribution and rural poverty, further intensifying the migration of peasants to urban areas.

This deteriorating quality of life has harvested a wave of mass social protests that has overrun the traditional scheme of politics (political parties and trade unions), fuelling social movements whose protagonists are those largely excluded and most damaged by neoliberal policies (unemployed, retired, youth, indigenous peoples and sectors of the middle class who have been forced into the ranks of the so-called "new poor."

In the sphere of public consciousness and political action, there has emerged a growing anti-neoliberal sentiment that has made it increasingly unattractive for political candidates to aggressively defend neoliberalism in the face of voters. But neoliberal policies continue in force in the economic sphere, cemented into place by the policies of the international financial institutions (IFIs) and by other mechanisms of the global capitalist order. This includes the risk of losing new capital investment, capital flight, monetary destabilisation and other dissuasive factors that are managed by the international financial oligarchy. In the face of these overwhelming forces, what real prospects are there for systemic change?

Another Latin America is Possible

In our view, the emerging scenario is anything but pessimistic. We believe that these real social consequences of neoliberalism have provided the fundamental basis for its own negation. The ideological monopoly of neoliberalism has without doubt been fractured, and if indeed the anti-neoliberal turn of the masses has not managed to totally sweep away those policies, it has put them in check while opening up new spaces for other possible development strategies.

Various Latin American governments have been brought down over recent years as a result of mass street actions, including the spectacular cases of Peru (2000), Argentina (2001), Bolivia (2003 and 2005), and Ecuador (2000 and 2005), the latter case of which in a certain sense is paradigmatic. The common pattern in these processes of mass popular mobilisation directed at their governments has been one of "emergency response." Under certain social conditions, mass action has proven able to sweep away those regimes that attempted at all costs to impose the most extreme varieties of neoliberal policies.

Notwithstanding these important examples, it is fair to say that the optimism which they awake has not been accompanied, at least not yet, with the kind of mass alternative political organisation capable of mounting a decisive break with neoliberal domination and its imperialist sponsors. In this context, the traditional actors of the political establishment have for the most part managed to contain and process these situations through existing institutional channels, preventing the accumulation of forces necessary to initiate a sustainable popular revolt and the consolidation of revolutionary regimes.

At first glance, this successful containment of resistance to neoliberal policies would seem difficult to explain. In some pockets of the region, such policies have resulted in nearly genocidal proportions of exploitation. In almost every country of the region, those on the losing end have included working people, the excluded sectors and various fractions of what remains of the middle-class. But with electoral systems neatly responding to the social fragmentation brought about early on by the instalment of neoliberalism, the established institutional orders have played an important role in minimising the advances of the popular upsurges alluded to above. This may in large part explain why Washington has emerged as a steadfast "defender" of existing "democratic" institutions operating within the structured parameters of neoliberal capitalist domination.

However resilient that this system of domination may be, we believe that an insistence on imposing and prolonging neoliberal policies in the face of sharpening social contradictions will continue to produce conditions propitious for new social explosions. It is our view that under certain circumstances, these contradictory social processes can ultimately lead to different, unanticipated and possibly more transformative results.

The electoral results that have traditionally served to preserve the system, as elaborated in the so-called Democratic Charter of the OAS, have created something of a headache for its imperial architects. Undesired results are requiring open interventions in electoral processes throughout the hemisphere in order to slow the rise to power of leftist and centre-left parties that has included Chávez in Venezuela, Kirchner in Argentina, Lula in Brazil, Tabaré Vázquez in Uruguay, Bachelet in Chile, René Preval in Haiti, and Evo Morales in Bolivia.

To appreciate the special significance of the victory of Evo Morales, one needs to ponder the problematic of the indigenous peoples in the hemisphere. Subjected to humiliation, exploitation, marginalisation and repression for over 500 years, indigenous people have been the protagonists of numerous resistance struggles and upheavals throughout the entire history of the continent. In recent years, popular indigenous forces have become well-represented among most active social movements in various Latin American countries, especially in the Andean region where native peoples constitute a strong presence of numbers.

Evo Morales and the Movement towards Socialism (MAS) were swept into power amidst the collapsing fortunes of the preceding governments. MAS proved able to show its force in the struggle for reclaiming ancestral roots and defending the rights of peasant producers including those who have maintained a centuries old tradition of cultivating coca. The MAS programme calls for reclaiming Bolivia's sovereignty over natural resources, expanding its share of the rent derived from the commercialisation of these commodities, redistributing income, addressing the highly unequal distribution of land, and confronting the most urgent social problems of the country. The nucleus of this programme is centred on dignifying the ethnic roots of indigenous culture and traditions, which among the first points of priority will involve the decriminalisation of coca cultivation and extending legal recognition to Aymara and Quechua as national languages.

With the re-nationalisation of hydrocarbons enacted by the state and the initiation of land reform in the course of 2006, the MAS government represents a rupture in the prevailing trends of the region. This has been accompanied by Bolivia's participation in the ALBA (Bolivarian Alternative for the Americas) initiative and the Peoples' Trade Agreements that stand in opposition to the hegemonic free trade agreements being peddled by Washington. In a country that has been disassembled, privatised and handed over to the greed of the transnationals, the move toward these kinds of social objectives is tantamount to revolutionising Bolivian society. As Evo Morales himself pointed out, Bolivia needs to be re-founded and this will require a Constitutive Assembly that is genuinely representative and that can facilitate incorporation of the entire panorama of changes proposed by MAS into the legal order. The realisation of these objectives will not be easy going and the enemies of the process have begun to show their face but there can be little doubt that the political panorama of Bolivia has changed.

In the case of Haiti, the United States ultimately had to accept and recognise the victory of the *L'Espwa Party* of René Preval. The Haitian case illustrates that it is not sufficient to just win elections. The mobilisation and participation of broad sectors of the population is necessary to ensure that an electoral victory of this sort is recognised in a country under occupation. While other means of controlling the island obviously remain in place, the

Haitian popular sectors have opened the door to a path clearly not preferred by Washington or the Haitian ruling class.

Another scenario could be found in Chile with the election of Michele Bachelet. If indeed few believe that her victory offered the prospects of significant change in the Chilean neoliberal model, it deepened the questioning of some of the most perverse remnants of the Pinochet era. Bachelet's election as a female representative of the centre-left in a highly conservative society is remarkable and has occurred in a country where women as a whole have been among the most battered by neoliberal policies. Just months after taking office, her government was confronted with an explosion of student protests who demanded fulfilment of their right to education. The government reaction to these and similar kinds of demands will continue to place the rhetoric of the Chilean Socialists under popular scrutiny.

We maintain that the redrawing of the continent's political map through these and other electoral developments have helped reduce the manoeuvring room of U.S. imperialism. If this is correct, it is nowhere more evident than in the case of Venezuela. The government of Hugo Chávez in Venezuela has pursued a novel process of Bolivarian transformation that has proven quite resilient in the face of various destabilisation manoeuvres on the part of imperialism, including a counterrevolutionary coup d'etat attempted in 2002. This has led the opposition which includes the traditional parties (AD and COPEI) to transform themselves into a minority among the Venezuelan population, their leaders forced to act in accordance with the guidelines that their imperial sponsors have recommended.

The consolidation of the Bolivarian Revolution has proceeded to move forward in developing social programmes aimed at responding to the needs of the popular sectors. The importance of Venezuela as a major oil producer and exporter has helped bolster its regional initiatives of solidarity and support for popular alternatives to the hegemonic schemes of regional integration being pursued by Washington. The most significant of these alternatives crystallised in the ALBA initiative.

ALBA and the Struggle for a Genuine Regional Integration

In our judgement, one of the most important results of the changing political map in the hemisphere was the failure in 2005 of Washington to win ratification of the FTAA (Free Trade of the Americas). The FTAA was not, as father-Bush had declared at its launching during the First Summit of the Americas, the "brilliant dawn of a splendid new world." Rather, it was a veritable project of economic recolonisation for the Americas. It promised to impede any possibility for development or genuine integration of Latin America by converting free trade with the North into a legal commitment of the state. The envisioned project encompassed not only issues of trade but also those related to investments, intellectual property, biodiversity and others. While an FTAA agreement was essentially torpedoed at the 2005 Mar de Plata Summit, it certainly did not signify the abandonment of the overall project. Imperialism's best efforts are now being dedicated to the consolidation of bilateral and sub-regional Free Trade Agreements (FTA's).

The ratification of FTA's by the parliaments of signatory countries converts them into laws of the Republic, rendering existing legislation as secondary, as can be seen in labour codes, environmental defence laws and other regulations. Indeed, the FTA's seek to fundamentally transform the relations to transnationals, according them the right to loot the country by giving them equal treatment to national companies, access to public licensing, and referring any disputes with the national state to international tribunals in order to guarantee the sanctity of investments.

For all intents and purposes, the FTA's practically constitute an FTAA in progress and they serve an overarching political purpose of sowing division between Latin American countries. Just as the possibility of unified action begins to evaporate, the pressure mounts upon those states that attempt to resist. Existing Free Trade Agreements include those signed with Mexico, Chile, the Central American countries along with the Dominican Republic (CAFTA), and the project underway with the Andean countries. With the FTA's cemented into place, Washington has greater possibilities for imposing the main objectives of its regional agenda and so these agreements cannot be seen as anything other than a path towards the same imperial project.

The FTAA and the FTA's represent one-half of a "twin tower project" for hemispheric domination. The other half consists of an aggressive militarisation of the region, disguised as a struggle against terrorism and illegal narcotics trafficking. The latter is quite conveniently compatible with the growing necessity to strengthen the mechanisms of repression while at the same time installing bases in the neuralgic points of the region that can constitute strategic platforms for launching future military interventions.

It was in opposition to this twofold campaign of militarisation and hegemonic integration that the Venezuelan initiative known as ALBA (Bolivarian Alternative for the Americas) was launched. This project is based in the genuine development interests of the region, with principles of complementarity, cooperation, solidarity and respect for the sovereignty of nations. It is a concept of integration that cannot be reduced solely to economic dynamics. Rather, it treats the social dimension as a substantial part of integration and addresses itself to the most pressing development problems of the region.

ALBA is the first project of Latin American integration that is based in regional solidarity and cooperation rather than trade and profits. While it does not reject the latter, it accords priority to the former. ALBA is a reality in progress that can be seen unfolding in Latin America through the concretisation of various agreements and initiatives. Here, we will just mention four of these:

The first materialisation of ALBA involved an agreement of collaboration and integration between Cuba and Venezuela signed in December of 2004, amounting to a strategic plan for the application of this alternative framework in April of 2005. This agreement not only contemplated mutually beneficial measures for both countries that extend into the spheres of health and education, but also a project that can benefit the entire continent, such as *"Operación Milagro* (Operation Miracle)" through which thousands of vision-impaired Latin Americans of humble origins are receiving free eye operations in Cuba, backed by Venezuelan funding.

Another important example of the progress of ALBA has involved various cooperation initiatives for the peoples of Latin America and the Caribbean. The most advanced in operation is the Energy Cooperation Agreement with the CARICOM countries of the Caribbean which in June of 2005 led to the creation of PETROCARIBE. The philosophy behind this accord is that the resources generated by savings in petroleum imports and energy cooperation by virtue of discounted prices offered by Venezuela become utilised to fund more effective social and economic development policies. PETROCARIBE not only guarantees the satisfaction of petroleum needs under preferential conditions to a group of smaller countries, but also contemplates a better coordination of energy policies, taking advantage of alternative sources of energy, greater technological cooperation and technical exchange in the field of energy while establishing a significant fund for social and economic development. This ALBA Fund for the Caribbean was supported by an initial quota paid by Venezuela of US$50 million.

Third, as mentioned earlier, the electoral victory of Evo Morales opened an additional space for projecting ALBA into the Andes. This was concretised with the People's Trade Agreement signed in April 2006 in Havana between Venezuela, Cuba and Bolivia. The idea behind People's Trade Agreements, in contrast to FTA's, is to explicitly take into account the development needs of each participating country and to address existing asymmetries in a spirit of mutual support.

Finally, we can mention the creation of TELESUR. This regional media project under the directorship of Aram Ahronian, an Uruguayan, constitutes a strategic means of breaking the information monopoly that is exercised by the large transnationals that dominate the mass media. TELESUR is a medium based in Venezuela that has hemispheric reach, allowing Latin Americans to disseminate their own values, imagery and content on a more free and equitable basis. It is no coincidence that imperialism has greeted the appearance of this regional media project aggressively. TELESUR is without doubt an important tool in the regional battle of ideas against neoliberal globalisation.

Beyond ALBA, we should note the trade agreement signed in October 2004 between MERCOSUR and the Andean Community of Nations (CAN) that created a new free trade area that is the fifth largest in the world, known as the South American Community of Nations. This has occurred alongside of the signing of a strategic alliance between Brazil and Venezuela, and later, a technological cooperation agreement between Uruguay and Venezuela. We do not claim that these agreements are harmonious in nature. On the contrary, the fact is that there exist basic contradictions between the principles and objectives of these proposals and the practical economic policies being carried out on the part of some of the governments involved, notwithstanding the potential opening that now exists for another *possible* Latin America.

We cannot help but stress that the path to such an end will not be an easy one. The inheritance of neoliberalism is not only one of greater poverty, inequality and informality among our societies, but also of states with lesser resources, dismantled by the elimination of some of its agencies and the privatisation of public enterprises, riddled with corruption, all with a massive external debt and the pressures of the international financial institutions weighing down upon them. In the end, the state reshaped by neoliberalism has limited the means for confronting the enormous problems that have been inherited. It faces a powerful, wealthy elite that perpetually accuses it of the very same deficiencies that they themselves have created, pointing to its inefficiencies and never hesitating to resort to capital flight, boycotting investments, and practicing speculation while paying bribes, all as a means of preserving their interests. Latin American states also face an international scenario with greatly enhanced power on the part of transnational monopolies and a fundamentalist government installed in the United States. The latter ensures that a wide arsenal of resources will be continually utilised in order to discipline all those governments that resist in an effort to serve the interests of their peoples.

The clearest example of this is Cuba whose socialist project has earned it a relentless series of punitive policies and aggression on the part of the United States. The Cuban Revolution has been climbing out of the crisis that began with the disappearance of the international economic relations of the former Soviet Bloc (CMEA) in which it was previously inserted and has advanced in the reconsolidation of its economy.

In 2005, Cuba registered an 11.8% rate of growth, contributing to a gradual improvement in the quality of life of the population. Moreover, Cuba has shown its humanistic face in the extraordinary assistance sent to numerous Third World peoples in the health and educational sectors. The paradigmatic example of this was the medical aid sent to Pakistan after the 2005 earthquake that caused extensive damage to that country, including 1700 health workers, 1300 of which were doctors. With health and educational personnel dispersed throughout the developing world, this is an area where the imperialists cannot hope to compete with the example of Cuba. Indeed, the Cuban Revolution's longstanding policies of solidarity and internationalism not only helped to inspire ALBA and the new generation of solidarity-based cooperative agreements but also the very generation of new leaders themselves who are bringing such initiatives to fruition.

Reducing Imperialism's Room to Manoeuvre

In 2005, Washington proved unable to impose its candidates for the General Secretary of the OAS (ex-president Francisco Flores and Mexican Chancellor Luís Ernesto Derbez). Rather, they had to accept the candidate of the Southern

Cone, the Chilean José Miguel Inzulza. In a certain sense, this was analogous to the failed tour of duty in the same year conducted by Secretary of State Condoleezza Rice that had sought to win condemnation of Cuba and Venezuela from the region. Her failure corresponded to a similar setback sustained a few months earlier when Donald Rumsfeld attended the Conference of Ministers of the Armed Forces of the Americas and attempted to place the region's armed forces under U.S. command in name of the struggle against terrorism and illegal narcotics.

There can be little doubt that the shifting balance of political forces in the region has thrown some wrinkles into the imperial project and in this sense have helped to reduce imperialism's room to manoeuvre. Again, we do not seek to portray all of this as the new land of milk and honey. We insist that there are serious challenges facing the broad range of popular movements in leading towards the accumulation of forces sufficient to opening the way to an anti-capitalist alternative. Imperialism's available resources to punish those that resist its hegemony seem at times to be virtually unlimited. From the Pentagon to the CIA, the "diplomatic" presence in the region to the mono-polistic presence of U.S. based mass media, and the enhanced power of transnationals to their counterparts in the local fractions of the transnationalised bourgeoisie, the totality of forces that line up against the region's popular resistance is formidable.

But learning about the complexities, obstacles and emerging cracks in the imperial edifice forms part of the movement towards the construction of another possible world. It is precisely with this idea in mind that the present collection was compiled. Our aim was to assemble diverse points of view on the impact and vulnerabilities of neoliberalism in crisis. Part of this involves examining some of the distinct experiences encountered by the left in power around the region as it struggles to chart alternative paths to development. It was also essential to draw into consideration the social movements and political parties of the region in their capacity as important fields of struggle in the creation of an anti-capitalist alternative. These are the processes that interact in a multitude of complex ways to reduce the manoeuvring room of imperialism. Far from that situation not so many years ago where some pro-claimed the end of history, we suggest that Latin America's human history is only just beginning. It is another history, one that places its peoples, rather than capital, at the epicentre of its universe. In the present work, the goal is to help arm ourselves with the elements necessary for a better understanding of a continent that is reaching the boiling point.

Jose Bell Lara, Havana,
Richard A. Dello Buono, Buenos Aires

February 2003 assembly in Bruhman Factory over a year since 'recovered' by its workers, Buenos Aires

Part I: NeoLiberalism in Crisis

José Bell Lara and Delia Luisa López
The Harvest of Neoliberalism in Latin America

Beginning with the Mexican default of 1982 and all
of the dynamics associated with turbulent debt renegotiations, the debt crisis became transformed into
the pivotal point of articulation for contemporary
forms of developmental dependency. This is something we referred to well over a decade ago as the
"latest dependency" in the region (Bell and López,
1993). As the debt burden evolved into a key instrument for imposing neoliberalism all across the
Americas, the experience of more than a quarter century now allows us to evaluate its consequences. The
cumulative social impact resulting from the application of neoliberal policies in the region is what we
refer to here as the "Harvest of Neoliberalism."

If it is true that some of the phenomena analysed
in this work were already present in Latin American
societies prior to the installation of neoliberal regimes,
there can be little doubt that neoliberal polices have
contributed to cementing them into place. Following
a synoptic discussion of the core premises of neoliberalism, we will proceed to discuss the principle tendencies of what in our judgement consists of the
harvest of neoliberal policies in Latin America.

The Premises of Neoliberalism

The ideological content of neoliberalism enjoyed a
broad and comprehensive dissemination across the

continent. It is not our goal here to subject its proliferation to a full anatomy. At the risk of oversimplifying matters, we are instead seeking to identify its essential dimensions.[1]

The neoliberal worldview can be characterised by its individualistic, utilitarian and ahistorical vision of economy and society. It begins with the premise that freedom of choice and the rational calculation of economic actors, be they producers or consumers, is the underlying principle underlying human behaviour. It postulates the need to eliminate "interferences" that limit the supposed free play of the market, above all, anything which involves state intervention. Capitalism is assumed to be the best possible regime because it supposedly operates free of exploitation. The distribution of earnings between capitalists and wage-workers is the rational scheme of compensation that corresponds to each social group. The capitalist system, if left to its own devices, is stable and efficient. It further considers that state interventionism generates inefficiency, reinforcing the above-mentioned necessity to eliminate this kind of "interference" with the "natural order of things."

With all of these assumptions in place, policy arguments become inevitably stacked in favour of free trade and the unrestricted mobility of capital. A self-reinforcing image results in which it is supposed that "those countries that today are industrialised have prospered on account of these free trade policies" (World Bank, 1991:27). This in turn signifies that developing countries have no other real alternative than to pursue the same path that leads to progress. In this harmonious world of assumptions where domination and structural asymmetries do not exist, countries can move freely in the international arena.

In reality, neoliberalism shows itself to be a fundamentalist form of thought, ahistorical and with little capacity for taking into account either distinct forms of social realities or the particularities of developing countries. Independent of its rhetoric, the underlying objective of neoliberalism has always been to create better conditions for capitalist accumulation. This real foundation is that which best explains its policy recommendations as well as the results of such policies.

---

[1] For the interested reader, consult Delia Luisa López in "El significado multidimensional del neoliberalismo," *FLACSO Documentos de Trabajo*, FLACSO-Cuba Programme, 2002.

The practical application of neoliberal policies has been inextricably linked to the interests of transnational monopoly capital. The debt crisis of the early 1980s resulted not only in a "lost decade" for Latin America as it was called by ECLAC but also to ensure that the region lost any possibility for negotiations with the hegemonic countries. These were the conditions in which the Washington Consensus arose and was put into motion. The Consensus expressed the position of the U.S. government, the international financial institutions (IFIs) and the right-wing think-tanks that continuously spun out neoliberalism's slogans.

The Washington Consensus identified ten aspects that served as a base for the political economy reforms that debtor countries ought to have as their goals. These goals included fiscal discipline, public spending cuts, tax reform (including indirect taxes and expansion of the tributary base), financial liberalisation, competitive exchange rates, trade liberalisation, foreign direct investment, privatisation of state enterprises, deregulation and protection of private property rights (Ahumada, 1996:26). The imposition of the Consensus was effectively contingent upon cementing four basic components into place:

- deregulation of the economy which can permit privatisation to take place;
- strict control over wages (resulting in their reduction);
- opening up the economy to foreign interests and liberalisation of the flows of commodities and foreign capital (but not labour);
- prioritisation of the interests of financial capital (Valenzuela, 1997:16).

Sustaining this policy orientation required a continual ideological reproduction of a central thesis, namely, that regulation of economic relations generates inefficiencies in the allocation of resources and adversely affects overall social wellbeing. "Neoliberals yearn for a minimalist state that places the market above all else because it is considered to be the most effective mechanism. The least possible amount of restrictions imposed on the free reign of the market is considered to be the best for the national economy, society and government" (Kay, 2001:81).

In reality, the state always intervenes in neoliberalism albeit at a more macro level so as to create better conditions for the operation of capital. This involves orchestrating the means of opening the economy, privatising public institutions, regulating the labour market through the imposition of more flexible norms of contracting wage labour, establishing exchange rates, levying taxes and other measures. In reality, the juxtaposition of state and market in neoliberalism amounts to the real promotion of a different type of state, i.e., the neoliberal state. The neoliberal state apparatus becomes utilised to promote a realignment of social forces and groups, of companies and workers with a redefinition of grand proportions in their access to resources, welfare and future prospects (Vilas, 1999).

Ever since the problem of development took centre stage following the end of the Second World War and the initial elaboration of development thought appeared in the North under the heading of modernisation theory, the market has always remained at the core of these proposals. Over the course of six decades, the argumentations have varied but the message has been the same: "There is only one way to industrialise and adopt the base institutions of modernity: the market above all else, and with the market, the autonomy of civil society, political pluralism and secularisation . . . In the end, it means to accept as a positive and inescapable fact that which Trubeskoi in the 1920s did not vacillate in calling the 'nightmare' of universal Europeanisation (Pelicani, 1992:113).

In this, we are not seeking to bedevil the market. Since the absolute contraposition between the state and the market in development does not exist, the real problem is the following: What kind of state and market do we need and for doing what? For social actors at large, the state and market are instances of mediation that permit the accomplishment of specified economic, political, cultural or other types of objectives (Vilas, 1995:11). There exist various studies that demonstrate the decisive role of the state in the promotion of development, including those dealing with the experience of the Asian tigers in installing forms of export-oriented capitalism.

Historical experience indicates to us that the "invisible hand" of the market has been incapable of promoting the development of any underdeveloped country. "Under present conditions, the goods and services markets as well as that of capital (the latter with growing autonomy) are internationalised and highly monopolised, dominated by a small group of transnational companies that operate under the protection of the governments of their countries of origin" (Sontag, 1994:280). An analysis of the behaviour of Latin American economy and society over the last couple of decades in the neoliberal era demonstrates that neoliberal policies have constituted the instrument for a greater subordination of the region to transnational monopoly capital. To this should be added the extraordinary social costs that its application has signified.

A study carried out by Pablo González Casanova showed that neoliberal policies have definitively contributed to increasing the transfers of surplus from the periphery to the centre, thanks to interest rates and debt payments, the declining terms of exchange, and the high level of profits remitted back to foreign capital investors. All of this has taken place at a far greater magnitude during the latest phase of capitalist globalisation. According to Gonzalez Casanova: The number of countries that transferred net assets to the developed countries rises to forty-one from Africa, twenty-three from Asia, nine from Central and Eastern Europe, ten from the Middle East and thirty-two from Latin America and the Caribbean (2001:102).

In spite of the outpouring of criticism from a majority of the affected population due in large part to the disastrous social consequences that it has provoked across the continent, neoliberalism has remained the dominant paradigm, albeit in crisis, and constitutes the most obvious sign of the contradictory advance of capitalist globalisation. Independently of the intellectual value of arguments put forward by Hayek or Friedman, if their theorising had not corresponded with the strategic interests of the transnationalised monopoly bourgeoisie, neoliberalism would not have otherwise enjoyed its paradigmatic ascent. The underlying class interests that it represents explain how it achieved ideological hegemony among establishment policy-makers.

This is necessary to emphasis here because our continent continues to live with the illusion that a simple change of cabinet, of one or another minister, or a campaign of pressure brought to bear upon the president, can bring about fundamental change. In short, there is a generalised tendency to ignore the determinant class forces that rest behind the possibilities for real social change. Even when a populist president is elected and manages to become positioned to threaten the class interests of the transnationalised monopoly bourgeoisie, the IMF promptly begins its work to establish the limits and commitments of the new government.

This structural quagmire is further reinforced by the effective role of the mass media of communications. The media works alongside of local policymakers to present neoliberal suppositions as the only possible route for modernising the economy, attracting foreign investments, enhancing the competitiveness of the economy and best capitalising upon increasing globalisation (Kay, 2000:78). All of this points us to an inevitable conclusion, namely, that a complex set of elements will be necessary for the reconstruction of popular forces and the materialisation of a viable systemic alternative.

In the remainder of this essay, we shall reflect upon some of the key social tendencies that have become established in Latin America up to and into the twilight of neoliberalism.

An Increasingly Unequal Society

The application of neoliberal policies involves a twin process of social class redistribution, redirecting wealth from workers to owners as well as between sectors within the ruling class, i.e., from those who produce for the internal market towards those sectors aligned with exports. Reports on the early years of the debt crisis and the application of IMF policies were dismal. They showed that Latin America during the so-called "lost decade" witnessed a decline in workers' earnings on the order of 25% while investor profits increased more than 15% during the same period. The 1990 World Bank Development Report indicated that in spite of Latin America's per capita earnings at between five and seven times greater than those of South Asia and Sub-Saharan Africa, it had an income distribution that unfavourably contrasted with those regions. For example, while the South Asian countries displayed a seven-to-one ratio between the 20% richest and 20% poorest, the difference in Latin America between these groups was almost 19-to-one (World Bank, 1990).

Over the course of the 1990s, the situation involving social inequality did not improve and in fact tended to worsen. One ECLAC study revealed that the five per cent wealthiest portion of the population increased its income not only in relative but in absolute terms. By 2001, the high level of inequality could be seen everywhere, such as in the elevated proportion of total income captured by the ten per cent wealthiest households which brought in 19 times more than the 40% poorest households (ECLAC, 2001a:67). Note that the difference was no longer simply between two quintiles, but rather between a one-tenth fraction versus the sum of two quintiles, or double the persons in the preceding comparison.

The vast majority of Latin Americans (83.6%) reside in countries where social inequality became more pronounced between 1975 and 1995 (ECLAC, 2001a:4). In this regard, a study reported the variations of average income, measured in dollars, between the one percent wealthiest and one percent poorest over the course of 15 years. In 1980, the difference between the two groups was 237-to-one while in 1990, the difference had grown to 360-to-one and in 1995, reached a level of 417-to-one (ECLAC, 2001a).

This tendency towards social polarisation was corroborated by numerous sources. For example, an IDB report issued in 2000 showed that one-forth of total income was being received by only 5% of the population. The 10% wealthiest sector was receiving 40% of total income. In contrast, the distribution figures for the most industrialised capitalist countries show that the 5% wealthiest received an average 13% of national income (IDB, 2000:5).

The figures also show that those Latin American countries with the most equitable distributions of income display concentration indices that are higher than the world average, thus helping to conceal other countries with some of the worst income distributions in the world. Among the countries with the highest levels of inequality are Bolivia, Brazil and Nicaragua where the difference between the richest 20% and the poorest 20% is more than 30 times. In Bolivia, the difference is almost fifty times in magnitude (ECLAC, 2001b:3).

In summary, the data available since 2000 confirms that Latin America continues being the region with the highest concentration of income. Unfortunately, the current trend is towards an unfavourable convergence among those countries in the region towards greater inequality. In 1990, 8 countries were classified among those having high or very high levels of inequality while by 2002 the list grew to 11 countries in that category. ECLAC has concluded that "with respect to the distribution of income, Latin America continues being the region of the world with the worst indicators, something which is become further aggravated by the trend observed in some countries towards an accentuation of the concentration of income" (CEPAL, 2004:5).

The regressive character of the distribution of income in Latin America has produced some of the most acute social contrasts in the world. Mexico provides us with a graphic example. In that country, the number of billionaires grew from only two in 1988 to twenty-four by the first decade of the 21st Century. Just one of these billionaires netted earnings that equal the sum total income of the 17 million poorest Mexicans, i.e., US$ 6.6 billion.

Inequality reaches perhaps its most extreme manifestation in the area of health where the figures reveal an unjust distribution in people's right to continue living. For example, an extremely high proportion of infant mortality is concentrated in the poorest sectors as a result of completely preventable diseases. It has been estimated that each year in Argentina, 15,000 children die as a result of curable sicknesses that defy control by health authorities due to cutbacks in the national health budget. Atilio Borón, a noted sociologist, pointed out that neoliberal policies had provoked a crisis that exterminated the same number of people in two years that state terrorism had disappeared in seven years. Predictably, this social class stratification also coincides with life expectancy where there is up to twelve years of difference between the wealthiest and poorest sectors. Latin America is today in every sense the most unequal region of the world.

A Society with Increasing Unemployment, Underemployment and Job Insecurity

The final portion of the 20th Century was characterised by the "employment problem," i.e. increased unemployment and underemployment on a global scale. In 1993, the UNDP pointed to the phenomenon of "growth without employment," a trend in which economic expansion no longer necessarily implied increasing levels of job creation. The prognosis at that time suggested a growing gap between the size of the labour force and the availability of actual employment. For Latin America, it was predicted that from 1990 forward, the labour force would grow by 27% while employment was likely to only grow by 14%. The realities that subsequently materialised proved that such predictions were if anything too optimistic.

At the beginning of the 1990s, the region's labour force was estimated at 180 million people. Over the course of the decade, it grew by 44 million while the demand for labour failed to keep pace due to a considerable increase in the number of idled workers that expanded by 10.1% per year. The unemployment rate which began at just under 6% ascended to close to 9% by the end of the decade (CEPAL, 2001b:2). This tendency continued into the new decade, with the ILO reporting that the 2002 unemployment rate had reached its highest level in the last 20 years. According to official estimates, for example, Argentina displayed an unemployment rate of 25%.[2]

An important part of the neoliberal policy package involved the opening of the region's economies to foreign commerce. In Latin America, this resulted in the closing of numerous local industries due to an inability to complete with their counterparts in the more developed countries. The deindustrialisation of the labour force signified a sharp decline in the regional economy's capacity to absorb employment in those sectors that formerly provided the most stable occupations, best pay scales and highest social benefits.

---

[2] This was reported by Reuters from the Mexican daily "Por Esto", section 4, p. 6. Quintana Roo, Mexico.

As a consequence of these processes, increasing unemployment has brought with it a decline in the quality of new jobs created. Seven out of every ten new jobs created in urban areas were located in the informal sector. Indeed, more than half of the employed labour force became relegated to the informal sector. At the same time, the increasingly flexible nature of work schemes has reduced work security, substantially intensifying the instability of employment. This has become clearly reflected by the increase in the proportion of work-ers with precarious employment, part-time jobs or temporary work arrange-ments (CEPAL, 2002:332–333). Moreover, the number of companies that systematically practise subcontracting has grown rapidly. All of this promoted a permanent feeling of insecurity for workers as a study completed in 2004 reported, revealing that 76% of those who are working believe that they will be idled at some point over the upcoming year (Latinobarómetro, 2004:48)

While unemployment affects all age-groups and categories of the labour force, it has a particular impact on two age-groups: young adults who have not yet worked and older workers who may not be able to return to work again. For example, the unemployment rate among adults under the age of 25 is around 2–4 times higher than those over the age of 25.

This is not only a problem of monetary income. Employment or the prospects of gaining employment is an important element of the overall quality of life. The failure to obtain work results in frustration, insecurity and psychological harm. The resulting alienation and desperation translates to a certain extent into a higher level of delinquency and antisocial behaviour among youth. Among older workers, the psychological and physical stress that results is associated with higher rates of alcoholism, domestic family abuse and other acts of violence.

From the beginning of the crisis, adjustment policies applied during the debt crisis were aimed at reducing state spending, above all in the sphere of social spending (health care, education, reduction or elimination of food sub-sidies, cutbacks in public transportation, etc.). The longer range goal involved downsizing the state apparatus and the public sector. The cumulative effect of these policies was to erode income levels and reduce employment, even for the middle classes. For each new year in 21st Century Latin America, there are around five million people becoming incorporated into the labour force, the larger part of which have little prospects of finding permanent and respectably-paying work. Indeed, over the 1993–2003 period, between 60% and 75% of the population received a per capita income that was less than the general average (CEPAL 2004b).

In summary, the achievement of a decent standard of living through stable employment has become possible only for a minority of Latin Americans. In general terms, the era of neoliberalism brought about an ever more precarious employment situation. This has led not only to greater inequalities but also increased poverty, social vulnerability and social de-stabilisation.

A Society of Increasing Poverty

During the 1970s, it was estimated that the percentage of people living in poverty fell by 40% throughout the region. But during the 1980s, the so-called "lost decade," the percentage began to grow once more, reaching 48.3% in 1990 according to ECLAC. By the turn of the century, Latin America displayed a poverty rate of 43.8% of people living in official poverty, with 18.5% living in absolute poverty (ECLAC, 2001b).

The above figures signify that in 1999, more than 211 million Latin Americans had joined the ranks of the poor, with 89 million living in absolute destitution. Between 1990 and 1999, official poverty grew by 11 million persons. Interestingly, this increase consisted of nearly four million for the 1990–1997 period, while for 1997–1999, poverty grew by 7.6 million (CEPAL, 2001b). More recent figures show that the poverty and absolute poverty rates remained essentially stable at these high rates over the first three years of the 21st Century, with the overall number of poor people reaching 224 million, with 98 million in absolute poverty (CEPAL 2004a). All of this suffices to say that after three decades of struggle for development, poverty in Latin American remains at around the same level as 1970 or perhaps even a little worse.

Poverty has a number of technical definitions with respect to the level of income or the satisfaction of basic necessities. In essence, however, it is a qualitative state of degradation characterised by inadequate diet, poor health, precarious employment with high unemployment, and in general a poor standard of living. The majority of poor households are characterised for their lack of access to safe drinking water, poor quality and overcrowded housing, and heads of household who have less than three years of formal schooling. In general, there is a low employment density, with few or no members of the nuclear family having stable unemployment.

Half or more of households have a female head, part of a phenomenon that became widely recognised as the "feminisation of poverty." In Latin America, poverty has also assumed a child's face, with minors under the age of 18 being disproportionately poor and more than 50% of children living in poverty while they constitute only 40% of the total population (De la Barra, 2002:9). Studies have been carried out, showing that the average income of the poor reaches only 55% of the level defined as the poverty line, just barely above the level of absolute poverty (PNUD, 1992). Indeed, among the majority of poor households, individual income of those employed generally bring in only enough to cover their own basic necessities, but lacking a sufficient margin to meet the needs of any other member of the household (CEPAL 2004a).

Poverty has become transformed over the last 20–25 years into a predominantly urban phenomenon, even though the intensity of poverty remains greater in the countryside. In 1999, 54% of the region's rural households were poor while 30% of urban families were in the same situation. In absolute numbers, however, the urban poor grew to 134 million persons while 77 million were living in the countryside. This was largely due to the systematic migration from the country to the cities in what amounted to a rural-to-urban transfer of poverty.

While there exists a Millennium Goal of reducing poverty rates by one-half by the year 2015, the prevailing economic predictions over the short and medium term strongly suggest that this modest target will be impossible to reach.

Table 1

Latin America: Poor and Absolutely Poor Population (1980–1999)

	Poor b/					Absolutely Poor c/					
	Total		Urban		Rural		Total		Urban		Rural	
	Million	%	Million	%	Million	%	Million	%	Million	%	Million	%
1980	135.9	40.5	62.9	29.8	73.0	59.9	62.4	18.6	22.5	10.6	39.9	32.7
1990	200.2	48.3	121.7	41.4	78.5	65.4	93.4	22.5	45.0	15.3	48.4	40.4
1994	201.5	45.7	125.9	38.7	75.6	65.1	91.6	20.8	44.3	13.6	47.4	40.8
1997	203.8	43.5	125.7	36.5	78.2	63.0	88.8	19.0	42.2	12.3	46.6	37.6
1999	211.4	43.8	134.2	37.1	77.2	63.7	89.4	18.5	43.0	11.5	46.4	38.3

Source: ECLAC based on special tabulations from household surveys of the respective countries included in the sample.

a/ Estimate based on 19 Latin American countries.

b/ Persons living in households under the official poverty line, including the portion of the population living in absolute poverty.

c/ Persons living in households in absolute poverty.

An Increasingly Informalised and Technologically Unsophisticated Society

Poverty has become concentrated in an extremely heterogeneous, informal sector that includes all of the diverse types of activities that the poor can manage to perform. This includes self-employed work, artisans, home-based shops, small repair businesses, and so on. It is a sector that includes people who perform and sell practically any kind of good or service, guided by the logic of survival, with their own physical existence serving as principal asset.

Indeed, one of the initial impacts of the 1980s debt crisis was the significant growth of this sector. The informalisation occurred as the rhythm of employment creation sharply declined, producing a widespread expansion of formal unemployment and underemployment. In the first half of the 1980s, the informal sector grew at a rate of 8.5% per year, while during this same period, industrial employment contracted at an average 2% per year. Between 1980 and 1990, the ranks of the informal sector expanded by 75%. At the onset of the 1990s, 80% of all new employment was informal in nature. The extraordinary expansion of this sector played a cushioning role, helping to absorb the flash growth of unemployment and ameliorate the urgent necessity of survival for those recently losing their jobs.

Through this process, one of the most exploited sectors of our societies was formed. The informal sector is home to more women than men, more young adults than older adults, more children than young adults, more migrants than traditional residents of the urban and surrounding areas, and more people of African descent, indigenous and mixed-race peoples than whites. These demographic realities are all expressions of the structural nature of poverty.

The growth of the informal sector was not only quantitative but also qualitative in nature and can be seen in the structures and social dynamics that materialised all across the continent (Bell, 1993). Together with this

Table 2

Distribution of the Employed Population 1990–1999 (%)

SECTORS	1990	1999
Formal Sector	58.9	53.6
Informal Sector	41.0	46.3
Total	100.0	100.0

Source: ECLAC, 2002; 2003.

informalisation is a tendency towards growth in the tertiary sector of the labour force. As a general trend, the service sector has a growth dynamic that is higher that the other sectors of the economy, resulting in a progressive accumulation of the labour force becoming dedicated to these activities compared to industry and agriculture. In 1960, close to a third of the employed labour force could be found in the tertiary sector of the economy while about half were involved in agriculture. Today more than half of the employed labour force works in the tertiary sector.

If this situation mirrors the modern tendencies of economic transformation, in Latin America it reflects to a far greater extent the incapacity of the region's formal economies to absorb the growing labour force. In sum, it constitutes an increasingly more common form of concealing unemployment, above all through the increase of service activities that are classified within the informal sector.

Table 3
Distribution of the Labour Force (1999)

	(%)
Agriculture	20.5
Industry and Construction	21.3
Transportation and Communications	5.1
Trade and Services	52.7

Source: ECLAC, 2002; 2003.

A Society of Declining Standards of Living and Downward Social Mobility

At the onset of the debt crisis, the austerity measures and resulting restrictions on demand produced a spiralling unemployment and decline in the real salaries of workers, leading to substantial downward mobility during the lost decade. This was attributable to a combination of the cumulative impact of inflation as well as the implementation of structural adjustment policies effectively designed to reduce peoples' standard of living. Average inflation across the continent managed to reach levels over 1000% in 1989 and 1990. During the 1990s, inflation rates steadily declined but salary increases failed to compensate for the drastic preceding downturn. As a result, workers' real wages were reduced by percentages of nearly 50% in some countries relative to 1980 levels and in the larger part of the continent, fell to 1960s levels. In general, the evolution of real salaries was negative and this produced a decline across all sectors. In some countries, the relative share of salaries in the GDP fell by ten percentage points.

Declining salaries most drastically affected agricultural wage workers, employees of the public sector, and wage workers in industrial manufacturing. However, this trend did not remain confined to these wage earning sectors but also affected the income of the middle sectors. This formerly more affluent portion of the population saw their relative advantage shrink for those living above the poverty line as well as for those who precipitously fell below this threshold. In those countries where adequate statistical data existed, it could be seen that middle income earning urban households experienced a significant decline in their relative participation of total income, accompanied by an absolute downturn in their income. This process yielded the phenomenon that became known as the "new poor," i.e., people whose income fell below the official poverty line while not displaying the other common deficiencies in their levels of education, housing and health.

A large portion of the new poor included those public employees who were either idled as a result of state downsizing or who retained their jobs but suffered a drastic reduction in their salaries, in some cases of up to one-half since the beginning of the 1980s. Even in the countryside, legions of the new poor have appeared among small landowners, landless and indigenous workers along with broad segments of temporary agricultural workers, female heads of households and young people obliged to migrate due to lack of work. It is this newly poor segment that constitutes the clearest expression of a generalised downward social mobility.

One measure indirectly linked to this is the decline of the per capita income level of Latin America relative to other regions of the world. In the 1950s, Latin America surpassed the per capita earnings of all other regions of the underdeveloped world, reaching roughly one-half that of the industrialised capitalist countries. By 1999, the region's per capita income was less than 30% that of the more developed countries and lower than the levels achieved by South East Asian countries, the Middle East and Eastern Europe.

A Society with Increasing Levels of Violence and Criminality

Part of the syndrome associated with social decline following the application of neoliberal policies across the continent has been the extraordinary growth of criminality and violence. Clearly, this trend is not unique to Latin America. There is an estimated average annual growth of 5% of this problem world-wide, higher than the rate of population growth or economic growth in a majority of countries. The increase in violence is linked to social inequality, chaotic urbanisation, excessive consumption of alcohol, widespread circulation of firearms, corruption, pervasive impunity and police abuse. For its part, Latin America has an annual rate of 30.7 homicides per 100,000 inhabitants, 6 times greater than the world average (Iglesias 1997).

There are various countries on the continent where despite a deteriorating health situation murder remains the second cause of death. El Salvador had the highest rate of criminality in the world during the 1990s, with 152 murders per every 100,000 inhabitants (Iglesias 1997). It can be inferred from this that the average Salvadoran faces a sixty times higher risk of violent death than those who live in Western Europe. Indeed, homicides today are causing more deaths than the civil war that scorched this Central American republic in the preceding years. In some Caribbean countries, the rate of homicide has reached levels of up to 40 per every 100,000 inhabitants, four times the rate of criminality of the United States (Iglesias 1997). It is said that in Brazil, a homicide is committed every three minutes. In Colombia, violence remains the principal socio-political problem of the country and it holds the world's record for the number of kidnappings with an average of one every 3–4 days.

To this must be added the problem of the illegal narcotics trade. Driven by the huge demand for illegal drugs on the part of the United States, narcotics trafficking has expanded throughout the region, opening routes through Mexico, Central America and the Caribbean. Tightly associated with this phenomenon is money laundering and the extensive network of banks, companies, administrators, public officials and security agents that are corrupted by the narcotics trade both in the North as well as the South of the continent. This has intensified the risks in various cities in the continent such as Sao Paulo, considered the most dangerous city of all with an average of 20 homicides daily.

A survey carried out in 18 countries, designed to be representative of Latin America, showed that a third of those interviewed indicated that they or a family member had been the victim of a crime during the last 12 months.

In 16 of the 18 countries surveyed, more than half of the population believed that renewed efforts to combat crime are failing (Latinobarómetro, 2004).

One element particularly noteworthy is the increase in juvenile delinquency where the average age of delinquents has declined significantly. Whereas previously it was concentrated in the 20–35 year range, the average offender is now between the ages of 15 and 25. However, children and adolescents are also highly victimised by the violence. For example, 27% of deaths by homicide in the region involve children and youth between the ages of 10–19. In addition, six million minors under the age of 18 are victims of severe aggression each year and 75 thousand die as a result of family violence (De la Barra, 2002: 11).

This high level of violence has also had destructive effects on the economy. According to the World Bank, Latin American countries have sustained losses of US$200 billion over the last 15 years attributable to the violence. In the sizable Brazilian economy, violence causes economic losses of US$7.5 billion or 1% of the country's GDP. In Latin America as a whole, the losses reached 2% of the regional GDP. The situation can be summarised in a single sentence by Eduardo Galeano: "Going for a walk in large Latin American cities has become transformed into a high risk activity."

A Society Whose Citizens Are Progressively Expropriated of their Political and Social Rights by the Market

The mechanism of conditionality and the processes of debt renegotiation constitute political-economic interventions through which decision-making in the area of economic policy came to be defined by IFIs. This extended through policies regarding finance, investment, public property, taxation and government spending. In this manner, it strongly affected monetary, taxation and subsidy policies as well as social policies including education, health, social security, and in general, the overall prioritisation of government spending. Citizens effectively ceded the possibility of their dominion over the economy. They can decide with their vote who governs, but the decision-making centre concerning economic policy and those measures to be implemented is now located outside of the country. Democracy in this context is converted into a mechanism for electing who is going to execute the decisions of transnational actors as national policy-making becomes emptied of its powers.

The case of Argentina is illustrative. IMF pressures at their peak even forced the country to modify national legislation in the interests of transnational capital and systematically pressured the Argentina state. On the other hand, neoliberal policies, together with the restructuration of social spending, forced the privatisation of public enterprises and social services in the name of a supposed efficiency. In this manner, social services once seen as the rights of citizens became transformed into goods whose access is partially mediated by the government. What was a social right is now a private commodity whose delivery is mostly regulated by the supply offered by its owners and the demand constituted by consumers' purchasing power. In other words, it is a process in which the citizen loses rights over that which capital is acquiring. Private enterprises now provide these services at prices that guarantee them a profit, including private schools, private service insurance companies, private retirement account agencies, and so on. The operation of the market does not pretend to guarantee rights or justice but rather the acquisition of profits. In this manner, the advance of neoliberalism effectively restricted the political rights of the citizens of Latin America.

It is not strange, then, that between 30–40% of the region's population believes that their vote lacks the power to change their reality according to the survey cited earlier (Latinobarómetro, 2004). In 16 of the 18 countries included in the study, more than 60% of the population consider that their country is governed in the interests of the powerful and not by the people. Overall, 71% of Latin Americans feel that way. In 14 of the 18 countries, citizens also manifested the belief that their country is heading in a bad direction. Discontent is nearly total in Ecuador and Peru, with a 92% unfavourable response, followed by Mexico with 84% indicating the same (Latinobarómetro, 2004).

These responses reveal the depth of dissatisfaction with democracy of the neoliberal type, i.e., a democracy emptied of its content where the scope of real state decision-making is systematically reduced. It is the market that emits the signals that regulate the state's conduct. Support for democracy has declined from 61% of the population in 1996 to 53% in 2004. One of the manifestations of this discontent is found in the high level of abstention within many of the electoral processes across the continent. It is moreover significant that 55% of the population is indifferent to the option of a non-democratic government, willing to tolerate it if it were able to resolve pressing economic problems.

On the other hand, when a government responds to popular expectations, it has shown that it can win the support of the masses. This has been the case in Venezuela in spite of the tremendous media war waged against the government of Hugo Chávez. Venezuela has "cultivated support for democracy which has significantly increased for three consecutive years" (Latinobarómetro, 2004:6). As a corollary, "Venezuela is the Latin American country that is least perceived by its people to be governed for the benefit of the powerful and which most feels that it is governed for the good of the people" (Latinobarómetro, 2004:17).

A Society that Offers No Future

The future of Latin American society depends upon its children and adolescents as they will be its future protagonists. In 2000, UNICEF published a summary of a regional survey *The Voice of Children and Adolescents in Latin America and the Caribbean* (UNICEF, 2000) and its results merit comment. Children and adolescents generally expressed a low level of confidence in their governments. In addition, they indicated that they are viewed with scant importance by government officials, with 62% of those surveyed feeling that they considered to be of little or no importance to their governments. If we extrapolate from this data to the existing population of children and adolescents between the ages of 9–18, we are talking about 63 million or more people that feel little confidence in their governments. "This situation reflects a lack of confidence of a significant part of the citizenry, along with the perception that economic and political policies do not give priority to children and adolescents and their rights as people in the process of development, leaving them at risk for various types of personal and social harm" (UNICEF, 2000:26). This same report indicates that children do not admire their political leaders, indeed, only 2% even mention them and those who were most discouraged during that period included the young people of Brazil and the Southern Cone. Subsequent governments that have assumed power in those countries clearly had their work cut out for them at the onset.

With respect to the future of their countries, there exists a great pessimism among children and adolescents, with 67% of them (representing 70 million children and adolescents of the region) feeling that the country is going to remain the same or become even worse in the future (UNICEF, 2000:26). Finally, a third of those interviewed manifested the opinion that they rarely feel happy. Predictably, it is not only the children that feel that way. When the opinion of Latin Americans is consulted, practically one-half of the population considers that the economic situation is in bad shape and 60% consider that their quality of life has declined with respect to their parents' generation (IDB, 2000). In 2004, a year where the region's economy grew by 5%, 59% of the population feel that their future economic situation will be worse and half feel that their children will eventually live in worse conditions than they (Latinobarómetro, 2004:44).

The total set of factors analysed here are indicative of a trend towards social discontent that can be perceived in the greater part of the region. The neoliberal project has begun to encounter its limits and to hear the movement of the region's popular forces. The slow and protracted advance of these forces has proven able to install governments that are clearly not the preferred flagbearers of the neoliberal project. While it is barely the beginning, it definitely suggests that the future can be different. It is upon the resurgence of the region's popular forces and the leadership of their political parties and social movements that this future depends.

Ximena de la Barra
THE DUAL DEBT OF NEOLIBERALISM[1]

"Humanity must understand that it will have to
fight for its survival"
Fidel Castro
Mayday Speech
Havana, Cuba, 2004

"We have no other alternative but to put an end
to the neoliberal model"
Evo Morales
Social Debt Summit
February 26, 2005

Introduction: Anatomy of a Failed
Development Model

The currently prevailing neoliberal development
model has brought with it various technological
advances and economic and commercial growth.
However, these results ultimately benefit fewer and
fewer people while augmenting social inequality,
injustices, and promoting serious social and ethical
setbacks. It is definitely not eradicating poverty.

[1] This paper is a revised and extended version of "Who Owes and Who Pays? The
Accumulated Debt of Neoliberalism" that appeared in *Critical Sociology* Volume 32,
No. 1, 2006. It emerged out an inaugural lecture "¿Quien Debe y Quien Paga? La
Deuda Social Tiene Muchos Deudores" originally presented at the FLACSO-Cuba
Seminar "Agenda Latinoamericana" at the University of Havana in June, 2004.

On the contrary, it creates conditions for a growing tendency towards political, economic and social exclusion for the majority of the world's population.

The model exacerbates poverty, social disparities, ecological degradation, violence and social disintegration. Loss of governability flows from its systematic logic of emphasising an ever cheaper labour force, the reduction of social benefits, the disarticulation and destruction of labour organisations, and the elimination of labour and ecological regulation (de la Barra 1997). In this way, it consolidates a kind of cannibalism known as *social dumping* that seeks to lower costs below the value of social reproduction rather than organising a process of progressive social accumulation. For most of Latin America and the Caribbean, the present minimum wage levels only allow for a portion of the basic consumption package needed by working people (Bossio 2002).

At present, the global income gap between the 10% poorest portion of the world's population and the wealthiest 10% has grown to be 1 to 103 (UNDP 2005). According to this same source, around 2.5 billion people, almost half of humanity, lives on less than US$ 2. per day (considered the poverty level), while 1.2 billion of these people live on less than US$ 1. per day (considered the level of extreme poverty).

Given its neoliberal character, globalisation failed to produce the benefits that were touted. Indeed, the process has greatly harmed the most vulnerable social sectors produced by the previous phase of capitalist development. The lack of social and ethical objectives in the current globalisation process has resulted in benefits only in those countries where a robust physical and human infrastructure exists, where redistributive social policies are the norm, and where fair access to markets and strong regulatory entities are in place. Where such conditions do not exist, globalisation has led to stagnation and marginalisation, with declining health and educational levels of its children, especially among the poor. Some regions, including Eastern Europe, the former Soviet Union, Sub-Saharan Africa, and more recently, Latin America and the Caribbean, as well as some countries within regions and some persons within countries (poor children and adolescents, rural inhabitants and urban slum dwellers, indigenous peoples, children of illiterate women, illegal immigrants, etc.) have remained mostly excluded (UNICEF 2001).

It is interesting to note that in May 2005, a group of NGOs in Spain where this author currently resides launched a campaign to denounce the causes and consequences of the external debt under the name of ¿Quien Debe a Quien? (Who Owes Whom?)

It is not hard to envisage a different kind of globalisation. Prominent political and religious figures have been calling for a change in its current nature in order to achieve the globalisation of solidarity. Developing countries need markets for their products but they also need fair rules of trade. Curiously, the free market principles imposed upon developing countries have in large measure been eschewed by the most developed countries. The latter continue to maintain protective barriers directed at the developing countries and to spend massive resources not in development co-operation as they have agreed to do, but rather in subsidising their own producers. In this way, they effectively jettison from the market those countries that lack conditions to do the same, thereby limiting their capacity to generate resources and employ their people. This extremely unfair situation is pivotal for the developing countries. It has been estimated that if Africa, Southeast Asia and Latin America were to experience a 1% increase in their respective participation in world exports, the resulting increase in income could lift 128 million people out of official poverty (OXFAM 2002).

The United States, presently the largest agricultural exporter of the world, provides a good case in point. The dumping of its products threatens the food security of other countries as well as the effectiveness of poverty reduction programmes by weakening the capacity of affected countries to generate needed foreign exchange. Worldwide, dumping only benefits a handful of large, agro-export transnationals, the majority of which are based in the United States and Europe (IATP 2005).

Beyond the need for fair trade, the poorest countries need a positive transfer of resources. In spite of numerous international commitments, development co-operation is not reaching its targets and due to its reduced and conditioned nature, it causes more harm than relief. Similarly, foreign capital investment has been erratic and largely speculative, to the point of being mostly damaging in nature. The main financial transfers rather than coming towards the developing countries are those flowing to the developed world originating in foreign debt servicing. In the final analysis, the transfer of human and financial resources as well as non-renewable natural resources from the South to the North has remained negative on balance.

Another form of expanding south – north financial flows is denationalisation of natural resources, national production and public services. For example, privatised public services in the hands of transnational monopoly providers have become increasingly exclusive in nature, restricting access to the poorest consumers from essentials such as safe water, sanitation, electricity, telephone communications, and highway use. Health care reforms imposed on the developing countries have created dual track systems, effectively eliminating mechanisms of solidarity with the poor. Having already saturated the existing demand in the United States, health care transnationals such as Aetna, EXXEL and CIGNA now fill the effective demand of the most populated developing countries as a means to further expansion and profits. These corporations also see the surviving social security funds in developing countries as a great new source of financial capital waiting to be exploited (Stocker, Karen, Howard Witzkin, and Cecilia Iriart 1999). In this manner, they can skim the cream off of the solvent market while contributing to the abandonment of the poor, the chronically ill, and the elderly, leaving them to fend for themselves in an ever degraded public service sector that has become badly de-capitalised. As the public sector itself is increasingly forced to contract portions of its service delivery to the private sector, public resources are still further drained.

The legacy of structural adjustment programmes has led, in the worst cases, to an acute decline in public spending in the areas of health and education. In the best of cases, it has led to an inadequate level of improvement in social spending levels. Foreign debt payments and military spending have consistently had a higher priority status than essential service provision (World Bank 2005). The privatisation of basic services, the recovery of costs, and the elimination of universal basic subsidies have together placed additional limitations on poor people's access to necessary services. The quality of education and health care services has worsened and disparities in access to these and other services have been exacerbated, completely stratified by socioeconomic level, ethnicity and geographical location.[2]

Lack of family income and absence of government role as service provider and as an instrument for disparity reversal, have progressively accumulated a social debt of huge proportions of immediate negative effects and with unquestionably worse projections towards the future. Nowhere is this debt

---

[2] This is taken from the SAPRIN Report (*Informe SAPRIN*), *Structural Adjustment Policies: At the Roots of Poverty and the Economic Crisis* (*Las políticas de ajuste estructural, En las raíces de La crisis económica y la pobreza*), SAPRIN Secretariat, Washington D.C., November 2001.
SAPRIN is the International Civil Society Network for Participatory Review of Structural Adjustment Policies (La Red Internacional de la Sociedad Civil para la Revisión Participativa de las Políticas de Ajuste Estructural).

causing more damage than in children, who are disproportionally poor, since children under 18 only constitute one third of the world's population, yet they amount to more than half of the world's poor.

The social development of children and adolescents is a particularly urgent aspect of the larger picture. For them, there exists no second opportunity. Their biological and intellectual development cannot wait until their family manages to escape poverty or until the promised benefits from economic growth manage to trickle down. The harm due to malnutrition, poor health, and inadequate treatment during infancy is often irreversible and destined to be transmitted across generations. The Convention on the Rights of the Child (CRC) is very clear in assigning responsibility for the development of children and adolescents to the families and the state. Additionally, the state is assigned the duty of creating the necessary conditions for families to comply with their responsibilities. Nevertheless, states have not created those conditions. They have failed to eradicate unemployment and to create safety nets. By transferring coordination of basic service delivery for children to the market via privatisation policies, impoverished families lose access. Simultaneous public investments in children and in the creation of stable formal employment for adults, with dignified salaries and social benefits that cover not just workers but also their families, have now become the indispensable priority for genuine development.

While there have been some important achievements in the area of child welfare, such as lowering infant mortality and increasing primary school enrolment, positive trends are slowing down and are extremely uneven. Current poverty reduction rates are one fifth of what they were during the 1980–1996 period (UNDP 2005). Achievements have mostly benefited the middle and upper-income segments of the developing countries while the most vulnerable sectors have benefited far less so, or in some cases, have suffered greater decline (Minujín 2001). Child mortality rates among the poorest 20% of the population are falling at less than one-half of the world's average. Closing the gap in child mortality between the richest and the poorest 20% would cut child deaths by almost two thirds, saving more than 6 million lives a year (UNDP 2005). This is why, the fact that disparities are increasing world wide, is such bad news for children.

Society is in debt to its children. One billion children are currently limited by poverty. One in every three children live without adequate housing or sanitation; one in every five, without access to drinking water; one in every six without adequate nutrition; one in every six dies before reaching five years of age with 29 thousand daily preventable child deaths; one in every seven has no access to adequate health care; and one in every eight has never gone to school (UNICEF 2006).In addition, around 500,000 women also die each year from complications related to pregnancies or giving birth and approximately 14,000 new HIV infections now occur daily (UNDP 2003). As a consequence, there are currently two million children under 15 who are infected and 15 million children under 18 who are orphaned (UNICEF 2006).

A social and macro-economic system which so highly values individualism, competitiveness, and aggressiveness is progressively destroying the micro-economic setting of families and contradicting their traditional values of affection, solidarity and belongingness. The structure and capacity of the family as a basic socio-economic unit has become progressively weakened, likewise degrading the primary environment for protecting and promoting the rights and well-being of children.

The worsening of local economic conditions increases the pressure on young people to begin working at an early age. Children are attracted to the labour market given the poverty of their family. They make desirable labourers because they are easy to exploit. This way, while the neoliberal development model creates unemployed or underemployed adults, it likewise yields alarming figures for child labour, child abandonment, school dropouts, and frustrated children and adolescents. As this poverty cycle snowballs, the personal and social aspirations of the poor become ever more impossible to fulfil.

The International Labour Organisation (ILO) has reported an estimated 246 million child labourers worldwide, 180 million who are employed in the worst and most dangerous forms of child labour, 73 million of whom are under the age of 10. No country is immune from this trend as evidenced by the fact that 2.5 million of the above work in the most developed countries, with another 2.5 million found in transitional economies of the former Soviet republics. In addition, an estimated 8.4 million children are trapped in slavery, human trafficking, family debt servitude, sexual exploitation and other illicit activities. It is estimated that 1.2 million children are victims of child trafficking, forced to cross national border or lured into situations of sexual or commercial exploitation.[3]

---

[3] See ILO, *Facts on Child Labour*: http://www.ilo.org.communication.

Unemployment transforms young people and adults into illegal economic migrants. The dismembered family often remains behind and in most of these cases, the family never manages to reintegrate. The feminisation of migration forces desperate mothers to abandon their children, something most often exploited by third parties, leaving children in conditions that are even worse than when they experienced hunger with their mother.

Although young people have expanded their access to education in many cases, they become restricted from access to dignified work. To the extent that their access to mass media grows, they also become transformed into the victims of consumerist publicity, precisely when their access to consumer goods is being ever more restricted. Meanwhile, the health care infrastructure not only excludes them but fails to even contemplate providing the kinds of differentiated services required by youth in areas such as reproductive health, HIV/AIDS prevention and treatment, drug prevention and treatment, violence, accidents, and so on (ECLAC/OIJ 2004).

Meanwhile, environmental management remains on a permanent collision course with the neoliberal, agro-export model of production. The incessant search for expansion, consuming ever more non-renewable resources in the process, fails to assume the accompanying environmental costs and results in an irreversible deterioration. Technological innovation concentrated in the hands of just a few private transnational corporations is unable to act as an engine for social transformation and reduction of environmental risk, instead serving as a vehicle for intensifying exploitation of labour, social exclusion, and environmental destruction. Globalisation and the growth of industrial production and commercial advertising have created new patterns of consumption catering only to select sectors while increasing the production of wastes and pollution. At the same time, there has been no corresponding rhythm of increasing the capacity for waste reduction or even recycling the valuable resources being lost in waste, including water.

This loss of balance has degraded ecosystems to an alarming extent. In the last 50 years, the overall level of deterioration has sharply accelerated. Climatic change is increasingly providing us with a painful reminder of this. The availability of water per capita is now less than half of what once existed and these supplies are being contaminated by pesticides, fertilisers, and untreated human wastes. Air quality is likewise worsening, resulting in at least a 50% increase in registered respiratory infections. Five times more combustible fuels are being burned and four times as much emissions of carbon monoxide are being produced. The proportion of urban inhabitants relative to the total has grown from 17% to 50%, while the investments being made in urban infrastructure are being reduced. The use of cement has multiplied four-fold and the expansion of built areas has limited the natural drainage capacity, especially in urban areas, causing more frequent and more severe flooding. Over the last 25 years, the planet has lost a third of its natural resources in terms of forests, fresh water, and marine species. Meanwhile, a high proportion of vegetation that fulfils a hydro-regulating role has been lost, and global warming has come to threaten our future as a species (UNDP 1998).[4]

Growing environmental risks therefore constitute an additional negative consequence of the dominant development model. Coupled with increased social vulnerability, the result is a breeding ground for the so-called "natural" disasters that continue to increase in frequency and intensity.

All of the tendencies identified above are linked. Financial debt opens the gates to debt conditionality – to the disempowering of government via public policy impositions contrary to those they were elected for – to unfunded public budgets – to the desperate competition for financial resources among developing countries – to export led economies – to unfair trade – and along with it, death, poverty and hunger. They constitute the main manifestations of a mistaken approach to development, one oriented towards growth with the illusionary hope (or purposeful misrepresentation) that the benefits reaped by the few will eventually trickle down to all.

The fact remains that the current trend which is slowing down the rate of poverty reduction is happening in spite of a global context of growth recovery and of an increase in the per capita growth rate (UNDP 2005). Growth or no growth, unemployment soars and salaries and benefits dwindle. Moreover, the emphasis on the accumulation of wealth fails to assign moral primacy to the kinds of investment that have historically built safety nets and have shown to yield the highest human and economic returns, i.e., social investment.

Only countries that have guaranteed universal primary education for its people have reached high levels of social and economic development. In the United States, every dollar that is invested in early childhood education

---

[4] See also: The World Resources Institute, The United Nations Environment Programme, The United Nations Development Programme, and The World Bank, *1998–99 World Resources, a Guide to Global Environment*, Oxford University Press, New York, 1998–1999.

programmes yields future profits to society of more than 7 dollars (Karoly, 1998). The International Labour Organisation has estimated that the elimination of child labour and its replacement by universal education would produce a high economic return over and above the evident social benefits. At the global level, the economic benefits would outweigh the costs of this initiative by a 6.7 to 1 ratio (ILO 2003).

Recent history had amply demonstrated that the neoliberal model is fixated on monetary stabilisation and expanding markets for transnational corporations. This is an approach that has proven incapable of considering the ethic, social and ecological costs of its financial actions. The dominant paradigm is now routinely confronted by this evidence and dissident voices have begun to gather momentum. Even some who contributed to the imposition of this development model have now begun to question it publicly.

On the other hand, it has been amply demonstrated that high levels of social development can be reached even in the absence of robust economies. This can only happen if the correct priorities are set and the necessary political will is present. One study of ten national case studies suggested that the redistribution of goods and income will not happen automatically and that there is no guarantee that the distribution of income in a market economy is going to be neutral (Lewis 1997). The study concluded by affirming public policy makers will do well to build upon the potential synergy that exists between investments in education, water and sanitation, and health and nutrition in order to maximise the possible levels of social development in a context of highly limited resources. The study also concluded that growth in itself will not reduce poverty in terms of income nor in terms of human development, unless there are public policies that are specifically oriented to this objective (Lewis 1997).

Millennium Development Goals: Universalising the Rhetoric of Commitment

In recent years, the flood of international attention placed on poverty led to negotiations for setting urgent goals for poverty reduction and linking these efforts to a commitment to human rights. The fundamental goal agreed upon during the United Nations Millennium Summit was the worldwide reduction of extreme poverty by one-half over the 1990–2015 period, as defined by the portion of humanity whose income is less than one US dollar per day (United Nations 2000).[5] It is already known that only Southeast Asia is likely to fulfil this commitment while the rest of the developing world's regions will have serious difficulties in even closing in on the goal.

Innumerable international conferences in pursuit of forming viable goals for global development have arrived at strikingly similar conclusions. The ritual is for each conference to extend the deadlines for compliance. For example, the goals established in 1978 at the Conference on Primary Health Care in Alma Ata, including access to health, water and sanitation services for all by 1990 had to be re-adjusted for later dates at the World Summit for Children in 1990, the Earth Summit in 1992, the Social Summit in 1995, the Summit on Cities in 1996, the Millennium Summit in 2001, and so on. The funding commitments established at the Monterrey International Conference on Financing for Development in 2002 have likewise not been complied with.

With respect to the "Millennium Development Goals" (MDGs), we are dealing with a commitment to which all countries of the world signed on to. There was a similar generalised commitment made in the Universal Declaration on Human Rights. More specifically, commitments have been made by practically all countries of the world with respect to the Convention on the Rights of the Child (CRC). (Only the United States of America and Somalia have yet to ratify.) The 2001 Millennium Summit managed to conclude that humanity now has the resources, knowledge and specialised capacities for eradicating poverty during the lifetime of a child born at the moment in which the Millennium Declaration was approved. It was likewise thought that if the global progress observed during the decades of the 1970s–80s were to continue during the next two decades or until 2015, it was possible during the life of a single generation to achieve the stipulated goals.

Unfortunately, nobody predicted the exponentially cascading consequences associated with the deepening of neoliberalism. Consequently, it was either with naivety or opportunism that the following eight goals were established in the Millennium Declaration, each of which were operationalised with various concrete targets:

1. Eradicate Extreme Poverty and Hunger
2. Achieve Universal Primary Education

---

[5] See: http://www.unmillenniumproject.org/goals/goals02.htm.

3. Promote Gender Equality and the Autonomy of Women
4. Reduce Infant Mortality
5. Improve Maternal Health
6. Combat HIV/AIDS, Malaria, and other Illnesses
7. Guarantee Environmental Sustainability
8. Develop a Global Partnership for Development (United Nations 2000).

These Millennium Goals have become generally defined as a pact between nations for the elimination of poverty (UNDP 2003). Seen from the systemic point of view, the first objective would appear to be the most important since it constitutes the results of the latter goals, which are in large measure instrumental to achieving the former. Nevertheless, the systemic vision has not yet permeated all development circles, be it due to a basic lack of comprehension or for the sake of political convenience. Poverty continues to be seen largely in terms of income.

Equally important is the eighth goal that already implies eliminating the principal obstacles to the achievement of the preceding goals. Regrettably, this goal, despite being qualified by a series of more focused targets, remains suspiciously vague, devoid of clear indicators, and the official follow-up given to it has demonstrated very little enthusiasm. Compliance would not be impossible but the obstacles are now in plain view and the prevailing incapacity and lack of political will to comply with this goal is hardly surprising.

The *Human Development Report 2003* of the United Nations Development Programme (UNDP 2003) has pointed to the low levels of development assistance that industrialised countries offer and to the existing agricultural barriers that these countries maintain, as major obstacles. In addition, it has identified vast disparities including discrimination against women and the spread of HIV/AIDS as key factors in limiting progress towards the goal of reducing extreme poverty by one-half for the year 2015.

The 2004 Secretary General's Report on the Follow-up to the Outcome of the Millennium Summit identified the following additional obstacles: 1) the growth of transnational forms of criminal activity; 2) high level corruption and terrorism; and 3) wars, which in the last decade have cost more than 5 million lives (United Nations 2004). For his part, Jeffrey Sachs who was appointed Director of the United Nations Millennium Project, argues that there are four principal sets of obstacles to reaching the Millennium goals: 1) failures of governance, marked by corruption, a mistaken political economy and violations of human rights; 2) countries caught in the poverty trap with national and local economies too poor to carry out necessary investments; 3) pockets of poverty that are excluded from the rest of the society; and 4) negligence in public policy towards addressing key issues such as the environment, exclusion of adolescents, and maternal mortality (Sachs 2005). Unsurprisingly, all of these obstacles are depicted as endogenous to the Third Word.

To these, we can further add: 1) the foreign debt that accumulates under conditionality agreements and which actively imposes the "erroneous policies" that Mr. Sacks alluded to; 2) the lack of democracy at all levels, including and especially within the multilateral agencies; 3) the level of violence, both personal and institutional; 4) the unlimited drive for profits and power without any concern over the means and consequences associated with this profit seeking; 5) the lack of respect for the state of law at international, national and local levels; 6) the ecological vulnerability that goes hand in hand with social vulnerability in generating risks that inevitably result in so-called "natural" disasters; 7) unfair markets and the manipulation of foreign exchange rates; all these among other factors. Although the United Nations does not like to dwell on this, we could summarise by saying that overcoming these obstacles and reaching these goals amounts to a direct contradiction with neoliberalism. In this, it is not difficult to predict on what side the majority of governments will fall be it by their own political volition or imposed from abroad.

The United Nations *Human Development Report 2003* indicated that 21 of the 67 countries it analysed experienced a decline in development indicators during the decade of the 1990s. In 54 countries, per capita income fell in spite of the economic growth that some of these nations experienced. In 34 countries, life expectancy declined, while in 21 countries, hunger levels increased. In 14 countries, a greater number of children under the age of 5 died during that decade while in 12 countries, primary school enrolment rates had fallen (UNDP 2003).

The good news is that the indicators for extreme poverty at the world level had on average declined, albeit very modestly, over this period. The bad news is that this reduction is largely due to successes obtained in China and India, while many people actually experienced greater impoverishment across large areas of Africa, Latin America, Eastern Europe and Central Asia (World Bank 2004). At this moment, 1/6 of humanity or 1.1 billion persons live in conditions of extreme poverty, leading the United Nations[6] and the World Bank to

---

[6] This according to the follow-up to the outcome of the Millennium Summit, A/58/323, September, 2003.

express their concerns about the present trends and to acknowledge the fact that the majority of developing countries will not reach the Millennium Goals (World Bank 2004). Recent past president of the World Bank, James Wolfensohn, warned: "At present, five out of the six billion people alive on Earth live in developing countries that subsist on 20% of all global income. In 50 years, eight of the nine billion people projected to be alive will be found in the developing countries. This doesn't seem to much matter since we continue walking down the same old [failed] path" (World Bank News Service 2005).

Adding to the bad news, it has been calculated that at the current rate of progress, 90 countries will not reach child mortality goals of reduction by two thirds by 2015, 52 will not comply by 2035 and 44 will not comply by 2050. Sub-Saharan Africa would only manage to comply by 2115. Similarly 67 countries will not comply with universal primary education in 2015, 47 countries will not comply in 2035 and 39 countries will not comply by 2050 (UNDP 2005).

While the custom is to monitor the social progress of developing countries, the novel aspect of the Millennium Goals is that it locates the "debtors" everywhere, including among those who "supposedly comply." The 1995 Copenhagen Social Summit constituted an important step toward this change in the order of things. At that time, it sought to give follow-up to the previous commitment made by the developed countries to allocate 0.7 of their national income to the development of other less fortunate countries. It was also thought opportune to stipulate that 20% of development aid be destined towards basic social services. As a counterpart measure, the developing countries committed to dedicate 20% of their public budgets to essential social services.

In essence, the Millennium Summit went far beyond all that. Not only did it want the more developed countries to increase their assistance to developing countries, but it also called upon them to lift the barriers that act as a brake on the latter's development. As a result, the more developed countries committed themselves to ending hostile trade and financial practises, particularly with respect to those poorest countries. They further agreed to establish mechanisms to avoid that the foreign debt continues to drown any possibility of compliance on the part of the most heavily indebted countries (United Nations 2000).

Although one frequently hears news about debt reduction, we should remember that the foreign debt of the developing countries was acquired in large part to confront poverty. This debt has spiralled and now limits the potential for further development. The mechanisms established for condoning or exchanging the debt of the most Heavily Indebted Poor Countries (HIPC) have been so cumbersome as to be practically impossible to follow for those countries that so desperately need them. The few that have benefited from the financial provisions of this initiative have had to pay dearly, mostly in terms of the conditions imposed for admittance to the program. Indeed, even once a reduction on the order of 50% of their annual debt service payments is acquired, they continue to pay more on servicing their debt than on education and health.[7]

During a 2005 meeting of Finance Ministers and Central Bank Presidents of the G-7 countries, a proposal was made by British Minister Gordon Brown, inspired by the call made by Nelson Mandela in Trafalgar Square.[8] This led to the participants agreeing on a historic reduction of up to 100% of debt service payments on the part of International Financial Institutions with these countries. Although it appeared to represent a huge advance, it effectively translated into an indeterminate gesture in that it pertained only to a yet to be clarified proportion of debt servicing and not to the cancellation of the outstanding debt itself. Even vaguer was the lack of a mechanism that would equally benefit all HIPC, relying instead on a case by case determination basis.

It is well known by now how differentiated negotiations invariably result in a further weakening of the debtor countries and their capacity to negotiate on a collective basis, allowing for the imposition of even greater conditionalities. At one point, it was suggested that the resources necessary for financing this initiative should originate in the gold reserves of the International Monetary Fund. However, this proposal unleashed a tidal wave of rejection on the part of the G-7 countries due to fear of the impact that release of these gold reserves could have on world markets. In the end, it all appears to add up to empty promises.

---

[7] This openly reported at the G-7 meeting of February 7, 2005.

[8] "Sometimes it falls on a generation to be great. You can be that great generation" Nelson Mandela, Trafalgar Square, London, 2005 as part of the Make Poverty History Campaign.

Is the Developed World Complying?

It has always been supposed that the industrialised countries have by definition fulfilled their development obligations. Lurking behind successful averages, however, are all kinds of injustices that fall heavily upon the most vulnerable sectors of these societies, especially immigrants and ethnic minorities (UNDP 2005). Rather than become lost in the sordid and somewhat obvious fact of the growing disparities and related injustices among the most developed countries, I propose to focus in on the issue of *compliance* with Goal 8 of the Millennium Development Goals and its associated targets. This is where the worst debts can be found hence the root of many other problems.

It should not be forgotten that the neoliberal model of development imposed upon the Third World originated in the North and has essentially only served to benefit international banking, transnational corporations and arms manufacturers. It must also be remembered upon whose backs the industrialisation of the most developed countries was forged. This exercise in historical memory is not superfluous as there is no shortage of countries that fail to recognise their debts and existing obligations.

It might also be useful to remember that in the year 2000, an evaluation was conducted in Geneva on the progress realised thus far in complying with commitments made at the Copenhagen Social Summit. Alarmed by scant progress, a broad questioning took place as to the effectiveness of market-based macroeconomic policies. In the end, it was proposed that a general policy reorientation take place towards job creation and the reduction of poverty (United Nations 2000b). In 2005, ten years after the commitments made in Copenhagen, the United Nations reaffirmed that little or no progress had been made. Moreover, considerable alarm was raised over the growing focus on combating international terrorism and the way it had effectively diverted attention and financial resources away from development (United Nations 2005).

Promote Development: *Goal 8, Target 12: Further development of an open, rule-based, predictable, non-discriminatory trading and financial system, with a commitment to good governance, development and poverty reduction, both nationally and internationally.*

The farcical nature of trade negotiations both in the sphere of the World Trade Organisation (WTO) as well as in the Free Trade Area of the Americas (FTAA) speaks for itself. The present systems of commerce are asymmetrical to the detriment of the developing countries. Free market principles are still being imposed on the developing countries, while they have not been assumed by the more developed countries. Agrarian subsidies, patents, speculative financial flows, and the political manipulation of the foreign exchange market, constitute the most crucial issues with respect to this development target.

Developed countries' tariffs remain high on goods that are strategically important to developing economies, such as textiles and farm products. Developed countries continue to maintain barriers against the products of developing countries as they continue subsidising their own products. Spending on agricultural subsidies presently totals to US$ 350 billion dollars (World Bank News Service, 2005). As a point of reference, six times as much is spent on achieving a false competitiveness of products originating in the North than is spent on overall assistance and co-operation with countries of the South. Exclusively considering the agricultural sector, what the industrialized countries spend in a year in development assistance to the sector is equivalent to what they spend in a day subsidising excess agricultural production in their own territory. It is currently estimated that developing countries lose close to US$ 24 billion yearly in agriculture due to developed country protectionism and subsidies (UNDP 2005).

While official development assistance has recently enjoyed a small resurgence after years of reduction, it remains well below the commitment of 0.7% of gross national income of the donor countries. The global figure fell from 0.33% in 1999 to only 0.22% in 2001, modestly increasing to 0.25% in 2003, amounting to about one-third of what was internationally agreed upon. Some NGOs calculate that this amount should be reduced by 50% to close to 0.1% GNP if double accounting, overpricing, inefficiencies, uselessness, donor procurement tied aid, high administrative costs, lack of coordination, and many other similar causes are taken into consideration.[9]

This grievous lack of compliance has occurred in spite of numerous ratifications in each passing summit and in spite of all of the additional commitments agreed to in conferences such as the International Conference on Development Financing held in Monterrey back in 2002. It is worth remembering that the doubling of resources agreed upon in Monterrey would only increase the level of assistance by the donors to a level of about 0.44% of their gross income. This would fail to comply with the established amount targeted

---

[9] Action Aid International USA, www.actionaidusa.org Real Aid: An Agenda for Making Aid Work.

(0.7% GDP) and instead only reach the levels of assistance that existed during the 1960s.

In terms of the volume of resources allocated, the figure for all developing countries grew from US$ 53 billion in 1990 to US$ 52.3 in 2001, US$ 57 billion in 2002[10] and US$ 68.5 billion in 2003.[11] This last figure surged primarily on account of the allocations made for debt relief and for the reconstruction of damages caused to Iraq by the invasion of foreign forces. Whether debt cancellation can be computed as development assistance is an issue being defended by donors but contested by many important NGOs. The reality is that countries in dire need of fresh resources and who consider their foreign debt illegitimate, find little relief in official debt relief. Whether it is legitimate for governments representing corporate interests to profit through mass destruction so as to then profit reconstructing is equally at issue.

If indeed there are donor countries that meet or surpass the agreed upon commitments, such as Norway, Sweden, Denmark, Luxembourg, and the Netherlands, others, regrettably those involving the greatest volume of product such as the United States and Japan remain far from complying with the target. The United States, for example, dedicates only 0.1% of its product on development (OECD 2004). The commitment in the field of development co-operation included the agreement to earmark at least 20% of the total amount to basic social services. Nevertheless, this has only grown at the global level from 9% in 1996–1997 to 15% in 2000–2001.[12]

Efforts at quantifying all of this have been made by the journal *Foreign Policy* in conjunction with the Centre for Global Development, yielding a Developmental Commitment Index that takes into account development co-operation policies as related to policies with respect to trade, the environment, immigration, investment and contributions made to peace-keeping. The two countries that contribute the highest volume of development assistance although the lowest percentage of their Gross Domestic Product are Japan and the United States. These same two countries were precisely those with the worst Developmental Commitment Index ranking. None of the world's most powerful industrialised countries making up the G-7 achieve a good ranking in this index (Centre for Global Development and Foreign Policy 2003).

---

[10] United Nations, A/58/323.
[11] United Nations, A759/282.
[12] United Nations, A/58/323.

In February 2001, then World Bank President James Wolfensohn declared in a press conference that the world spends less on development in percentage terms than it did forty years ago. He argued that with US$ 1 trillion annual expenditures on defence, twenty times more is being dedicated to military spending than to giving hope to people by way of development assistance spending (Flickling 2004). He later said, jokingly, that if the world would spend US$ 1 trillion in development co-operation, it would only need to spend US$ 60 billion on defence. In reality, his quip was probably pretty accurate. The establishment of a just international order could allow savings of both the US$ 1 trillion as well as the US$ 60 billion. In any case, the World Bank under his direction proved entirely incapable of achieving anything remotely similar to Wolfensohn's commentary during his ten year term prior to stepping down in mid-2005.

One of the arguments commonly utilised to dismiss the lack of compliance on this issue is that developing country governments are incapable of absorbing larger quantities of development funds. This is where development assistance meets structural adjustment. With the soft, benevolent mask on, concerns are expressed regarding the urgency to alleviate – not to eradicate – poverty. Without the mask, developing country government hands are tied via structural adjustment. If it were true that there is an inability to absorb additional aid, it is precisely structural adjustment, to which most aid is tied, that is destroying those abilities.

So violently meagre is the amount of development co-operation and so poorly distributed and heavily conditioned is the assistance they offer that the Group of 77 countries (G-77)[13] decided to create a High Commissioner on South-South Co-operation[14] as an impartial mechanism of their own that will be more disinterested and more democratic in its functioning. The effectiveness of South-South co-operation has been increasingly demonstrated. The way in which Cuba has provided extensive scholarships for young students from excluded minorities across the region to study medicine on the island as well as the large scale co-operation of Cuban doctors working in health programmes in some of the most underdeveloped countries[15] constitutes

---

[13] The group of countries formerly known as the non-aligned countries.
[14] Group of 77, Declaration of Caracas on South-South Co-operation.
[15] Presentation of Cuba at the XVI Meeting of the International Co-operation Directors of Latin America, in reference to the more than 6 thousand young people from various Latin American countries that study at the Latin American School of Medicine in Cuba.

one of the most uplifting examples and potential for this type of co-operation. More recently, there are notable co-operation agreements between Venezuela and several other Latin American and Caribbean countries across a wide range of areas, including, and most importantly, in the field of petroleum. The most commendable feature of this kind of development assistance is that it is based on recipient countries needs and on donor countries capabilities, with no hidden costs.

Beyond the issue of the amount of development assistance and its distribution is the issue of the strings attached to most of it. It is frequently allocated to specific countries according to geopolitical interests as is evident when the list of largest aid recipients is unveiled as compared with the list of countries most urgently requiring assistance. Here, the main concern is its manipulation and it certainly does not go for free. Recipient countries have to pay back with political and even military complicity, with trade concessions or with the agreement to have their natural resources looted. The most flagrant misuse of development assistance currently ongoing is the subversion of democratic processes. Even though democracy promotion is paid lip service as the main imperial interest, great sums of money are used to get "friendly" governments in place. Nevertheless, when democracy puts leaders in office who are not in line with the preferences of the powerful, development assistance suspension is one of the first measures of retaliation. The disrespect for the decisions of the Palestinian people after the election of Hamas into government constitutes a recent case in point while certainly not the only one. The United States is the main political manipulator of foreign aid but the European Union is quick to follow. The intention of conditioning development assistance to thwarting emigration at the source in the developing countries is just another example.

Notorious is the case of aid related to reproductive heath and HIV/AIDS. Much of it is rendered ineffective due to conditions imposed by the United States which constitutes one of the worst forms of aid manipulation. Funds are conditioned to action according to particular religious beliefs which are certainly not universal. These actions have proven to be counterproductive in causing great human pain and have totally failed in halting the AIDS epidemic. These conditionalities are not only limited to their bilateral aid but are also imposed upon the multilateral agencies which they contribute to with funding.

Least Developed Countries: *Goal 8, Target 13: Address the special needs of the Least Developed Countries. (This includes tariff- and quota-free access for Least Developed Countries' exports, enhanced programme of debt relief for heavily indebted poor countries [HIPC] and cancellation of official bilateral debt, and more generous official development assistance for countries committed to poverty reduction).*

The Secretary General's 2004 Report indicated that between 1990–2001, the portion of development assistance allocated to the lesser developed countries actually diminished – especially that which was allocated to Africa – falling from US$ 14.4 billion to US$ 11.8 billion. This is an especially astonishing fact. On the other hand, the percentage of imports by more developed countries originating from the lesser developed countries that were allowed to enter freely remained largely unchanged. The contradiction lies in the fact that the percentage received by the developing countries showed an overall tendency to increase.[16] The lesser developed countries have not been privileged either in terms of development assistance or in terms of lowering protectionist barriers. Consequently, the additional efforts needed by the least developed countries in investing in the achievement of the Millennium Goals necessarily depend upon their own resources. At this moment of fiscal, economic, social, political and institutional crises, such a proposition is particularly difficult, especially for those countries furthest behind (de la Barra 2002).

The money dedicated to the Debt Reduction Initiative of the Heavily Indebted Poor Countries (HIPC) has definitely resulted in an increase in social spending as is the case in Bolivia and would therefore seem to be a positive initiative. Nevertheless, to continue to qualify, Bolivia has to continue paying those amounts which have not been eliminated which means that 20% of its public budget still goes to debt repayment (UNDP 2005).

HIPC funds to all countries increased from US$ 34 billion to US$ 41 billion between the years 2000–2003.[17] Nevertheless, the 27 countries under HIPC programmes still devoted US$ 2.6 billion in 2003 to pay their creditors (UNDP 2005). On the other hand, the sharp price drops for commodities produced by these countries have reduced the progress that would have otherwise been made by this initiative. Additionally, the qualification requirements and the conditionalities imposed have limited the utility of this kind of initiative. This

---

[16] United Nations, A/58/323.
[17] United Nations, A/58/323.

has led many countries in this category to fall further behind. The need to recur to additional borrowing as soon as the funding provided by this initiative is exhausted has demonstrated its lack of sustainability.

Adding insult to injury, the world's highest trade barriers are erected against some of its poorest countries. Moreover, WTO rules on intellectual property present a twin threat since they raise the cost of technology transfers and potentially increase the prices of medicines, posing grave risks for the public health of those in poverty (UNDP 2005).

Landlocked and small island developing states: *Goal 8, Target 14: Address the special needs of landlocked developing countries and small island developing states.*

In the case of landlocked countries, the proportion of development assistance received relative to their gross national income remained practically unchanged. Worse yet, it fell off drastically in the case of the small island developing states.[18] In the case of the island state of Cuba, blockaded for decades, its special needs have been exacerbated by hostility instead of being provided with assistance. In recent years, the blockade was further intensified and the United States has dedicated US$ 56 million to destabilisation efforts, a figure expected to grow (Noriega 2004).

Debt: *Goal 8, Target 15: Deal comprehensively with the debt problems of developing countries through national and international measures in order to make debt sustainable in the long term.*

According to the World Bank Debtor Reporting System, in 2003, overall Third World external debt reached 2.4 trillion dollars following a prolonged and exponential increase. On the one hand, debt servicing obligations continue to increase and continue to be a major obstacle to public investment in social services. On the other, external debt continues to be a weakening factor for governments subjected to conditionalities which again impact the social sector negatively. Even though bilateral debt cancellation has benefited some countries, especially HIPC countries, this has not been the case for multilateral debt where debt servicing costs have continued to rise.

The well-publicised G8 announcement in July 2005 concerning their decision to cancel debts, one re-broadcasted in a similar World Bank announcement

---

[18] United Nations, A/58/323.

on April 2006, in reality provided nothing more than a large smokescreen. It serves to hide the fact that cancellation will be available to just a handful of countries and not necessarily the most needy countries. Moreover, the draconian conditions under which these reductions are to be provided will worsen living conditions for the vast majorities while at the same time allowing transnational corporations to intensify their plunder. Only 54 billion out of the 2.4 trillion dollars of overall developing country debt will be cancelled. This certainly does not change the fact that maintaining high levels of indebtedness in the Third World remains instrumental for maintaining their dependency and their servitude to the interests of their creditors. Needless to say, it also keeps the reimbursements flowing. The more they pay, the more they owe.

> **Youth employment:** *Goal 8, Target 16: In co-operation with developing countries, develop and implement strategies for decent and productive work for youth.*

In the case of this final target associated with the eighth Millennium Goal, the youth unemployment rate of those aged 15–24 decreased in the 1995–1999 period across the developing world as a whole. Nevertheless, it has increased in Latin America and the Caribbean,[19] with all sorts of repercussions such as illegal migration. The developed countries also have high rates of youth unemployment, albeit half of those existing in Latin America and the Caribbean, and youth reactions are highly visible in the streets of Europe. Of the 185 million jobless people worldwide, just under half are young people aged 15–24. In developing regions, young people are three times more likely than adults to be unemployed. The total number of young people has increased by over 115 million since 1990, to nearly 1.2 billion in 2004, and is expected to grow by an additional 64 million by 2015. In 6 out of 9 developing regions, unemployment rates are higher among young women than among young men (United Nations, 2005b). Youth unemployment is simultaneously a violation to their dignity, a drag on national economies and a waste of a country's most important resource.

Is Latin America Complying?

The region of Latin America and the Caribbean exhibits the greatest inequalities in the world in terms of income distribution. The per capita income of

---

[19] United Nations, A/58/323.

the 20% wealthiest segment of the population is 17.8 times greater than that of the 20% poorest segment. Latin American countries, on average, have per capita levels of income barely more than the midpoint of the world's average income at the same time that it has a three times greater unequal distribution (Hintze 2003). The benefits of economic growth achieved during some periods have not yet arrived to the lowest income sectors. On the contrary, the income disparities continue to intensify and constitute an important underlying factor of poverty in the region. Households in the bottom 20% of the distribution scale receive between 2.2% (Bolivia) and 8.8% (Uruguay) of total income, while the top quintile holds between 41% (Uruguay) and 62.4% (Brazil) of total income (ECLAC 2005).

Disparities among countries are a concern as are disparities within countries. The region is highly indebted and highly dependant on external financing which remains highly volatile. The financial servicing of the debt becomes a crushing burden that seriously impairs the capacity of states to implement public policies. The region is also dependant on the prices of the raw materials it exports such as oil, gas and minerals which have recently had a positive turn due to increased military demand and to China's increasing production needs. However, the region is very negatively impacted by global agricultural trading systems while the share of development assistance it receives is insignificant.

Among the region's most pressing problems is the shortage of jobs with unemployment rising from 6.9% in 1990 to 10% in 2004 (ECLAC 2005). According to the International Labour Organisation, Latin America has a formal employment deficit of at least 126 million jobs, considering the 23 million unemployed and the 103 million precariously employed people that amount to more than half of the economically active population. Meanwhile, research has indicated that in order to obtain relatively "decent" jobs in the region, no less than 11 years of formal education are required (ILO, 2006).

Are Latin American and Caribbean countries complying with the goals they have committed themselves to? In a target by target analysis, it can be seen that they are not. For the existing realities of the region, the Millennium Goals are not particularly ambitious. Having been globally set, they correspond more to the realities of other regions of the developing world. This makes the failure to achieve them doubly dubious.

Poverty: *Goal 1, Target 1: Halve, between 1990 and 2015, the proportion of people whose income is less than $1 a day.*

The level of extreme poverty (less than US$ 1 per day) remains high in the region and shows no signs that it will reach the target. It went from 11.0% of the population in 1990 to 9.5% in 1999[20] and has worsened since then, especially since 1997. Between 1997–2003, 27 million new individuals became added to their ranks. After six years of low per capita growth and weak labour markets, 40% of the region's population by year 2000 were living under the poverty line (US$ 2 per day). In 2003, that figure increased to 44.4% (or 227 million people) with 20% of the total population living in extreme poverty (US$ 1 per day).

The economic "recovery" of 2004 which witnessed a regional growth of 5.5% was accompanied with a considerable increase in remittances on the part of immigrants living abroad and an increase in employment, all of which helped to reduce poverty to a 42.9% level and extreme poverty to 18.6%. These changes were insufficient given continued population growth to allow for much hope in reducing the total number of poor people now reaching 222 million with 96 million living in extreme poverty. Official unemployment remained high but fell from 10.7% in 2003, to 10% in 2004. Seven out of every ten new jobs are created in the informal sector. Economic growth when it has occurred has not reduced poverty and has not created new jobs or improved salary levels.[21]

The United Nations Economic Commission for Latin America and the Caribbean (ECLAC) in conjunction with the UNDP and IPEA, carried out an analysis with the aim of assessing to what extent a sample of 18 different countries in the region would comply with the Millennium Target of reducing extreme poverty by 2015 if they maintain the trends and advances in the reduction of disparities achieved during the 1990s. The conclusion was very convincing. Only 7 of the 18 countries would reach the target. Six other countries would continue to reduce the incidence of extreme poverty, but at a rhythm too slow to reach the targeted goal. The last five countries would actually increase rather than reduce the incidence of extreme poverty due either to an increasing income disparity or to reductions in per capita income, or both. The study also concluded that the high levels of income disparity in the region constituted the most powerful obstacle to reaching this goal. It was made quite clear that economic growth free of any redistributive

---

[20] United Nations, A/58/323, September, 2003.
[21] See various publications of ECLAC in this regard, including their annual *Social Panorama* and *The Millennium Development Goals: A Latin American and Caribbean Perspective.*

mechanism is a very weak factor for poverty reduction. Much more effective than economic growth by itself are policies designed to reduce disparities (ECLAC, et al. 2002).

On the other hand, ECLAC also calculated that upon completing nearly half of the time allotted towards the goal of reducing extreme poverty in half, the cumulative progress made by 2002 had only achieved 27% of the goal. The pace of reducing extreme poverty, looking back at year 2000 when poverty was at 40%, has not just slowed but in fact suffered a significant setback as a result of the economic and social crisis of the next several years.[22] The relative progress made during 2004 improved the regional situation with respect to this particular goal, but it remains far from keeping pace with the targeted rate of steady advances.[23]

More recent analysis concludes that not enough progress has been made towards this target. Only one country has already complied and five others are making substantial progress. All the other countries have made little progress or have suffered setbacks (ECLAC 2005).

It should also be mentioned that the indicator utilised for measuring extreme poverty – that of less than US$ 1 per day – is a global indicator adjusted to the situation of other developing regions of the world, with the end result that it remains quite low for the highly urbanised region of Latin America and the Caribbean. Again, this renders even more dismal the conclusion that compliance with this inadequate standard is not going to be achieved.

Hunger: *Goal 1, Target 2: Halve, between 1990 and 2015, the proportion of people who suffer from hunger.*

The incidence of hunger has been reduced but not to an extent sufficient to achieve this goal. In 1990, 11% of children under the age of 5 were underweight, something that was only reduced to 8% by the year 2000. The portion of the region's population falling under the minimal level of caloric consumption went from 16% to 10% in the same period.[24] Meanwhile, the absence of food subsidies, low salary and employment levels, the systematic destruction of subsistence agriculture and the high levels of urbanisation, all

---

[22] ECLAC, *Panorama Social de América Latina 2002–2003*, Santiago de Chile, August 2003.

[23] ECLAC, Panorama Social de América Latina, 2004, Santiago de Chile, November, 2004.

[24] United Nations, A/58/323.

contribute to a convincing scenario that makes it impossible to believe that this regional target to dramatically lower hunger can be achieved.

Education: *Goal 2: Ensure that, by 2015, children everywhere, boys and girls alike, will be able to complete a full course of primary schooling.*

Latin America and the Caribbean is the only developing region where reaching the goal of primary education is possible. The enrolment rate in primary schooling for each 100 school-aged children went from 86.9% in 1990 to 95.7% in 2001/2002.[25] Unfortunately, this indicator is extremely limited. It is not sufficient to know how many children enrol. It is also important to know how many reach the fifth grade and overall quality of the education received. The calibre of teaching, the relevance of the curriculum to practical working skills, and the overall educational level reached show severe deficiencies in the majority of countries. The high drop-out rates of children prior to reaching the fifth grade in part constitutes a reflection of this situation (ECLAC/UNICEF 2002). UNICEF has established that no matter how good the quality of primary school instruction, if pupils have not received any early childhood or pre-school education, they do not tend to perform well in primary school. Pre-school education of children 3–5 years of age increased from 31.4% of coverage in the region in 1990 to 48% in 1997, although these are basically localised in the urban areas and among the higher socio-economic strata (ECLAC/UNICEF/SECIB 2003). Regrettably, there were no goals set for these educational levels.

Nor was any goal proposed for the secondary level of education. It has been amply demonstrated that a primary level of education is insufficient to provide for an exit out of poverty in Latin America and the Caribbean (ECLAC/UNICEF/SECIB 2001). Minimally adequate to the task is 11 or more years of education. The secondary enrolment rate was at 64.1% in 1996, the best year of the decade and so it is difficult to imagine that it could reach universal coverage by 2015. Both pre-schooling and secondary schooling should be universal, regardless of the absence of a dedicated Millennium Goal. Moreover, in a region where the most excluded children are from indigenous and Afro-descendant families, universal intercultural education cannot continue to be postponed. So while this goal has a high potential to be achieved

---

[25] United Nations, A/59/282.

in Latin America and the Caribbean, it is in reality an insufficient goal that will bring little sense of jubilation when such a limited target is finally reached.

Gender: *Goal 3: Eliminate gender disparity in primary and secondary education, preferably by 2005, and in all levels of education no later than 2015.*

Latin America and the Caribbean is the only region in the developing world where girls have higher rates of literacy than do boys, where enrolment rates in primary schooling is almost as high for girls as it is for boys, and where secondary school matriculation rates for girls is slightly higher than those for boys.[26] Consequently, this goal can be considered achieved in advance according to these indicators, although gender inequality in work, pay levels, and political participation leaves women still far behind.

Child Mortality: *Goal 4: Reduce by two-thirds, between 1990 and 2015, the under-five mortality rate.*

The mortality rates for children under the age of five fell from 54 per thousand live births in 1990 to 35 per thousand in 2002 although this trails far behind the eight per thousand figures for the more developed countries.[27] Infant mortality (under the age of 1) fell from 43 per thousand live births to 28 per thousand, also lagging far behind the six per thousand figure for developed countries. Both indicators declined but not sufficiently to reach the targets, and given that the average figures conceal the huge disparities that exist, it is effectively the case that little progress has been made among the poorest segments of the population.

The percentage of children vaccinated against measles by age one went from 77% in 1990 to 93% in 2003, approximating the figures of the developed world.[28] Nevertheless, some countries in the region will not be able to sustain their achievements in vaccination coverage due to the crisis in recent years, both because of the lack of resources for the purchase of vaccines as well as the outmoded infrastructure for administering the vaccinations.

Maternal Mortality: *Goal 5: Reduce by three-quarters, between 1990 and 2015, the maternal mortality ratio.*

---

[26] United Nations, A/58/323. A/59/282.
[27] United Nations, A/59/282.
[28] All of the above figures derived from United Nations Report A/59/282.

Maternal mortality has only slightly improved and the Report of the Secretary General found it difficult to discern a trend. The regional average for the year 2000 was 190 maternal deaths for 100,000 live births, this in spite of the fact that the percentage of assisted births by trained personnel increased from 76% in 1990 to 85% in 2000.[29] The probability of dying due to causes related to pregnancy and giving birth is almost ten times greater in Latin America than in the more developed countries.

HIV/AIDS: *Goal 6: Have halted by 2015 and begun to reverse the spread of HIV/AIDS.*

In 2002, 0.6% of the population in Latin America between the ages of 15–49 were living with HIV/AIDS, increasing to 0.7% in 2003. In the Caribbean, this same figure was 2.4%, the highest rate of infection in the world after sub-Saharan Africa.[30] Only Cuba and Brazil have had success in containing HIV/AIDS as a result of a prevention and treatment programme differenti-ated by risk group, in conjunction with free treatment being offered to those affected by the epidemic. The spread of the virus has elsewhere become more serious, particularly in the rest of the Caribbean and Central America.

Progress will not be easy in a Region which has allowed neoliberal poli-cies to destroy its public health systems and in a world which for the same reasons has placed research in the hands of private, for-profit enterprises. The lack of progress towards this goal puts all of the remaining goals at risk.

A Human Rights Perspective: Contradictions in the Millennium Initiative

A critical look at the Millennium Initiative can be enhanced from a human rights perspective. The guide for this is provided by the principles of vari-ous human rights instruments that emphasise the inherent dignity of human beings both as individuals and as societal members. Such human rights are universal and inalienable, which means that they pertain to all and cannot be renounced.[31] The principles of the indivisibility and inter-dependency of rights further convey their over-riding importance and inter-related nature.[32] They imply that the realisation of any one of these rights depends upon the

---

[29] United Nations, A/58/323, A/59/282.
[30] United Nations, A/58/323, A/59/282.
[31] Universal Declaration of Human Rights, 1948.
[32] Conventions on Economic, Social and Cultural Rights and on Civil and Political Rights, 1996.

realisation of all of these rights. What is needed in both thought and action is a multi-sectoral approach. It obligates us to look integrally at economic, social, fiscal and budgetary policies when addressing development issues.

The principles of equality and non discrimination grant equal rights of equal quality to all. The right to participation and inclusion along with the principle of responsibility before the law imply rights as well as obligations. The realisation of human rights at the very least depends upon:

- Legislative concordance
- Effective independent functioning of the three branches of state power
- Adequate public policies at the global, national and sub-national levels
- Public institutions capable of implementing essential public policies
- Organised civil society capable of monitoring and demanding rights.

It should be remembered that the Declaration of the Rights to Development ratified back in 1986 defined development processes as inalienable human rights.[33] Like every right, the right to development is an integral construct that depends upon the implementation of all other civil, cultural, economic, political and social rights. It was also established that the purpose of development co-operation is to contribute to the development of capacities of the duty bearers (states) to comply with their obligations and the capacities of the rights holders (members of civil society) to demand their fulfilment. With these notions in place, we can point to a variety of contradictions.

From the point of view of the universality of human rights, the right to inclusion and to non-discrimination is already implied. The mere fact that the Millennium Goals were established for only a fraction of the global population is in clear violation of elementary human rights principles. Even if we understand these goals to constitute a tool for measuring progress, i.e., the establishment of minimal standards that all are invited to surpass, and even if they only signify a critical path for achieving ever broader development objectives, the goals are exclusionary with respect to those social sectors not contemplated by them. Worse yet, it is easily predictable that in seeking to achieve the goals as stipulated, emphasis will be placed on those segments where compliance is most realisable, i.e., on the segments of the population

---

[33] Declaration on the Rights to Development, 1986; World Conference on Human Rights, 1993.

that already have the necessary income to help compensate for the state's chronic inaction.

As we have argued, not only has global progress been insufficient in fulfilling the Millennium Development Goals, but the poor have not benefited from the scarce progress made thus far. Worse yet, progress towards achieving the goals have only deepened existing disparities (Minujín 2001). This latter observation would seem unthinkable and yet it can be easily seen if the trends in the area of relative and extreme poverty are jointly analysed. While in some cases, relative poverty has been reduced, extreme poverty has increased and the region has become further polarised. The manner in which development efforts have been designed to gloss over this ignominious fact rests in the way it collects information on development progress, deliberately failing to disaggregate data in essential areas. Strong preference is given to averages and in this manner, the worst injustices and most extreme disparities among specific age-groups, genders, geographical territory and socio-economic groups as well as others are all concealed.

Over recent years, relative poverty as well as absolute poverty have both intensified in Latin America, with the latter growing much more rapidly as a result of the overall exacerbation of disparities. Take for example the year 2002, the worst year of the recessionary first half decade of the century in Latin America. Of 7 million new poor people, 6 million fell into extreme poverty (ECLAC 2003). The Millennium Goals lacked an indicator for measuring disparities that would have ensured avoiding the absurd possibility of, for example, achieving the proposed development goals while completely excluding the entire indigenous population (Molina 2004) or even completely missing the lowest 10% socio-economic stratum.

Another form of violating the principle of universality consists in putting the wrong kind of policy into practise. This includes, for example, those being imposed by International Financial Institutions (IFIs) that focus only on the most excluded. If indeed this kind of positive discrimination is seen as an available formula for reversing existing disparities, in the present context, it has come to signify that the poor need to be included but with inferior quality services, i.e., "poor people's services." This kind of formula would obviously be discriminatory for those who are not being classified as the poorest as well as those who are just on the edge of cut-off, consequently leaving them excluded. In other words, positive discrimination ends up contravening its laudable purpose of contributing to levelling the terrain. In the current political context, however, where there is so little solidarity to be found, there will regrettably be greater opportunity to approve budgets, laws and policies that ostensibly aimed to benefit everyone.

The Millennium Project formulated a Practical Plan for Achieving the Millennium Goals,[34] although in reality, it more resembles the goals themselves rather than recommendations for achieving them. One of its ten principle recommendations flagrantly ignores the principle of universality by proposing that donors should identify at least a dozen countries whose good governance and capacity for absorbing assistance would make them more apt for achieving the goals over a shorter time. The recommendation essentially calls for concentrating development assistance in those countries so identified in order to improve the average level of achievement. Shamelessly, it proposes a statistical solution to the problem, ignoring the ethical consequences which such an approach signifies in terms of increasing the existing regional disparities.

From the point of view of the indivisibility of rights, a series of fallacies can be identified. The most flagrant is the delinking between social policy and economic, fiscal and budgetary policies. Social issues are handed over to under-financed social cabinets or decentralised to the municipal level where technical and financial resources are woefully lacking. It is frequently the case in Latin America that the responsibility for guaranteeing the rights of children fall to persons that are accustomed to de-linking the task from public policy and transforming it into a charitable or even religious activity.

A great step forward has been taken by some organisations in linking the achievement of social policies with the politics of budgetary allocation. However, this battle is just beginning. Not only is it failing to comply with the committed levels of investments but in fact, it has cleverly been de-linked from the issue of fiscal and tax policies. This results in something unforgivable in a region that displays the lowest tax loads in the world and whose systems of taxation are plagued with opportunities for tax evasion (IDB 2004). Latin America is a region characterised by highly regressive tax systems that are imposed most systematically on consumption instead of capital, disproportionately impacting upon the poorest sectors as a consequence.

---

[34] It is called the *Millennium Project, Investing in Development: A Practical Plan for Achieving the Millennium Goals*, New York, 2005.

From the point of view of the inter-dependence of rights, recognising that the realisation of one right depends upon the realisation of all rights, we can scrutinise some of the recipes for development presently in circulation. The World Bank, for example, affirms that a focus on primary education yields the best payoff in terms of development and therefore conditions its loans upon that premise. We know well, however, that without preschool and early childhood education, the performance in the primary educational system will suffer. But performance levels will also suffer if children are not guaranteed their right to nutrition, health and a family. Perhaps greater work should be devoted to studying why their parents are unemployed.

In the same vein, the magical formula for achieving development as proposed by the Bretton Woods institutions consists in trade for growth. It remains blind to the necessity that growth be accompanied with redistribution policies designed to benefit the majority. It also ignores the fact that commerce, in order for it to yield development benefits, must be a fair trade, with rules of the game that are the same for all commercial parties. In Latin America and the Caribbean, even when there was growth for the first half of the 1990s, this did not reduce poverty and it simply did not result in significant net job creation.

The World Bank itself now recognises the fact that it is not the quantity of growth that matters in development but rather the quality of growth (World Bank 2000). According to Malloch Brown, Head of the United Nations Development Programme (UNDP) during the period 1999–2005, the figures have destroyed the myth that if a country followed the so-called "Washington Consensus,"[35] by liberalising its economy, bringing its macro-economy into line, and cutting public spending, it would result in economic growth. The great decade, heralded as the decade of economic reforms, the liberalisation of the market, the integration of world markets, and all of these other good things has ended with a significant nucleus of countries in a worse situation and with more poor people than there was a decade earlier, according to Brown.[36] So numerous have been the voices critical of the Washington Consensus that one now hears more and more of a post-Washington Consensus era.

---

[35] This expression is well known in Latin America and it refers to policies imposed by Washington.
[36] According to his comments before The Inter-Parliamentary Union Conference, Address by Mark Malloch Brown, UNDP Administrator, Santiago, Chile, 7 April 2003.

A similar example is the "magic formula" developed based upon the direct correlation posited between social investment and human development (or the inverse correlation between social investment and poverty). Those countries in the region with the greatest level of human development (equal to or greater than 0.760) or with the least poverty (less than or equal to 10%) have social investment of US\$ 150 per person per year or more. This figure consequently would appear to represent a minimum level of per capita social investment that could allow more acceptable levels of development and poverty reduction to be achieved.[37] It can be inferred that by carrying out adequate levels of social investment, countries could achieve the development of their peoples, reduce the poverty that exists and effectively pay the social debt.

However, development cannot be achieved solely by social investment, no matter how redistributive it may be. It is indispensable to review the totality of public policy. This is so that economic, fiscal and budgetary policies can produce and allocate the necessary resources to comply with its commitments and so that social policies can be specifically designed to achieve it. Parallel to this, it is also indispensable that the strengthening of public institutions be prioritised since they are the only instrument with the possibility of reversing existing disparities and effectively complying with the goals.

Even more contradictory is the fact that increased social spending falls into a collision course with the adjustment policies previously put into place by neoliberalism. Although these adjustment policies have been universally reviled in recent years, in some cases even by their own authors, the policies remain imposed as conditionalities on the borrowing countries, and even more so on those countries with ongoing debt reduction programmes. Payment of the foreign debt and continued arms spending have instead assumed priority over social spending. In Latin America and the Caribbean, social spending has historically been pro-cyclical. This means that significant contraction occurs during periods of recession, precisely when it is most needed.

Another contradiction can be seen in the World Bank proposal made at the Shanghai Conference on Poverty Reduction. Good practises were looked for in distinct contexts in order to replicate them and increase their scale so as

---

[37] This came from a draft document of UNICEF: "Actualización de la estimación de las Necesidades de Inversión en la Infancia para alcanzar las Metas de la Agenda del Plan de Acción Iberoamericano" (April 2004).

to more effectively reduce poverty. In so doing, they failed to recognise that good ideas do not prosper unless they address the generalised context that reproduces injustice.

Equally unsustainable are the so-called "Quick Win Initiatives" that are contained in the document of the Millennium Project[38] as one of the ten Principle Recommendations for achieving the Millennium Development Goals. The same document advises that these are not the only interventions needed for achieving the Goals, but they are simply those with the greatest potential of making a short-term impact if placed into immediate practise. Other interventions, they advise, are more complicated and will require more prolonged efforts that only show their effects in the long term.

From the point of view of the right to participation, the new formulas created by the IFI's are equally plagued with contradictions. Their very nature seems to poke fun at this right in the processes of dialogue set up prior to the formulation of the Poverty Reduction Strategies. An independent study concluded that all of these strategies, no matter how distinct the countries involved may be, end up being very similar. Worse yet, they suspiciously resemble the old programmes of structural adjustment. Economic growth, macro-economic stability, financial de-regulation and commercial liberalisation continue to be considered prerequisites in order to end poverty,[39] while remaining blind to all existing evidence to the contrary. The Millennium Project sets forth a recommendation to create strategies that can align Poverty Reduction Strategies with the Millennium Development Goals. There is nothing to indicate that these are going to have any better luck in their outcome.

Needless to say, participation in important stages of the development process such as policy development, budget allocation or trade negotiations has yet to be conquered. The emblematic exception to this rule has been the participatory municipal budgets in a handful of Brazilian local governments. On larger issues, important social mobilisations trying to stop Free Trade Agreements with the United States have largely been ignored by governments in Ecuador and Peru. On the other hand, social mobilisations have been powerful enough to bring down some governments in Latin America.

---

[38] Millennium Project, *Investing in Development: A Practical Plan for Achieving the Millennium Goals*, New York, 2005.
[39] See: Frances Stewart and Michael Wang, "Do PRSP Empower Poor Countries and Disempower the World Bank, or is it the Other Way Round?" University of Oxford, Queen Elizabeth House Working Paper #108.

The four broad sets of observations outlined above suggest the contradictory nature of the MDGs from a human rights perspective. The late James Grant, former Executive Director of UNICEF, argued forcefully that the problem is not that we have attempted to eradicate global poverty and failed. The problem is that there has never been a serious, concerted attempt to achieve this objective (Grant 1999). The resources to do it exist. It only remains to allocate them in a better, more prioritised, and more equitably distributed manner.

The tendencies currently in place are reversible only through a collective political will to do so. The universal instruments of existing human rights place a moral and legal obligation to act accordingly. A development agenda that combats disparities and eliminates exclusions will require a public policy of a new type, a change in institutions, and a change in societal values. Action should be aimed at the transformation of the structures of power at all levels, from the global level to the local level, to the level of the family and the community, so as to eradicate the deep-seated causes that impede the welfare of the majority. The need for an increase in the capacities to govern has become a survival issue (Dowbor 1998).

In a unipolar world engaged in an asymmetrical process of globalisation, where conflicts are resolved by the use of armed force and where relationships between countries are strongly conditioned in favour of the strongest, the sum total of these social relations amounts to an antithesis of democracy. Consequently, the urgent task is to achieve global democracy; to establish regulatory mechanisms over the flows of speculative finances and over the extraction of non-renewable natural resources; and to reform global institutions, especially those that impose failed development models which only exacerbate existing asymmetries.

What is needed are macro-economic policies that benefit the vast majorities and that can guarantee compliance with human rights. At the national level, a democratic development is needed to ensure that governments respond to collective interests and work to promote greater inclusion. It is moreover necessary to evolve from a representative democracy to more participatory democracies. Significant spaces for social participation must be created at all levels of decision-making processes, including in those decisions that link national processes to transnational processes. For that to be effective and to not become easily manipulated, good educational levels are needed along with a mass media working at the service of people rather than big capital.

Beyond the open expression of opinion, the exercise of voting, and greater participation in major decision-making, a true democracy cannot exist if there is no equitable participation in the fruits of development. This requires a state that can play a strong role in guaranteeing rights, in the redistribution of wealth, in the protection of the most vulnerable, and in crisis prevention. To that end, it is indispensable to impede the negative impact of the commercially monopolised mass media and of the private financing of electoral processes in order to be able to achieve true democracies and a state that can represent the majority. Independent mass media plays an essential role in informing public opinion, in promoting transparency in the relations between those who govern and those who are governed, and in helping to reverse the accelerated tendency of the use of disinformation on the part of world leaders in order to achieve their narrow objectives.

In Latin America, there exists a very particular relationship with democracy. The region is largely still caught up in a process of re-democratisation following a prolonged period of military dictatorship. In many cases, the acquisition of justice and equality before the law is still felt to be only a utopia. Conquering the right to know historical truths seems equally unreachable. Corruption throughout the region is not rare within the incipient democracies and the opportunities that the neoliberal development model has offered for the growth of corruption have been plentiful. But on the other hand, it has to be remembered that the era of neoliberalism in Latin America was imposed by the hand of authoritarian governments and dictatorships.

We must insist that a change in values is needed to promote solidarity over competitiveness, to put an end to the supremacy of one country over another, of capital over labour, of one gender over another, of one race or culture over others, and of one age-group over others. A change in values is needed that can go from self-interested individualism to social responsibility; where the principle value of growth and development is not the accumulation of wealth but rather the democratic achievement of a minimal human morality that can guarantee the priority of human rights.

The principles that support international human rights instruments can contribute towards orienting the change of approach. The consideration of these principles implies the decision to develop inclusive societies based in values of solidarity and shared responsibility, where basic needs are considered rights and where the concept of the expansion of citizenship includes both civil and political rights as well as social and economic rights.

Development of a new type of public policy is needed that is based on these values. This must be policy with an economic base that puts the available resources where they are needed in promoting the conditions for all families so that they may remain viable. It should privilege the concept of "right to access" to basic services over the concept of "free access" to the market of basic services. Public policy must work to reverse existing disparities rather than just confronting the worst symptoms of poverty. It must re-orient technological development towards human development. Public policy must establish permanent systems of social protection in order to prevent social crises before they occur. Policy must permit everyone to become participating actors in the processes that affect them. This kind of public policy is one that ultimately guarantees the right to change existing structures of oppression.

Resistance and the Upswing of Hope

Submerged in recurring and multi-dimensional crises, with permanent outflows of resources to the North, and inextricably intertwined ties to the interests of the United States, Latin America is producing resistance. Out of this resistance comes the kind of creative proposals necessary to confront the present status quo and they provide the region with hope that a more just world is possible.

There is a growing consensus on the urgency to define a regional development agenda responding to regional demands and interests rather than to continue with imposed agendas like the Washington Consensus which only responds to external interests. Several alternative initiatives for liberation have emerged and are being tested. The development of a club of debtors to collectively confront creditors is one of them. The creation of Compensatory Structural Adjustment Funds in order to compensate the deficiencies of international financial institutions and to fund the adjustment processes derived from the opening of the markets is another. There is the creation of a Regional Monetary Fund to provide early and unconditional financial assistance in order to prevent crisis by contagious international monetary crisis. A South – South Cooperation Agency has been envisioned in order to sideline the imposition of foreign agendas. The creation of TELESUR represents a milestone in order to counteract media dependency from transnational conglomerates geared towards the manipulation of information and minds. There is the creation of PETROAMERICA integrating PDVSA (Venezuelan oil company) and PETROBRAS (Brazilian oil company) in order to increase the region's clout in the field of energy. Finally, the creation of a South University can be included in this group which are among just some of the many new emerging initiatives.

A growing movement towards paying outstanding foreign debt in full in order to liberate countries from IMF and World Bank impositions, which debtor countries are forced to accept, is one emerging road towards freeing up countries from the Washington Consensus.[40] The region is simultaneously producing concrete proposals to reform both the IMF and the World Bank. Even more impressive is the proposal put forth by Venezuelan President Hugo Chavez, with support from the Group of 77, for creating an International Humanitarian Fund to act as a financial support mechanism to those countries that present alternative models of development in defiance of the prevailing model being imposed from the North.

The proposal of a Social Charter for the Americas as a framework for a free and integrated Latin America constitutes a new way of understanding integration and cooperation with important projections towards a future of independence. This Charter includes concepts such as the social control of government function, the rights of the indigenous population, and the right to work and to social protection. It has been promoted by Venezuela in contraposition to the OAS Democratic Charter which is merely an instrument for political domination.

Also hopeful is the fact that supra-national organisations are emerging with greater capacity to confront the assault of global capital. To this end, the South American Community of Nations has been formed not only for commercial integration purposes but also for political, social, energy and infrastructure integration, just like MERCOSUR was formed earlier in the Southern Cone as a means of uniting forces in negotiating better commercial terms in a unipolar world. In fact, the imperial trade project known as the FTAA and slated to be concluded in 2005 ultimately met intense resistance and was forced onto the backburner. The United States has tried to rescue this project by lowering the bar of expectations, settling for a more symbolic agreement (the so-called "FTAA light") while focusing on bilateral and sub-regional trade agreements which are also encountering substantial resistance.

The Venezuelan decision to abandon the Andean Community of Nations (CAN) was based on the argument that it was unwilling to risk being negatively

---

[40] This initiative is not free from its detractors who consider that the debt is illegitimate and should not be paid, i.e., the resources could have been better utilised by paying the social debt.

impacted either by limitations to the production of generic medicines or by the impact on its weak production infrastructure by competition with North American products coming in through Colombia and Peru. This was in effect, a response to the bilateral free trade treaties that these countries signed with the United States. Venezuela has stated that it would only reverse its decision should Peru and Colombia retreat from their agreements with the United States and should Ecuador stop its ongoing negotiations. A similar move by Uruguay to prepare for negotiating a bilateral trade agreement with the United States will most likely force that country to decide if it intends to remain in MERCOSUR.

Both CAN and MERCOSUR have their own internal weaknesses that need to be overcome. In the case of MERCOSUR, small countries like Uruguay and Paraguay fear becoming powerless in relation to Brazil and Argentina, their comparatively gigantic partners. Moreover, public criticism has been building that MERCOSUR constitutes only a commercial mechanism for the integration of capital while ignoring crucial issues such as the external debt, the asymmetries between countries, and more importantly, the larger interests of its people.

New and more positive forms of regional integration based on maximising solidarity, complementarities, and compensating for asymmetries among countries are emerging. These offer new hopes for the future that go well beyond traditional commercial objectives. The Bolivarian Alternative for the Americas (ALBA) is "the mother" of all these alternative integration projects. Rather than just integrating markets, it mainly integrates peoples. Rather than promoting free trade which solely benefits the strongest, it promotes fair trade and cooperation, developing compensatory measures to level the ground for smaller economies.

With ALBA, integration ceases to be a matter for governments who may be more or less submissive to imperial interests and becomes transformed into a matter of the people. Considering the highly conditioned forms of development co-operation, unjust terms and anti-democratic nature of global trade, the insight once espoused by the Cuban patriot José Martí more than a century ago still prevails in this new initiative, namely, that the region must create its own internal logic for development.[41]

---

[41] At the Monetary Conference of America held in New York in May 1891, one hundred and fifteen years ago, visionary José Martí stated "In order to ensure freedom,

Parallel to this, the active arena of regional commercial negotiations is expanding well beyond the United States and is now taking place with non-traditional partners such as China and others. This is not without its risks. A free trade agreement (FTA) with the European Union is now being considered even though there is no guarantee that it will differ much from those with the United States.

The main issue behind all of this consists of the persisting asymmetries among countries. The viability of integration processes therefore depends in large measure on the management of this issue. For the same reason, national integration depends on the ability to solve intra-country disparities. The fact that Latin America is the region with greatest disparities will need to be overcome as a matter of urgency if all these initiatives are to succeed. The reverse is also valid. Fidel Castro pointed it out as long ago as 1972 when stating that "solidarity cannot be achieved nationally if at the same time it is not achieved among all nations."[42] This is why aiming at competitiveness of one country over another, as neoliberalism proposes, has always been the wrong way to go. We should aim instead for the systemic competitiveness of all countries together in order to come close to Bolivar's dream of the region as a single nation. This is also why alternative international integration and cooperation based on solidarity turn into instruments of justice when compensating for asymmetries and disparities.

Another positive feature of this more genuine kind of integration is constituted by the region's social movements which are multiplying and acting ever more in concert such as in the World Social Forums and elsewhere. Over and above its many critics, the Social Forums offer a space for sharing counter-hegemonic thought and for confronting the World Economic Forum, the club of the powerful. Similarly, social movements confronting the FTAA have created their own Hemispheric Forum and have expanded their agenda to include the rejection of U.S. policies such as increased regional militarisation, neoliberal policies and the foreign debt. This particular movement inflicted upon the United States and its creation, the OAS, a resounding defeat in Mar del Plata at the end of 2005 as Washington made a last ditch effort to rescue the FTAA.

---

commerce needs to be balanced . . ." "The first thing a country does to dominate another country is to separate it from other countries . . ." "What needs to be done is whatever integrates people and makes their lives more ethical and liveable" (translation from Spanish original).
[42] Speech during a mass event in Poland in June 1972.

Large public demonstrations in desperate reaction to poverty, unemployment and other such bitter fruits of neoliberalism have in less than two decades proven capable of bringing down nine elite-dominated governments closely allied with the interests of imperialism. The movements of indigenous peoples, beginning with the Zapatista uprising in Mexico, have gained increasing clarity in actions to defend their rights, their territories, their natural resources and their autonomy. They are even managing to bring their leaders into office at the highest levels as is now the case with President Evo Morales in Bolivia. In sum, there are resurgent hopes for moving towards a more participatory democracy in the region.

The most unusual of the current social movements has been the show of force of Latin American immigrants in the United States who have found courage in numbers in spite of the consequences they face. Even though the movement originated in protest of the draconian new immigration laws being designed by the U.S. Federal Government, the sheer volumes of protesters, mainly of Mexican origin, evidenced the huge failure of the North American Free Trade Agreement (NAFTA) in improving living conditions in Mexico, forcing millions into illegal immigration. NAFTA essentially annexed Mexico as a low-wage industrial suburb of the United States and opened Mexican markets to heavily subsidised agricultural products from the United States which have destroyed local producers and national food security in Mexico. It is yet too soon to project the impact of this new effort but it certainly gives food for thought for other emerging movements in the region.

The enemy is of course learning from its failures and evolving. Dissident groups are covertly financed to pursue tactics similar to those of legitimate social movements. Without any disguise whatsoever but rather with the excuse of the fight against drugs and later terrorism, Plan Colombia has been well funded, allowing the proliferation of paramilitary death squads and the installation of U.S. military bases that act as counter-insurgency centres across the region.

As history continuously teaches us, advances acquire different speeds in different areas and territories, and are always accompanied by some retrenchments. There are governments that seek to redistribute wealth in favour of the poorest social sectors. Others seek to create mechanisms that can break with the servile traditions engendered by imperialism, seeking at least to reduce the vulnerability of their nation in this context. Still others, whose parties in power call themselves socialist, move towards a more representative democracy but to a large extent remain submerged in the contradictions arising from attempting a reformist approach within the dominant logic of neoliberalism. Under such adverse conditions, they have abandoned all audacity and creativity and continue to be subordinated to the interests of big capital to the detriment of the vast majority. They argue that they are in no position to frighten off potential foreign investors or even to pressure judicial authorities to bring those responsible for the crimes of the recent past to justice for fear of "destabilising" ongoing democratisation.

In spite of its limitations in size and diversity of natural resources and the constant harassment by its enemies, Cuba remains a great hope for the region and for the world at large because it demonstrates that if policy decisions remain firm, it is possible to accomplish ambitious goals. Not only is it the only country in the region that practically has the Millennium Goals achieved at the onset, but it continues to set higher standards for its development in spite of the need to cope with continuing aggression. Cuba has prioritised education, nutrition, health care and hygiene. It has also prioritised the productive sectors that can best help guaranteed its independence. Any other country in the face of such adversity would have abandoned its people and supported the large corporations, thereby relinquishing development efforts to whatever trickle down mirage these may offer.

Cuba is also an exemplary country in solidarity with other developing countries as shown in the large quantity of resources it has dedicated to South-South co-operation and to regional integration in general. Not only does it train doctors from socially excluded sectors from all over Latin America at its Latin American School of Medicine, but it also sends Cuban doctors to practise free of charge in 18 countries in some of the most backward and abandoned regions of the developing world, six of which are found in the region.[43] Cuba has also provided technical assistance to a large number of countries where the effectiveness of its social programmes has been amply recognised. The programmes "Yo Si Puedo" ("Yes, I can") and "Educa a tu Hijo" (Teach your child)" are revolutionising early childhood and pre-school education in the region. The same occurs with its food security and HIV/AIDS prevention programmes.

Venezuela is also a country under constant attack from the United States and its cronies, and is rapidly recovering from its recent opposition-promoted

---

[43] See: Cumplimiento de los Compromisos del Milenio. Informe del representante de Cuba ante la Conferencia del SELA, July, 2003.

crisis. In spite of everything, it continues to insist on supporting the traditionally excluded sectors of its population, so much so that UNESCO has now declared it an illiteracy – free territory. It is simultaneously engaged in a struggle to create a participatory democracy and a non-classist state. This in large part explains why it is being so aggressively attacked by global capital and perhaps also helps explain how it maintains such massive popular support. The petroleum reserves of this country, savoured by the powerful during this critical historical juncture of high fuel costs, both complicates and intensifies the country's present situation. This divided and harassed country nevertheless continues to demonstrate a capacity for expressing its solidarity towards other countries in the area of petroleum supply[44] and has the strategic vision of using its oil resources in contributing to regional welfare and unity in the face of continuing threats from International Financial Institutions (IFIs).[45]

In this context, President Chavez has formulated the historical project of liberation for Latin America, with Bolivarian principles guiding a transitional phase towards a Twenty-First Century socialism. The proposal of the Bolivarian Alternative for the Americas (ALBA), as discussed earlier, is based on co-operation and not competition, with a regional energy infrastructure forming the foundation of other proposals such as the creation of a Latin American Central Bank, a Social Charter for the Americas, a Development Bank of the South, and the creation of TELESUR, a television system serving regional information and cultural needs. It is unquestionable that at this historical point it is President Chavez who is capturing the imagination and support of the people in the Region and who has taken the lead in producing initiatives oriented to break the back of neoliberalism.

There are other important signs of resistance across the continent. Since President Kirchner came to power in Argentina, his government has displayed a creative manner in confronting the unjust impositions of the Breton Woods Institutions. We can just point here to the innovative series of negotiations which were led in defence of public spending on children, seeking to exempt it from the cutbacks imposed by the adjustments; the debt swap for educational spending; the request in alliance with other countries to the

---

[44] By way of the Acuerdo de San José and the Acuerdo de Caracas, Venezuela provides petroleum under very favourable conditions to various countries in the Region.
[45] Presentation "Venezuelan Proposal: Creation of Bolivarian Alternative for the Americas." III Hemispheric Meeting of Struggle against the FTAA, January 2004.

IMF to win recognition of spending on infrastructure as investment and not as an expense; the proposal to the Inter-American Development Bank to play a counter-cyclical role; the proposal that structural adjustment programmes be replaced with genuine development programmes; the denunciation of the devastating effects of the erroneous economic policy imposed on Argentina by the IMF and the affirmation that it should be the IMF and not the Argentine people that should pay for such errors; and the call to neighbouring countries to heed the risks implied by the unrestricted entry of foreign financing in view of its largely speculative component that harms recipient countries.[46] All of these positions taken by the Kirchner government, whether they were successful or not, involved principles the majority of countries in the region would have generally preferred to ignore.

Equally important, Argentina has been steadily supporting regional integration initiatives. More recently, after the replacement of Minister Lavagna with Ms. Miceli, the Argentinean position continues along the same confrontational lines, accusing the IMF to be responsible for its part in the recent crisis and the harm it inflicted on the population. Moreover, Argentina is demanding that more consideration be given to a labour market policy that can allow workers to receive a salary compatible with their productivity and with effective social protection.

Unquestionably, where Argentina most radically broke into new territory was on the issue of its foreign debt. It proved to the world that it could suspend payment to its private creditors for an extended period until the time was ripe for settling with them at a considerable discount. Later it went on to set the lead in repaying the IMF in full so as to set itself free from its perverse policy impositions.[47] Others are now following along the same steps and it is evident that if individual countries can free themselves from IFIs, regional integration can help pave the way for all of them to do so. Now it is the IMF that will have to learn how to find a role and how to make do without the steady financial flows it received from its debtors.

When President Lula came to power in Brazil, he put forth the idea that rich nations should accept a reduction of the Third World's foreign debt and end protectionism, actions which jointly can help fight the generalised misery

---

[46] Speech by Economic Minister Lavagna to the Board of Governors of the Inter-American Development Bank in March, 2004.
[47] As mentioned earlier, there are detractors with regard to this initiative on both sides of the political spectrum.

found in the developing countries. "Poverty must no longer be treated as a social problem and instead be thought of as an issue of economic policy of the highest order at the national and international level," he declared. At the Shanghai Conference for the Reduction of Poverty organised by the World Bank, Lula affirmed that the international agenda had concentrated too much on security issues and had ignored the fact that "poverty was the worst arm of mass extermination and that hunger was the worst arm of mass destruction." He also said that "there will be no peace without development and no development without social justice."[48]

In addition to Brazil's well known global campaign for "zero hunger" and the national programme of school meals and scholarships that offer stipends to families who keep their children in school, what has most distinguished Brazil's presence in the region are the efforts that have been made to establish greater alliances between countries. The objective is to establish mechanisms of integration that can allow for a more consolidated negotiations process with the globalised economy. Exemplary is the creation of the G-20, today recognised as a legitimate mediator of the developing world in global commercial negotiations. So too are the efforts made to strengthen MERCOSUR and to create the Southern community of Nations as a form of joining forces in improving the terms of negotiation.

Both Argentina and Brazil are countries that have sought to maintain an often impossible balance between "the possible" and the oppressive regional trade system. Regretfully, in spite of the initial wealth of new ideas, both leaders are constantly reducing "the possible" in response to increasingly stronger external pressure. This renders them incapable of continuing to capture people's imagination the way they once did or to respond to their hopes. They are both however, displaying efforts to recover their support, have excelled in backing the recently elected government of Bolivia, recognising Bolivia's sovereign right to nationalize gas and in offering to invest in its development.

Bolivia is one of the countries with a historical tradition of committed social movements, including indigenous organisations that have exhibited considerable strength and ability for defending their interests, their natural resources and in electing their own leaders. Shortly after taking office, President Evo Morales, an Aymara and former coca cultivator union leader, has shown the

---

[48] World Bank Information Services.

ability to take the lead in regional matters and in the fight against neoliberalism, but also to devise new avenues for liberation. Since his election, the possibility of an FTA with the United States has fallen off the map in Bolivia, the announcement has been made that Bolivia will not renew its financial agreements with the IMF, and support is being given to all positive instances of regional integration, especially ALBA to which Bolivia has become a new member.

Where Bolivia has brought in new initiatives has been in the re-nationalisation of its wealth in energy resources. President Morales has been revered by the vast majority in his country and received the full support of his partners in integration, but has also been reviled in the United States and Europe whose transnational companies operating in Bolivia have been challenged. Another innovative idea receiving immediate support from his partners are the People's Trade Agreements (TCPs) as opposed to the bilateral free trade agreements which are treaties benefiting big corporations. These new types of treaties are based in the complementarities among countries which go beyond commercial interests. They recognize the state as the main regulator and articulator of commercial activities and aim to benefit small producers as well as to create bilateral enterprises, projects and operations. Unlike the FTAs, the TCPs do not interfere in issues such as intellectual property, privatisation of public services, government procurement, etc, which remain in the hands of individual governments. TCPs are based on solidarity because the stronger country concedes special benefits to the weaker one while benefiting nonetheless.

Conclusion

In the neoliberal capitalist system, everyone owes but those who most owe are those who least pay. Nobody dares to collect their debts and those who ultimately pay are the children, the Afro-descendents and the indigenous peoples. The winners are the multinationals, the banking establishment and the arms manufacturers. For Latin America to comply with its obligations, effective strategies with adequate public policies need to be put in place. For hope to be possible, what is missing is a change of values, a more just international order, a more genuine national and global democracy, and a radical change in the regional development model. There are cracks in the imperial edifice and we know that no imperial power can survive eternally. It is quite possible that we have entered into a period that is propitious for change, albeit one that will be neither rapid nor painless.

The innovation of the struggle for liberation is no stranger to the history of our region. I mention here just two manifestations of this historical current: The teachings of José Martí[49] more than a century ago, and the more recent example of Salvador Allende[50] who led an attempt to structurally transform Chile on behalf of the Chilean people. The fact that both paid with their lives well before their time in advancing the region's struggle does not translate into a meaningless failure. History does not advance in a linear manner, and no people can liberate itself without a transformative vision. Today, the region is witnessing another resurgence of its vision for liberation. Its potential, as well as the threats that are amassing against it, provides an intensifying echo of the slogan "Union or Death" put forth by President Chávez at the 5th World Social Forum at Porto Alegre.

---

[49] In 1989, at the Washington Congress, Martí stated that the time had come for Ibero-America to declare its second independence.

[50] In New York during the 1972 general Assembly of the United Nations Allende stated that "the perspective facing my nation, as many other Third World countries, was a model of modernisation in which technical studies and a tragic reality coincide in demonstrating that it condemned to exclusion millions and millions of people from the possibilities of progress, wellbeing and social liberation . . . This is the model that the Chilean working class upon becoming the architect of its own destiny has resolutely chosen to reject, opting instead for its own autonomous and accelerated development while revolutionising its traditional structures." (original in Spanish).

Darío Salinas Figueredo

Democratic Governability in Latin America: Limits and Possibilities in the Context of Neoliberal Domination[1]

Introduction

It is becoming increasingly clear that if one wishes to embark on a political analysis using the analytical approach of governability, it is no longer possible even in a strictly theoretical sense to take this concept for granted. This is even less plausible if we wish to employ a broad and more conceptually audacious version. We are mindful of the fact that the visibility of this perspective was originally attained vis-à-vis a focus on problems involved with maintaining political control over democracies. In that vein, governability referred to the process of managing democratic demands emerging from a context of crisis. This became urgent when such pressures were perceived as potentially destructive in their capacity to overwhelm the institutional framework of the system.

The transplantation of this conceptual category from the conservative branch where it first originated to the current reality of Latin America is taking place at a moment when the region's most pressing political problems have assumed a different character. The spectrum of problems that now

[1] This paper has appeared earlier in *Critical Sociology*, Volume 32, N° 1, 2006, pp. 105–123.

confront Latin America constitutes the antipode of the moment in which the notion of governability of the Huntington or Trilateral type was formulated. In Latin America, less democracy signifies greater instability and consequently the risk towards an involuntary hardening of the system and a closing off of its possibilities for change. Rather than signify a perfectioning of institutional and state control, i.e., the construction of effective institutional floodgates for conflict management, governability can instead be employed in the search for consensual participation in the formation of institutionally legitimate proposals and solutions to pressing social problems.

To speak of governability in the present context of the region does not presuppose a debate about how to avoid tension, threats or social conflicts emerging from the modernisation of aging systems of coercion or control. Rather, it is to inquire about the conditional factors that could give rise to that possibility. A point of intersection with the neoliberal experience can be seen in those processes inspired by democratic expectations. This helps to sketch out an angle of visibility that can offer an alternative perspective.

In effect, the difficult insertion in the globalised world (Cadermartori 2004; Salinas 2002; García Canclini 1999), the profiling of new forms of collective action (Gilly 2004; Quijano 2004; Seoane 2003), the tensions between social demands and proposals (Salinas and Tetelboin 2005; Hardy 2004), and the complex bonded ties that exist between political regimes and the contents of democratic governability (Lechner 1995; Osorio 1997) are some of the central questions currently revolving around the axis of discussions on governability in Latin America. A productive exploration of recent political and economic experience can only take place through the recognition of a certain play of tendencies, although not exempt from identifiable counter-tendencies, that rest upon the fundamental referents of internal and external challenges. Democratic concerns can be apprehended as precisely situated in those referents, confronted by pressing and unresolved problems, and dynamic in a new field of options and possible transformational processes.

This general kind of perspective forces us to engage in a critical review of the tendencies and means for diagnosing the political processes of the region. The identification of spheres of political action that impact at the national, regional and international levels can be useful in anticipating the factors that shape governability. Although social and productive heterogeneity may be more pronounced than ever, the Latin American reality continues to have a historical, political and cultural significance. It is difficult to ignore that we are living a very specific period in capitalist globalisation in which the region as part of the periphery offers considerable competitive advantages capital that is highly mobile. In this article, the focus is on a matrix of change in which a whole set of emergent tendencies results in common problems and challenges that characterise a new era of historical movement in the region.

From the Lost Decade to the Frustrated Decade

It is possible that the climate of euphoria that accompanied the end of the Cold War, preceded by the very negative results from the economic performance of the 1980s, stimulated widespread hopes that the region's principal economic and social indicators were going to be more favourable over the next period. This positive climate of expectations for the decade of the 1990s also had to do with the beginning of a transition to democracy, in some cases building off of new advances in that direction, while in other cases being reconstituted after long experiences of military dictatorship.

In spite of all of the diverse lines of political interpretations in the region, what is clear is that an overall consensus was eventually formed about the 1990s. The decade became seen as a difficult period that fell far short of the initially optimistic expectations we alluded to. Moreover, it could be said that the emergent tendencies were ultimately quite negative. Expressions of social discontent over the achievement of democracy, the contraction in the productive capacity of the region's economies, the vicissitudes of a difficult international insertion, and the persistence or accentuation of poverty (in many cases) and social inequality were all in ascendance.

But the most difficult field to manage belonged to the political terrain proper. Strongly associated with the traditions of democratic-liberal politics, the diverse experiences of the past gave way to processes of change according to the transitional designs and shifts in the exercise of governmental action. In just a few short years, the majority of the region's countries moved from the optimistic expectation of greater democracy to pessimistic discontent. This was especially pronounced give the poor results achieved by new governments following their complex negotiations to conclude the cycle of authoritarian experiments and/or military dictatorship. Many of these states became consolidated behind a highly conditioned terrain that forced new elected governments to administer an economic situation with very little margin for manoeuvre. They were obliged to conduct difficult negotiations with powerful interest groups of political and economic opposition. Notwithstanding the outcome of such talks or the agreements eventually reached, it became clear that entrenched power interests were generally not inclined to cede control over the spaces envisioned by the democratic transition.

It might be worth remembering that the rate of GDP growth during the early years of the 1990s was relatively promising. This initial trend proceeded to steadily deteriorate following the Mexican economic crisis which exploded in December, 1994. The tendency from that point forward was ever more unfavourable, intensified by the Asian crisis in 1997. By 1999, notable declines in production resulted in negative growth rates, followed only by a slight recovery in 2002, before declining once again in the following year (CEPAL 2002a). In that same direction, per capita income was falling in 2001, as were the inflows of foreign capital, and became accompanied by a deterioration in the terms of trade and the net transfer of resources abroad at a time that the foreign debt was already over US\$ 730 billion (CEPAL 2002b). These setbacks all displayed similar characteristics of stagnation, with an aggregate dynamic that was highly unfavourable for the middle sectors, now more vulnerable than ever, and for the popular sectors that had already hit rock bottom, having eroded their salaries and last remaining reserves.

In that recessive framework, Latin America became converted into a setting for enormous political convulsions. We remember this period particularly with respect to the Brazilian economy during the last portion of the government of Fernando Enrique Cardoso as well as the final and dramatic decomposition of the Argentine economy. Further to the north, immense difficulties dogged the Andean and Central American countries where they had to confront not only the real dimension of their respective economies (that continued to be small) but also the difficulties of the international economic and financial setting. This includes Chile as well, which had maintained a relatively favourable counter-tendency, having erected a model of growth with World Bank and International Monetary Fund support, but which also fell into the recessive quagmire and experienced a declining growth performance after 1997 and actually went negative in 1999. Even with its strict parameters of neoliberal reference, it could not manage to sustain its growth trajectory. This signified its rendezvous with growing social discontent produced by a transition to democracy that had failed to achieve satisfactory levels of profundity. In the end, "exceptional" Chile came ever closer to being bogged down in the same syndrome as the other countries mentioned.

Neoliberalism as a System of Domination

In spite of the existentialism that seems to surround the socio-economic doldrums of recent years described above, no international agency has sought to conceal their negative prognosis for the region. Lurking behind the applied policies and encompassing their implementation, the economic model became consolidated and transformed into a system. The region served as the laboratory in which the neoliberal system had gestated and was now being consolidated. During those same years, the Latin American countries had to abandon their historical processes of "inward-oriented" growth in order to adapt themselves to the international economy and to open up spaces for their exports in external markets. The experience of dependency upon the export cycle was nothing novel in itself, but now it was occurring under conditions more adverse than ever. Transnationalised capitalism imposed an iron law of competitiveness over the region.

Following that itinerary, the region's economies were reconstituted by invoking the modernising effects of their reorientation to external markets. This in fact is the most sensitive part of the process still underway. The process tended to destroy the pillars of the old form of capitalist domination that created the "welfare state" in Latin America. In so doing, it managed to erode and later transform the remaining iota of legitimacy that the old form of domination had managed to cultivate.

In effect, previous capitalist forms had developed under a scheme of welfare states with all of its concomitant structures and had managed to meld it into a developmentalist form. This form was generally speaking inefficient in realising its objectives, including the reproduction of the system in its totality. During its reign, there had developed a whole context of mobilisations and conflicts, of struggle and negotiation, in which important spaces of institutional conflict resolution were developed. This took place in accordance with a measure of democratisation where the state, without abandoning what it has always been, had to by necessity exercise its role of mediation and create the conditions for constructing a politically necessary consensus.[2]

---

[2] This phenomenon of mutation had profound implications and has been enriched under the conceptualisation of the Latin American state-centred matrix (Cavarozzi and Casulla 2003:11) and by others in terms of a double process of transition, namely, one towards democracy and a market economy (Lechner, 1992).

But this old design for the organisation of capitalism was no longer adequate for the type of globalisation that was moving forward by the end of the 1970s-early 1980s with its strategic option in favour of "free market" driven development. In this context, the other process of transition was also being produced, that which has been the most important aspect of contemporary political history. We speak here of the difficult and painful transition from protected capitalist economies to open and unregulated capitalist economies.

With the results of the experience that have occurred over the last two decades, it was now possible to better perceive the early conceptualisation of Marx. In *The Communist Manifesto*, he suggested that the entire world could become one large market with a corresponding global character, with capital, labour and in general all commodities freely able to circulate. This new relationship with the international market as the culmination of the complex processes which constituted the globalised market became highly complex in conjunction with the dismantlement of the previously existing structures. The globalisation of markets implied a profound restructuration of labour relations. The opening to international markets of these economies in the periphery, under-developed, half-modern and half-traditional, put forward dramatic demands of competitiveness for the industries of our countries. Almost everywhere, requirements were being imposed to increase the rate of exploitation, informalisation into more precarious forms of employment, and the generation of diverse forms of social exclusion.

This signified that together with the globalisation of markets, the new stage of capitalism brought with it a demand for flexibilising labour relations, thus weakening the power of negotiation and representation of working people throughout all of Latin America. As shown in a recent study, "Economies of this type present difficult negotiations with political organisations based in formulas that imply an active participation of citizens and arriving at a stable consensus" (Osorio 2004:125). The present economic structure, whose politics accentuate polarisation, can only with great difficulty generate the requisite conditions for democratic governability. This is precisely what has happened in the process of constituting the neoliberal form of capitalism, distinct from its previous form, and subjected to brutal demands for competitiveness in international markets, resulting in a dynamic of deepening social class, regional, cultural and ethnic divisions.

The governments of the region, with little regard to either its ideological orientation or the system of alliances constructed within its respective administrations, generally fell over themselves in trying to get in tune with the new reality. Although with observable counter-tendencies in the process of becoming established, the predominate trend involved adapting governmental policies to the systemic readjustment of global capitalism. In political terms, this became accompanied with an extensive list of international agreements that cemented "economic complementarity" and "free trade" into place as the prerequisite for dynamising the export of capital.

Resulting from these actions was the consolidation of a different order of regional segmentation. Latin America at the beginning of the 21st Century consisted of the aggregation of four sub-regional spaces: (1) the complex, multicultural space of the Caribbean dominated by 15 Anglo-Caribbean islands plus Cuba, Dominican Republic, Haiti, and Suriname; (2) the Central America region with its traditional configurations being somewhat dressed up with aspects of modernity; (3) the Andean countries; and (4) the nations of the Southern Cone, the latter two of which have become reorganised into the Andean Community and MERCOSUR. To these, we must add Mexico that is seeking to establish a two-way bridge with ties to the Anglo-saxon nations to the north and the rest of Central and South America to the south. Not withstanding the existence of delicate strips of interdependence, the historical relations of dependency profoundly dominate and in many ways are more varied and wide-reaching than in the past. This dependency becomes ideologically displayed under the appearance of integrated systems of the exchange of opportunities. Only if the region could somehow remain confined to someone's theoretical drawing board could such a system be more equitable.

Restrained Democracies

As a tributary of the study of transitions, there is an analytical current that considers democracy to be only a political category in the most limited sense of the term. Political democracy is seen as a regime that in the final instance establishes institutional mediation between the state and society characterised by the operation of a multi-party system. The programmed process of elections resolves the problem of who and how to govern society in the context of respect for the normative body of legality. For all that to function, societies have sacred institutional norms and the hope is that they be scrupulously respected at all times. In reality, these norms of course never function in a manner entirely independent of more complex and less immediately visible structures.

If we try to make this conceptual perspective appear consistent with the social and political reality of Latin America, we would have to accept that the democratic order does not exist independent of its efficiency in addressing specific social dilemmas. Democracy, however, goes beyond simply being a regime along with its associated institutions. It is also a process of seeking integral solutions to the social, political and economic problems that confront the larger society. In societies such as ours, with their profound social inequalities and differences, democracy requires something more than elections and institutional proceedings for making possible a "good government" and constructing a "good society." In the final analysis, the proceedings and elections of post-dictatorial democracies and post-authoritarian regimes are a simple ritual that could just as easily be done without.

But what should be underlined here is that recent experience in the region places us closer to a restricted vision of democracy. When in the economic sphere, the system consists of reiterating the economic and financial decisions being taken abroad, then we cannot speak of a democracy capable of transforming and deepening itself but rather one of observance and compliance. In other words, it represents an economic power under a protectorate. This is a central characteristic of the transitions to democracy that we have seen evolve in Latin America since the latter half of the 1980s. In effect, the reconstituted ruling class immersed in the interests of neoliberalism, having already signed its pact abroad, has not had to sacrifice absolutely anything. The new configuration of political power, different from that of the old dictatorships or authoritarian governments, has produced a more polished systemic power limited to exercising its domination under electoral democracies.

For that reason, it should not be surprising when the conceptualisations we see being developed fall into arguing that democracy is a political regime proper and has nothing to do with the economy and the larger model which it forms part of. This can be considered as such, not because things are "naturally" that way, but rather because a correlation of forces has achieved another turn of the screw in the divorce proceedings between economic and politics. The extension of this hegemonic point of view has managed to eradicate from democratic discourse all notion of the principle of equality.

Although no governmental expression during recent history has failed to recognise the deficient social conditions that exist, i.e., the importance of addressing problems of poverty and inequality, no governmental platform has included the need to inquire into and recognise the profound causes underlying these problems. If explicit policies in this regard arise, it is only when the organised demands surrounding these social problems threaten to undermine the conditions of social stability.

Meanwhile, a large portion of governmental expressions have scrupulously omitted any kind of critique of the economic model currently in force. The principal blame probably consists in having "forgotten" that the administration of that model was a lesser evil, maybe even impossible to avoid and that the reforms that were put into place at some point did their part in remedying some of its effects. But it is well known that there is an enormous jump between tolerating a vice and transforming it into a virtue. Almost all governmental discourse in the region has assumed for some time now that the present economic system was somehow inevitable and that there was no other way to have proceeded. It was assumed, then, as something "given" that only waited for a better administration. "Evolution concerns us not so much because of its change but for its capacity to persist. The duration of the system will be regulated through a natural selection that depends to a greater or lesser extent upon its adaptation to the larger setting" (Lechner 2002:19).

The most important thing here is that in Latin America, a phenomenon seems to be spreading that in the language of Lechner is referred to as the "naturalisation of the social," i.e., that the system appears as a natural order, removed from political decision making and flagrantly obscuring the historicity of society and its political reproduction. Politics, then, or what occurs in its name, becomes reduced to the "possible" and this is what in discourse becomes seen as a virtue, cooked up as political realism. It is upon these kinds of invocations that the present democracies have been constructed.

Under such conditions, it does not seem so preposterous to advance a prognosis: Latin Americans, in spite of the fact that their political bets have been placed in favour of democracy, are unsatisfied with the results (Latinobarómetro 2003 Latinobarómetro 2004). For more than a decade, military coups and dictatorships have disappeared from our reality. The occasional attempts to bring about changes of this type ended in a total failure for coup leaders and this has constituted an important "vaccination" against the attempts of reducing the exercise of politics to *de facto* decisions. Elections appear as the general rule, although at an ever greater distance from the view that democracy and electoral exercise are the same thing. What people hope for is that democracy can produce results in the most determinant spheres of social and political life, helping to satisfactorily face crucial situations related to unemployment, informal work, and insecurity along with reinforcing and universalising social policies in the spheres of education, health and social security. These are all joined with the absolutely legitimate expectations of people to be able to participate in decisions that affect the general course being taken by their country.

A series of tendencies intersect around this situation in a way that reflects the state of perceptions. In this order, symbolic mutations that take place in the social vision of people are as important as those in the material realm. Its correlation rests in the values tied to the hegemonic discourse of neoliberal domination that has formatted the mind and the visibility of the individual. Identities are presented as anachronisms where sovereignty constitutes, at least theoretically, a "difficulty" that must be somehow integrated into modernity. In the absence of collective and organically rooted political projects that can transform growing frustration or disenchantment, all aspirations or expectations for change remain limited to simply individual or individualistic proposals.

The part that corresponds to the enabling process of identity, that which produces identification, tends to become divorced from collective referents. The citizen which neoliberalism produces remains devoid of the fabric of solidarity, and is no longer one whose integration occurs based on shared rights, but rather upon their "entrepreneurial" capacity and, ultimately in their aptitudes for acceding to "opportunities" that are at least in theory offered by the market through purchases or credit. In some sense, the social subject is the bearer of credit. The phenomenon of consumption in that arrangement is not only an everyday and indispensable operation, but an entire secular social dynamic that permeates the being of individuals. The individual now finds himself or herself thrown into the living uncertainty of the neoliberal society of globalised capitalism. "In its turn, propaganda creates and reproduces on a broad scale the desire of a sublime acquisition. It spreads before our eyes the delight of objects or of services, presenting everything in terms of beauty and comfort" (Moulian 1999:23). In the spirit of this citation, we must also be sure not to neglect an analysis of the media apparatus. It is no longer a secret for anybody how the mass media operates now more than ever as a virtual "fourth power." They control the hearts and minds of a large part of the population. They are true shredding machines for consciousness and producers of illusion and conformism.

Prolongation of the Restrained Democracies

Amidst all of these unfolding developments of the political establishment, there is another aspect that deserves attention. This relates to those governments that manage to secure backing for prolonging their political mandates. In the case of devising re-election mechanisms not previously contemplated in the constitutional order, this has occurred in the Argentina of Carlos Menem, in the Peru of Alberto Fujimori, in the Brazil of Fernando Henrique Cardoso and most recently in the case of the Uribe Administration in Colombia.

In the case of Chile, although strictly speaking, there is no re-election mechanism in place since 1990, there is instead a fundamental continuity in the basic governmental platform made up of *Concertación* or an alliance of parties in power. Their projects and programmatic contents are certainly not identical nor are their trajectories, but they nevertheless exhibit a fundamental common denominator. In short, they seek to capitalise on a "good political moment" in the progress of their programmatic experiments so as to assure themselves a more prolonged period in power. This can include making amendments to the constitution or seeking to solidify their support among the possibilities offered by the laws in effect which in all such cases they were able to impose over their opposition.

Beyond these observations, we can see an even broader common denominator to the present political regimes, namely, the economic backdrop that establishes a context for the region as a whole. The quality of life indicators have been deteriorating at a time when privatisation no longer appears to have the active consensus of the governed. The regional prognosis for Latin America and the Caribbean is for greater levels of social inequality in terms of income at the same time that the gap in per capita product relative to the developed world continues to increase. The momentary recoveries that have been registered here and there have not managed to reverse this overall tendency (Banco Mundial 2003; CEPAL 2004. It is with this regional prognosis in mind that we need to situate all those questions involved with the reconstruction of the essential conditions for democratic governability. In other words, we must shape our analysis in view of the criteria, interests and institutional responsibilities that both define prevailing policies and prop up the overall reproduction of the social and economic model. It is not unreasonable to propose that the increase of inequalities tied to the dynamic of that model we have described and the social conflicts that subsequently envelop it, will limit the possibilities for democratic governability.

Politics as Viewed from the Society in Motion

We turn to a phenomenon that has been widely observed in recent times to which we will refer to as the *social revocation* of the mandate. In our political history, political constitutions have provided for periods of government that have been generally complied with. Although this has not completely disappeared, there is a new development in the regional trajectory for an increasing number of countries. It refers to when a government fails to comply with the electorate's social expectations, giving rise to protest movements that generate serious challenges for governments and ultimately proving capable of forcing their destitution.

Many particular and even unique components of these diverse conjunctures exist within the multiple kinds of social protest movements witnessed in recent years throughout Latin America. But there is a basic component that repeatedly occurs and which displays a direct relationship to the social effects resulting from the implementation of neoliberal policies. There is an undeniable climate of outrage and rejection that becomes incubated in response to each adjustment or IMF package and this occurs to an even greater extent in opposition to privatisations.

The list of experiences in this rubric is relatively extensive. The crisis that developed in the wake of the "Caracazo" in 1989[3] shortly after the beginning of the second term of President Carlos Andrés Pérez in Venezuela. This process which ended with the destitution of his government can be viewed as the beginning of a tendency that has continued right up to the present. The expulsions of the Ecuadorian Presidents Abdalá Bucaram and Yamil Mahuad occurred after mass protests that included the mobilisation of indigenous peoples as its principal protagonists. The forcible ejection of President Raúl

---

[3] The "Caracazo" refers to the violent circumstances that unfolded in Caracas, Venezuela in 1989 when the government attempted to impose a neoliberal programme despite widespread public opposition.

Cubas of Paraguay, following the dramatic incidents that followed the assassination of that country's Vice-president Argaña and the creole politics that appeared under the name of the "Paraguayan March." The unusual spectacle of the Peruvian President Alberto Fujimori fleeing to Japan and the spectacular fall from power on the part of Argentine President Fernando de la Rúa in late 2001 all form part of this trajectory. We can add here the prolonged situation of confrontation that faced Bolivian President Gonzalo Sánchez de Losada. With majority participation of the indigenous population, the protests ended in his sudden abdication to Miami, something that provided only a brief pause in tensions in a still mostly unresolved situation.

In the Caribbean, a history of conflicts and mobilisations also resulted in the destitution of the government of Jean Bertrand Aristide in Haiti, a leader who was forced to leave power before the expiration of his mandate amidst diverse and complex expressions of discontent and allegations against his administration. The ominous aspect in this case, all of the multiple factions of Haitian opposition notwithstanding, was constituted by the "external factor" of North American intervention. Contrary to the OAS Democratic Charter, Washington precipitated the end of Aristide's government on February 29, 2004 under a series of actions that simulated a coup d'etat (Chossudovsky 2004).

In practise, the "revocation of mandate" has appeared only very recently in the politics of Latin America. The only place where the revocation of mandate is actually specified under a constitution is in Venezuela under the new constitution established by the presidency of Hugo Chávez. In the Constitution of the Bolivarian Republic of Venezuela, the procedures are set forth for revoking the mandate of a sitting president and they have in fact been used, albeit unsuccessfully, by the opposition forces in that country to attempt to remove his own administration from power.

This phenomenon will clearly require more extensive analysis since it ultimately constitutes a mechanism that favours genuine social participation in political affairs. In effect, universal and secret voting constitutes both the possibility and limit of participation in the neoliberal democracies, especially if in the exercise of citizenship, the possibility of participating in a referendum, ratification or revocation is not clearly specified in the constitutional norms. It can easily be concluded that the institutional and operative characteristics of neoliberal democracies are not impacted by its citizens in the definition of its objectives and the actual contents of its politics. This problem that directly competes with the democratic design of politics, finds some relief in the prospect of revocation or the principle of recall.

Another tendency from this same social current can be found in the changing profile of electoral results seen recently in Latin America where leftist parties seek to initiate a process of transformation within the established institutions. In this vein, we can identify important spaces for the forces and coalitions that have sought to consolidate the chain of progressive democracies in the continent. The rise to presidential power in 2003 of the social and political forces led by Luis Ignacio Lula da Silva in Brazil can be cited here as well as the assumption of President Néstor Kirchner in the case of Argentina. While Lula was one of the emblematic leaders of the Latin America "New Left," Kirchner has resulted as a kind of "surprise," particularly with respect to his firm postures in defence of a more independent economic reconstruction project.

The majority of analysts have probably not examined the consistency in his political biography since he was an active leader of the Peronist Youth in the decade of the 1970. His formulation of governmental proposals, his support for the investigation of crimes against humanity committed by the previous military dictatorships and the firm position that his government has assumed in negotiating the foreign debt have all converged to create a precedent in forging a new regional style of politics. This tendency appears to be reinforced with the election in Panama of Martín Torrijos, the son of the legendary Colonel that recovered the sovereignty of his nation over the canal with the signing of the treaties with President Carter in 1977. It still needs to be evaluated what possibilities, if any, the election of Torrijos and the return of the PRD to power can offer Panama.

We can say something very similar about the political processes that have resulted in Montevideo, Uruguay with the election of Tabaré Vásquez in November of 2004. Here, the leftist *Frente Amplio* (Broad Front) triumphed convincingly in the first electoral round. With coming elections in Nicaragua, Peru and Mexico, it remains to see how dynamic this tendency actually is. The experiences and concrete situations are not identical. But there is a manifest intentionality when the sense of politics actively seeks to retake the road of independence and renovation of national sovereignty. In the midst of these recent electoral experiences, the form of politics projected displays an orientation, albeit a variable one, looking to distance itself from pragmatism and the docile acceptance of the conditionalities imposed by international economic and financial powers. They seek to directly confront the national project of their countries, reordering national priorities and manoeuvring within what are undoubtedly very restricted margins, particularly if we consider that the underlying economies are highly indebted.

The project of creating the South American petroleum agency PETROSUR can help nurture a very healthy counterweight to transnational monopolies, the latter of which in their near-sighted, short term interests are proven experts in making decisions that contradict the possibility of development in our countries. One example to illustrate this latter point is the conduct of the English-Dutch oil transnational Shell that in early 2005 decided to raise the prices of their products to inflationary proportions for the economy of Argentina. On the other hand, an additional example regarding the former process rested in completing agreement on the TELESUR project. This media project will now offer transmissions that can help offer a counterbalance to the monopolised information media presently entrenched in the region. These and other regional initiatives are among the democratically progressive expressions that are being profiled in this part of the continent.

Clearly, it is not possible to extract triumphal conclusions in this brief survey of recent trends. For every democratic measure being incubated, an anti-democratic response is lurking somewhere behind it. The forces identified with a vision critical of the neoliberal experience in Latin America have important challenges lying ahead. There are big issues wrapped around trying to successfully distance from the interests and expressions of the great political and financial powers that seek to invoke their own objectives with respect to democracy. A conjuncture of country visions must be identified in the area of development strategies within the real context of the global reality. The principal challenge has to do with articulating the accumulation of social and political forces. The experience of neoliberal domination has already done its part in provoking an entire generation of diverse forms of social resistance, mobilisation and rejection of systemic exploitation, exclusion, and violations of social and human rights.

Conclusion

Three essential points of discussion can serve to conclude the reflections set forth in this article. They include the social backdrop of democracy, a need to rethink the importance of the role played by the United States in the region, and a need to consider the ideological weight of democracy in Latin America.

The continent as a whole has seen an increase of poverty in absolute terms. Indigence, in spite of focused compensatory policies designed to combat it, has proven to be resilient. To a greater extent, the overall distribution of wealth has proven to be especially difficult to mollify. This presents a whole set of problems. There needs to be greater caution exercised in implementing economic policies aimed at devising remedial measures. It clearly implies a struggle since the availability of resources necessary to address these deficient situations continues to be an important issue. It is indispensable to avoid creating unrealisable expectations that can ultimately serve to validate the claims often made by the prevailing economic regime.

It is therefore important to know how to distinguish when a social mobilisation rooted in poverty contains the active elements for deepening democracy or when such movements are simply reactive or clientelist forms of expression that only complicate the prospects for a more democratic political establishment. In any case, the ultimate responsibility continues to rest upon the predominant political system in the sense of looking for proposals to face existing problems and to implement profound and enduring changes.

Accumulated social urgencies puts any government in power at risk when it becomes situated between the necessity of successfully resolving pending demands by way of concrete policies and the urgency to negotiate the debt load or other financial commitments with international creditor agencies. Any agreement with the latter carries the risk of conditionalities, frequently tied to the aims of imposing privatisation, whose impact inevitably erodes what remains of an internal social consensus. Moreover, this makes politically implausible the argument for allocating greater resources to social spending or job creation, resulting instead in arguments about the limitation of resources and the need to continuing to making payments on the foreign debt.

With respect to the need to rethink the role of U.S. policy, it requires us to think through the implications of the commercial trade agreements that currently predominate in Latin America. The application of their politics of "preventive war" has not translated into favourable results for their economy. The art of threatening to make war and actually making war has not yielded the expected benefits anticipated by Washington. Everything would seem to indicate that the U.S. economy is experiencing a tendency towards decline, plagued by problems of productivity, competitiveness, technological sluggishness, high fiscal deficit, weakness in their investments and elevated indebtedness. I underscore these points here because the package we are perpetually being sold asserts the need of our countries to solidify our integration with this rather questionable business partner.

Among the few comparative advantages exhibited by the U.S. economy is its absolute military supremacy that none of its allies can compete with. Their principal competitive resource, then, is the ability to maintain or increase the imperial rent. This unchecked military power permits Washington to violate any of the rules of the market game that it claims to venerate in theory. The operative example is when it exercises internal protectionism at the same time that it demands unrestricted and unregulated economic opening from all other countries. Such is the case in their treatment of key commodities that form the primary basis for U.S.-Latin American ties.

We could also identify here the issue of agricultural subsidies. Or the manner in which it imposes upon its allies, without prior consultation, mechanisms of negotiation that in the end also end up violating the free play of supply and demand. An example of this can be the law of commerce with Cuba, as well as the laws that it seeks to impose upon third countries in its drive to economically strangle that country. Under these political "rules," there is no hesitation to tighten restrictions over the flow of remittances as well as travel on the part of Cuban-U.S. citizens.

North American power politics is thus seen from the Latin American point of view not only as a permanent risk of military invasion, in a literal sense, but also as a process of other forms of invasion against our economic sovereignty. This involves the application of interventionist policies that seek to certify our democratic practices as in the explicit case of Venezuela. They seek to qualify the treatment of human rights of other countries and emit political judgements concerning their efforts in fighting the illegal narcotics trade. All of this should not be seen as much more than another part of the process that closes the pincers around our countries. I can also refer here to the decision-making influence that U.S. policy has upon the multilateral financial organisations with which our economies maintain disadvantageous relations. Take the case in point of appointing Paul Wolfowitz to the presidency of the World Bank. The very fact of having proposed a candidate who played an active role in the U.S. actions in Afghanistan and Iraq, and then seeing the candidacy accepted, suffices to show the level of U.S. influence over this multilateral agency.

My final reflection concerns the ideological weight of democratic conceptions. I refer here specifically to the ideological collapse of anti-systemic alternatives.

In effect, every one of our countries has witnessed the unfolding of a discourse concerning the anachronism of socialism. The "end of history" atmosphere that flooded the region, although waning, has not yet faded from sight. To the extent that it continues to gravitate through the schemes and designs of neoconservative thought, it permeates the politics that predominate in the region.

The pervasive stupor of de-politicisation in the sense of politics being reduced to the art of administration still carries more weight than does a consistent line of thought oriented towards substituting the capitalist system. This notwithstanding, there are anti-systemic currents to be found everywhere, for example, in defence of water as a strategic resource, electricity, gas, or energy resources against the threat to privatise them, or when a population pronounces itself in favour of a provisional system that is not managed by private capital. This bodes well for new possibilities in formation.

Since the end of the Twentieth Century, we have passed into a political phase with new profiles that are exploring development strategies corresponding to a new and more democratic formulation of politics. Although they still have yet to be expressed in open convocations and ideologically articulated plans, they are moving in that direction and will almost certainly yield results very different from the political forms that currently prevail.

Marco A. Gandásegui, Jr.

Social Security Crisis and Popular Mobilisation in Panama

Prior to completing nine months in office, President Martin Torrijos launched his proposal to reform the Panamanian social security system in May of 2005. After a serious confrontation with the popular sectors that were already prepared to reject the initiative, the Torrijos Administration was left weakened with a significant decline in popularity. In this article, the economic and social background to the political crisis will be briefly analysed so as to provide a context for understanding the popular struggle unfolding in Panama. The continuing importance of the Panama Canal will then be discussed in the context of the objectives being pursued by the Torrijos Administration. This will in turn frame an analysis of the proposed neoliberal reform of the social security system and how the popular organisations have sought to confront them with demonstrations, marches and a month-long strike.

The protests and the strike ultimately forced Torrijos to hold a national dialogue. Torrijos eventually decided to impose a resolution against the will of the popular sectors. The high political cost in doing so has consequently placed in jeopardy the government's pending plan to widen the Panama Canal.

Economic and Social Policies in Panama

Beginning with opposition to the first structural adjustment programmes implemented in Panama during the 1980s, the popular movement has been steadily developing its capacity to confront the state. New ideological elements have become incorporated in the popular struggle and its scope of coverage has expanded. Its overall message now displays increased consciousness of issues concerning the environment, the rights of women and ethnic groups, and regional concerns. The struggle has also grown to incorporate the demands of the unemployed, workers in the formal sector, marginalised groups and newly impoverished middle strata.[1]

In spite of this increased capacity for mobilisation that can force a standing government to pause and grapple with their discontent, the working class and the popular sectors more generally do not yet possess a political organisation that can permit it to effectively confront the initiatives of the traditional ruling groups. It is the most advanced fractions of the working class that continue to form the central nucleus of the popular movement and this is a reality that can be readily seen in Panama as elsewhere.

Neoliberal economic and social policies have been on an offensive against the Panamanian working class and the popular sectors for over twenty years. At the global level, the fledgling rate of profit has forced the agents of capital to search for formulas designed to minimise its losses. In the particular case of Latin America, the successive waves of structural adjustment programmes signified the means by which to ensure that capital transfers continued to flow "properly" from the indebted countries to the lender countries.

In Panama, the percentage of the annual national budget allocated for debt service payments has hovered above fifty per cent since the 1980s. This change in priorities signified a significant reduction in public investment in programmes of education, health and development. The resulting deterioration in the quality of life began to be felt almost immediately. But this also served

---

[1] "The heterogeneity of the forms of work is nothing new, either in capitalism or in earlier modes of production. Two theoretical conceptions, related to the advance of salaried work in modern societies . . . [have contributed] to the concept of work. One was the neoclassical conception according to which there is no other work to be considered other than wage-labour, that which is bought and sold for wages. The other conception was the classical Marxist version where the concept of labour did not remain confined to wage-labour, and in which labour is conceptualised as all forms of activity related with the material wealth of society, not just that which is involved with the creation of exchange value." (de la Garza T. 2005)

to weaken the social organisations, especially those of the urban and rural workers, communities, youth and the middle sectors.

In the 1990s, structural adjustment policies became complemented by the privatisation of public services, including those services that were based in the savings of the popular sectors over the preceding three or four decades. These privatisations in effect constituted transfers of national savings to transnational companies based in the United States and Europe. As part of the same process, the Labour Code was reformed as a means of putting an end to prior advances made by the unions over a protracted period, including their prevailing salary levels, expanded freedom of organisation and work security.

The tariffs that had previously protected national manufacturing and agricultural industries from the unfair trade practises of the United States and Europe were substantially reduced. This promptly resulted in factory and shop closings as well as a collapse of agricultural production in rural areas. The combination of all those aspects increased the rate of unemployment and poverty while further accelerating the informalisation of the economy. In just twenty years (1985–2005), the rate of unemployment went from 6% to almost 14% while the percentage of the population living below the poverty line went from 15% to 40%. The informal sector that practically did not exist two decades earlier swelled to over 40% of the economically active population.

At the same time, however, the successive governments that applied the recipes conforming to the "Washington Consensus" found it ever more difficult to govern. In 1983, a military regime applied the first structural adjustment programme at the same time that it consolidated itself with the creation of the Panamanian Defence Forces (FDP), simultaneously increasing the portion of the national budget earmarked for that sector. The confrontation between different factions of capital and the growing repression of the popular sectors resulted in a pervasive crisis that could not be resolved until Washington militarily invaded the country in 1989, killing around 600 people, mostly civilians.

The various governments that have materialised since the 1989 invasion have with greater or lesser success dedicated themselves to applying neoliberal policies in the absence of deployed military forces. These governments, some disguised as social-democratic, have seen their conservative programmes confronted with strong popular resistance. A corrupt and anachronistic system of political parties has nevertheless enabled civilian regimes to defy this popular protest and impose their policies upon the popular sectors. This fact notwithstanding, it is important to see how at certain specific moments, popular mobilisations have managed to neutralise some of the most abhorrent neoliberal initiatives. Examples of these include attempts to privatise drinking water, extend U.S. military base rights, enact reactionary constitutional reforms and other anti-popular measures.

The Panama Canal and the Government of Martin Torrijos

It was during the above-mentioned period that the Torrijos-Carter Treaty signed in 1977 went into effect, ceding the Panama Canal to the national government. This finally put an end to the U.S. colony known as the "Canal Zone" and in the process, U.S. troops were evacuated from its longstanding bases on Panamanian territory. Thanks to their neoliberal policies, the conservative governments of the 1990s turned the transoceanic passage into an instrument to save money for cargo companies while the "reverted areas" of the former Canal Zone were transformed into a giant real estate business. The U.S. military presence has continued to be felt via its control over the Panamanian Public Security Forces that have become ever more militarised.

In spite of the denationalisation of the economy, the weakening of the labour unions, and the loss of momentum among the student federations and civil society organisations in general, the popular movement showed in 2005 that it is still alive in Panama. It has proved capable of mobilising the most diverse social sectors for protests against the government irrespective of the party in power, targeting its neoliberal policies and defying state repression.

The latest of the four conservative governments to materialise since the 1989 U.S. military invasion is led by Martin Torrijos whose *Partido Revolucionario Democrático* (PRD) assumed power in September 2004. The PRD was founded in 1978 by Torrijos' father, General Omar Torrijos. The programme that the PRD presented in 2004 was plainly neoliberal in content, aimed at privatisation, more flexible labour policies and state decentralisation. Martin Torrijos was preceded by the administration of Mireya Moscoso of the *Partido Panameñista* whose 1999–2004 period of presidential rule was characterised by an incompetent team of presidential advisors and a high level of corruption that affected all governmental levels. Indeed, Torrijos gained considerable electoral sympathy during the 2004 campaign with the slogan "zero corruption."

The three principal proposals put forward by the Torrijos Administration included fiscal overhaul, reform of the social security system and a major project based in widening the Panama Canal. These three proposals are intimately related and directly affect the interests of the popular sectors. The first two were demanded by the World Bank in order to position the Panamanian government as a borrower, something which is important for the governing sectors given that they will be initiating implementation of their plans for expansion of the canal. This mega project of canal expansion will require an investment calculated to run between US$ 5–8 billion.

The fiscal reform, approved in March of 2005, principally affected the productive sectors, professionals and above all, the popular sectors. The manufacturing and agro-industrial sectors (including agricultural and livestock producers) asked for a set of incentives and subsidies. At the same time, independent workers were affected by tax increases. The fiscal reform represented a price increase for the products found in the country's basic food basket and at the same time, a loss of employment in the most dynamic sectors of the Panamanian economy. Fiscal reform did not, however, affect the sectors that control banking, maritime services, commercial services (e.g., the Colón Free Trade Zone) and other speculative services (including the tourist industry). According to the government's statistical reports, services represent more than 80% of the country's gross domestic product.

The fiscal reform awoke sharp opposition among the country's producers who protested the new legislation. Professional associations actually managed to partially reduce the effects of the reform upon their interests. The popular sectors, however, beyond some isolated pockets did not organise a mass mobilisation.

The Social Security Reforms

The reforms relating to the Law of the Social Security Fund (CSS) as proposed by the Torrijos government included increasing the retirement age of the workers, increasing the mandatory payment quota and extending the number of quotas (density) that had to be paid by the insured worker. In accordance with the new proposal, the majority of workers would never be able to retire and enjoy their earned benefits.[2]

---

[2] The reforms of the Social Security Fund (CSS) contemplated changes that clearly harmed the interests of Panamanian workers. In the first place, the retirement age would be increased (to 65 years for men and 62 years for women). Moreover, the quota paid by salaried workers would be raised. The reforms also proposed to increase the total number of monthly quotas that should be required to be paid by the ensured from a total of 180 months (15 years) to a total of 300 months (25 years).

The initiative to reform the Organic Law of the CSS was introduced by the preceding Moscoso government. During her administration, she had created a process of national dialogue that ultimately failed under the combined weight of irreconcilable demands on the part of the World Bank, the workers and the business owners. Torrijos for his part proposed to leap over the failed dialogue process and seek rapid approval of the reform that would satisfy the demands put forward by the World Bank.[3] However, he did not antici-pate the obstacles that would appear along the way. In the first place, the population was already sensitised to the issue and did not accept the argu-ments put forth by President Torrijos. The mass media, usually supportive of the government in power, showed only meek support while at the same time giving considerable space to those who rejected the official proposal.

Secondly, it was during the Administration of Mireya Moscoso that the popular sectors had created the National Front for the Defence of the Social Security Fund (FRENADESSO) in order to lead the struggle against the pri-vatisation of the CSS along with all policies being enacted against the poor.

The government did not cede in the face of popular pressure. On 18 May 2005, President Torrijos sent the proposed law containing the reforms of exist-ing social security legislation to the National Assembly of Deputies. In an expedited manner, the reform project passed through the required three debates in the Assembly. On May 27, only ten days after receiving the pro-posal, the Assembly approved the reform of social security. On 1 June 2005, Law 17 (the "Death Law" as it became referred to by the Panamanian People) was published in the *Official Gazette*.

This process was not a smooth one, however, as intense confrontations occurred between FRENADESSO and the government. Torrijos nevertheless managed (with much publicity) to gain the support of the majority of the unions belonging to the National Council of Organised Workers (CONATO),

---

[3] "The reform package at once sought to earmark 25% of the CSS reserves for pri-vate banks, both Panamanian and foreign, so that they could speculate on interna-tional markets. These proposed reforms responded to World Bank guidelines that were made public in 2004. The Bank recommended that countries increase their col-lections from users of social security systems in order to lower their costs. The World Bank also recommended that countries with social security systems should not pri-vatise the reserves of their systems since prior experience in doing so had been neg-ative." Marco A Gandásegui, Jr., "Reformas a la CSS perjudican a los trabajadores," *Haciendo Camino*, No. 14, May, 2005.

the old labour confederation created by the President's father General Torrijos during the 1970s. This created divisions between the health care workers, teachers and retired sectors of the working class and would have important repercussions in the aftermath. In the following section, we will walk through the whole tumultuous process.

Popular Protests

The popular rejection of the proposed reforms to the Organic Law of the CSS presented formally by the Head of the National Assembly on 18 May 2005 was immediate. Without regard to organisational or ideological affiliation, the population demonstrated against the reforms as more than 800 thousand members of the nation's economically active population of nearly two million were to experience the first "shock" of the Torrijos government.

The Torrijos initiative had been delayed by FRENADESSO after it had organised its first mass demonstration on 17 March 2005, even prior to the time that Torrijos had submitted the reforms for consideration by the National Assembly. The massive protest presented the President of the Republic with signs of a well-organised movement with evident representation of all social sectors and a spirited level of combativeness.

The high point of tension was to occur on 25 May 2005 when FRENADESSO organised a march on the National Assembly in which close to 40,000 persons demanded a national debate for approving any reforms of the Social Security Law. During the march, various opposition political parties made a symbolic act of presence. At the *Plaza Cinco de Mayo* right in front of the Assembly, the popular organisations and its leaders congregated in order to express their rejection of the reforms to a Commission of Deputies. Once the leadership of FRENADESSO was inside the parliamentary chamber, a group of provocateurs began to convincingly throw objects at the contingents of police that had surrounded the Assembly. The police responded by attacking the congregation of the popular organisations, forcing their retreat.

In all, the police detained close to 100 members of the popular organisations without showing much concern for pursuing the provocateurs. In fact, they were left to continue causing damage to traffic lights and other nearby public properties. The repression, however, did not stop FRENADESSO from redoubling its efforts to stop the Assembly from proceeding in its attempt to approve just two days later the reforms aimed at the retired pensioners.

FRENADESSO is made up of fifty popular organisations among which includes the Construction Workers Union, the professors and teachers' associations of the Republic, and the organised workers of the health sector (including the doctors although excluding the nurses' organisation). The success of FRENADESSO can be attributed to its constituent organisations and to its complete convergence with popular demands. In a campaign against reforms of the CSS, FRENADESSO managed to organise five marches in the course of two months that mobilised all of the social organisations of the country in repudiation of the proposed reforms.

Once the Law that reformed the social security system was approved by the National Assembly, FRENADESSO declared all of its organisations to be on strike for an indefinite period. For one month which lasted up to June 27th, construction throughout the entire country was paralysed, educational offices were closed, health services were seriously affected, and other sectors declared themselves on a state of alert. The general population supported the strikers, especially the construction workers, and the strike funds were augmented by donations that were collected all across the country.

The demands mounted by FRENADESSO were developed across two phases. During the organised marches, it had insisted in overturning the "parametric" measures that increased the retirement age and raised the density of payment quotas. Moreover, the organisation of health care workers emphasised the necessity to reject those measures that would privatise the medical services offered in CSS hospitals. Later, it was demanded that the government open a national dialogue so as to prepare a new law that better contemplated the interests of the ensured and of the working people in general. After a month long period of strike, mass mobilisations, and significant repression, the government was forced to cede on the latter demand. The country had turned against Torrijos whose opinion surveys now showed his initial popularity plummeting to a 28% acceptance rating and losing ground.[4]

---

[4] "If we are all here today – and in this we want to be very clear and emphatic – it is exclusively because FRENADESSO called for, led and conducted a national strike of more than 30 days in which tens of thousands of Panamanian men and women participated in all of the provincial capitals and which the citizenry had to pay a high price: more than 1,600 detained, of which 3 remain unjustly imprisoned, 3 were wounded by firearms, 3 were badly beaten, one lost his sight, one with multiple fractures, 25 with probation, 15 free on bail, and more than 60 police files were opened by security forces and the Ministry of Government and Justice." FRENADESSO, "Presentación al Segundo Diálogo Nacional por la Seguridad Social," Press Release of 5 July 2005.

The Dialogue

On 24 June 2005, Torrijos announced that a national dialogue would be held to submit the reforms of the Social Security Law to a broad debate, thus responding to the popular demands and the demands made by FRENADESSO. He also acknowledged the "supplication" made by the Bishops of the Catholic Church. FRENADESSO demanded that the reforms to the law be overturned. In a second television appearance, Torrijos announced on 25 June 2005 that he would be sending a legislative proposal to the Assembly that would "suspend all effects of Law No. 17" for a period of three months. While the Assembly proceeded with processing the proposal for temporary suspension, the government organised the Dialogue, appointing Salvador Rodríguez, President of the Council of Rectors, to facilitate the talks while the Episcopal Conference and the Ecumenical Council of Churches were designated to serve as guarantors. Meanwhile, a list of participants was drawn up among which a clear majority were government officials.[5]

FRENADESSO did not join the Dialogue that began on 28 June 2005, indicating that it would not do so until the law that suspended the effects of the reformed CSS entered into force and became published in the *Official Gazette*. When it subsequently joined the Dialogue on July 5, it found that the government had everything regarding the dialogue prepared and had even initiated deliberations. In principal, FRENADESSO only had the support of three of the 13 organisations selected by the government to participate in the Dialogue: themselves, with Professor Andrés Rodíguez as spokesman; the National Confederation of Unified Labour Unions (CONUSI), represented by its General Secretary Gabriel Castillo; and the National Unitary Union of Construction Workers (SUNTRACS), represented by its General Secretary Genaro López.

The Dialogue promptly resulted in sharp confrontations between the government (represented by the Ministry of Health and the spokesperson for

---

[5] The named members of the National Dialogue on the Social Security Fund (CSS) included representatives from: the Confederation of Retired and Pensioned Workers; the National Private Enterprise Council (CONEP); National Association of Nurses; National Coordinating Council of Health Associations and Professionals; National Medical Negotiating Commission; Federation of Professional Associations (FEDAP); National Front for the Defence of Social Security (FRENADESSO); National Confederation of Unified Labour Unions (CONUSI); The National Unitary Union of Construction Workers and Affiliates (SUNTRACS); National Coordinating Council of United Teachers; National Council of Organised Workers (CONATO); Social Security Fund (CSS); and the Ministry of Labour.

the CSS) and FRENADESSO. These clashes elicited reactions among the other dialogue participants that began to generate sympathy for the workers. Indeed, the public battle had now become shifted from the streets to the halls of the Council of Rectors. The government had manoeuvred to cool down the popular protests whose high political costs were reducing support among important sectors of the country. For its part, FRENADESSO has achieved its principal objective, i.e., the suspension of the application of Law No. 17. Nevertheless, the continuation of the strike demanded material sacrifices from the workers that were deemed too great at that moment to continue to ask for. In this case, it was especially true for the construction workers.

For the government, the convocation of a National Dialogue had the political aim of recovering its image and preparing itself for future political initiatives. President Torrijos formally invited the workers, business owners, retired pensioners, and professionals to sit at the table with the government, in all, a total of 13 organisations. In the Dialogue, CONEP represented business, FEDAP represented the nation's professionals, the Confederation of Retired Pensioners sat for those most directly affected by the reform, and eight other associations that included CONATO and CONUSI represented the labour unions, the doctor and nurses associations for the health care sector and the teachers and professors that were part of FRENADESSO.

President Torrijos announced that all articles of the suspended law could be altered. At the same time, he limited the dialogue to a period of three months. In joining the Dialogue, FRENADESSO argued that it did not want to debate about which portions of the reform to sustain but instead move to shape a totally new law based on principles that took the interests of retired workers into account.

It was therefore from the onset that the government and FRENADESSO collided. FRENADESSO demanded that the government publicly present the calculations utilised to justify the increases in the retirement age and density of quotas. The government never actually presented the numbers, however, and this began to erode its credibility in the Dialogue. In the end, the Dialogue was reduced to discussing, one by one, each of the articles contained in the suspended Law No. 17.

The proposals of the popular sectors present in the Dialogue were ruled to be out of order by the facilitator named by President Torrijos. Nevertheless, the facilitator could not easily manage to overcome the confrontations, especially given that a significant number of organisations now sympathised with

FRENADESSO. The government had previously calculated that it would have ten votes at the Dialogue table against only three for FRENADESSO. It therefore came as a rude surprise to the government that by the first confrontation, it could only count solidly on four votes, with the remaining organisations fluctuating in accordance with its interests.

From Dialogue to Imposition

The situation that evolved during the Dialogue gave FRENADESSO some manoeuvring room to present alternative recommendations to the four working commissions that were set up as part of the process: "Administration," "Disabled, Elderly and Death Benefits," "Health," and "Professional Risks." The government meanwhile decided to introduce some old tactics into its management of the Dialogue. On the one hand, it attacked those organisations that sought to maintain their independence. On the other hand, it unilaterally modified the rules on how to determine when a majority was reached in approving an initiative or other article of law that the commissions had studied.

In the case of the latter tactic, when a majority of nine organisations approved a FRENADESSO proposal that questioned a financial aspect, the facilitator decided to change the rule. According to the facilitator, from that point forward, the table would be formed of five "sectors" and not thirteen organisations. The five sectors would be the government, private enterprise, workers, retired pensioners and professionals or independent workers.

The government would now only need four votes in order to impose its criteria upon the rest. They would consist of the two of the government, private enterprise, and the retired pensioners. If this rule were to be applied, the workers even when they were to garner 9 votes (out of a total of the original 13) would be unable to approve its initiatives. Given this new situation, FRENADESSO backed away from the dialogue on 27 July 2005. They requested meetings with the Episcopal Council and the Ecumenical Council in order to solicit an intervention on the part of the guarantors in what appeared to be the end of the Dialogue process.

The Panamanian churches proved to be timid and did not demand any correctives on the part of the government and the facilitator. However, they did make a commitment to be more vigilant and seek to ensure that no new backsliding would occur on the part of the government. Now at the point of leaving, FRENADESSO decided to rejoin the Dialogue process. The government was well aware of the fact that its victory could prove to be Pyrrhic one if it did not move quickly to modify the correlation of forces in the Dialogue. It rapidly analysed the weaknesses of each organisation and proceeded to subject them to a process that would ultimately leave them internally divided and inoperative at the bargaining table.

In the case of the doctors, it managed to orchestrate a resolution to a pending legal problem such that its present director would now be replaced by a previous director. Upon retaking his post, the previous director assumed the role of representation in the Dialogue and lined up behind the government. In the case of the teachers, the government utilised a divide and conquer tactic by placing their internal issues before the public, helping to discredit them to the rank and file. This led the position of the teachers in the short term to also fall in line with the government.

The attempt to achieve something similar among the Federation of Professional Associations (FEDAP) proved to be more difficult. FEDAP is dominated by independent associations that rarely participate in political debates and who instead mostly defend their own specific interests. In a meeting prior to the beginning of the Dialogue, a FEDAP Assembly elected an ex-president, Luis Chen, to represent them in all issues related to the reform of the Social Security Law. Julio Zúñiga, President of the Federation, was named as a contingent substitute. This arrangement, however, resulted very unfavourably for the government since Chen did not automatically align himself with the government. Zúñiga understood the situation and proceeded to call an Assembly into session where he attempted to displace Chen. Even when this proved to be unworkable, he notarised an act with his signature that indicated that he was the elected representative of FENAP in the National Dialogue. While this document had absolutely no legal standing, the facilitator accepted it and deposed Chen from the table of Dialogue.

Chen for his part did not accept the improvisation of the facilitator and insisted on arriving to the Dialogue. The members of FEDAP accepted a truce in the dispute and held another Assembly. On this occasion, the constituent members of the FEDAP gave their support to Chen to represent them at the Dialogue. But the President did not attend and denounced the Assembly. The facilitator in turn continued to recognise the President without representation while Chen continued to attend as well. The drama only ended when the Dialogue facilitator forced FEDAP to exit from the Dialogue process, providing another victory for the government.

When CONUSI was designated to coordinate the activities of CONATO during September/October, the unions affiliated with the ruling PRD of President Torrijos opposed this. By way of a missive signed by a majority of the members of CONATO directed to the facilitator, the unions loyal to the government disavowed the internal rules of CONUSI, assumed its role and installed themselves in the offices of CONATO and assumed the corresponding place in the Dialogue.

A small mob attacked the offices of CONATO, trying to expel the members of CONUSI. Even when the local was destroyed, the mob did not achieve its objective. A spurious order subsequently issued from a municipal authority forced CONUSI to abandon the local in order to avoid any further violence. At the same time, the facilitator of the Dialogue disregarded the internal rules of CONATO and continued recognising the previous representative. FRENADESSO opted to abandon its confrontation with the government on this point.

The nine members of the Dialogue that would continue supporting the initiative of FRENADESSO now became reduced to just four. In short, the original nucleus around FRENADESSO was now joined only by the Medical Commission. For the popular movement, the Dialogue had accomplished its objective, namely, to force the government to take the organised voice of the workers into account. Even though the Dialogue was controlled by the government at the onset, it also served as a forum where FRENADESSO could publicly expound its alternatives to Law No. 17.

Conclusion: The High Political Cost

In a sense, the Dialogue served to make clear that the reform of the Law of the CSS would not contribute to the resolution of what some referred to as a "deficit." The government in power has taken this notion of the "deficit" to frighten the pensioned and attempt to convince them that the CSS was bankrupt. Against the backdrop of the demographic numbers game, the government justified the incorporation of extreme reforms at the expense of the insured pensioners. On the one hand, it increased the retirement age and the density of quotas needed to qualify for benefits while on the other hand, it increased the amount of payments and opened the reserves of the institution to private market speculation.

President Torrijos and his closest circles justified these measures in order to "save" the CSS. Nevertheless, the agenda of the government was not driven by the problems faced by that institution. Rather, it had to do with the overall strategy being developed by the Ministry of the Economy. Ricaurte Vásquez, the economic minister, had already shown his hand at the outset of 2005. In order to comply with the demands of the World Bank, Panama had to reform its fiscal system and reform the Law of the Social Security System (CSS) so as to guarantee a greater entry of funds into the State. The additional funds would permit the government to clean up some areas of its finances and become a more attractive borrower. Between the fiscal reforms and the reforms of the CSS, it was calculated that a tributary increase of approximately US$ 750 million per year would be realised. This sum would be obtained in large part from the most impoverished sectors of the population thanks to the neoliberal adjustment measures instituted since the preceding decade.[6]

The reaction of general protest on the part of all social sectors had been rapid and convincing. In spite of the mobilisations and the resistance mounted against the reforms to the Social Security System, Torrijos refused to turn back. The government insisted that the increase of the age of retirement and the density of payments could be attenuated. In October of 2005, President Torrijos was to send his reform law back again with some new touches added.

Torrijos recognised at the onset that his confrontation with the organised popular sectors would have a "high political cost." According to the opinion polls that were conducted, his acceptance plummeted to 28% in May and later stabilised at 45% by August. Those same polls indicated that only 30% of the public supported his administration's imposition of reforms to the Social Security System. Complicating the entire matter, however, is the fact

---

[6] In February of 2005, months before the presentation of the government proposal, FRENADESSO pointed out that "at the base of the arguments put forward by the alliance of the government and the ruling sectors, coinciding fully with the authorities of the International Monetary Fund, is the idea that the root of the problem is to be found in the *excessive generosity* of the system. The solution, according to this approach, is to be found in reducing this generosity, including an increase in the retirement age, the number of quotas that must be paid in order to obtain the right to a pension, the reduction of the calculation of the base pension, and an increase in the amount payable by the insured worker. The second central aspect of the strategy put forward by the alliance of the government with the dominant economic interests rests in the idea that the solution to the identified problems must come about through a *shared sacrifice*, something that hides the reality that the real idea is to place the entire costs of the reform of the CSS upon the workers." FRENADESSO, *Diagnostico alternativo sobre la problemática de la CSS* (executive summary), February, 2005.

that Torrijos' negotiations with the World Bank are related to his mega project for expanding the Panama Canal.

On the one hand, the President felt obligated to carry out social security reforms in order to comply with the World Bank and thus open the doors to the additional credits necessary for investing in the Panama Canal (between US$ 5–8 billion) in the short term. On the other hand, however, he has suffered a drop in popular support that will be indispensable in winning a favourable vote on the Canal project. By Panamanian law, the expansion of the Canal must be submitted to a constitutional referendum.

In the end, the popular struggle of 2005 in Panama centred on battles for the defence of the social security system led by FRENADESSO. New confrontations loom ahead in the near future over the Panama Canal project. With the prestige of the Torrijos government now seriously weakened by the battering it took over social security reform, it will have to face a popular movement that is certain to demand greater transparency. The question in the pending case of Canal expansion will be quite simple: a canal for the benefit of global capital or a canal at the service of national development?

Carlos M. Vilas[1]

Neoliberal Meltdown and Social Protest: Argentina 2001–2002[2]

The Economic Background of the Argentine Crisis

The asymmetric *apertura* or liberalisation of the Argentine economy was carried out from the beginning of the 1990s in the framework of a scheme of monetary convertibility. A broad de-regulation of economic and financial activity and a persistent over-valuation of the national currency encouraged an accumulation of stiff external deficits, de-industrialisation, and a disarticulation of the chains of production. This was accompanied by the growth of unemployment and under-employment, the fall of real salaries, and an increase in the number of households under the poverty line. Relative prices favoured non-traded goods such as basic services, transportation and communication, run by privatised enterprises. The combination of these factors conspired against an export-led economic reactivation of the type usually recommended by the multilateral financial agencies. The effects that could have been derived by the higher initial rates of both product and productivity growth were appropriated

[1] I wish to thank Juan Pablo Ferrero for his collaboration in the statistical illustrations.
[2] This paper has appeared earlier in *Critical Sociology*, Volume 32, N° 1, 2006, pp. 163–186.

by the most concentrated groups of the economy along with those who participated in the privatisation of state-owned enterprises. The share of wages in the total product fell to the very lowest levels in the history of official statistics, while open unemployment rose in a corresponding manner. As the overall macroeconomic scheme relied on an ever-increasing public foreign debt, the need to keep public spending under tight control became a number-one priority – particularly as growth started to slow down after the *Tequila* effect and eventually entered into a recessionary phase.

Due to the convertibility scheme, monetary emission was pegged to foreign currency reserves. Thus, every increase in the domestic monetary supply was tied to additional foreign currency inflows and the growth of production linked to the growth of foreign indebtedness. Since the overvaluation of the peso conspired against a dynamic export sector and on the contrary prompted cheap imports of any kind of goods, an accumulation of trade and payments deficits resulted from the entire macroeconomic design. As monetary emission was pegged to the amount of foreign currency reserves, every increase in monetary liquidity was contingent upon additional foreign currency inflows, thus tying the rate of GDP growth to the growth of foreign indebtedness. The state assumption of the external debt as part of the regime of monetary convertibility transformed interest payments into the principal category of public spending. As debt payments increased, a conflict arose between the creditor's timetable and the goal of fiscal and public accounts equilibrium that was a lender's condition for subsequent foreign currency inflows. To this must be added the fiscal impact of the privatisation of the pension and retirement system that shifted to administrative enterprises of pension and retirement funds (AFJP), aggravating the problem of fiscal disequilibrium being fuelled by the servicing of the public debt.[3]

Yet, indebtedness of the private sector exceeded the public one. Throughout the 1990s the capacity of the private sector to generate foreign currency inflows (either from exports or/and foreign debt) was less than its own remittances to foreign financial markets. The imbalance had to be covered by the state through its own indebtedness. Consequently, growth of the total debt (public

---

[3] More than two-thirds of the growth of the total public debt of the national government during the 1990s was due to interest payments on the external debt, while most of the other third was the effect of transferring the retirement and pension system. The payments of interest ultimately grew 275% in real value over the course of the 1990s (Vaca and Cao 2001).

+ private) ran parallel with the evolution of capital flight abroad, thus supporting the hypothesis that one of the very goals of the state's heavy debt load, well in excess of its own needs for foreign exchange, was the financing of the export of capital by the private sector (FIDE 2000; Basualdo and Kulfas 2000).

The accumulation of negative balances in foreign accounts fed into a growing under-valuation of the exchange rate, which in turn further contributed to the creation of larger external deficits. The exhaustion of the privatisation process marked the end of the period of steady inflows of foreign currency. Access to the amount of foreign exchange needed to feed the convertibility scheme relied on the capacity for further borrowing in capital markets that were only accessible at higher interest rates as the level of indebtedness steadily grew. For its part, the increasingly expensive character of credit in the domestic market rendered ever more vulnerable the prospects for survival of those firms that lacked ties with the most concentrated economic groups of the country or to the global economy.

With the deceleration of growth in 1998 and the beginning of the recession in 1999, capital flight from the financial system quickly accelerated until it reached in 2001 the proportions of a stampede. The impositions of the convertibility system, the commitments assumed over an entire decade with multilateral credit lenders in the framework of the "Washington Consensus," and the economic ideology that predominated in government circles, led the successive administrations of Carlos Menem and Fernando de la Rúa to paint the growing crisis as merely a fiscal one, thereby depicting the symptom as the cause. The policy conditions set by financial lending agencies together with the prevailing monetarist approach, plus the need for the government to appeal to external markets in order to gain access to much needed additional funding, all converged in economic policy decision-making that gave highest priority to commitments with foreign creditors at the expense of investment in infrastructure and social services as well local creditors – such as public sector employees, government contractors, and retired elderly. The permanent fiscal adjustment, alongside of steadily decreasing levels of activity, employment and social welfare, was one of the most visible aspects of the economy during the second half of the 1990s.

The Social Impact of the Macro-Economic Crisis

Social inequality in Argentina experienced a sustained growth over the last three decades. During the final years of the 1990s and the initial years of the subsequent decade, this tendency accelerated. While there are various causes for this persistent trend and they have lined up differently in specific moments, there is broad agreement that the main factor promoting inequality during the 1990s could be attributed to the effects of the macro-economic strategy adopted at the onset of the decade within the framework of the so-called "Washington Consensus" (See Altimir and Beccaria 1998; Altimir et al. 2002; Schvarzer 1998; Schorr 2000).

In October 2001, the richest 10% of households in the Buenos Aires Metropolitan Area accounted for the same portion of income than the poorest 60% of households in the same area. Their income level was almost 34 times higher than that of the poorest 10% of households, or almost 80% more than those of a decade earlier, and 25% more than in the hyperinflationary period of 1989. This increase in social inequality accelerated the growth of poverty among households, both with respect to the proportion of the population living in poverty and in terms of the intensity of poverty. This was in turn the result of a significant growth of unemployment as well as the down-grading of salaries. At the end of 2001, the rate of under-utilisation of the workforce (open unemployment plus under-employment) was around 35% of the urban EAP (economically active population). In that year, more than 830,000 people fell into poverty. Towards the end of 2001, the average household income in the Buenos Aires Metropolitan Area reached no more than 46% of the retail price of the basic foodstuffs basket and even less in several provinces (INDEC 2001).

The transfer of resources towards the highest socioeconomic sectors led to a sharp deterioration in the economic standing of middle-income sectors, including professionals, small and medium sized business owners, and skilled labourers in the service sectors. The explosion of "new poverty" grew above all among these once prosperous groups of Argentine society. Having little experience in managing their new social situation and with a memory still fresh of the well-being that had been rapidly lost, these middle-class sectors now came face to face with the "historically" poor, transforming themselves into one of the most highly visible components of the social ire that erupted in 2001–2002.

The Political Landscape of the Crisis

Going against the commitments that afforded an electoral victory in October 1999, the coalition presided over by Fernando de la Rúa maintained continuity in the economic policy implemented by the previous government of Carlos Menem.[4] In more than one area, such as tax policies, the new administration deepened it, thus aggravating the already worrisome external financial imbalances which in turn resulted in greater vulnerability to the pressures from the most powerful economic actors (e.g. the banking system and financial corporations) as well as the multilateral lenders. Shortly after his inauguration in early December 1999, a tributary reform of the most regressive type took square aim at the earnings of the middle class, who in large part constituted the electoral constituency of the new government. In March 2000, a severe cut in public spending at the expense of the government sector delivered another blow to this important part of the same political base. Shortly after, the Congress passed a law enacting a new regime of labour relations.

This new regime, which substantially encroached upon long-time workers' rights, was publicly sponsored by the IMF as a central conditioning ingredient for additional liquid disbursements to the government. Openly rejected by both labour unions and left-wing political parties, the reform was eventually passed amidst accusations of bribes to members of the Senate that were never totally dismissed, leading ultimately to the resignation of the Vice-President and substantial changes in the presidential cabinet (Vilas 2001a).[5]

From that point on, the government became involved in a process of rapid disintegration. The most conservative elements in the original coalition gained

---

[4] The coalition was formed by President de la Rúa's Partido Radical and FREPASO, a convergence of centre-left parties led by Vice-President Carlos "Chacho" Álvarez. The coalition had made its debut with a resonant victory in the legislative elections of October 1997.

[5] The Parliamentary Secretary of the Senate at that time confessed under oath to the payment of large sums of money to various Senators of the Justicialista (Peronist) Party in exchange for their vote for the approval of the reform. According to that statement bribing those senators had cost the public around the five million dollars, with alleged involvement in this episode of then President Fernando de la Rúa together with the Secretary of State Intelligence, the Minister of Labour, the president of the bloc of senators of the governing Allianza, the president of the block of Senators from the Justicialista Party, and the accuser himself, plus the Senators that collected the bribe. See the editions for December 13–14, 2003 in the newspapers La Nación, Clarín, Página 12, Crónica and La Prensa, of the City of Buenos Aires. Also, the newspaper La Jornada (Mexico City, DF) for December 14, 2003.

political leverage together with a greater willingness to give in to the pressures of the multilateral lending agencies as the financial crisis went on. At the same time, the dispersion and shift into opposition of a number of political parties and minor organisations that had earlier contributed to the formation of the governing coalition drove President de la Rúa and his reconstituted cabinet to rely upon parliamentary collaboration with the Justicialista Party (PJ) from early 2001 on. Being the main political party backing the neoliberal policies implemented during Carlos Menem's government, the PJ had suffered a severe setback in the 1999 elections. This allowed the de la Rúa-Alvarez coalition to gain control of executive power. Born out of necessity, the new congressional accord was interpreted by not a few sectors of civil society as clear evidence of the convergence the two traditional parties (the Radical Party of President de la Rúa and the Justicialista Party) in an underlying continuity of neoliberal policies at an increasing social and economic cost, along with greater subservience with regard to the domestic and external financial actors.

In March 2001, the appeal to a crude monetarist approach to manage the economic crisis triggered an outburst of angry street opposition that forced the government to step back from its implementation just a few days later. The package of proposed measures included severe cutbacks in the public education budget, further reductions in the already badly shrunken public sector workforce, a variety of cuts in social spending, among other measures, all of which was met with broad opposition from organised labour and significant sectors of the middle class. The subsequent appointment of Domingo Cavallo as Economic Minister contributed very little, if at all, in improving the climate of opinion much less in solving the economic conundrum. Having served as Economic Minister for a good portion of the Menem Administration, Cavallo was well-identified as the "father" of the neoliberal political-economic model of which an ever broadening social base throughout the Argentine society was now blaming for the crisis. By designating Cavallo to return to the post and with the unfolding continuation of his neoliberal management of the economy, a growing majority of the population became convinced of the de la Rúa Administration's betrayal of electoral promises and the submission of his government to the pressures of powerful economic and financial elites. Indeed, the social rebellion that was to break out nine months later was largely due to Cavallo's second term of service performance as the economic tsar of the already crumbling de la Rúa Administration.

During the period of Cavallo's renewed tenure as Minister of the Economy (March to December 2001), there were distinct moments when Argentines became ever more embittered as the puncture hole in their purses grew larger. The partial reprogramming of the most pressing foreign debt payments resulted in new accusations of government corruption. A 13% reduction in government salaries, retirement payments and the unsettled debts of the state with its providers further aggravated the situation. For broad sectors of the society, what began at the end of 1999 as a political as well as moral commitment for progressive change and public accountability had turned into nothing but evidence of unfulfilled promises, a degradation of the rule of law, an explosion of financial speculation, social inequalities, internal quarrels and a seemingly endless parade of absurdities. The delegitimisation of the government was also projected to the Justicialista Party that was providing parliamentary support to the economic initiatives of the Executive that required Congressional approval. While the PJ's support was presented as a contribution to governability, it can be interpreted as a follow-up of its disciplined endorsement of neoliberal reforms during the two Menem's Administrations. Consistent ideological persistence, not just crass opportunism, was underpinning this party collaboration.

Social Protest and Electoral Rejection

Increasing social deterioration reinforced social protests, mainly in the Metropolitan area. Weakened by the growth of unemployment and by the reorientation of state management in the previous decade, and in fact, compromised in large part by the governmental policies of Menem, the labour unions channelled the widening social mobilisation with little efficacy. In contrast, an array of social organisations, with a protagonist role displayed by the unemployed workers and women, gained increased public notoriety thanks to a variety of new forms of social mobilisation. The so called "picketers movement" (*piqueteros*) soon became the most prominent actor of this period. Consisting of unemployed persons and their families, they developed innovative modalities of protest, including street and highway blockades. By channelling their dissatisfaction and demands out of the roots of a growing urban poverty and unemployment that had been fostered by privatisation of state enterprises and de-industrialisation, the resulting movement most evidently linked the crisis to the political-economic scheme that had become installed in Argentina.

Throughout 2001, the picketers' movements up-graded their public positioning and ability for recruitment as persistent unemployment threw new
ranks of jobless out of the labour market. They proved to be quite able in
carrying out strong protests (blocking strategic public arteries and access
routes to the city of Buenos Aires) capable of disrupting everyday life, while
in the process providing convincing evidence of a vast co-ordination that
transcended ideological differences. But it was not only the deterioration in
the labour market that fuelled the growth of the picketers' movements.
Constituted by unemployed workers, these activists provided the new movements with their own "social capital" stemming from their prior trade union
experience as well as their political ability in negotiating with government
agencies. As a matter of fact, the initial blow-up of the picketers' protests
took place in the poles of industrial activity with a labour force involving
those with very high skill levels: refinery workers, transport and communications workers, steel workers, and similar occupations, which had been badly
hit by privatisations and the overall economic policy. Moreover, many of the
initial leaders of the "picketers" were former union cadres and leaders, thus
providing an organisational "know how" to the new breeds of layoffs. These
former union organisers shared their experience with the incipient social
movements appearing in this period, helping to account for the especially
strong impact that the picketers' organisations were able to make in their
demands.

To this, we must add two additional elements that are clearly linked to the
political system. On the one hand, there was a dynamic network of articulations
between the organisations of the unemployed and the more or less radical
political parties of the left.[6] While neglected by most academic analyses of
the *piquetero* movements which tend to emphasise their spontaneity and autonomy vis-à-vis more conventional social or political organisations (Fradkin
2002; Svampa & Pereyra 2003 etc.), these articulations contributed in no small
measure to strengthening the movement's course of action and helped orient
them towards a rational administration of resources, including employment

---

[6] For example, the close ties of the Combative Class Struggle Current (*Corriente
Clasista y Combativa*) and the Revolutionary Communist Party, between the Workers'
Pole (*Polo Obrero*) with the Workers' Party, and between the Neighbourhoods Stand
Up! Movement (*Movimiento Barrios de Pie*) and the Patria Libre. These relations also
developed among less radical organisations, for example, between the Land and
Housing Federation (Federación de Tierra y Vivienda), Frente Grande and Central
Union of Argentine Workers (*Central de Trabajadores Argentinos*, or CTA).

training and the food assistance that they were able to obtain by pressuring various governmental agencies. This placed even further into relief, the relative marginalisation of the Justicialista Party and their local leaders with regard to social protest. On the other hand, the manner in which the government of Fernando de la Rúa packaged the implementation of emergency assistance policies created opportunities for strengthening the autonomy of the picketers' movements and provided the impetus for aiming the demands directly at the national government, thus eliminating or limiting the various intermediate bureaucratic levels where the conflict could have been somewhat cushioned or absorbed by provincial or municipal authorities.[7] The initial demands for work became increasingly articulated with broader critiques of macro-economic policy and the political system, and demands for human rights which pointed to police harassment of protesters. To a large extent, the social assistance policies implemented in this period can be understood as an outcome of the effective ways in which these organisations pressed forth their demands.

The legislative elections of October 2001 made explicit the orphaned politics of the government and the overall extent to which the principal protagonists of the political system had lost their legitimacy. There was a 26.3% national average of absenteeism, several points higher than that of the previous legislative elections in 1997. But the most notable and widely publicised ingredient of the elections was the so-called *"voto bronca"* (anger vote) where the voters went through the effort of voluntarily annulling their ballots as a form of protest against all of the candidates and parties participating in the elections. A new phenomenon in its magnitude, the *voto bronca* amounted to 21% of the total vote recorded across the country. In seven electoral districts,

---

[7] With the twofold aim of neutralising the political build-up in the Buenos Aires Province where the Justicialist (Peronist) Party was traditionally hegemonic and limiting the growth of small groups of picketers in the Metropolitan area, the de la Rúa's administration changed the distribution pattern of emergency job programmes which up until then were channelled through the municipal governments. In the new system, jobs were assigned in "packages" to non-government organisations that assumed responsibility for distribution to individual unemployed. Far from containing the picketers' organisations, this helped institutionalise them and created conditions for their subsequent strengthening. The picketers' organisations began to create their own NGOs, acting moreover as co-ordinating agencies of the small groups that were appearing in the very poorest neighbourhoods of the Greater Buenos Aires area. All of this helped them become transformed into an organised social movement with greater power to pressure the government and to self-administer the subsidies received from the same.

which included among them the City of Buenos Aires, the proportion was considerably higher. In all, almost half of the Argentine electorate either abstained from voting or utilised their vote to repudiate the entire political system. The governing coalition lost more than 5 million of the votes that it had received in the previous legislative election in October 1997.[8] Just in the City of Buenos Aires alone, the government lost a third of the electoral total it had received in 1997, while in the province of Buenos Aires, the loss was over 70%.

The protest vote also scorched *Acción por la República*, the political party of Economic Minister Cavallo, which lost around 1.2 million votes and practically disappeared in the province of Buenos Aires. On the other hand, the small parties of the left experienced notable advances. Their traditional inability and unwillingness to forge electoral coalitions greatly reduced the impact of these advances. The Peronist Justicialist Party therefore resulted as the winners with almost 5 million votes cast, about 1 million less than the legislative elections of 1997. In the province of Buenos Aires, a district already governed by that party, the Justicialists lost one-third of its electoral vote, but won it any case, thus keeping control over the most populous province, as they did in Córdoba, Entre Ríos, Formosa, La Pampa, La Rioja, Mendoza, Misiones, Salta, San Juan, San Luis, Santa Cruz, Santa Fe, Santiago del Estero, Tierra del Fuego and Tucumán, allowing them to win control of both legislative houses, i.e., deputies and senators (Vilas 2001b).

The electoral results of October 2001 can be interpreted as a punishing expression of the frustration over what a significant portion of the society felt was the dishonesty and lack of compliance with earlier promises for progressive change, something that only two years earlier had permitted the governing alliance to win control over national government. This was also a repudiation that involved the party of Economy Minister Cavallo as well the Justicialist Party that collaborated strategically with the government in the parliament. But at the same time, the October turnouts showed the capacity of the Justicialist Party to preserve, in spite of setbacks, the vote of an important portion of the electorate and to recover as the country's leading political organisation. This is what allowed it to win election in the province of

---

[8] Comparison is made with the October 1997 elections since both were legislative elections, while that of 1999 was a general one – i.e. including, in addition to Congress seats, a Presidential as well Provincial Governor' election. See Escolar et al. (2002) for a comparative analysis of the elections of 1999 and 2001.

Buenos Aires, a situation that was of crucial importance in the culmination of the crisis that was detonated two months later.

Far from attempting corrections in the economic path taken or even a major reshuffling of his cabinet, President de la Rúa insisted on the courses of action that had already led to political isolation. The government had definitively lost all capacity to take control over the economic crisis. Towards the end of November, the big operators of the financial system had drained the national economy of almost half of its reserves, further aggravating the pressures on the fixed and undervalued exchange rate. Overcome by the turn of events and the increasing disaffection of other members of the presidential cabinet, Cavallo either did not realise or did not wish to come to terms with the gravity of the nation's economic problems. Clearly, such a recognition would have implied an acceptance of the inevitability of changing the macro-economic scheme which he himself had designed a decade before. On the contrary, he insisted, with a strong presidential backing, on further implementation of convertibility at any and all costs.

Economic Meltdown and Social Explosion

At the beginning of December, Cavallo made a fateful decision that would later prove to be his undoing and that of the President who against all advice to the contrary, accepted his Minister's stubbornness until the bitter end. In order to prevent further capital flights and a huge banking system crackdown, a drastic freeze on banking accounts was decreed in what came to be known as the *corralito*. Cash withdrawals of more than US$ 300 per week per person were prohibited at a time when just the price of a basic goods basket for families cost more than US$ 550 per month. Any transaction over this sum had to be carried out by way of checks, credit or debit cards. The attempt to stop or at least slow down capital flight was late since by then, outflows sponsored by the biggest financial operators, including banks, had already assumed massive characteristics. It was also a badly targeted decision since it fundamentally affected the banking deposits of small and medium customers in the formal sector of the economy, with a heavy impact upon the informal sector and the poorest segments of the middle-class.[9] In the final

---

[9] Of the US$ 69,843 millions that were "corralled" by the government, more than half (US$ 38,568 million) corresponded to deposits made by 12.3 million individual persons, affecting accounts with an average size of deposits of slightly over US$ 3100.

analysis it was also a foolish decision because it relied on a drastic change in many people's personal behaviour – a shift from cash transactions to those mediated by the financial system which usually takes place in a longer time span-something badly needed by Cavallo. It not only required a "cultural change" in people's way of conducting everyday transactions, but also subjected the banking system to a gigantic expansion in order to service the exponential growth of small customers and micro-transactions.

Due to the low index of bank mediated activity in the everyday Argentine economy, the measure generated a severe reduction of total transactions, with a resulting crash in the chain of payments.[10] The impact was particularly grave for low and middle-income groups, and in the informal sector of the economy, whose transactions are most frequently if not exclusively carried out in cash. Mobs of enraged customers and the general public amassed at the doors of the banks where people tried to open rolling savings accounts that would permit them to continue carrying out their routine transactions. The paralysis of activities was especially hard felt in the sectors of small shops and personal services. A swarm of small establishments, small service providers, and micro-enterprises were left out of the game. The system now made it impossible for them to actively or passively operate in accordance with the new financial rules. The timing of the decision also contributed to making its impact more severe, i.e., the onset of the Christmas season and the eve of the period where a great deal of Argentines usually make additional purchases or take their summer leave. Many Argentines were suddenly faced with the imperative of shelving their travel plans and seasonal purchases. If indeed the vacation issue represented a severe blow to the middle classes that during the 1990s had grown accustomed to travel abroad to a variety of tourist destinations, the curtailment of basic consumption drastically affected families of the lowest income-earning sectors. This latter sector has a strong tradition of making some small extraordinary purchase during the Christmas season, albeit simply the traditional cider and *panetone* of Christmas Eve and some small present for the children.

But while the average amount of fixed term deposits was around US$ 18,350 per account, the average amount of rolling deposits was at US$ 860 per account (Cafiero and Llorens 2002).

[10] In the last trimester of 2001, the relation of deposits in rolling accounts/M1 was 50.1%, while the relation of deposits in rolling accounts/GNP was 3.5%, this according to estimates of the (IEFE) Institute of Fiscal and Economic Studies (Instituto de Estudios Fiscales y Económicos) over the base figures of the Central Bank and the Ministry of the Economy.

All of this suddenly evaporated under the *corralito*, helping to explain the mass discontent, anger and above all the insecurity that befell an enormous portion of the nation. For many, it was the sensation of the floor dropping out from beneath them, of not knowing what to do, where to go, and to whom to submit their claims for compensation. Trying desperately to rescue the financial system now perched on the edge of total collapse by the capital flight that the system had itself sponsored, the government of Fernando de la Rúa was now roasting under the intense ire of nearly the entire society. The magnitude of the anger went far beyond the effective hijacking of the nation's finances. The "*corralito*" represented the end of the fantasy held by millions of Argentines for well over a decade that the country in which they lived somehow belonged to the "First World." The image of a society whose currency was as worthy as the U.S. dollar and whose citizens lived in a cosmopolitan outpost was abruptly shattered. This was the grand fantasy that had been conspicuously nourished by the official discourse of successive governments, with a concerted collaboration of the media networks while the unpleasant ingredients of the convertibility scheme – such as massive poverty, social exclusion, growing unemployment, and deepening social polarisation, as well the increasing fragmentation of the social fabric – were systematically dismissed.

It was precisely in the face of this no longer hidden side of the convertibility scheme that the first explosions of social rage began. People living in a new world of unemployment and hidden under-employment, a rapidly proliferating poverty, and a culminating de-monetarisation of the informal sector caused by the "*corralito*" became transformed into historical actors. The mass disturbances that developed in mid-December, which included sacking and pillaging of food shops, supermarkets and the like, were the expression of an accentuated climate of social exhaustion and aggravated impoverishment in the framework of an overwhelming rejection of most of the conventional actors of the political system.

By the afternoon of December 19, thirty-seven people had died throughout the country as a result of the reaction to businesses being ransacked and the subsequent intervention of the police. Under total duress by his political isolation and by the emerging social situation that was effectively now beyond government control, President de la Rúa fired Cavallo and enacted a state of siege, thus legalising the intervention of the armed forces to repress the swelling social protest. Far from calming the situation, this proved to be the final straw that broke the people's patience, dispelling any residual doubts that might have remained among the capital city's middle classes.

Pressed up against the wall by the "*corralito*" and astounded by the arrogance of the presidential discourse that announced the state of siege, with all expectations of change frustrated beyond repair, first hundreds and then thousands of citizens from Buenos Aires City middle-class neighbourhoods (Palermo, Belgrano, Flores, Almagro, Caballito) spontaneously began to express their rage with street protests and the blaring horns of their cars, shouting their denunciation of the government and joining in a massive two-pronged march, with one column heading to the Plaza de Mayo, directly in front of the Government House, and the other to the Plaza Congreso, directly facing the parliament. Others chose to amass and loudly protest in front of the official residence of the President. The protest continued well into the night, with the middle class leaving behind their traditional fear and dispersion that had been nurtured through years of military dictatorship and democratic passivity, now putting their bodies directly on the line. It was a mix of people fed up with the "*corralito*," some continuing the process that began with the October vote, others celebrating the resignation of Cavallo, but all united in the slogan "*¡Que se vayan todos!*" (All of them must go!). That night in the Plaza de Mayo, traditional site and symbol of mass citizen action from the very days of independence from Spain, a people who had reached their limits gathered together behind a single slogan without prior planning or organisation. After the first wave and the ensuing police repression, the people returned to the streets the following day, December 20. The government's response was even more brutal, leaving six demonstrators dead, but serving only to accelerate and make more inevitable the final end. By that evening, President de la Rúa had announced his resignation and abandoned his post.

Institutional Recomposition

An important aspect of the aftermath of the December social explosion rests in the institutional procedures that were carried out through the existing constitutional mechanisms. While an act of the masses in rage brought down the government of Fernando de la Rúa, the presidential succession was carried out in accordance with already existing institutional procedures. The spontaneity of the collective protest and consequently its lack of organic make up contributed to the management of the crisis falling back into the hands of the very political actors who had been submitted to citizen's rejection in the October polls. The slogan "All of them must go!" fed the fires of the mass popular uprising but the acceleration of its dynamics worked against its long-term efficacy as the initial moment of a reformed political system. Moreover, the social uprising that ousted de la Rúa was a mostly Metropolitan event, without anything similar in the rest of the country. It was an act brought about by mass agitation in the capital city, leading to the subsequent measures that were taken without any concerted base in political activism (Bonasso 2002; Camarasa 2002).

This geographical concentration of social mobilisation would continue to be manifested throughout 2002. Facilitated by the tolerance of the new authorities, the social protests against the *"corralito"* and most of traditional political actors fused together under the "All of them must go!" slogan, reaching an unprecedented intensity and magnitude (See Graph 1).[11] Yet it was basically Metropolitan in scope, with 20% of the protest actions and a similarly large portion of participants residing in the City of Buenos Aires (who make up less than 8% of the national population), and with similar percentages pertaining to the neighbouring municipalities of the Buenos Aires Province.[12]

Institutional tolerance of street rallies and protest throughout 2002 significantly reduced their potential for conflict despite the obvious fact that the social environment continued to deteriorate. Poverty, inequality and social polarisation became sharply accentuated, in some cases doubling the levels that contributed to the social explosion of December 2001 (See Table 1).

---

[11] The acts of social protest quantified in the graph include road, avenue, highway and bridge blockades, public demonstrations and rallies, mass mobilisations and marches, and other mass demonstrations of repudiation and demands for change against institutions or persons considered to be representatives of some power structure (government, government officials, political parties and their leaders, legislators, judicial figures, business leaders, banking officials, police authorities, etc.). There is no systematic record of protest actions prior to January 2002. The series is interrupted in October of that same year because from then on this information was no longer considered to be public.

[12] The figures refer to the number of persons who participated in protest acts and only have an indicative value in terms of magnitude. The same person is counted in accordance with the number of protest acts in which he or she participates in. The eminently Metropolitan character of the social protest of December 2001 and throughout the following year contrasts with the way in which some media portrayed these events. In any case, this was not the first time that mass concentrations of people in Plaza de Mayo eventually ended up in political changes of national scope. In this sense the events of 20 December can be seen as adding to a long list of transformational moments in Argentina's political history which include the installation of the first independent government on 25 May 1810, the spontaneous massive rally on 17 October 1945 that gave decisive leverage to Juan Perón's popular leadership, just to name a few other examples.

Graph 1

Evolution of social protests, by number of actions, Jan.-Oct. 2002

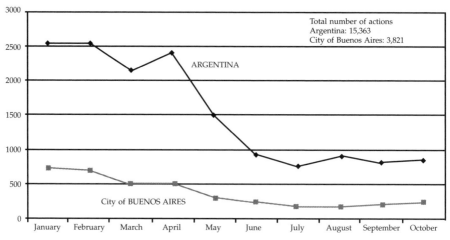

Source: Subsecretaria de Seguridad y Proteción Civil

Table 1

Evolution of poverty and inequality in the metropolitan area, 2001 and 2002

Date of observation	People living under the poverty line (%)		People living under the indigent (very poor) line (%)		Ginni Coefficient	Index of polarization*
	Households	Persons	Households	Persons		
Oct. 2001	25.5	35.4	8.3	12.2	44.8	33.9
May 2002	37.7	49.7	16.0	22.7	45.2	46.4
Oct. 2002	42.3	54.3	16.9	24.7	53.7	39.3

(*) Relationship between the median income of the 10% wealthiest and the 10% poorest households.
Source: INDEC, Encuesta Permanente de Hogares.

Several factors played a role in this shift in the society's mood. First, the above-mentioned tolerance for protests. In spite of calls for a repressive approach stemming from right wing media and political organisations seeking to criminalise social protest, the national government generally opted for a strategy of dialogue and political negotiations.[13]

---

[13] Representative of the right's demands for repressing social protest was the editorial of the conservative daily newspaper *La Nación* published on 10 August 2002.

There was also a re-orientation of social protest. The strongest and more organised mobilisations with respect to the *"corralito"* made the banks their principal targets. In the popular imagination of the victimised citizenry, the banks had essentially kept the money that the people had deposited there. In this sense, the rule of several courts to endorse demands for compensation, together with some government decisions to ease the *corralito*, all contributed to the decompression of social tensions.

For their part, the state's management over the instruments of political economy managed to provide a timid economic reactivation, among which included a strong currency devaluation. The new exchange rate drastically increased the price of imported goods, making them extremely expensive, while generating a favourable conjuncture for the substitution of imports and in stimulating exports. The fact that none of the catastrophic predictions made by economists and spokespeople of the financial establishment occurred as a result of these measures (e.g. hyper-inflation, melting down of salaries, exchange rate stampedes, trade sanctions and other external punitive policies as a result of defaulting on the debt, etc.) contributed to an overall improvement in collective perceptions. Table 2 shows the positive evolution of real salaries both in the formal sector of the economy as well as in the informal sector. These rather modest improvements were accompanied with a slow but persistent reduction in the unemployment rate.[14]

Table 2

Evolution of real salaries.   (INDEX – Oct. 2001 = 100)

	October 2002	October 2003	October 2004
All sectors	106	119	130
Private formal sector	115	133	149
Private informal sector	94	102	113

Source: Ministry of the Economy, Press Release, Jan. 5, 2005.

On 26 June, two militants of the protest organisations died as a result of Buenos Aires' Province police forces in the neighbouring municipality of Avellaneda.

[14] The urban unemployment rate fell from 19.7% by the end of 2002 to 14.5% at the end of 2003 and to 13% by the middle of 2004 (Figures from the Ministry of Labour).

However, the main factor conducive to lowering the level and scope of social mobilisations had to do with the government's management of emergency assistance policies. The implementation of a broad plan of social subsidies aimed at the unemployed heads of household throughout the entire country permitted a minimum level of monetary assistance to be provided to the most indigent groups. With a coverage of close to 2 million beneficiaries, 800 thousand of whom were living in the Metropolitan area, this relief programme put money back in the pockets of the unemployed and contributed to an aggregate stimulation of the local economies in the most impoverished districts. Small neighbourhood merchants were in position and ready to match the resurrected consumer demand of the most vulnerable social sectors.[15] At the same time, the programme served to open the channels of dialogue and negotiation between the national government, the municipal governments and the organisations of jobless people, articulating the latter into the institutional network of public policies.

These policies managed to change the character and organisational forms of social protest. In the City of Buenos Aires, the demonstrations that continued tended to revolve around issues of how the national government should best intervene in the crisis, for example, with respect to the "*corralito*" and in moving from US dollar-denominated transactions to transactions in pesos. In a number of provinces, local issues gained relevance vis-à-vis national ones.[16] Yet alongside of the exhaustion that affected many protesters and their fulfilment of specific demands, there was also an improvement in the organisation and logistic support for protest mobilisations. While less frequent than in the summer months, protests were now becoming more massive, better organised and more politicised. The role of some smaller political parties of the left seems to have been decisive in this regard.

Graph 2 shows the ascending tendency of the average amount of participation per event. The data should not be regarded as anything more than an illustration of the tendency in which the quantitative weight of hundreds of small demonstrations gradually gave way to less frequent but exponentially larger rallies and marches. The large organisations of the unemployed and

---

[15] The programme distributed the equivalent of $150 per month to each beneficiary, in national government bonds that operated as a quasi-currency in free circulation. This was complemented by a plan of subsidised distribution of medicines and foodstuffs in kind.

[16] For example, see Izumi (2002); Gallo (2002); Márquez (2002).

Graph 2

Average participation by protest action.
Jan.-Oct. 2002, in number of persons

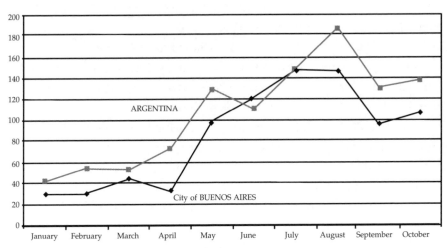

Source: Subsecretaria de Seguridad y Proteción Civil

the small political organisations that moved around them turned into the
main driving force. In contrast, the neighbourhood assemblies that channelled
the demands or at least the complaints of the City of Buenos Aires middle
classes, and had led in no small way to the creation of a differentiated and
eventually autonomous space of political expression with respect to the institutional framework, had towards the end of 2002 lost much of their capacity
for mobilisation and practically disappeared.

The definition of an electoral schedule by mid-2002 that was to culminate
ten months later in the election of a new national government further contributed to the decompression of social tensions. Consequently, the traditional
political parties came back to the centre of the institutional forum to re-assume
their hegemony, addressing themselves to the expectations of more traditional groupings rather than those represented by the organisations that had
led the social protests.

Thus, the presidential elections of 27 April 2003 displayed the capacity of
the traditional institutions of the political system to contain and channel the
political options of a population whose social unrest was already being mod-
erated by the above-mentioned policies and changing environment. A high
level of electoral participation (almost 82% of the national electorate) was
recorded. Most notable was the virtual disappearance of the "voto bronca",

which reached a total of only 541 thousand – slightly more than 2% of the total votes cast or 3% of the validated votes). More than half of the votes cast went to the three presidential candidates advocating reforms to the neoliberal macroeconomic scheme, while candidates advocating for renewed endorsement of neoliberal policies gathered around 40 percent of the turnout. The high electoral participation significantly diluted mass support for the slogan "All of them must go!" that previously reigned the streets. Ironically, this slogan ended up being the proposal of a small party of former army offers that were involved in a number of attempted military coups in the late 1980s.

Two-thirds of the valid votes cast were oriented towards a collection of presidential formulas headed by figures who were relatively marginal to the political commitments and styles of the administrations of Carlos Menem and Fernando de la Rúa, consisting of two governors from smaller provinces, a former Congress-woman heading a small, new political party, and a neoliberal economist who for the first time presented himself as a political contender, now being supported by a recently formed political party.[17] The parties and coalitions of the left including the *Partido Obrero* (Workers Party), *Izquierda Unida* (United Left) and others, had a very prominent street presence in the social mobilisations of 2002, but experienced a very strong setback in the electoral process, above all in comparison to the elections of October 2001. In the April elections, their combined turnout was only 4% of the validated votes.

Upon taking office, the new administration led by Néstor Kirchner defined a broad package of social policies that promoted a diverse and heterogeneous set of opportunities for a genuine re-insertion back into work of the swollen ranks of the unemployed. These policies included the formation of work co-operatives linked to state investment programmes in the area of housing, regional networks of public drinking water, associations of workers to self-manage their enterprises in facilities abandoned by their former owners during the height of the crisis, etc. At the same time, the social policies introduced tensions as well as fragmentation in more than one social organisation. The

---

[17] On 18 May, the electoral showdown was set for the two formulas that had gained the highest number of votes on April 27, i.e., those let by ex-President Carlos Menem (who won 24.4% in the first round) and by Governor Néstor Kirchner (with 22.2% of the first round vote). In view of a convincing coincidence of all opinion polls that predicted a strong electoral polarisation in favour of the reform programme of Kirchner, ex-President Menem decided to withdraw from the runoff election three days prior to the actual voting.

cleavage now widened between those that accepted the new opportunities of re-insertion in the labour market and more generally accepted the "reformist" character of the resolution of their demands and needs, and those more radicalised sectors whose organisations denounced the new direction of state policies as a strategy of co-optation designed to displace popular demands for radical changes.

Conclusion

The failure to comply with the electoral promises for reform of the macro-economic model, greater institutional transparency, and a more balanced distribution of social costs and benefits, i.e., the package of promises that permitted Fernando de la Rúa to win the 1999 elections, led to deep seated feelings of frustration, anger and injustice in large segments of Argentine society. These feelings went in tandem with unemployment, a deterioration of income, and a drop in consumption as the convertibility model was additionally stretched beyond its own limits. The policy decisions made during 2001 deepened the fragmentation of the Argentine social fabric. Poor management of social communications that promoted relentless publicity of frivolous styles of living on the part of members of the presidential family added to the widespread feelings of injustice by an impoverished population. The preservation of the mechanisms of representative democracy permitted broad sectors of the electorate to express their opposition to that state of affairs, as the government's inertia only accentuated its own political bankruptcy.

The violent change of scenario prompted by the state freezing of bank accounts and people's savings was the fuse that detonated the outbreak of violence and social rage. The blow dealt to the purses as well as the fantasies of the middle and lower classes had a tremendous destabilising effect, one perhaps even greater than the actual long term deterioration in the quality of life being suffered by a large majority of the popular sectors. The social downgrading that was experienced over the course of 2000 and 2001 had a certain gradual character that had been going on since the final years of Menem's Administration. The policy decisions involving the heaviest impact on the pockets of the population had been justified by arguments seen as plausible by many, and this gradualism provided the opportunity of a certain process of re-accommodation towards a declining position on the part of those most affected and already well-accustomed to sliding downhill.[18] In contrast, the *"corralito"* affected everyone and was understood as a measure aimed at saving the banks, thus lacking any plausible justification. It was implemented in a scenario of isolation and obvious governmental weakness emerging out of the October elections. The declaration of the state of siege with all of the potential for repressive violence that this normally implies, along with the police repression that was unleashed in order to smash the protests, all converged to seal the fate of the elected ruling government.

The impact of the *"corralito"* involved a sharp break with normalcy, worsening the on-going concentration of income, growing poverty and exacerbation of social inequality. The gradual nature of things became transformed into an abrupt fall from night to day, putting an end to the survival strategies that could have been adopted until then. On this particular point a parallel may be traced between the social collapse of mid-1989 that forced an early end to the Presidency of Raúl Alfonsín, and the one that was triggered off in 2001. In both cases, government decisions made in the framework of profound crisis altered the rhythm of social decline, liquidated the people's spontaneous family or personal mechanisms of adaptation which up to then had been appealed to in order to soften the deteriorating situation, and triggered off a massive social uprising in the face of the incapacity or disinterest of political actors to take charge of affairs and address the people's grievances.

From the point of view of institutional representative-democracy, the events of late 2001 yielded ambiguous results. On the one hand, they point to the manner in which conditions of grave deterioration and profound social fragmentation, along with unwise political decisions, feed the potential for serious social distress. When a sense of injustice, illegitimate authority, undeserved punishment, and of shutting the light off at the end of the tunnel all becomes

---

[18] For example, the cutbacks in public spending in March of 2000 affected a distinct set of social sectors, namely, public employees. This was a process that had steadily advanced since the times of Menem. The official language and the way in which the mass media presented the typical public employee as a bureaucrat opposed to modernisation, with a lazy and bumbling profile, vegetating behind a window or playing games in the computer. To this image the new government added accusations of complicity with "menemismo" and even corruption, while the already mentioned 13 percent cutback of pensions and government wages involved a new blow to the lower middle class families' budgets. (See for example *Cash. Economic Supplement (Suplemento Económico)* of the daily newspaper *Página 12* (in Buenos Aires), January 16 and 23 editions in 2000).

widespread among the population, the conditions for rebellion are ripe. The resulting social upheaval reduced to rubble a government that had carefully placed the explosives and lit the fuse. But the dynamics of this period also demonstrate the capacity of the institutional system to process and contain social conflict within its own parameters, neutralising pressures of the most reactionary sectors who called for repression and an authoritarian response to the popular mobilisations.

The lack of success in the demand that "All of them must go!" was evidenced not only in the high rate of electoral participation and the stunted renovation of the candidates lists put forth by the political parties in the electoral contests of 2002, but also in the poor showing made by the political organisations of the left, notwithstanding the role they played in the organisation of mass social protests. The lack of correspondence between the social arithmetic of street actions and that of electoral participation confirms the profound disjuncture between social protest and electoral behaviour that has been shown over the years as one of the central characteristics of the political scenarios prevailing in various countries in the region (Vilas 1999).

Finally, there is a specific issue that makes it possible to pair up the events of December 2001 in Argentina with the outbreaks of mass social protest that have since occurred in other countries in South America such as Peru, Bolivia or Ecuador. In all of these cases, we can observe the prior implementation of the so-called "Washington Consensus," the objectives and interests of financial and economic elites, and the ensuing level of popular bitterness that overflows in the face of the subsequent de-legitimisation of the corresponding political systems. To this, we must add the objective capacity of the established political system, once compelled to process the crisis, to adapt itself to new social scenarios and to orchestrate a re-orientation of mass protest into less violent and less-threatening arenas.

Chávez, Fidel and Evo Morales sign a 2006 People's Trade Agreement

Part II: Leftist Paths to Development

José Bell Lara

Cuban Socialism in the Face of Globalisation

Introduction: Prior to Globalisation

Capitalism brought an end to local civilisations. Beginning with the 15th and 16th Centuries, a process of the formation of a single world economy had begun which crystallised when the system reached its imperialist phase. It was Lenin who had affirmed that upon having finished carving up of the world and then having moved towards a new process of incorporating the spoils, capitalism had achieved a global scale (Bell 1968). From that point forward, all societies, independent of their level of development, moved together in a parallel way towards a new society (Dos Santos 1980: 284), although that does not necessarily imply that they would follow the same path of development.

Prior to capitalist development, humanity lived under diverse civilising processes which exhibited their own dynamics and their relations with other civilisations were minimal or non-existent. In general, it can be said that there was a great historical epoch in which the course of development of these distinct civilising processes displayed a large degree of autonomy. Their markets were localised and their commercial ties were very weak. There existed wars and prolonged conquests between these diverse civilisations but the global totality did not share a common focal point of expansion.

The disintegration of feudalism in Europe coincided with the expansion of trade throughout the region and the birth of capitalism. From the very onset, this emerging system displayed a clear dedication to domination and it rapidly manifested its universal extension in search of riches. The conquest and the colonisation of America ultimately formed part of this process of expansion of capital and the rise of a global market (Marx 1959: 683).

For the first time in history, all of the territories on the planet began to articulate themselves in terms of a common denominator, i.e., the exchange of commodities, with the centre of this articulation process based in Western Europe. The process was no longer simply an aggregation of empires, rather, it now constituted a process of incorporation and subordination to the world system of capital. Capitalist relations penetrated to the interior of all other existing systems and impregnated its internal structures, either modifying them, destroying them, or adapting them in the service of obtaining the maximum benefits from domination over them. This process of capitalist development was carried out by both economic and non-economic means which together combined in a multitude of complementary ways to favour the hegemonic centre of the system. In the process, it generated the condition of underdevelopment of vast areas which became subordinated or rendered dependent upon the world system of capital.

Beginning with these elements, we can begin to visualise an inherent reality of capitalism as a world system, namely, that development and underdevelopment are two sides of the same coin which is global capitalist development. The significance of the industrial revolution for the development of humanity was analogous to the invention of intensive agriculture which had occurred some ten thousand years earlier. After each of these revolutions, humans lived in a different manner. The first of these types of civilisations took thousands of years to spread across the globe while the second took only three-hundred years (Toffler 1982: 22).

The capitalist epoch has been characterised by the creation of new productive forces and new commodity-products. Important historical examples such as the utilisation of new energy sources such as steam, electricity, petroleum and the atom; the shortening of distances via the development of transportation means such as the railways, the automobile and aviation; and the revolution of the means of communication such as the telephone, radio, television, fax and internet illustrate how all have contributed to the increasing productive forces.

The large factory, the conveyor belt and the assembly line style of production have made possible large scale manufacturing at ever lower costs and higher profits while unleashing torrents of commodity products that have inundated all spheres of life. The continual introduction of technical change, like Taylorist methods and Fordist systems within the rationalisation of work and the social organisation of production, have all made their imprint upon this world civil-isation. Through successive jumps and moves forward, something which accel-erated in the imperialist era, industry constituted the nervous system of world development (to the point where in some ideologies, industrialisation was made synonymous with development) and capital grew, becoming ever more concentrated and internationalised in preparation of the base for the next leap forward. All of the above-mentioned processes have never been linear but instead full of conjunctural advances, reverses, contradictions and inequalities.

Globalisation

In the light of day, the so-called process of globalisation is a new stage of capitalism, a transnational stage in the accumulation of capital characterised by the appearance of global oligopolies, the transnational companies (TNCs), which constitute the principal actors of the international economy. Their eco-nomic power is greater than that of many national states.

The level of accumulation and expansion of the TNCs and the concentra-tion of capital have encouraged the process of the internationalisation of the economy, all of which is supported by extraordinary advances in the means of transportation and communication. This new internationalisation which has become associated with the term "globalisation" presents a series of char-acteristics which include the following tendencies:

- The growth of trade and international investment increases at a rate faster than that of the aggregate production of countries (Dabat 1994: 146).
- A change in the composition of direct foreign investment in which the ser-vice sector predominates (Dierckxsens 1994: 3).
- A growing mobility of capital that increasingly favours the unification of the financial markets in one unitary circuit (Dabat 1994: 148).
- A growing dominance of finance capital in the world economy. It has been estimated that for every dollar backed by real production, between 30 and 50 dollars circulate in the finance market of the global economy.
- An internationalisation of the productive process. Today, the components of a single product can be manufactured in various countries, assembled in one and commercialised in others, without losing any control over the larger process.

- Last but no less important are the changes in the organisation of the labour process.

The new model that is generally referred to as "post-Fordist" integrates thought and action at all levels of operation and seeks to combine some of the advantages of artisan and craft-style production with Fordist production. This synthesis involves long term changes in the entire chain of aggregate value.

Among its essential characteristics include: simultaneous engineering (design and production are not separate processes, rather they are integrated into a face to face production between designers and producers); continuous and gradual innovation (workers constantly participate in the improvement of products and processes, not just the experts); and team-process work (organised by flexible work groups that display relative autonomy and are made up of workers who are "susceptible to training" and who possess multiple skill levels). To these characteristics can be added the techniques of "just in time production," the principle of total quality, and the integration of the chain of inputs (Oman 1994). The above-mentioned factors lead to a new work situation in which flexible manufacturing,[1] computerised management and the management of work based upon self-controlled quality circles are incorporated and combined, as is an overall decentralisation of productive processes, including the spatial dimension at the international level, with continuous flows of information that permits the preservation of control over the process of product configuration (Dabat 1994: 147–8).

International competition leads the TNCs to search for lower production costs, relocating various moments of the production process where they are more profitable. The new technologies which are available permit the spatial decentralisation of production and an elevated division and subdivision of labour such that it becomes possible for a minimal skill level when appropriate to carry out specified parts of the production process. For the first time in history, the creation of a world market of production has been accompanied

---

[1] "The cross-juxtaposition of computer design with computerized manufacturing (CAD/CAM) permits rapid and successive modifications in the productive planes, the final result of which is the production of variable volumes of broad range of differentiated products, as much in fine details as in essential characteristics. Given its greater capacity of coverage and its enormous adaptability to the variances of demand, the flexibility within manufacturing can be found in the higher level of economic efficiency." In M. A. Ramírez (1999: 923).

by a world labour market along with a world reserve army of workers (Finkel 1995: 62).

Nurtured by all of its systemic potential and intimately interrelated with the process of globalisation, the extraordinary scientific and technological revolution continues to unfold. There is no doubt that modern biotechnology and the creation of new materials and information technologies are central elements of the new scientific and technological revolution. Some authors emphasise that its central link of articulation is constituted by information technologies as manifested in distinct specialty areas such as microelectronics, optical electronics, robotics, informatics, telecommunications, and so on.

The common element of all these developments is that they are strongly based in the development of scientific knowledge: "the cycle of capital accumulation increasingly depends less upon the intensiveness of labour inputs and even the intensiveness of productive physical capital so as to concentrate itself in an accumulation based in knowledge-intensive production. The concentration and centralisation of technological knowledge is more intensive and far more monopolistic than other forms of capital, augmented by the large gap between the North and South" (Gorostiaga 1991: 5). The weight of this knowledge component in production can be evaluated by observing that in high tech branches such as microelectronics, the costs associated with this factor represents around 70% of its total value. In older industries such as automobile production, the percentage is closer to 40% of the final product's total value (Marini 1996).

These extraordinary developments are monopolised at the hegemonic centres of capital and do not become readily transferred to the underdeveloped world. Better put, productive processes become transferred but not the *creation* processes of scientific and cutting-edge technologies.

In fact, the present scientific-technical revolution has a distinctive trademark: the industrialisation of knowledge through permanent systems of innovation that permit enterprises and nations to compete. When innovation is the rule rather than the exception, the human factor acquires a singular importance in the production process. Above all, the fraction of the labour force which is highly skilled plays a preponderant role in economic processes whose successful operation selectively requires a given technical level within its labour inputs. In recognition of this phenomenon, the factor of "human capital" is increasingly regarded as a leading sector in the dynamic areas of the world economy.

Amidst these rapid technological changes and the changing organisation of work within global capitalist competition there can also be observed a growing worldwide rate of unemployment. This increase of unemployment and the structural demand for ever greater flexibility in the labour market is a concurrent tendency of globalisation, something which makes work increasingly precarious for many and in the final analysis results in greater levels of poverty and inequality across the globe.

Capitalism continues being a regime of exploitation, replete with multiple contradictions, which negates the possibility of dynamic development for the underdeveloped world. This is to repeat the earlier assertion that development and underdevelopment are two sides of the capitalist coin of expansion and world domination in its globalised phase, something it shares in common with the preceding period. Taking this fact to heart would suggest that the possibility of genuine development is associated with a rupture of dependent capitalist relations, something that in a strict sense would signify an exit from the world system of capital.

In reality, breaking with dependency is primarily a political issue. The taking of power opens the possibility for initiating a complete reordering of the whole society in favour of the majority sectors. This restructuration can be supported by a different form of distribution of the economic surplus, one more to the benefit of the popular classes where the satisfaction of their basic needs can elevate the dignity of their life. At the same time, this begins to ignite larger transformations in the economic order where a struggle unfolds to guarantee the continuity of this process.

Overcoming underdevelopment is nonetheless a historical process. The taking of political power creates the necessary prerequisites for social transformation; it is the *sine qua non* condition but is in itself insufficient to guarantee success. As the poet would say, it is only the beginning of a long path "fraught with difficulties and ripe with hope" in which the past constitutes not only a distinctive inheritance but something against which must be struggled. The legacy of the past continues to impinge upon society just like the present world system of capital.

Due to the high level of the internationalisation of economic life, there are no countries which function totally at the margin of the world economy in the current phase of capitalist globalisation. For this reason, a country with a socialist revolution has to search for ways of surviving and for developing by taking full advantage of the contradictions of the system.

Cuba's Prospects for Development under Globalisation

Cuba is confronting one of the greatest challenges of its history, a challenge which is replete with great risks and which can be summarised in just a few words: How can a socialist revolution survive in the new, fundamentally capitalist world order and in permanent confrontation with the active aggressions of the hegemonic superpower in a historic moment of conjunctural strengthening of the world capitalist system?

At first glance, it might appear paradoxical to dedicate our efforts to analysing the possibilities that Cuba has for devising a coherent and strategic paradigm of development, when the highest priority at present is its survival as a nation and as a revolution. But in fact, it is precisely a question of survival which renders necessary the search for a path to development. In the configuration of that strategy, the underdeveloped countries must pay serious attention to a series of factors that have emerged out of the current processes of capitalism.

Among these factors, a highly important one is the way that classical comparative advantages tend to transform themselves into *disadvantages*. This occurs precisely because on the one hand, the demand for primary products which have been traditionally exported tends to decline. On account of the permanent, structural deterioration of the terms of trade caused by the increased availability of new and synthetic materials as well as the overall tendency towards a de-materialisation of production, the result is a regressive trend among the prices for traditional exports on the world market.

With respect to the terms of trade, if we understand their deterioration as the tendency towards decline of those products with a small knowledge component incorporated in their aggregate value relative to those products which are highly knowledge-intensive, then this tendency is irreversible (Arocena 1994: 105). On the other hand, a widely available, cheap labour force which was at one time a decisive factor of industrial development and an important impulse for the rise of the newly industrialised countries, now increasingly becomes disadvantageous. Now it becomes necessary to have a skilled labour force and a deployment of human capital which includes education as part of the investment process for development.

There exists, of course, other factors to consider but the above-mentioned elements are sufficient to formulate a key question: What kind of strategy can be pursued by a small, underdeveloped country with a socialist revolution in power that has achieved a certain level of accumulation accompanied with widespread, non-capitalist sentiments?

This advance, as has already been showed, it not only a technical and material accumulation. In so far as the creation of an infrastructure and broad industrial development is above all a social accumulation, part of this is formed by the economy while another part has to do with other aspects of human development such as the prevailing levels of education and health as well as the creation of values and diverse forms of participation in the country's everyday political affairs.

In the economic realm, the Cuban Revolution has created industries and an infrastructure that few countries in the so-called Third World possess. "Some factories have expanded in a considerable way and new branches have been established in steel, nickel, oil refining, machinery production and the production of capital goods, tools, electronics, nitro-fertilisers, textile products, construction materials, paper, glass and seafood products" (Figueras 1992: 1149–1155). This constitutes a material base for any strategy of development, although in the case of an open economy such as that of Cuba, the levels of production are affected by its capacity for importing a large variety of necessary inputs.

The problem is not just one of insertion into the world economy, seeking niches within it, but also how to organise the larger society which is going to enter into new relations with the global economy, while at the same time, how to maximally preserve the project which the Revolution had brought to life without letting capital, operating in accordance with its own laws, to peacefully devour it. This constitutes a political problem of the first order.

The issue is framed by a basic premise: Today, a total rupture with the world economy is not possible, i.e., a "total disconnection" (to use Samir Amin's notion)[2] like that which Paraguay had at one point accomplished from France, because the dependent reproduction of society passes through the exterior (Bambirra 1973: 35–64). Dependency "configures an internal situation in which it is structurally tied, making it impossible to break free and

---

[2] See S. Amin (1989). A study of the economic history of the Cuban Revolution would show that in the decade of the 1960s, a process of relative disconnection from the capitalist system, being the consequence of the U.S. blockade, led Cuba to reorient its external economic relations and to realize a reconversion of its economy. During the decade of the 1980s, the external economic relations of the island were now around 87% with the former USSR and Eastern Europe and only 13% with capitalist countries.

to achieve isolation from foreign influences, something which would simply lead to provoking chaos in an internal structure which is deficient in its essence" (Dos Santos 1980: 308). The question must consequently be recast in terms of which structural changes become fundamentally necessary.

In the Cuban case, these changes have to be brought about in order to avoid a new dependency, particularly since in a certain sense, its former integration into the CMEA system was basically just that, a dependency based in the export of primary products. Cuba is moreover a small country whose level of self-sufficiency is markedly limited.

That being said, it is also true that a total connection with the global economy would bring along with it the reproduction of underdeveloped capitalist relations within the internal structures of Cuban society because the world market functions under capitalist profit criteria as based upon the law of value. For the underdeveloped countries, it is an asymmetrical market where their structures of exports have a pronounced weight upon primary goods. As we have already shown above, these kinds of commodities are affected by a recurrent instability of prices and a permanent, structural tendency for the terms of trade to decline.

That the economy of a country depends upon the export earnings of products with declining prices on the world market clearly cannot offer a solid base for any revolutionary project. So if the relations of dependency cannot be broken by isolating the country, the only remaining solution is the cultivation of political power which can transform internal structures and establish a new type of relationship with the system of international capital that can better accommodate the social project of the Revolution. This can only be accomplished within the objective limits that prevailing conditions impose upon the country.

In the cultivation of this external relationship, an important role is played by the country's exports and so this is where the structural changes must ultimately focus, giving high priority to products which display a greater aggregate value such that the tendency in prices will exhibit a greater stability.

In terms of economic security, the internal economic and social project can only be successful if it guarantees a high level of welfare for the population and a certain accumulation which can facilitate the need to attain a competitive position in the world economy. To the contrary, the revolutionary project will become transformed into simply a dream. To repeat, the problem is not just insertion or reinsertion into the world economy. In one form or another, all countries display such an insertion. But we are not seeking to be inserted like Haiti, Honduras or any other underdeveloped country because it is precisely that link which ultimately reproduces their structures of underdevelopment.

An insertion based upon the traditional export products of Cuba such as sugar, nickel, citric fruits or tobacco, will in the long run simply maintain the country in permanent underdevelopment, even if the country retains certain comparative advantages in its production. It is necessary to seek a competitive position in the world economy, that is, a kind of insertion which allows for a dynamic accumulation and a strategy for leaving underdevelopment behind. This type of insertion has to be associated with the process of the contemporary scientific revolution whose technological floor is extremely mobile and is based on knowledge-intensive production.

The current problematic of development consists of the acquisition of a capacity for technological creation, for the social incorporation of a potential for and realisation of innovation. In this sense, development strategies have as one of their basic components the policy of constructing a national system of innovation (Arocena 1994: 100–114). Beginning from this basic component of knowledge, it becomes possible to construct an advantage or comparative advantages if a certain accumulation of knowledge is achieved. Based on that achievement, production can take place in specific high-tech branches such as biotechnology, informatics, etc. For a country which attains a place in the international market based on its knowledge intensive products, the result is greater income than what could be achieved with more labour intensive products.

In such branches, having the monopoly over certain specific products can generate a monopoly profit in so far as other potential competitors are unable to develop the same products. In accordance with some of the literature, this situation can sustain itself for periods of between three to five years. It is a kind of dynamic comparative advantage which fluctuates in accordance to ongoing technological development.

Some authors more properly call this "competitive advantage." Achieving it and sustaining it depends upon the country's endogenous capacity,[3] such

---

[3] Various authors refer to the relationship between knowledge, competitive advantages and competitive position. Aldo Ferrer (1993: 807) shows that the generation of competitive advantages in the world market have a common nucleus: knowledge and skilled human resources. For her part, Carmen García (1993: 157) asserts that the position of countries in the global sphere depends upon their competitiveness and this depends more and more upon knowledge.

that in order to compete on this terrain, it is necessary not only to be capable of obtaining specific kinds of products and generating specific kinds of discoveries, but also to achieve the conditions that permit the conservation of this kind of comparative or competitive advantage. In other words, a *critical mass* of knowledge, materialised in a certain quantity of highly trained technical personnel (scientists, engineers, etc.) is required that together with an adequate infrastructure can permit a sustained kind of chain reaction for proceeding to go about incorporating new innovations. All of this corroborates the decisive importance that human resources have for development, i.e., the importance which human capital has for achieving the sustainability of this dynamic.[4]

The above elements can help us to configure the important aspects of the strategy that should be developed and which can be considered the central core of development policy. These aspects can include the following:

- The construction of comparative advantages which provide for a competitive position in the world economy as one part of the national economy, while the other part maintains its traditional insertion in underdevelopment, such that both branches work together to achieve the famous "take-off" which Rostow had spoken of.[5]
- The formation of human capital.
- The selection of the cutting-edge branch or branches in which the country possesses conditions to compete.
- The creation of an endogenous capacity for constructing competitive advantages in those selected branches.
- The construction of a national system of science and technological innovation capable of promoting scientific creativity and technical capacity in the principal areas of need as well as in the society at large.
- The promotion of a culture of innovation and of competitiveness as part of a globally competitive society
- Above all, the materialisation of an infrastructure capable of transforming scientific and technological capacity into high value-added products.

---

[4] In Cuba, by way of example, during the decade of the 1980s, the costs of education represented 6.1% of the GNP and 13.2% of the national budget (See G. Trueba 1993). In the 1990s, these costs ranged between 11% and 13% of the national budget.
[5] See W. Rostow (1967).
A theory can be wrong and yet have certain valid components to be analyzed. We don't share the conceptions of Rostow, which in the final analysis figure within the various versions of the theory of modernisation; but this notwithstanding, we think

What has Cuba accomplished thus far in these areas? In the formation of human capital, Cuba has made notable efforts with results to show for it. Over the course of 40 years, the advances of the Revolution in the educational sphere have been extraordinary. At present, the country has 1.8 scientists for every 1000 inhabitants; there exist some 600,000 graduates of higher education, of which 64,000 are doctors; and one of every five workers have studied in a university. In higher education, there are 46 centres of college level instruction in which 21,600 professors are employed.[6]

With respect to the selection of "cutting-edge" branches in which the nation can compete, a reading of the unfolding of the Cuban economy shows that the principal thrust moves in the direction of what can be called the "scientific-productive constellation of health."[7] This comprehends the biotechnological and chemical-pharmaceutical developments, as well as the design and the manufacture of short-series medical equipment with a computational base. It also includes the commercialisation of health services with a high knowledge component, based in specialised installations at recognised international standards, as well as the exportation of these services.

This constellation has demonstrated a notable development in its scientific-productive results. Over recent years, the country has developed more than 200 biotechnological products that represent a significant export potential. Many of these products are currently being commercialised in some twenty countries. In this area, various vaccines with a high degree of effectiveness have been developed, some of which have no counterpart in the world, including vaccines against meningitis, hepatitis B, leptospirosis, and an experimental vaccine under development which is designed to fight AIDS.

Currently under a national patent are medications such as Malaginina, the only known treatment for vitiligio; the anti-cholesterol drug PPG, whose known secondary effect is the increase of sexual potency; and other medications in the process of elaboration and testing, including monoclonal antibodies,

---

that some of the concepts which he used can be of a certain utility in focusing upon certain problems of development, although perhaps they require a substantial re-elaboration. Examples of theses would be the notions of the "leading sectors" and the "take-off."

[6] Cited in *Granma*, January 12, 1999.

[7] We utilize this concept and not that of the productive scientific complex because the latter is used in Cuba to refer to the entire apparatus in general, and in this case, the idea is to specify only that part related to health.

interferon, recombinant estreptoquinaza, a factor which favours the regeneration of damaged skin, among others.

Some high-tech medical equipment items have been designed and constructed, such as the SUMA kit, an ultra-microanalytic system which detects AIDS and twelve other illnesses; the Neurónica which is used for measuring visual and audio perception; the Diramic which provides a microbiological diagnostic profile, just to mention a few. In Cuban institutions of health, thousands of people have been attended to from forty-two different countries for illnesses ranging from psoriasis, retinitis pigmentosa, and vitiligio as well as for neurological restoration and complex orthopaedic treatments.

In 1996, Cuba presented 124 applications for patent registration and 32 were granted. In 1999, 237 applications were submitted and 77 were approved, giving the country an invention coefficient (total number of national applications per 100,000 inhabitants) of 0.99, up from 0.76 from the earlier year. Likewise, the country has sustained an effort in the creation and registration of patents in the industrial sector. In 1996, 106 applications were submitted and 20 were granted while in 1999, 93 applications yielded 53 approved patents.

All of this demonstrates that Cuba has managed to create and maintain an endogenous capacity for the construction of competitive advantages. Behind this capacity rests a material and organisational base. The country has 221 research centres and invests 25 dollars per capita in research and development, the highest figure in all of Latin America, such that scientific activity receives 1.45% of the Gross Domestic Product.

The pivotal institutional link for coordinating this effort is found in the Scientific Poles where high priority research is carried out. At first glance, they appear to be organised along the lines of high-tech industrial parks. But in reality, Cuba's scientific poles have some very particular characteristics. In the first instance, they are organisations of cooperation between research centres and production centres, reflecting a spatial distribution designed to create certain synergies among them.

The scientific poles are the highest expression of scientific activity in Cuba. They interface units that group together multiple institutions with the common objective of participating in the economic and social development of the country. They represent the ideal environment for integrating the everyday work of political, scientific, productive and commercial factors towards the end of transforming scientific ideas into productive realities. "Their principal virtue resides in the cooperation of knowledge, of equipment and installations, all of which favour a considerable shortening of the time periods between the execution of important projects and the assimilation of advanced technologies.[8]

In the country at large, there exist 15 scientific poles, twelve of which are territorial with the remaining three being specialised. These poles tie together some 465 entities, institutions and working groups which pertain to 24 different organisations. More than 23,000 persons work in the scientific poles, 43% of whom are university graduates.

Of particular interest are the research-production centres, entities that not only conduct research but are equipped with the necessary infrastructure so as to actually carry out production of the results of their activities on an industrial scale. There are oriented towards the creation and operation of their own technologies rather than just being consumers of imported technologies (See Majoli 1999).

The objective to achieve a competitive national position also makes it necessary to create the socio-organisational conditions that permit the integration, to the maximum extent possible, of the generation of scientific and technological knowledge with the social and economic utilisation of these, all of which constitutes the principal function of a national system of innovation.

Properly speaking, it was the decade of the 1990s in which Cuba created this system in its modern and current concept, with the creation of the scientific poles, the conversion of the Forum of Spare Parts into the National Forum of Science and Technics, the creation of the Ministry of Science, Technology and Environment (CITMA), the definition of concepts and the consolidation of a scientific policy which is better adjusted to our realities and to our international demands. Moreover, the infrastructure was completed for entering into new areas of advanced technology (Garcia 1998: 16).

The Cuban system of innovation, referred to as the System of Science and Technological Innovation, is "constituted by a network of relations which involve private, state as well as mixed entities, both national and foreign, and whose activities and interactions generate, import, modify, and disseminate new technologies" (Garcia 1998: 19).

It is a ubiquitous system that goes well beyond any one sector, making CITMA a kind of coordinating organism which supervises the overall process.

---

[8] Cited in *Granma*, May 14, 1999.

Its scope spans over the entire society and it forms an essential component in the development strategy which is promoted by the Cuban state. As such, it performs organisational evaluation and strategic decision-making concerning the optimal means for articulating the relations between other entities and institutions, and between those agencies and the market. A recent CITMA document evaluated as its principal strength its human resources, and among its greatest weaknesses, its scarce productivity in terms of publications and registration of industrial property, the insufficient connection between social and technical investigations, and the lack of an overall policy for commercialisation (CITMA 1998).

If it is necessary to increasingly project ongoing innovations within the larger society, nurturing that which is known as a society-wide culture of innovation, something similar must occur within the realm of information technologies. In the era of globalisation where the idea is to construct a "cutting-edge economy, it is necessary to advance towards the informatisation of the overall society.

The recognition that the use of information has a direct relationship with economic growth has resulted in a situation where numerous countries establish particular government programmes for the creation of informational infrastructures as well as more generally developing an informational industry (Chao 1998: 20). Most studies on the issue argue that contemporary society is increasingly dependent and immersed in the use of informational products and services. More than dependency, it can be said that this process of informationalisation progressively permeates all spheres of social activity, beginning with the most technologically advanced areas and gradually extending into the affairs and habits of everyday life (Castells 1997: 47).

For this reason, Castells prefers the term "Informational Society," given that information and its use has existed in all societies, and so what must be characterised is the really new element: "the term "informational" indicates the attribute of a specific form of social organisation in which the generation, processing and transmission of information becomes converted into the fundamental source of productivity and power, this due to the new technological conditions of this historical period (Castells 1997: 48). Before long, these developments become unequal and segmented, not just between countries but between classes and social groups, and under capitalism, they serve to reinforce the positions of the dominant nations.

Beginning with an analysis of this phenomenon at the world level, its political context and the development needs of the country, the Cuban government created its strategy for the informatisation of the Cuban society. This strategy contemplated among its objectives the creation of an informatic and information-oriented culture, the utilisation of information technologies in all areas of social life, and the encouragement in Cuba of an informational industry (Olivé 1998: 42). Likewise, it anticipated the formulation and implementation of the national information policy, with an eye towards the development of resources and services of this type.

In this area, it can be said that Cuba has displayed various strengths and weaknesses. Its strengths rest in its human resources and in the organisation of industries dedicated to providing information technologies, particularly in the area of informatics. As for its weaknesses, we can include technological backwardness in the provider industries of information technologies, weak application of the new technologies in terms of production, distribution and use of specialised information goods and services, and the lack of expertise in the mechanisms of commercialisation. This latter aspect is of particular importance with respect to the prospects for strengthening the exports of tangible goods, the incorporation of Cuba in electronic commerce via the system of virtual shopping sites on the internet, and the implementation of the Quick Cash system so as to more efficiently manage family remittances sent from abroad. Cuba's use of some of these means are still in their initial phase and it necessary to advance in the efficient utilisation of each, but the reality up to the present has been that these kinds of more advanced types of transaction have not been susceptible to being blocked by the embargo, including transactions between parties residing within the United States itself (Gil and Fernández 1998: 42).

Based on our earlier analyses, it can be deduced that the country possesses a potential for a competitive insertion in the world economy in the area of activities at the cutting-edge and it is presently immersed in the process which can create the platform for enabling this strategy. In spite of the fact that Cuba has a capacity for seeking a competitive insertion in these areas, based upon its availability of human capital and because theoretically the nation is capable of effectively articulating the generation, transfer, mobilisation and utilisation of knowledge, the real context surrounding the implementation of this strategy introduces some highly unfavourable elements. Among these can be found the monopolisation of the international circuits of commercialisation by TNCs as well as various extra-economic obstacles which in this case include the blockade. To this we can add the lack of resources for development and the necessity for what can be called a process of social learning in this area.

Development is a slow and complex process and the future cannot be entirely staked upon a strategy of converting one part of the economy into a competitive sector while the other is abandoned to underdevelopment. As promising as certain emergent new branches may be, all efforts cannot be based solely upon them in the hopes that they can provide some sort of magical wand for overcoming underdevelopment. The struggle against underdevelopment is an integral process and this is an essential aspect of a social project like Cuba's.

In accordance with the possibilities of results in distinct branches and in their strategies, the principal directions of the economy and the hierarchical organisation of efforts have to be maintained. That implies that together with the principal direction in a strategic sense, the main tactical directions must be maintained and efforts must be developed in the overall direction of the economy in accordance with the prospects displayed by each of the distinct branches and sectors.

This obliges us to expend energies simultaneously in the emergent sectors and in the traditional ones. At the same time that some of those traditional sectors play a strategically important role in the economic recovery such as sugar, tobacco, citric fruits and nickel, there has likewise been a strong effort in the development of tourism.

In the traditional sectors, there are accumulated productive experiences, historical articulations with the national economy, and knowledge about their markets which require that they not be left unattended. Some of these products such as sugar have a decisive weight in the formation of the GDP. For example, sugar can come to determine around 3% of overall GDP growth. In these more traditional areas, the need exists to look for ways of expanding the margin of aggregate value and greater diversification of products. In every case, the critical problem becomes the need for additional investments.

The traditional sectors of production have recovered and in some areas such as that of tobacco, citric fruits and nickel, certain advances have been registered. Sugar has been more problematic and it will be a slow process to overcome the compounding difficulties of this sector. Also problematic has been the production of basic foodstuffs, something which requires the country to continue to have a high dependence upon imports in order to satisfy the needs of the population, although significant deficits continue to exist in this area.

Tourism which became transformed into a priority area relatively recently is now one of the leading sectors of the economy. It has demonstrated its capacity for stimulating other branches of the economy, such as the cultivation of foodstuffs, light industry and construction, the development of commercial trade, and some aspects of the informal sector (notably artisan crafts), all by generating a demand for products and services. Tourism constitutes an important source of liquid foreign exchange in the short term, something which was very important for Cuba in the context of the blockade. Overall, tourism is a generator of employment and contributes to the articulation of the economy in the world economy. In particular, it makes possible the creation of new relations within the Caribbean, owing to the fact that the region is an important tourist destination.

There are of course negative aspects of tourism associated with certain social phenomena which tend to accompany it, such as prostitution and the black market, but these constitute challenges that are being confronted. Between 1989 and 1998, the Cuban archipelago sustained an annual rate of growth of 17.9% in terms of the number of incoming tourists. In 1999, more than 1.6 million tourists were received and by 2001, the island had closed in on the two million figure.

As part of the effort which the country realised in order to develop, it is necessary to implement a very active policy of exports of goods and services that have specific characteristics for entering into niches of the world economy. Examples are services of high intellectual aggregate value (doctors, professors, etc. who engage in temporary work abroad); products and services of cultural content (art, music, etc.); types of agroexports which due to their characteristics of being dedicated to specific segments of the world economy have a higher aggregate value such as organically cultivated products; and certain specialised forms of tourism (ecological, scientific, conventions and events, etc.). With varying results, these efforts have been working towards conjunctural solutions to the shortages of resources which were produced by the crisis.

As part of the economic recovery of the country, a process of technological updating has been put into effect so that in a gradual manner, taking into account the availability of resources and the problem of unemployment given that the new technologies tend to reduce the demand for labour. Also put into effect has been a modernisation of services, with priority accorded to the bank and insurance sectors.

The idea has been to diversify the competitive capacity of the country with the participation of the greater part of the productive and service apparatus. An economy cannot be competitive if the society in its totality cannot reach certain qualities, and in this case, that has to be accomplished by putting limits on the type of rationality which presides over the capitalist world economy. In other words, the challenge is to simultaneously achieve a competitive society and to the save the revolutionary project. This leads the country to a strategy of relating to the world economy that has to do with the form in which the national economy will operate alongside of the law of value.

In the Cuban scheme, one part of the economy has a greater relationship with the world capitalist system, with the function of being a source of accumulation, while the other operates in accordance with basic needs. In this overall context, the strategy has to be understood in terms of a selective connection/disconnection which permits the larger operation of the economy at the national scale in view of the law of value. In some areas such as health, education, basic foodstuffs, social security, etc., the criteria of socialist rationality will govern, while in others such as tourism, agroexports, cutting-edge technologies, etc., they will function in accordance to the logic of the world market. The problem rests in creating the mechanisms which can permit this articulation, mechanisms which cannot be purely administrative but economic as well. Those sectors grouped in the area administered by socialist criteria must be understood as part of the national security of the revolutionary project. The revolution was made in order to resolve social problems. To cede these gains would be to lose the sense of the Revolution and to put the entire project at risk.

Every development strategy had a class character. Who benefits? Who stands to lose? A country which proposes to break free from dependency must logically have to confront the opposition of those who benefit from that dependency. This presents a political-economic and a political-military reality, namely, that the strategy cannot win without allies. In a world in which wealth dictates power, alliances must be formed with the wealthy in order to beat the wealthy.

The strategy could be approximately formulated as follows: a policy of alliance with some sectors or fractions of the international bourgeoisie so as to successfully resist and overcome imperialist harassment, and to achieve paths towards development. This is the objective of the policy of the economic opening to foreign capital, with the socialist revolution firmly in power, actively seeking out diverse forms of association with foreign capitalists. This is the sense that the mixed enterprises have in Cuba. It is a policy which seeks to integrate capital in the overall development effort, without at all thinking that capital is disposed to renounce its central objective of seeking profits.

Moreover, the idea is to open the possibility of obtaining profits so as to most aptly utilise them in support of the development of the country, this based on the returns for actions which Cuba owns, not by the hands of capitalists of national origin but rather by the revolutionary state that fixes the overall terms under which the conditions and time frame of the association is governed.

The Cuban government proposes association in those areas and spheres deemed most convenient for the development of the country, in search of capital, technology, markets, management, and so forth. The foreign counterpart can count on a series of incentives, i.e., they can freely repatriate their profits without being obligated to reinvest and they have no taxes levied against their gross earnings or against the earnings of their personnel.

The Helms-Burton Law, promulgated in 1996, had among its principal objectives a scheme to obstruct and impede foreign investment in Cuba. This notwithstanding, investments of this kind continued after the law went into effect. To have an initial idea, there were 50 economic associations with foreign capital in 1990 and at the beginning of 1998, there were 340 in existence.

In Cuba, the economic associations with foreign capital were established fundamentally as mixed enterprises and the state maintains a percentage of the actions in these entities. In 1995, the legal framework to regulate such investments was established in the Law on Foreign Investment. Since then, a very cautious policy has unfolded in which the field of action for direct foreign capital has slowly expanded. Initially centred in tourism, direct foreign investment has since moved into other branches of the economy. Basic industry has 93 enterprises while tourism has 54. Together, these sectors have displayed the greatest presence of foreign capital and are indicative of the utilisation of foreign investment in support of development.

In some activities, the role which mixed enterprises occupy is highly significant. Associations with foreign capital constitute 100% of oil exploration, telephone services, and the production of lubricants, soaps, perfumes and the exportation of rum. They form more than 50% of the firms involved with the citric fruit industry, the production of nickel and cement (Everlenin Pérez

1999). In spite of the opposition and hostile actions on the part of the United States, the tendency has been towards growth in the magnitude of direct foreign investment in Cuba.

There is another dimension of direct foreign investment which is less well known. This has to do with the necessity for Cuban revolutionaries to learn about the world of capital and the laws of the market so as to work efficiently in this area in procuring resources for the country. A good example of this is in the area of Cuban investment abroad in capitalist countries. Cuba operates more than 100 entities abroad with Cuban capital invested in either mixed enterprises or as foreign branches of Cuban enterprises. These include a bank in London, a nickel refinery in Canada, health clinics in Latin America and various enterprises in Africa and Asia (Everlenin Pérez 1999).

This practice not only represents profits for the country but likewise serves as a training ground for human resources management, based in operational experience in the capitalist world, learning about the market and the political factors which influence business. These activities have been developed in spite of all of the hostility emanating from Washington where numerous forms of pressure have been brought against those who decide to invest in Cuba or who provide openings for the operation of Cuban enterprises.

Foreign investment in Cuba in partnership with the state as well as Cuban state investment abroad generates profits which are utilised in function of the interests of the country and in accordance with the overall strategy for development. This association with foreign capital is an important element in the development process which we must continue to stimulate but such activities remain only complementary in the final analysis. The principal efforts being made by the country are carried out with its own resources. ". . . today the banking system can allocate working capital and back up investments of the enterprises, and this makes even clearer the policy on foreign investment in which only those fields where it is deemed desirable will promote this activity in the search of capital, technologies, and markets, i.e., only in areas where we cannot resolve this by ourselves, thus placing it in the country's interests" (Lage 1999: 3).

Capitalism is a regime that has among its social characteristics the tendency to destroy and/or re-articulate the relations of production of other social formations, all in its own interests of expansion. For this reason, there always exists the risk that the influence of capitalist social relations can expand beyond that which has been foreseen, by means of consumerism, social relations, etc.

We need to be realistic and assume that Cuban revolutionaries will have to coexist and work with the most advanced forms of capitalism if they want to find the path that leads to a society which can overcome the economy of scarcity. This implies knowing the world of capital, mastering its laws of the market and working efficiently with them, while taking care not to be absorbed by them. It is a marriage of convenience, not of love, and although tensions exist and will continue to exist, the policy with respect to foreign capital has a limit, namely, the possibility that it can this activity can trample the struggling model of the country's development. This is the challenge which faces us.

The guarantee that this does not happen rests in the maintenance of revolutionary socialist power, which through economic and extra-economic mechanisms can track the path of development and retain the force and operational capacity which can hold the destructive forces of capital in check, harnessing its forces in favour of the goals of the revolutionary project which directly contrast with the logic of a free market society.

The process of globalisation is not uniform, nor is it exempt from contradictions. Indeed, the old contradictions have been maintained while new ones have emerged. The contradiction between North and South has been maintained and the gap between the two groups has actually grown. The contradictions and competition between the economic blocs within the system persist and they likewise thrive within the interior of each of them. The contradictions and competition between the principal actors of the globalised economy, the transnational enterprises, are increasingly acute in their need for expansion and their struggle for profits, this leading to a corresponding struggle on the part of the transnational fractions of the bourgeoisie, both in the countries of the North as well as the South. For Cuba, the important thing is for the revolutionary state to fully exploit the contradictions which are generated in the globalisation process with the aim of gaining increased room to manoeuvre. The Cuban Revolution is showing that this is possible.

Accompanying the process of globalisation are the diverse schemes of integration both in the North as well as in the South. By the nature and tendency of such groupings, Cuba has proved capable of establishing growing economic relations with them, thus forming a nexus in wider markets. For example, economic ties with countries that form part of MERCOSUR and CARICOM establish a nexus with Europe as well as with the Latin American Integration Association. This logic even applies to the North American Free Trade Agreement (NAFTA) in that Cuba maintains highly significant economic relations with two of its members, namely, Mexico and Canada.

As we have argued earlier, development is not only an economic process, although the economy is of primary importance, but rather, it is a socio-political process of transformations characterised by quantitative and qualitative changes in economic, political and social structures as based in specific social class interests. Nor is it simply a goal to be reached, or an object strictly delimited, but it is rather a concrete historical process that should provide society with a new mode of life, seated in an economic base which permits a greater autonomy with respect to the international capitalist system and which can provide comfortable levels of satisfaction for the material and spiritual needs of the population.

In other words, development needs to be seen from the point of view of the class struggle, and in this sense, it is a process which is pushed forward by groups endowed with the power to respond to a class or an alliance of classes. This implies a totality of technical measures with a high political content which imprint upon society determined courses that impact upon the proportions between accumulation and consumption, distribution of social wealth and the strengthening, weakening and/or transformation of classes and social groups.

Most evident is the necessity for state power to guide the process of development, and this process must avoid bureaucratic centralisation of the type associated with real socialism just as it avoids submission to the vagaries of the free market. The guiding and regulating role of the revolutionary state is essential for concentrating resources, defining priorities, and negotiating with other actors of the international area. The state command over the economy gives the Revolution the equivalent management power of a transnational conglomerate. The loss of this power leads to the loss of the revolutionary project, but that does not mean that the state should avoid seeking new forms of organisation and management which can transcend and outperform the scheme of centralised planning that was inherited by the model of real socialism.

In this area, what is needed is the creation of a model for economic management that implies efficient systems of information management and economic projection, with an adequate balance between centralisation and decentralisation, flexibility and agility in decision making as well as in the assignation of resources, and the creation of mechanisms that can really promote the reduction of costs, the assumption of risks and the introduction of innovations.

As if it were little to ask, that model must learn to function within the larger logic of a socialist economy. With this, I want to express the idea that it should

be an economy whose reproduction tends towards socialism, but which operates with the presence of foreign capital and private property. The model
must combine the state as proprietor and manager as well as regulator so as
to create a society which displays widespread initiative without losing its
social justice component.

The task is not easy and the model of management will not arise overnight.
Rather, the path is a long one of trial and error because, in my judgement,
the capacity for managing an economy which engages at the cutting-edge of
global production is not only an economic act but also the result of a certain
level of social efficiency of the system in its totality.[9] At this level of analysis,
the characteristics of the Cuban paradigm for development can be elaborated,
always remembering that the point of departure for this model is a country
which has completed a phase of primitive socialist accumulation.

The principal elements of the paradigm would be the following: the possibility of achieving a development *from within* via the articulation of a complex of strategies that imply the construction of competitive advantages,
supported by the development of knowledge-intensive branches of the economy; a strategy of selective global connection-disconnection and a policy of
accords (or alliances) with certain fractions of the international bourgeoisie
so as to gain greater access to capital, technology and markets while maintaining the political commanding heights over the economy based in socialist political power. This is what can permit the promotion of a sustained and
sustainable, autonomous development capable of realising a type of accumulation that breaks with the throes of dependency and which tends towards
socialism.

The kind of development strategy being visualised here overcomes the
dichotomous discussion of "inner-oriented" verses "export-led" development.
The goal is not to create a socialist version of the import substitution model
nor is it aimed at creating an export platform model oriented towards
the world market, although certain elements of both are present. Rather, the
goal is to programme the productive structure so that it is supported by the
endogenous capacities of the country, searching for combinations and

---

[9] In an economy in which innovation is the rule and not the exception, the socio-
organisational factor plays a decisive role. "To innovate strictly within a technological plane accomplishes nothing if there is not simultaneously an innovation at the
level of social practices, at the level of social organisation, at the level of knowledge-
able practice." (García 1993: 159.)

complementarities between production for the internal market and production for the world market; an intensive production in capital and/or knowledge intensive production in balance with more traditional, labour-intensive exports; and an ongoing search for exports which display a high aggregate value.

Conclusion

As for the internal factors which conspire against Cuba's competitive insertion into the globalised world economy, four basic factors can be alluded to by way of summary. In the first place, there are the conditions of underdevelopment and the complex processes that are required in order to break with the structures of dependency. This factor has its greatest significance in the mono-crop structures which the island has maintained over long centuries. Cuba since 1790 has been profiled as the world's sugar producer and this is something which has only begun to change since the final decade of the Twentieth Century.

Secondly, there is the inheritance of real socialism. This has influenced many spheres, but particularly all that is related to vertical structuring in the forms of management, including an excessively centralised administration based on a micromanagement from above with little space left for the realisation of initiatives and the assumption of risks. This inheritance does not remain confined to the economic realm but in fact has impregnated the society as a whole. For that reason, the struggle against these aspects is a complex and protracted one. Their elimination is gradual because simple directives are insufficient to the task. It can only be effectively carried out through a social learning process about new methods of work and an emphasis on participation which can become gradually incorporated into the mentality and behaviour of thousands of persons.

Thirdly, there are the persisting vulnerabilities which resulted from the island's former insertion into the CMEA system. This refers to the low level of integration which exists between the distinct sectors of the national economy. It must be remembered that the reproduction of dependency passes through the external sector. In the case of Cuba, the singular sector with the greatest link to other sectors of the economy is the sugar industry. These vulnerabilities also have to do with the high dependency upon imported components which are necessary for national production. This implies that installed capacity does not determine productive potential, but it is instead determined by the import capacity of the country. Under the present conditions, this characteristic greatly limits the rate of national economic growth. For this reason, among the policies which have been implemented is the completion of a nationwide chain of technical-productive institutions.

Another aspect of this inheritance from CMEA is the physical organisation of the installed plants, in which a kind of gargantuan, overly large-scale model prevailed, utilising technologies which were highly inefficient in the consumption of energy. At the end of the 1980s, Cuba consumed, in per capita terms, double the energy of the United States (See Figueras 1994).

Fourth, there is an element strongly implied in the previous obstacles, namely, the lack of efficiency. The search for efficiency is at the heart of Cuba's economic battle. The challenge in this area is to reach greater levels of efficiency without losing the social gains already accumulated.

Taken together, these four internal obstacles refer to the problematic of the creation of an economic culture which can allow us to develop within globalised capitalism. This is not a problem of individuals, e.g., of training one or another leader, but rather one of a social learning process about new forms of regulation and economic functioning so as to successfully achieve a competitive insertion. At the same time, this culture must contain the necessary components which can nurture an ongoing resistance against the socially invasive tendencies of capitalist social relations.

Given that human resources are decisive for development, a task of the highest order is to restore the stability of consumption for the population as a way of recovering the subjective element of social efficiency. This implies technical means and policies as well as the increase of production and productivity. It does not signify egalitarianism, but it does require the maintenance of a basic social minimum and a range of remuneration that can guarantee a comfortable life for all members of society. This notwithstanding, it is almost certain that over the short and medium term, the contradiction between the historic paradigm of the Revolution and the prevailing standard of living which the economy can deliver to the whole population will persist.

Lastly but no less important, there is something that cannot be left unmentioned in any analysis of the prospects for the Cuban Revolution, namely, the blockade. This economic war against the island, in my judgement, forms part of the tradition of low intensity warfare and constitutes a principal obstacle for any future development of the Revolution. The policy implemented by Washington has assumed various forms. The is the hard-line policy of the sort associated with the sanctions imposed by the Helms-Burton Law as well as the "soft" policy version as exemplified with the "Track Two" approach. This latter example had to do with the so-called relaxation of relations between the countries, with the means put into place by Washington so as to strengthen those social groups on the island which could most likely transform themselves into protagonists of capitalist restoration.

In Cuba, socialism constitutes the guarantee for the continued existence of the nation. In the geopolitical conditions of Cuba and in the context of U.S. aggression, a capitalist restoration would imply an associated/dependent/subordinated bourgeoisie as a local ruling class whereupon their resentment could lead to an attempt to forge a closer integration with imperialism.

Socialism means the continuity of the Revolution. That signifies a class option that limits the scope of action within the national arena of those tendencies which are imposed by globalisation, this so as to defend a certain alternative form of social development. With these elements in place, the prospects remain present over the long run for the formation of a sustainable, non-capitalist society.

More than a decade following the fall of the Berlin Wall, socialism in Cuba continues displaying its validity as a political option in so far as it signifies the preservation of national independence and of a social project that responds to the interests of the popular majority. In the short term, socialism legitimates the current struggles for development. If this banner and objective were to disappear, an extraordinary mobilising element would likewise be destroyed.

Knowing where one is headed is one of the premises for not losing their way, even though circumstances may sometimes impose partial delays, detours, and even reversals in some areas. But the real options are clear: The choice is between underdeveloped, dependent capitalism in conditions of capitalist globalisation or the project of a viable socialism that offers the potential for a society rooted in social justice.

These are the conditions in which the Cuban Revolution must unfold, whose conscious challenge is to try to maintain the project of a societal alternative to capitalism. If, in doing so, we may have to sometimes use capitalistic instruments, our intelligence and will remain at the side of our heart: *to the left*.

Without doubt, the new global conditions will affect the profile of the Cuban society of tomorrow. If the policy of development we have described is successful, that society will not be the one which the revolutionaries of the 1960's had dreamed of. But it will be an alternative to capitalism, a plausible socialism. Only within that framework will Cuba be able to maintain its independence and its national sovereignty.

Emir Sader
Brazil's Workers Party in Power:
A Lost Opportunity

At the beginning of the 21st Century, Brazil seemed
like an exception to a worldwide left in disarray. The
strength of the organised Brazilian left and the
capacity of Brazilian social movements to mobilise
remained nothing short of impressive. Home to the
Brazilian Workers Party (PT), the largest leftist party
in the capitalist world, and the Landless People's
Movement (MST), the massive trade union *Central
Única de los Trabajadores*, of the participatory budget
policies and of the Social World Forum, the country
seemed to offer an ideal opportunity for the left at
a historical juncture where popular forces elsewhere
seemed to be wallowing in one of their weakest
moments ever.

The election of Luiz Inácio da Silva ("Lula") as
president seemed to be a logical consequence of that
accumulation of forces, affording the Brazilian left
the possibility of becoming among the first to make
a decisive break with neoliberalism. The situation
could not have been so easily predicted based on the
country's trajectory over the course of the Twentieth
Century. Until the final decades of the last century,
Brazil was not characterised for having a particularly strong political left, especially when compared
to some of its neighbouring countries. A particular
historical convergence came about which permitted

the country to enjoy what Trotsky called "the privilege of historical backwardness," allowing it to attain a confluence in the accumulation of forces that helped catapult the Brazilian left into a favourable situation.

The history of this evolution is fundamental for understanding the real significance of Lula's victory in the 2002 presidential elections as well as its potential, its limits and its contradictions. It is also indispensable for situating this historical juncture of the Brazilian left within the process of a hegemonic transition within the international arena associated with the rise of liberalism as the dominant model as well as within the particular evolution of Brazilian capitalism.

Lula, the PT and Liberalism

The 1964 military coup in Brazil happened in a relatively premature way in comparison with the greater strength of the left in other Southern Cone countries such as Argentina, Chile and Uruguay. A combination of U.S. strategic interests in Brazil, this as evidenced by episodes involving Nelson Rockefeller and oil, the Amazon and other natural resources, and the relative weakness of Brazilian popular forces during that period, all promoted the triumph of the military coup with a lower overall level of repression compared to that which was experienced by the rest of the Southern Cone. It was not necessary to close the Congress or shut down the Judicial System given that they proved their ability to functionally co-exist with the Dictatorship. Unions on the contrary were shut down and this placed in clear evidence the class character of the military coup.

Liberal analyses attribute the relatively lower level of repression to a supposed liberal ideology present among one sector of the military coup leaders. In this scenario, the first dictator, Humberto Castelo Branco, is considered to have been a liberal. Certain quarters of the conservative press began to talk of another military coup in 1968 at which time "the repression began to harden." This is put forward as if in 1964, there has simply been an occupation of government left vacant by the "flight abroad" of President João Goulart. This vision gives us a measure of the force of presence that liberal conceptions have in Brazil.

The Brazilian military regime benefited from final years of post-World War II expansion with the availability of the so-called "Eurodollars." This helped it to reconvert the economic model and impose a new, short term expansive cycle during the 1967–1973 period. Following that period, the cyclical trend arrived to a point of definitive exhaustion in global expansion. While the expansion period lasted, the Brazilian economy grew at more than 10% a year. Beginning in 1973 and supported by a rigid control over wages and the attraction of foreign capital, it was possible to maintain the unprecedented rate of growth over the long recessionary cycle at around 7% a year. The difference this time, which would subsequently result in devastating effects in the following decade, was that the Brazilian economy was no longer attracting foreign investments but simply loans, contracted at a floating rate of interest. This amounted to the construction of a time bomb that would explode around the end of the 1970s and the beginning of the 1980s.

From the left's point of view, the repression brought to a close the hegemony of the Communist Party and its trade union leaders. At the same time, the Party was held responsible for leading the popular movement down a dead end alley that culminated in a virtual absence of resistance to the military coup. The new internal cycle of expansion renovated the social structure of the labour force and paved the way for the emergence of a new left in the country. The return of foreign capital, principally from the United States, about halfway through the 1950s had permitted the creation of a large scale automobile industry in a manner similar to what occurred in Argentina. This had established the material base for the creation of a new working class in tandem with a great exodus of inhabitants out of the country's northeast caused by a prolonged and severe drought. It was out of that historical situation that Lula along with hundreds of thousands of people from the northeast arrived to the south-central region that included the metropolitan region of Sao Paulo. That area was to become the economic and financial centre of the country in the years to come.

The economic model of the military dictatorship rested upon high levels of consumption and exports of automobiles and electric appliances. At the same time, the sector of the working class residing in this "ABC" region (São André, São Bernardo and São Caetano) adjacent to Sao Paulo experienced a correlation of factors highly favourable for generating a grassroots trade unionism, this despite being under military intervention. Union activism managed to break apart the rigid wage structure imposed by the military government and by the end of the 1970s, large scale strikes were being aimed at the dictatorship itself under the leadership of Lula and a new generation of trade union leaders.

This new trade union nucleus was formed politically out of the struggle against the dictatorship, the existing form of the state at that time. This followed their earlier struggle against a highly restrictive labour code that blocked labour union autonomy and which had been imported into Brazil by Getulio Vargas from Mussolini's Italy. The union leadership often had less conflictual relations with their employers than they had with the state. With the former, they frequently advanced through ongoing negotiations, although at times interrupted with police intervention. With the latter, they were subjected by a rigid doctrine of national security in which any movement towards a strike left them branded as "subversives."

Across the totality of opposition to the Dictatorship following the suppression of the armed movement of the latter 1960s, liberal ideology was hegemonic, spearheaded by the activities of the legal opposition party, the Democratic Movement Party of Brazil (PMDB) and accompanied by social movements, civil movements, and NGOs of a liberal democratic character. The theoretical discourse of authoritarianism expounded by those such as Fernando Henrique Cardoso emerged as the ideology of a competing front. What the opposition shared in common was a strong, anti-state feeling seated in the civil society opposition to the dictatorial state that crystallised into a paradigm of liberal hegemony.

At the international level, the Cold War was moving towards a final triumph of the West as anticipated by the proponents of liberal hegemony. This promoted a liberal, ideological convergence of the anti-dictatorial struggle in the Latin American Southern Cone and the opposition struggle against the East European regimes under a common mantle of "anti-authoritarian" struggles.[1]

This scenario of liberal ascent conditioned the reconstruction of the Brazilian left that coincided with an overall weakening of the left at the global level. This is symbolised by the fact that during the year of the collapse of the Berlin Wall, Lula was almost elected president of the republic. In any case, the PT began to occupy a strategic space in Brazilian politics and emerged as a real alternative for national governance. Since the Communist Party of Brazil no longer carried decisive weight in the Brazilian left and in fact did not even participate in the political front led by the PT, the fall of the Berlin Wall did

---

[1] It is worth remembering here that Lula's first international trip was to meet with Lech Walesa, prompted by the PT's international secretary, Francisco Wefort.

not directly affect Lula's party which had taken to openly criticising the Soviet regimes and the Leninist party model. However, this movement in opposing directions also served to demonstrate the ideological particularities and differentiated trajectories of the Brazilian left in relation to the correlation of forces at the global level.

At the historical moment in which the Brazilian left, under pressure of the military dictatorship, incorporated the democratic question as a strategic element of its proposals, the international setting was one where liberal hegemony was in full ascendance. In this sense, the incorporation of the democratic question took place at the expense of its class nature which for the left signified the disappearance of capitalism as the general historical context of argumentation.

A left that had historically developed under the hegemony of the Communist Party and which had lived under military dictatorship and its repression was now accused from both the left and the right for underrating the importance of the democratic question. Under the model of Getulio Vargas, democracy has been subordinated to the national question and the CP had aligned with Vargas as a strategic ally. Indeed, the issue of democracy was best appropriated by the liberal-oligarchic opposition to Vargas which had always accused it of forming a dictatorial project. This same slogan later played a central role in the destabilisation campaign against João Goulart' government and helped paved the way for the military dictatorship. These campaigns were developed in typical Cold War style and relentlessly harped on the risks of installing a statist, totalitarian, Soviet model in Brazil.

In suffering the effects of the military dictatorship, the Brazilian left nevertheless moved to revaluate the democratic question. The armed resistance movements that struggled from 1964 to 1971 did not form part of that tendency, have built their affiliations with Cuban or Maoist platforms. But once those movements were defeated, the space was opened up for a liberal hegemony and this also affected the Brazilian Communist Party.

The international communist movement was living out the contradictory effects of the period of "de-Stalinisation" that was projected out of the XX Congress of the Communist Party of the Soviet Union. In that period, the Eurocommunist tendencies took up one side while the tendency that gravitated towards the Maoist Cultural Revolution made up the other extreme, forming two important political expressions of this period. Brazil had experienced the first Sino-Soviet split in the world with the rise of a rival Maoist

Communist Party formed in 1961. With this, the Eurocommunists eventually took control over the non-Maoist faction. The text that was most ideologically important for them was authored by the communist intellectual Carlos Nelson Coutinho who was exiled in Italy, entitled *Democracy as a Universal Value*.[2]

On the cover of Coutinho's book is a quote from Enrico Berlinguer, then Secretary General of the Italian Communist Party, to the effect that: "Democracy today is not only the territory where the class adversary is forced to recede, but also a historically universal value on which an original socialist society is to be built." Berlinguer's insight was formulated in the light of the failed experience of the Popular Unity Government in Chile by stating that it is not sufficient to gain majority support but also necessary to garner support from the determinant political forces in the reproduction of capital, which in both the case of Chile and Italy meant the Christian Democrats. In this formulation, the anticapitalist dimension was lost in the struggle for democracy among this Eurocommunist style of politics.

In that same year of Berlinguer's quote, the Italian communists and socialist won a majority for the first time in that country's history but the communists were denied entry into the government, with the establishment alleging the need to preserve democracy of the "really existing" liberal variety. The subsequent development of the largest communist party in the West whose self-dissolution and replacement by a political force modelled after the U.S. Democratic Party makes it easier to understand how this approach shared greater affinity to the basic suppositions of liberalism as opposed to an anticapitalist line.

In Brazil, the text of Carlos Nelson Coutinho had big repercussions in the Communist Party that later helped to further divide the group. On one side was the group that abandoned socialism, opting to form a centrist party that lacked any firm ideological or political line. On the opposing side was a smaller group that intended in vain to maintain communist ideological positions. All of this was to impact significantly upon the formation of the Brazilian Workers Party (PT).

---

[2] See C. N. Coutinho, "A democracia como valor universal", in *Encontros com a Civilização Brasileira*, Rio de Janeiro, n° 9, March 1979, pp. 33–48; and later, in an expanded second edition, in *A democracia como valor universal*, São Paulo, Ciências Humanas, 1980, pp. 17–41 (e *A democracia como valor universal e outros ensaios*, 2ª ed. ampliada, Rio de Janeiro, Salamandra, 1984, pp. 17–48).

Coutinho in his text tried to make the linkage of democracy to socialism, also citing Lenin from 1916 in the introduction: "Socialism is inconceivable without democracy in two senses – 1) the proletariat cannot make a socialist revolution if it is not prepared for this task by way of a struggle for democracy; and 2) a victorious socialism cannot consolidate its victory and lead humanity forward towards the eradication of the state if it lacks an integrally structured democracy. This latter reflection shared the same sense that Gramsci later argued. Nevertheless, the linkage is made based on the interpretation that the Italian Communist Party made of Gramsci as analysed by Perry Anderson (2002), suffering from the same contradictions.

This legacy was incorporated by the PT via Coutinho when he affirms in the preface to the second edition of his book: "My conviction is that Brazilian modernity demands the creation of a socialist party, secular, democratic and of the masses, capable of retaining all that is valid in the inheritance of Brazilian Communism while at the same time incorporating the new socialist currents that originate from different political and ideological horizons." In identifying that new force with the Brazilian Workers Party (PT), Coutinho together with other intellectuals and militants of the Communist Party of Brazil were entering the PT by 1989, the year of the fall of the Berlin Wall, where they would warmly embrace this party right up to the first year of the Lula government in power at which time they would abandon it.

The second edition of Coutinho's book included an article that had been published in a major Brazilian newspaper, *Folha de São Paulo*, where a sharp critique of the 1981 military declaration of martial law in Poland was expounded. In this critique, language very similar to the Italian Communist Party was used including expressions such as "the degeneration of the Soviet model" and so forth. In addition, the Secretary General of the Spanish Communist Party was quoted in his support of Eurocommunism as the "contemporary representative of the best traditions of the communist movement" and as being in search of a "third way" between the "Stalinist or neo-Stalinist path" and the "limited reformism of social democracy" (Anderson, 2002:114).

That same equidistance would be searched for by the PT which would later proclaim itself as the first "post-social democratic party" at the same time that it would share in common with Coutinho, the position of radical condemnation of Jaruzelsky's regime in Poland while identifying itself with the *Solidarność* movement led by Lech Walesa.

Coutinho nevertheless worried that the critic of the Soviet model would turn into a liberal position and therefore lose that which was considered to be "positive moments" of the communist path, such as the "Leninist theory of the Commune, a workers state self-managed by the workers councils," among other elements. Meanwhile, a distinct line of political influence in contrast to that of Coutinho sought to articulate democracy with liberalism rather than democracy and socialism. This line emerged as the interpretation of Fernando Henrique Cardoso and his theory of authoritarianism and it became the dominant line during the transition away from the military dictatorship.

From this view, democratisation represented the de-concentration of economic power held by the state and of political power monopolised by the executive branch. The political aspect was placed into practise at the end of the dictatorship by the first civilian government (1985) and mainly with the entry into force of the new Constitution (1988). The economic aspect was put into practice by Cardoso himself as the President of Brazil (1994–2002) by way of his neoliberal programme.

Liberalism was winning out in the international sphere with the victory of the capitalist bloc over the socialist camp and it also became hegemonic inside of Brazil. This was largely true on account of the strictly political-institutional character of the transition from dictatorship back to democracy, one without any type of significant reform of a social or economic kind. The PT resisted this version of democratic transition, appealing for expanded citizens rights and social policies, but without proposing any alternative conception of democracy. The PT did not, however, place into question the thesis that democratisation of the country would resolve its basic problems. It did not immediately grasp that the historical moment of the dictatorship's exhaustion had also coincided with the exhaustion of the model of accumulation and form of state inaugurated in the 1930s by Getúlio Vargas.

The political and legal vision of dominant liberalism concealed the process of socio-economic crisis that underscored that historical juncture. The PT identified itself with democracy and talked about socialism but without giving it any precise content. Much greater attention was dedicated to differentiating the party from the Soviet model, always taking care to add the word "democratic" to socialism, something that redefined the meaning of the latter, submerging it into the contradictions of liberal democracy being offered to the country. What was missing in the platform was any analysis of capitalism, the indispensable reference for rethinking the nature of socialism.

The first document of the PT, its Letter of Principles, dated back to May 1979 in a year of great advances in the anti-imperialist struggle (PT 1979).

This was just prior to the Sandinista victory and the fall of the Shah's regime in Iran, the victory of the popular government in Grenada, and the election of Fidel Castro as President of the Non-Aligned Nations, all in a climate of favourable prospects for revolutionary movements worldwide.

The PT initially defined itself as a "party of the masses" that would express "the will of the political independence of the workers . . . The PT is born out of a decision on the part of the exploited to struggle against an economic and political system that cannot resolve its problems, one that only exists to benefit a minority of privileged Brazilians" (PT 1980). There was no mention here of capitalism when they spoke of the objectives of the party's struggle. Instead, the objectives are fragmented and do not constitute a socialist platform. What is mentioned is the "will for emancipation of the popular masses" and opposition to "the current regime and its development model that only benefits the privileged sectors" (PT 1980).

It is only after ten years following the fall of the Berlin Wall that the PT approved the document "PT Socialism" that treats the question of socialism. "It is capitalist oppression that results in the absolute misery of more than 1/3 of humanity. It is capitalism that imposes new forms of slavery on Latin America . . . It is capitalism that maintains and deepens the real bases of social inequality in Brazil." With this, it proclaimed that "the overcoming of capitalism is indispensable for the full democratisation of Brazilian life." It acknowledges that "although our greatest texts do not treat in detail the internal design of the alternative society desired, the historical ambition of the PT has been, since its origin, socialist in nature," thus affirming that a decade had gone by since its foundation during which time "they had only confirmed its anticapitalist conception and the PT's commitment to profound social transformation."

It was nevertheless at that moment when the PT faced the possibility of advancing following its narrow loss of the presidential elections of 1989. It began a process of ideological and political transformation that would pave the way for its eventual electoral victory in 2002, 14 years after its founding and initial electoral forays. What happened during that period? What took place during this period of regrouping?

On the international plane, the disappearance of the former Soviet Bloc, the first Gulf War, and the extension of neoliberalism around the world, including in Russia and the Eastern European countries, all contributed to the consolidation of neoliberal ideology and this was reinforced by the rise of self-proclaimed governments of the "Third Way", of Tony Blair and Bill Clinton, and a rejuvenation of the "Washington Consensus." In Latin America, the strong presence of "centre-left socialist" forces such as the Chilean Socialist Party (an ally of the PT), of the *Acción Democrática* of Venezuela, and the traditional nationalist parties such as the Peronists in Argentina and the PRI of Mexico all served to reaffirm the hegemony of neoliberalism across the continent. The PT tried to maintain its own space and to project this stance by way of its membership and prominence in the São Paulo Forum of regional left parties opposing neoliberalism. This grouping includes such parties as the PRD of Mexico and the *Frente Amplio* of Uruguay among many others.

Yet, the "centre-left" field continued to reveal the influence of dominant neoliberalism. A series of proposals was organised by Jorge Castañeda and Robert Mangabeira Unger which became known as the "Consensus of Buenos Aires" that, without calling itself so, identified with the "Third Way." This meant recognising the need for fiscal adjustment and monetary stabilisation policies while trying to preserve and expand social policies. Brazil's PT participated in the elaboration of the document but at the last moment decided not to sign it. This was due to among other reasons the fact that the Presidential candidate Ciro Gomes, with Mangabeira Unger as his advisor, was directly associated with the document and was in competition with Lula. All of this was occurring just as in a similar manner, Casteñeda participated in the candidacy of Vicente Fox, who was the conservative rival of the PRD but represented the electoral possibility of beating the PRI. But by this point, there was no real divergence between the PT and the Third Way-oriented "Consensus of Buenos Aires" despite the PT's initial attempts to remain at a distance.

In the presidential campaign of 1998, Cardoso was favoured to win re-election. Lula's campaign avoided pronouncements on the crisis state of a nearly bankrupt Brazilian economy and the preparations underway to devalue the Brazilian currency and open renegotiations with the IMF. This was to avoid becoming associated in any way with the impending catastrophe. Lula was nevertheless defeated in the first round of the presidential elections, culminating a campaign which did not propose any real alternatives. The Cardoso government which was already in negotiations with the IMF during the electoral campaign needed to prevail in the first round so as to avoid the risk that the deteriorating economic crisis might explode in its face. Less than three months after the elections when Cardoso inaugurated his second administration, he decreed a major devaluation of the Brazilian currency, concluded re-negotiations with the IMF, and raised the annual interest rate to 49%.

The organisation of the first World Social Forum (WSF) in Porto Alegre in 2002 had the direct support of the PT in the state of Rio Grande do Sul, one that had always favoured the more leftist tendencies within the party. The national PT leadership did not directly participate and continued investing its energies in the Sao Paulo Forum and in cementing its alliances with Europe's social democratic parties. It gave particular emphasis to an alliance with the French Socialist Party, while Cardoso was actively involved in building his credentials with "Third Way" currents. While Lula and other members of the PT attended and participated in the first WSF, the PT at the national level was not directly part of the organisation of the event nor did it sign on to its final declaration.

Recycled for Governability

The fourth candidacy of Lula in the 2004 presidential elections occurred within the framework of a complete exhaustion of the Cardoso governments. It was by this time clear that the economy had not recovered from the crisis of 1999 and that monetary stability had not been the precursor for a renewed development of the country, much less a renewal of social policies. (Cardoso's re-election campaign of 1998 had featured the slogan "He who put an end to inflation will put an end to unemployment.") This time, Lula appeared to be the stronger candidate although political polls showed that the electorate was looking for a candidate that would maintain financial stability while expanding social policies. This recipe most closely resembled the Consensus of Buenos Aires which was being advocated by the Popular Socialist Party candidacy of Ciro Gomes.

Prior to the beginning of the electoral campaign, the daughter of former president José Sarney was ahead of Lula in the polls but fell victim to a vicious set of allegations spearheaded by the government and its candidate José Serra which rapidly dragged down her presidential prospects. Her place in the pack gave way to the surging candidacy of Ciro Gomes who along with Lula and Serra became the leading candidates going into the elections.

Lula ultimately organised a programme that reflected not so much the platform of the PT but a political centrism that grew out of his analysis of his own defeat in the previous elections. This shift was bolstered by the formation of a shadow cabinet that Lula kept autonomous from the ranks of the PT, but allowing it to guide the projection of his new candidacy. Seminars with economists and other specialists from the areas of social policies, environmentalism, political reform, among others, were conducted to help formulate the programme of Lula's campaign. The final version placed emphasis on the need for a recovery in the nation's economic development as the precondition for revitalising social policies. Productive capital was favoured over speculative capital from among enterprises both big and small, without distinction between domestic and foreign capital. Economic reactivation was the main objective and the goal was a slow and gradual shift away from the neoliberal model. The campaign placed emphasis on "change" and "giving priority to social spending". This did not rely so much on a concrete plan but already suggested the modalities that a Lula government would eventually assume. Significant attention was dedicated to a commitment for combating hunger, something that Lula had mentioned in previous campaigns. This allowed him to repeat over and over again that his goal was to see to it that "every Brazilian ate three meals a day." Also mentioned was the need to maintain monetary stability and a proposal for a (counter) reform of the social security system.

As the campaign took shape, there were two elements that had a determining effect on the eventual outcome of the election. First was the surging popularity of Ciro Gomes and the difficulty that Lula was having in surpassing the PT's historical levels of support that remained around the 30% level. The second element involved a major league attack by financial capital on his candidacy, creating imagery that associated the PT with a possible destabilisation of the economy. This led to the so-called "Lula risk factor" which suggested that massive capital flight and a monetary meltdown would occur if Lula were to win, raising the spectre of another sharp devaluation of the Brazilian currency.

The first problem was ameliorated by the Cardoso government itself by virtue of an aggressive campaign of accusations aimed at Ciro Gomes, something orchestrated out of the fear that the ruling party's candidate Serra might not reach the second electoral round. The ensuing shootout brought down Gomes in the polls but Serra was unable to capitalise given the sharp responses coming from Gomes who took aim at Serra.

This allowed Lula some space to focus on the second problem in which he denounced the attacks from finance capital and issued a "Letter to Brazilians" in which he promised to maintain all of the government's existing financial commitments. This meant that there would be no renegotiation of the foreign debt and no other type of new controls placed on the circulation of finance capital.

The PT had been softening its position with respect to the foreign debt for some time. Together with the incorporation of a commitment to monetary stability, this represented one of the principle steps taken by Lula and the PT to "ensure governability." From its earlier positions of suspending debt payments and later to auditing debt payments, the PT finally arrived to its 2002 position of promising full compliance with the foreign debt payment. Similarly, the commitment to monetary stability had been gradually assimilated over the period since the 1994 elections when Lula had criticised Cardoso's plan of fiscal and monetary adjustment policies.

This reformulation of policy changed the relationship of Lula's candidacy to finance capital. In so doing, it changed Lula's relationship to the neoliberal model in which finance capital is hegemonic. This effectively charted the path that Lula's government would assume just months later.

Lula's conversion was reflected to some degree by the appointments made during the presidential campaign when he had shifted responsibility for the marketing of the PT campaign to Duda Mendonça, someone who had been previously in charge of several campaigns that promoted the candidacies of a well known politician on the right, Paulo Maluf. The turnabout was also foreshadowed by the appointment of Antonio Palocci, a former PT mayor of Ribeirão Preto, one of the richest cities of Brazil in the State of São Paulo, to oversee the Lula's economic programme. Mendonça created the campaign slogan "Lulinha, peace and love" to help soften and recast the overall image of a formerly combative labour militant while Palocci authored the "Letter to Brazilians." This twofold formula proved to be the winning combination in a campaign that had become increasingly Lula's and no long that of the PT.

Things became even clearer with the composition of the government, once Lula proved victorious in the presidential runoff elections. The most significant indication was the naming of Henrique Meirelles, ex-president of the Bank of Boston, as President of the Central Bank. When Meirelles had returned to Brazil after building his banking career in the United States, he managed to carry out a rather expensive electoral campaign and win himself a deputy's seat on the party ticket of former President Cardoso. With his appointment by Lula, he created a policy team made up of young neoliberals that had occupied posts in previous governments. Not a single PT economist or from any other leftist force was invited to form part of the government's economic unit, thereby sealing Lula's rupture with the PT's political trajectory and the left in general.

Preservation of the "Accursed" Cardoso Legacy

In its first moment in power, the new government argued that it would be unable to rapidly change economic policy due to the "accursed" nature of the economy it had inherited from the previous administration. Palocci, appointed to head the Economics Ministry, utilised the metaphors of his medical profession to declare that "the treatment cannot be changed while the illness still persists." While alleging that an economic policy of transition was underway, the goal was to maintain the confidence of the market, continue to attract capital and gradually reduce interest rates so as to optimally position the economy for future development.

The argument of the "accursed inheritance" had two basic components, the risks of external insolvency and the menace of an inflationary spiral. In the former, it is true that there had been a sharp deterioration in foreign accounts during the two Cardoso Administrations (See Paulani 2003). An unceasing economic liberalisation generated a large stock of private national capital that was cheap and of good quality that wound up in the hands of foreign capital. The process of privatising state companies in the industrial services sector contributed to much the same result. As a result, deficits grew in the balance of revenues and services given the rapid expansion of external indebtedness.

The deficit averaged $11 billion dollars in the 80's, increasing to $19 billion in 1997, in part as the result of an artificial overvaluation of the Brazilian currency. It was external vulnerability that led Cardoso's government to twice appeal for new IMF agreements after having already reached agreement with them in January of 1999. These renegotiations, first in June of 2001 and then in August of 2002, smack in the heat of a presidential campaign, was the context in which finance capital had launched its attack upon Lula's candidacy. It could be argued that the country was at the brink of an external moratorium on debt payments, with capital flight bringing the dollar to over 4 Reales (originally introduced by Cardoso on a 1–1 exchange with the U.S. dollar). It was also the context for Lula's "Letter to Brazilians" and the creation of the "Lula risk factor."

In spite of all this, the country's reserves remained unaffected throughout the entire electoral year of 2002 at around US$ 37 billion despite menacing conditions of financial instability. This allowed the government to continue meeting its foreign commitments. The commercial trade balance continued improving and it could be said that by the weeks prior to Lula assuming the presidency, the overall economic situation was considerably better than it had been just a year earlier. There was not much to justify the maintenance of a fiscal adjustment strategy, much less the enactment of new fiscal monetary measures designed to increase the fiscal surplus to levels even beyond those solicited by the IMF.

The other conservative argument related to the risk of a surge in inflation did not square with the increase of interest rates and the stagnated state of the economy. The unemployment rate was high, preventing any inflation associated with demand. In short, there was no indicator that could suggest that inflation represented any risk of going out of control.

The economic policy was essentially being maintained and even intensified with the prioritisation of a higher fiscal surplus. With the increase of interest rates, the fiscal adjustment of the previous decade was continuing on much the same path. In order to package its policies as a strategic option, the Lula government prioritised in its first year the approval of two World Bank styled economic reforms, namely, social security reform and taxation simplification.

The first involved a definite bias towards privatisation, increasing the payments burden on the retired who had already been paying all their lives so as to reduce the social security deficit. Pensions were capped for the public-sector workers, obligating them to turn to private pension funds and therefore working to the benefit of the banks. The proposal was strongly opposed by the trade unions, resulting in the expulsion of three deputies and a senator from the PT and this helped demonstrate to what length the Lula administration was willing to go in implementing its economic programme. While the tax reform was a bit more innocuous, it sought to make investment more attractive by reducing taxes on investments, something that only worsened Brazil's regressive and socially unjust taxation system while contributing to an already large public deficit.

Upon completing its first two years of presidency, Lula announced that the "predicted catastrophe had not taken place," confirming that his government had "reversed a process that had led the country to the brink." Roundly denying all evidence to the contrary, Lula proclaimed that "We did not continue the policies of the previous government, but did everything we had to do in order to reconstruct the economy, strengthen its institutions, and above all, regain credibility both within the country and abroad."

The recovery of economic growth would be essential to what Lula had grown accustomed to emphasise as a process of "recovering the self-esteem of Brazilians." "The economic indicators are the best that they have been for the last ten years. Growth of the Gross Domestic Product economical growth went beyond the most optimistic expectations. This is not something momentary . . . but rather the beginning of a consistent and lasting process. With the greatest recovery in employment since 1992, spectacular successes in foreign trade, and policies for bolstering agro-industrial exports, we have at the same time managed accounts in a responsible manner, thereby keeping inflation under control."

At that moment of completing two years in power, Lula had established a permanent shape to his administration. There may be significant modifications in some of its policies and there would certainly be some changes in its composition, but it was not increasingly unlikely that any of these would be substantial. The essential options chosen by the government would seem to indicate that they will remain in place at least during the present term, until 2006, given the declarations of Lula to that effect, the determinant weight of his economic team, and the special role that his economic minister Antonio Palocci has occupied within the government.

Economic policy became consolidated as the core content of the Lula government. Throughout the first year, the government talked about transition while in the course of the second year, the economic policies assumed a permanent character. The vice became transformed into a virtue when Lula proclaimed that his economic policies represented "the best of his government."

The eventual questioning of Palocci's policies was ironically softened after the political misfortunes of another initially important minister in the government, Jose Dirceu, who fell victim to allegations of corruption. Even more important was the consolidation of a mini-cycle of economic recovery in 2004, enabling the government to convince itself that the economy has taken the path of a sustainable growth. This cycle displayed a 5% growth in 2004 following stagnation during the two previous years, with significant recovery of idle capacity, and expanded primary goods exports that were especially robust in soy and agro-industry.

With the 5% growth achieved in its second year, the Lula government had presided over an average economic expansion of 2.7%, a little higher than the eight years of Cardoso government that came in at 2.3%. Nevertheless, the concentration of income in the export-oriented sector and in high income consumption coincided with employed and self-employed people experiencing a 2.3% decline in earnings, compared with a fall under the Cardoso government of just .68%. That drop in earnings came along with an increase in the super-exploitation of labour, with 4.9 million retired people forced to continue to work in 1996, increasing to 6 million in 2003. The number of workers with two or more jobs increased from 3.4 million in 2001 (4% of the work force) to 3.8 million (4.3%) in 2003.

The number of workers working extra hours from 27,132,000 in 1996 rose to 29,320,000 in 2003, while unemployment rose from 5.1 million (6.7%) to 8.5 million over the same period. From 1996 to 2003, 17.5 million new jobs with compensation of up to 3 minimum salaries were created while 6.3 million of higher paying jobs were lost. The balance was insufficient to attend to the growing demand for new employment as well as the serious decline in the level of employment. An "Asian pattern" of employment has become accentuated involving long days, low wages and scarce labour rights. The historical tendency towards an increasing concentration of income in Brazil continued. Employed and self-employed workers went from receiving 51.4% of national income in 1993, the first year of the Cardoso government, to 40.1% in 2003, continuing a steady decline. Between 2002 and 2003, 3.3 million people with a monthly family income of between 1–5 thousand reales have experienced a decline in their purchasing power, while the number of persons with family income under 500 reales has grown by 3.5 million.[3]

The proposed "priority for social spending" remained suppressed by the financial goals of the administration aimed at the public deficit and inflation. This notwithstanding, the administration did not manage to reduce the external fragility of the Brazilian economy. The budgetary restrictions were compensated for by high interest rates that for their part continued elevating the level of indebtedness of the economy. In 2002, the public debt was 623 billion reales and this rose to 812 billion over the two year period, with almost 50% of the increased indebtedness being short term, i.e., coming due in a year's time. The surplus obtained was almost half of the increase in indebtedness, resulting from some of the highest real interest rates in the world.

The relationship between investments and payment of interest on the debt resulted in a situation where in 2003, 6.9 billion reales were invested while

---

[3] See "Número de dois gumes," *Carta Capital*, December 15, 2004 and "No torniquete," *Carta Capital*, November 17, 2004.

interest payments increased by more than 10 times to 77 billion reales. This negative trend continued in 2004 when 1.7 billion reales in investments could be compared to 50.8 billion reales in debt interest payments. The state was therefore continuing to play the role of channelling resources from the productive sphere to the speculative sphere through its domestic system of taxation.

The monthly decisions made on the interest rate and the discussions regarding the minimum wage level remained firmly in the hands of the administration's economic team and the Central Bank. They continue to be the main force in defining the economic direction of the government and in serving as a filter for the allocation of resources to the various ministries, including those charged with social spending policies. After the welfare and tax counter-reforms of the first year, further reforms were announced in the areas of labour, university and political parties. However, these additional reforms began to stall in the second year as it was becoming increasingly difficult for the government to gain the necessary support.

After its tax reforms favouring investors was pushed through, the government proceed to promote the Public-Private Sector Partnerships (PPP) as an alternative to raising the necessary resources for public investment. This involved offering guaranteed, risk-free returns to capital as a means to help the government maintain its priority of showing a fiscal surplus and achieving economic growth at the same time. The end result is a deepening of the process of privatising the state. The government achieved approval of the law that permitted the use of this mechanism as a core strategy for restoring needed investments.

The municipal elections that were held in the latter half of 2004 constituted the first electoral test of the Lula government and the PT after its arrival to the presidency of the republic. A synopsis of the results is as follows: There was in increase in the total number of votes obtained by the PT, something relatively normal for a party recently victorious in presidential elections. At the same time, there were very significant qualitative defeats such as the loss of São Paulo, Porto Alegre and Belém, which has been controlled by the party for 4, 16 and 8 years respectively. In the case of São Paulo which constitutes the third largest budget of the country, the defeat was at the hands of Jose Serra, Lula's adversary in the 2002 presidential election, thus handing back control of the political and economic centre of the country to the PSDB, the party of Cardoso.

If Lula's first year of government was marked by opposition from the Left, especially on the part of social movements that mobilised against the reform of social security, the second year was to experience an increase of opposition on the part of the right. This is not any reflection of a move to the left on the part of the Lula government, but rather a sign of its political weakening. It has been unable to put forward effective social policies, significantly raise the minimum wage or reduce high unemployment. Agrarian reform has also failed to advance and the government's ineffective environmental policy is being confronted by the environmental movement. The PT has proven unable to either broaden its overall base of political support or free itself up from the lambasting coming at it from the press.

It has also been weakened by a proliferation of accusations that allege corruption on the part of key members of his government and this has dovetailed with municipal level electoral defeats. In the final analysis, its inability to leave behind the economic model that it inherited resulted in economic expansion that has not become reflected in the social sphere.

The traditional right has based itself in political alliances that were in power during the previous Cardoso government. While this alliance lost its bearings in the first year of the Lula government, it reappeared during the second year, bolstered by the growing accusations of corruption and the PT's electoral setbacks at the municipal level. The latter was particularly costly in São Paulo where Lula had made a particular presence designed to favour the PT's prospects. From that point forward, Cardoso's PSDB has regained its presence in the national press, with Cardoso himself now emerging once more as a regular voice in national politics. It resulted in a premature opening of political debate around a successor to Lula, with various pre-candidates beginning to surface.

Clearly, those forces hope to polarise the electorate against the government, directly supporting the economic policy that they recognise as theirs while attacking the progressive aspects of the government, demanding repression of the Landless People's Movement (MST), echoing the accusations of corruption and criticising what they consider to be uncontrolled social policies. In the face of all this, the government is forced to look for support among the followers of the centre and right parties in order to improve the prospects of Lula's re-election. Heading into his third year of government, polls still showed Lula as the favourite, perhaps due to the absence thus far of a strong competing candidate.

Conclusion: The Left and Lula's Government

The left was defeated in the municipal elections of 2004 in a period where the overall level of social mobilisation had diminished considerably. The exception to this rule was the Landless People's Movement (MST) who managed to maintain their pressure on the government. In 2004, they mounted a "red April" that involved a large number of land occupations, mobilisations and expanded publicity in support of its struggle. Electorally speaking, however, the left lost its control over important municipalities like Belém, Campinas, Rio Grande del Sur, Porto Alegre, Caxias do Sul, Pelotas, the latter considered a bastion of the PT.

The overall tendency towards dispersion was accentuated by the foundation of a party to the left of the PT, the rapidly-constituted PSOL that in place of congregating the discontents with the core tendencies of the government, simply created another party out of the group surrounding Senator Heloisa Helana (who was expelled from the PT) in support for her presidential candidacy in 2006.

The ideological and political battles within the left have led to a process of fragmentation, increasing the distance between contending positions at a time when a reunification will be necessary. The struggle against the economic policy of the government, revolving around neoliberalism, has not been taken as the point of reference for unifying the left. This is unfortunate since it could in fact serve as the best means for overcoming the isolation of the left during the present period. The matrices of critique have polarised the debates and led to confrontations in place of building bridges between discontented sectors both within and outside of the PT.

The most important discussion today for the Brazilian left revolves not so much around the greater or lesser degree of radical critique of Lula's government, but rather about the best way of accumulating forces for a reconstruction of a social and political bloc that can advance the profile of the left. For those that left the PT, this meant forming something new. Their logic, however has led them to demonise everything that has the PT brand associated with it. This included, for example, soliciting an annulled ballot in the municipal elections that were already quite polarised between the right and the left in dispute of municipal PT governments that had clearly been privileging social concerns in the case of São Paulo and Porto Alegre. That exemplified their posture of direct confrontation with everything PT, something which not only presupposes an incorrect and reductionist interpretation of the PT that is incapable of distinguishing between the federal and local levels of the government, but also serves to further isolate a large mass of left militancy that remains loyal to the PT. The forming of a new party in this context represented more of a divisive strategy than one favouring the consolidation of left forces.

For their part, the tendencies that remain in the PT, wielding leftist critiques of the federal government, have erred in continuing to participate in that government, offering their support to the general orientations of the Lula administration and a direct loyalty to Lula in place of developing a political and ideological course of struggle within the PT in concert with the larger social movements of the country. Not one important tendency has ceased to participate in the government on the basis of political principle while it would be perfectly possible to do so and remain in the PT.

Actions remain pending that can permit the left to regain the initiative and to create a space where an accumulation of political forces can effectively take place. This could include a proposal by the Brazilian Lawyers Association of presenting a law by popular initiative backed by thousands of the signatures that can result in forcing a popular consultation by referendum or plebiscite concerning those decisions that involve committing the future of the country. The campaign of initiatives has already begun and if the law were to become approved, it would be possible to hold a plebiscite around the core issues of the Lula government's economic policies. In such a campaign, it would be possible to form an anti-neoliberal front with the participation of social movements, intellectuals, parliamentarians, and members of various political parties. This initiative could open up an important space for the left, help it to unify its forces and generate a field where the accumulation of forces could take place with the potential to amass considerable public support.

The big debate within the Brazilian left revolves around the character of the Lula government, in searching for analogies in the history of the international workers movement, and in deepening the analysis of the evolution of the PT, Lula and his government. The tone of these debates varies although the contents of the critique, are fairly consistent, namely, continuity and the failure to break with the neoliberal model. Nevertheless, the divisions among the left, a sub-product of the crisis created by the platform implemented by the PT government, contribute to their disempowerment and isolation. This in turn leaves the field even further open to the manoeuvres of the Lula government in the popular media, particularly among the most depoliticised.

The Lula government enjoyed the best conditions for transforming itself into a model experience for the left and breaking with neoliberalism. Even knowing that the expansion of market relations would strangle it and take the wind out of the state's sails, as Chomsky says, not by military coup but by the insidious action of the market, Lula at the moment of his election opted for continuity. He did so despite having the domestic and international support necessary for making a break with the neoliberal economic model and initiating a transition to a model focused on social priorities, just as he himself had promised to do in his electoral campaign.

He could have renegotiated the Brazilian debt, arguing precisely in accordance with his popular slogan during the electoral campaign that it is his obligation to ensure that all Brazilians eat three meals per day. He could have sought to adjust the Brazilian social deficit while subordinating the financial priorities to the social ones. However, the search for governability which was an essential part in securing an electoral victory in his fourth attempt, led him to compromise with financial capital as stated in the "Letter to Brazilians" and thus block that possibility. The Lula government has conformed with that letter and not with the original programme of his campaign, much less to the historical trajectory of the PT.

Finally, what does the cooptation of the Lula government signify for liberalism? In the Latin American framework, it means that the creation of a pole by Brazil, Argentina and probably Uruguay as a liberal social alternative. This pole will search for its own space in its international commercial policy by pursuing free trade and pressing capitalist superpowers to open their market. In doing so, they will be strengthening the regression of the continent's economies to an earlier stage as exporters of primary commodities with a renewed emphasis on agro-industry. This will weaken the levels of industrialisation that were previously reached, diminish the capacity for genuine regional integration and favour the consolidation of agreements of the FTAA kind, albeit seeking to negotiate in that framework somewhat less unfavourable terms for its primary export commodities.

Víctor M. Figueroa

Venezuela's Chávez: An Alternative for Democracy in Latin America?[1]

Introduction

Various studies have been published in recent years concerning the present state of "democracy" in Latin America. One of the most notable consisted of a large-scale survey conducted by the United Nations Development Programme (UNDP). Many observers were caught by surprise when they read the rather unexpected results about how the region's population perceives their political institutions. Among other things, the UNDP survey indicated that:

- Only 43% of citizens support democracy.
- Only 20% support political parties and their congresses.
- There is consistently less than a 40% trust level among the population when asked separately about their nation's judiciary system, national police forces, armed forces, and president.
- Television has a less than a 50% level of credibility.
- During the 1990–2002 period, only 62.7% of citizens with a right to vote actually cast ballots, but no more than 56.1% of the votes they cast were recognised as valid. Those countries where voting is not compulsory generally had lower rates of

[1] This paper appeared earlier in *Critical Sociology*, Volume 32, N° 1, 2006, pp. 187–211.

participation: Colombia, 33%; Guatemala, 36.2%; Venezuela, 45.7%, although the notable exception was Nicaragua with 78%.

• Electoral abstention appears to be growing. This is clearly the case in Mexico where abstention rates reached 42.3% in 1997 and 58.3% in 2003 (UNDP 2004).[2]

This data presents a convincing case that the political and ideological institutions of Latin American capitalism are at best providing for an anaemic social reproduction. They do not readily mobilise social energy and the population's commitment to them is increasingly precarious. For that reason, these institutions display an ever weaker capacity for legitimating state power. Indeed, they continue to contribute to the de-legitimation of established authority regimes.

How can this situation be explained? A very popular response circulating around the region is that we are living out a "political crisis." While this seems to square with reality, it does not constitute an adequate answer.

The present paper portends to offer an alternative response. First, some brief reflections will be offered on the various forms of democracy that exist under contemporary capitalism. These considerations will then be extended to Latin America with a focus on the contradictions of neoliberal democracy. The discussion will then turn to the exceptional case of Bolivarian democracy that has been established in Venezuela.

Two Forms of Democracy Under Contemporary Capitalism

By politics, we refer to the praxis which regulates social conflict based on the internal social class divisions of countries as well as the relations among states in the global order. Politics unfold around specific relations of domination and a world without politics can only be imagined as a world free of domination. In this, states constitute the main political agent. The particular form of domination and historical circumstances surrounding it actively condition the organisation and tasks of every state. This notion is valid for each particular type of state.

During the six last decades of capitalism, we have witnessed two main forms of political regulation. On the one hand, there has been authoritarian-

---

[2] The English version of this report (UNDP 2004) can be found at: http://democracia.undp.org/Informe/Default.asp?Menu=15&Idioma=2

ism as expressed in specific modalities such as liberal dictatorships, totalitarian states, and presidentialism.[3] On the other hand, we have seen liberal democracy that has operated under the two versions of *tendentially inclusive* and *tendentially exclusive* liberal democracies. These versions are directly linked to the forms of capitalist economic organisation that came into practice through Keynesianism and neoliberalism respectively.

The Keynesian framework was based on consumption with a strong emphasis on the expansion of domestic markets. For that reason, it paid careful attention to wage levels and systematically constructed a social pact that was emblematic of capitalist evolution from the post-World War II period (and even earlier in Latin America with the emergence of the populist states) up into the 1970s. The operation of Keynesianism was predicated on a steady flow of concessions negotiated between contending social classes. This made it possible for the popular sectors to be significantly incorporated into the enjoyment of the fruits of economic growth, allowing them to form reasonably viable expectations for steady improvements in their quality of life. The welfare state helped support these expectations, especially in the area of access to education, housing, and health services. For their part, political parties acted as dynamic agents in promoting this steady flow of class concessions, and this served to elevate their prestige among the population as effective agents of social mediation.

For its part, neoliberalism put an end to the above mentioned social pact and inaugurated a new era in the treatment of the labour movement and the popular sectors more generally. In reality, this was a prerequisite for overcoming the tremendous economic crisis that had incubated during the course of the 1960s, and which exhibited its first major manifestations in 1967–1968 and then again in 1974–1975. The challenge was to restore the rate of profit and this fundamentally required a new social correlation of forces.

The attacks on trade unions that became generalised during the latter part of the 1970s in the United States occurred when the same had already taken place throughout the Southern Cone of Latin America. The expansion of unemployment helped to politically weaken the labour movement everywhere. Technological innovations simply helped to intensify this process.

---

[3] "Presidentialism" can be understood as a state with the following features: a) a strong executive power which b) controls legislature and judiciary, c) corporativism, and d) elections are also controlled by the executive power.

State activity no longer focused on employment generation but rather on the deregulation of labour relations. This concerted policy of "labour flexibility" tipped the balance of political power almost unconditionally into the hands of capital.

Tendentially Exclusive Democracy in Latin America

Latin America is a region where governments remain highly vulnerable to the pressures from organisations, corporations and governments of the developed world. The social reorganisation that took place under neoliberalism resulted in particularly severe consequences for the popular sectors. Income redistribution now moved overwhelmingly in favour of the most economically powerful sectors. A perverse concentration of wealth, beginning during the 1980s, was firmly consolidated during the 1990s. In a group of countries that included Argentina, Bolivia, Brazil, Costa Rica, Ecuador, El Salvador and Nicaragua, the position of the popular sectors got steadily worse while the richest 10% of the population increased its share of total income. By 2000–2002, the 10% wealthiest stratum of the entire region received an income equal to 19.1 times that which was obtained by the poorest 40% of the population (ECLAC 2003).

Between 1980 and 2002, the portion of the total population living in poverty grew from 40.5% to 44.0%, i.e., from 135.9 million in 1980 to 221.4 million in 2002. Within the swelling ranks of these impoverished people, the number of individuals categorised as indigent (or severely poor) went from 62.4 million to 97.4 million. By the end of the 1990s, the number of serious malnourished people living in the region was estimated at 54 million (ECLAC 2003).

This oligarchic income distribution has been followed by the consolidation of a broad and growing sector of excluded people. Appeals to these segments of the population to participate in electoral democracy were something which the bourgeoisie only began to opt for during the second half of the 20th Century. Even then, it did so while guarding the contingency option of resorting back to dictatorship. The critical point is that these appeals for popular participation in elections have been notably accompanied with scant concessions in the economic sphere. Indeed, this fact is the main pitfall of electoral democracy. Political inclusion cannot possibly be successful if it goes hand in hand with economic exclusion. Such an obvious gap was bound to have an impact on the political evolution of Latin American societies and it ultimately did precisely that. The political game has dramatically failed to win allegiance by a large part of Latin America societies, thereby eroding its ability to legitimise the established concentrations of power.

There is no doubt that a large part of the criticism of the electoral democracies emanate from the excluded sectors of the population. In a survey concerning electoral abstention in Mexico during the 1990s, the following results were obtained:

- Electoral abstention and individual income level display an inverse relationship.
- The greater ones level of education, the lesser the rate of abstention, i.e., less educated people abstain more.
- Rural abstention is larger than urban abstention.
- Abstention is larger in districts with a large informal sector.[4]

In this extreme state of things, the survey suggests that the portion of the population who would tolerate having an "authoritarian government capable of solving their economic difficulties" has tended to grow. The survey indicated that the percentage of potential Mexican voters who expressed a willingness to revert to authoritarianism went up from 39% to 41% between November 2002 and April 2004.[5] It would be difficult to find a clearer and more convincing expression of the relationship between economic organisation and political regulation.

Surveys such as these, however, do not admit to a single, monolithic interpretation. Each society has its own image of authoritarianism that it has constructed based on previous historical experience. For example, while authoritarianism in Chile and Argentina is linked to murder, torture, jail, exile, hunger, unemployment, the absence of rights, open and arbitrary repression, "disappeared" people, and so on, Mexico under authoritarian governments experienced a much more moderate dose of these kinds of atrocities. Indeed, in its best moments, Mexican presidentialism even managed to form a pact between social classes, albeit a weak one, that lasted for quite some time, permitting a relatively wide range of social mobility.

---

[4] See: Centro de Estudios para un Proyecto Nacional S.C. *Estudio sobre el abstencionismo en Méxic.* http://www.deceyec.ife.org.mx/estudio.
[5] *El Universal*, Mexico, 17 May 2004.

So while it is very doubtful in the case of Chile and Argentina that authoritarian governance would any time soon win the widespread backing of the
popular sectors, the case of Mexico shows on the contrary that people have
a difficult time establishing a clear line of demarcation between the past and
the present. In this context, it is not so difficult to imagine why people trying to resolve the problem of their subsistence might at a given moment opt
for a "practical authoritarianism" over "democracy" as presently constituted.
They can realistically imagine that their votes, should elections even be held
under an authoritarian regime, could not possibly be any more ignored than
they are at present.

It seems clear, then, that the present form of democracy is engaged in an
enterprise working against itself. Its very logic constitutes an obstacle to its
own further development as it promotes rejection over adhesion. In this kind
of setting, the ultimate question must sooner or later arise: Is the behaviour
of the popular sectors fundamentally anti-democratic in view of their refusal
to support the present form of democracy? Professional politicians, so deeply
immersed in the ideology reproduced by neoliberalism, would most probably be inclined to think so.

We think, however, that in the first place, the popular sectors are not rejecting democracy, but rather the presently existing form of exclusion that goes
under its name. The vast majority do not feel that they are part of a project
that understands or takes into account their fundamental needs, much less
contemplates changes that can help alleviate their problems. On the contrary,
most people of the popular sectors feel assaulted by a project that sentences
them to misery, that employs coercion instead of consultation, and that offers
firm guarantees for market rights that they cannot exercise. The real solution
to the "crisis of democracy" does not consist in the desperate efforts of electoral authorities to bring the population to the ballot boxes, but rather in promoting a complete overhaul of the political and economic system.

To blame the people for the neoliberal debacle is to do nothing more than
ignore the inherent contradictions in the neoliberal project itself. These contradictions in the political regulation of the overall political economy are multiple in nature and in the following section, we shall turn our focus directly
upon them.

Contradictions of Exclusive Democracy

Neoliberal globalisation, driven by large transnational capital in the attempt to free itself up from all of the regulations and concessions imposed by historical conditions in the past,[6] has seriously narrowed the scope of national economic agendas in the region. No longer is even the orientation of economic processes being discussed at national levels since they are so clearly defined from abroad. Neoliberals try to hide this reality by peddling the belief that economic decisions have passed into the hands of the market, a mechanism that listens, reacts, promotes, put things in order, and whose wise and precise decisions set people free from state mistreatment. So goes the dominant ideological mantra.

But for all intents and purposes, the results are plain to see. Nations have been expropriated from a large part of their ability to make decisions. National fractions of the same ruling blocs have been pushed to a new height of subordination. The asymmetrical relations at the international level have appropriated an ever more important space, leaving behind an impressively small range of decision-making for domestic political processes. Institutions such as the International Monetary Fund (IMF), the World Bank and the Organisation for Economic Cooperation and Development (OECD) actively design and deliver their "recommendations" (read "decisions") on economic policy, health and social security or any matter of significant importance. At the other end of the imperial scheme, an insatiable need for credits and capital investment leaves Latin American countries on their knees, conforming to an autocratic decision-making process. The client-state simply confines itself to mimicking the slogans it receives from abroad as if they were its *own* creation. If the local state cannot approach the situation of the popular sectors as *its* own task, it is because this issue, like various others, is simply too important for foreign capital. In this context, much less can the state actually work *with* the poor towards a new relationship. Local political figures are pushed up against a wall, compelled to submit into mediocrity with the same force that once empowered them to impose this same mediocre system of democracy upon others.

---

[6] I have developed this point in "Globalización y lucha de clases", *Glocalrevista* 2(9). http://www.glocalrevista.com.

Along the same lines, neoliberal globalisation reduced the state's capacity to make concessions, and in this way pulverised the managerial power of national political processes. If this delimitation of the national agenda has indeed contributed to the loss of prestige of the congresses, neoliberal indifference to the problems of the popular sectors has decisively annihilated the prestige of executive politicians and their political parties. In a brilliant analysis, McPherson (1982) had concluded early on that the role of political parties was to blur class contradictions. But he would now probably be annoyed with the present environment where political parties seem to do nothing more than aggravate class contradictions. They can do this because they answer to nobody. Political parties as organisations that fight for control over governments have given way to *indirect* popular representation, thanks to that which they have developed independently of the demands of the people they supposedly represent. But in doing so, they have undermined their political function and have been left to simply support the legitimation of class domination. In that role, parties have widened a fissure which wins them criticism even from the most reactionary fractions of the bourgeoisie.

Both the structure of political parties as well as their internal dynamics have become converted into an expression of this hopeless task of legitimation. Panebianco (1990) envisaged this as an evolution caused by the internal logic of political parties, but today it appears to be a result at the very least accelerated if not orchestrated by external circumstances. A drastic reduction of ideas has been produced by these circumstances, fuelled by a sharp constriction in the range of local decision-making, the abandonment of great social causes, and resignation towards a situation that is slowly leading to their strangulation. Political parties at one time opted to the left in favour of transforming the prevailing social reality. They are now situated in a position where the entire focus of their activity is placed upon their own survival. "The best policy is to have no policy" seems to be the motto of politicians, thereby announcing their own irrelevance to the excluded sectors while demonstrating their role in reproducing neoliberalism.

The motivations of solidarity that once mobilised feelings and actions behind great social causes has given way to the administration of "selective incentives," doled out among the leadership groups of those clients and social organisations that remain loyal. Costly electoral campaigns and the need for access to public and/or private financing have further deepened the subordination of political party organisations. All of this has made it ever more difficult to aspire to democratic dynamics within internal party organisations, something particularly destructive to parties based in the popular sectors. The party congresses have turned into tremendous rituals of fraudulent consultations. In a word, these party organisations have become severely distanced from popular interests in a cordial neoliberal environment that enables them to espouse their irrelevance.

It would seem odd to think that electoral democracy in this neoliberal environment could have ever been even conceptually maintained. Guillermo O'Donnell is an author of theoretical work that has been extensively utilised by the United Nations Development Programme (UNDP) in order to provide a framework for its report on the status of democracy in Latin America. According to O'Donnell (2004), a democratic regime is one in which the main political posts (at least executive and parliamentary) are filled by means of fair elections. For an election to be fair, it must be: a) competitive; b) free (of coercion); c) egalitarian (one person, one vote); d) decisive, that is, the positions for which candidates are competing must be decided by the results; e) inclusive, in as much as every adult that meets the nationality requirement can participate; and lastly, f) institutional, that is, it must take place in a context of regulated electoral activity so that the population is confident about the overall process. In addition, he argues that for an election to be free, there must be freedom of expression and association along with free access to multiple sources of information (O'Donnell 2004).

O'Donnell thinks that this concept can currently be found in application in the developed Western countries. He believes, however, that its fundamental premises (i.e. universal political and civil rights, homogenous legality throughout the national territory) are not generally present in Latin America. In reality, his criticisms of the Latin American context are very acute. He points out that the popular sectors have no protection against public and private violence, that their access to public services is unequal, that they suffer from continuous humiliations, and so on. He also says that states are "economically colonised" by foreign interests and are invariably found to be "bureaucratically inefficient" whereby they do not accomplish their legal function nor can they can act as "filters and moderators" of social inequalities. Latin American states, he points out, are "deaf" to demands for equality and only serve to reproduce inequalities and the dynamics of globalisation in their destructive aspects. Further, they fail to achieve the necessary control over violence in the national territory, while certain zones persist that remain out of the reach of the national legal system.

Why then does he speak of democratic regimes in Latin America? He does so because he thinks that the political regime and the state are different entities, something which in strictly analytical terms could well be accepted as valid. In his way of reasoning, it seems fair to conclude that the democratic regime has to do specifically with the generalisation of political rights, not with social and civil rights, which is why these rights exist in diverse settings. But this is where his analytical approach quickly becomes depleted.

The political regime is the historically conditioned manifestation of the state and reflects the way in which the state regulates social conflicts at a given moment. Any regression to authoritarianism would not be a simple shift of the regime but rather a comprehensive transformation of the state. An integral approach to the state cannot leave aside the political regime. This recognises that the state and the political regime can be separated only for the purpose of study, but only even then by taking into account their historical relationship. The state, once it is separated from the political regime, only suggests to us the general conditions of its existence with respect to social classes and the underlying class struggle. But such abstractions become meaningless when deprived of their historical content. Class domination gives different types of state their form and capitalist class domination is one of those. The study of the capitalist state comes pre-formed with a specific relationship between social classes. The type of capitalist state is in every context conditioned by diverse modalities determined by the level of social development and existing class struggle.

The state as empirically conceptualised apart from any political regime, as if it were something with a regime operating parallel to it, most certainly represents a brilliant pile of rubbish. This can be easily seen in everyday affairs. When a topic such as the participation in "clean elections" is treated, one can than allude to the need to be well-informed as to the alternatives being offered. But this possibility is completely denied to those who suffer from hunger and who can therefore pay little thought let alone any money for the costs of information. Their right to "freely" participate in such a "clean" election is totally non-existent.

If O'Donnell asserts that it would be inconsistent to recognise rights when the means to enjoy them do not exist, it is for an essential lack of congruence. The argument that it is not possible to establish a minimum standard for the means of exercising rights does not free him from this inconsistency. His postulation that ". . . these rights, political, civil and social are analytically separable but in practice, each one presupposes the others . . ." (O'Donnell 2004:57), does nothing more than reinforce the confusion, one very analogous to his confusion of state and regime. This is particularly true if one is made to accept the notion that some rights, those tied with the political regime, are inseparable from the others, those tied to the sphere of the state.

O'Donnell should have concluded that democracy does not exist in Latin America. However, not only is it accepted that democracy is being practiced in various grades, but he further posits that there exist cases that basically comply with the requisites of his model. Here he refers to Costa Rica, Uruguay and Chile. In these cases, not only does the regime qualify as democratic but so does the state. The author does go on to accept that Chile seems to be experiencing an important regression in terms of social rights. For some unexplained reason, however, this does not seem sufficient to ultimately disqualify it.

Only with great difficulty could he sustain that the Chilean state is one adequately adapted to the democratic regime. He can further be questioned if he really believes that the state acts as a filter and moderator of social inequalities. Perhaps he would like to take on the notion that this state, unlike other states in the region, is somehow not "economically colonised." Is the Chilean state one that attends to demands for equality? Does he suppose that the popular sectors have equal access to the services of education, health, housing, and that poverty and indigence no longer exist? The list of questions can go on in making reference to the labour rights, monopolistic powers, etc., but we trust that the incongruence of the author which is in large measure a reflection of the incongruence of the democracy he discusses has by now been adequately established.

It must be recognised that to demand full democracy out of capitalism is a losing proposition, given that exploitation and social inequality is a fundamental characteristic of the system. Even a democracy that is tendentially inclusive, as a mode of regulation of social conflict and as a form of organising social domination, leaves something to be desired and with all the more reason, on the part of the underdeveloped countries. The history of democracy is a history of struggle against exclusions for varying reasons (economic, gender, race, policies, etc.) and this has not changed in the context of its contemporary forms where economic exclusion has become especially pronounced, particularly in Latin America. This kind of exclusion, because of the way that it appears isolated and able to co-exist with inclusive characteristics in terms of codified political rights, demands a fresh approach to the problems of democracy. In the framework of neoliberal globalisation, the formalisation of political rights has advanced but in the sphere of economic and social rights, the setbacks have been dramatic, leading the political rights won to lose their practical significance. For this reason, the formal generalisation of political rights appears at the same time as its real particularisation. It is this specific characteristic that still predominates in the democracy found in Latin America.

Democratisation is clearly a process, not a given situation. Taking this into account, it can be said that the democratisation taking place in Latin America is an inverted process. Popular support for congresses and for political parties has fallen. The size of the population that is dissatisfied with democracy as it presently exists has grown. The level of participation in electoral contests has diminished and the expectations with respect to changes to come about as a result of electoral processes have dramatically declined. All of this has come about, not as the result of any reduction in political rights. In Mexico, a notable effort has been made over recent years to build trust in the electoral system. Nevertheless, the portion of the population dissatisfied with Mexican democracy has continued to grow, reaching 59% in April of 2004 after having appeared to peak at 58% in 2002,[7] precisely during a period when all of these efforts at perfecting the electoral system have been taking place.

It is no coincidence, however, that this occurred at the same time that poverty and social inequality was deepening. The sectors most affected were unable to find a way of ensuring that their concerns could be addressed by the state. Nor could they even witness their own organisations being reactivated so as to pressure for more substantive changes. This is illustrative of the typical manner in which the state operates. In a fundamental sense, a given political regime does nothing more than to project itself in a given correlation of forces among social classes; it is at once the producer and product of this correlation. If the democracy can continue to operate without significant turbulence in its exclusive mode, it is because the capacity for mobilisation and for struggle on the part of the popular sectors has been demolished, in large measure due to the denial of their social and political rights. The control that party oligarchies and governmental bureaucracies exercise over them, reinforced by the ideological pressure provided by monopoly controlled mass media, would seem indisputable.

---

[7] *El Universal*, May 17, 2004.

The demonstrations against neoliberal globalisation place into evidence the crisis besetting that model and the signs of its exhaustion are increasingly multiplying. We insist that the decisive task before us does not consist in codifying rights but rather in constructing the material conditions that can permit their effective exercise. This means to reverse the present course of economic growth, placing the priority on internal markets, and simultaneously creating the conditions that can make it possible to overcome the present, subordinated insertion of the region in the global order. This implies negotiating a new arrangement with the imperialist countries and in the division of labour that can permit progress to be made internally.

Popular mobilisation can contain existing authoritarian tendencies, including those repressive tendencies that take a street form, and promote a change in the mode of capitalist-democratic regulation. But it must be said that if the regime, while in the process of transformation, fails to at the same time achieve a transformation of the social and economic organisation, the consolidation of an inclusive democracy remains all but hopeless.

Nonetheless, the popular sectors cannot simply ignore existing political institutions. Those who control the means of violence in society are in the best position to obtain advantages from the destruction of political institutions. That is how we find ourselves with cases like Brazil and Argentina where the two processes become unified. On the one hand, the marginalised masses have opted to resort to their own means and methods of struggle to ensure that their demands become heard. On the other, those means and methods that were not anticipated by the political regime end up pressuring for the search of effective transformations of the regime, something which is not always successful.

Venezuela represents a different case. In that country, it was not an initiative of the masses that pushed forward the process of transformation, but rather the decision to link up with a leadership that was outside of the neoliberal establishment and willing to combat it.

Venezuela's Bolivarian Democracy

The Bolivarian government of Hugo Chávez Frías represents an attempt to liberate Venezuela from the neoliberal framework that continues to predominate, albeit with growing difficulties, in the region. The character of the process being led by Chávez is not anti-capitalist or strictly speaking, even anti-imperialist. Rather, it is a process seeking to combat economic and social exclusion while opening the way to an inclusive democracy. From this point of view, there is no justification for the levels of violence that has occurred within the ongoing social conflict or for the elevated tone in the discourse that has presided over the process. In a published interview that was held with Tarik Alí, Chávez defined the basic content of the Bolivarian project in the following way:

> . . . I don't accept that we are living in a period of proletarian revolutions. This is what reality tells us day after day. But if they tell me that this is the reason that we can't do anything for the poor, I say that here is the point which separates us. I will never accept that nothing can be done to redistribute the wealth of society. I think that it is better to die in battle than maintain a revolutionary banner very high and very pure, while doing nothing. . . . We are trying to make our revolution, to go into battle, advance a little in the right direction, even if is just a millimetre, rather than sit back and dream of utopias" (Alí 2004).

The fundamental points of the Bolivarian programme of Chávez can be summarised as follows:

- Recovery and expansion of the state's ability to intervene in the economic process
- Increasing the standard of living of the popular sectors
- A radical transformation of the political regime

The state can act as a promoter and regulator of economic activity by means of a national system of democratic planning that is open to the influence of all kinds of social organisations. Coordination with the private sector is encouraged, although the state reserves the right to maintain control over strategic activities, such as the production of petroleum and liquid hydrocarbons. It nevertheless intends to promote foreign investment oriented towards the refining of crude oil, gas and petrochemicals. In fact, foreign investment is welcome in every other productive area, but the state gives preference to local investment in those areas related to managing the facilities that are under its control. In construction, infra-structure, tourism, and agro-industrial production, a mixed, public-private sector partnership is postulated as well as for banking and finance enterprises. Private property is guaranteed in all other industries, including the commercial import business.[8]

---

[8] An interesting analysis of the process leading to the design of the programme can be found in Yrayma Camejo (2002).

In proposing that employment and wage levels increase, priority has been placed on the diversification of production. Foreign and local investments are called upon to favour the expansion of the domestic market, particularly in the production of consumer goods, something that is aimed at alleviating the chronic commercial deficit in this area. Agricultural policies seek to revaluate the role played by peasants in economic growth, with a view of more favourably integrating them into society while reducing the country's food dependence. Complementary forms of production, especially cooperatives, are being promoted by means of the creation of production and consumer associations.

The social importance of the Bolivarian project is obvious. The rate of unemployment had continuously grown in Venezuela prior to Chávez assuming power, from 6.6% in 1993 to 14.9% in 1999 (Stallings and Seller 2001). The distribution of income had worsened as well, with the population's poorest 40% seeing its participation reduced from 16.7% of total income to 14.7% between 1990 and 1997; while the richest 18% increased its share from 28.7% to 32.8% during the same period. The percentage of the population living in poverty rose from 39.8% in 1990 to 48% in 1997, while the very poorest, indigent portion grew from 14.4% to 20.5% (ECLAC 2002). Figures like these would certainly tend to mobilise mass sentiments and political action, and that is precisely what happened.

It seems fair to note the fact that the Chávez government's effort to re-orient production back towards the domestic market takes place in a new and completely different global context than that of the 1930–1940s when a similar attempt was made in Latin America. In the present neoliberal setting, it can be asserted that the developed countries are not engaged in a large-scale resolution of their own problems as they were during the great Depression and the Second World War. On the contrary, they are fully committed to deepening their penetration and control over the region. On the same note, large transnational corporations are not primarily interested in the domestic markets of the Latin American countries. Rather, their penetration is mainly intended to improve their productive conditions for competing among developed country markets.

So, Latin America becomes most useful as an export platform. This all means that there is no major external stimulus for inwards oriented production in Latin America. On the contrary, neoliberal globalisation constitutes an obstacle to the expansion of the region's domestic markets. It is also important to note that there is a generalised lack of emergent bourgeois classes capable of stepping up to the plate and directing the process of accumulation. On the contrary, foreign capital hegemony was consolidated among the ruling classes of the region early on. Globalisation has served to *further* consolidate this hegemony of the transnationals, progressively displacing local capitalists to ever more subordinated economic roles.

There is no point, then, in evoking previous military leaders in the region such as Lázaro Cárdenas of Mexico or Juan Domingo Perón of Argentina. The broad social alliances of the past that included sectors of the exporting oligarchy are no longer possible. For this reason, the social base being led by Chávez cannot hope to find allies from within the ruling class who would be willing to join forces with Venezuela's popular and middle sectors.

This is why a radical transformation of the political regime is by necessity a fundamental aspect of Chavez' programme. The pre-condition for its success rests upon eradicating the established political system built mainly on the foundation of two political parties: *Acción Democrática* (AD) and *Comité Político Electoral Independiente* (COPEI). This system emerged in 1958, when the so-called "Pact of Punto Fijo" sealed an alliance between business owners, the Church, the armed forces, and trade unions. This alliance pioneered the distancing between the political regime and the larger society, creating a superstructure that could be reproduced without any real ties with the population and remaining largely indifferent to social demands. In order to transform this political regime, the Bolivarian government established under Chávez convened a Constituent Assembly in order to discuss and approve the Constitutional order that would define the contours of the new Bolivarian Republic of Venezuela.

Venezuela's Process of Political Transformation

Given the absence of any social support from within the propertied classes, the armed forces were called upon to play a fundamental role as agents of transformation. The accumulation of these forces required a long period of work inside the military before they were capable of assuming such a role. The point of departure for these efforts was the creation of the Revolutionary Bolivarian Movement 200 (*Movimiento Bolivariano Revolucionario 200*) or MBR-200 back in 1983. This grouping was formed by a group of young officers, Chávez among them, on the bicentennial anniversary of the birth of Simón Bolívar. The long period of crisis experienced during the 1980s helped strengthen the MBR-200, in spite of the relative political stability that prevailed throughout most of the decade. But in 1989, large sectors of the population mobilised in protest against the decision taken by President Carlos Andrés Pérez to put into effect the IMF´s neoliberal "recommendations" for structural adjustment. The ensuing repression of this mass mobilisation resulted in thousands of deaths and served to distance the government still further from the population.

Amidst the growing social discontent, Chávez led an attempted *coup d'etat* on February 4, 1992. The coup failed and Chávez was imprisoned until 1994 when President Rafael Caldera discontinued the legal case against him, clearing the way for his release from detention. For a time, Chávez continued his political activities at a distance from the electoral realm. Then, in 1997, the MBR-200 approved a re-organisation of its cadres, leading to the creation of the Fifth Republic Movement (*Movimiento Quinta República*) or MVR that now opened itself up to the participation of civilians, especially intellectuals. With the formation of this new movement, Chávez prepared for the first time to participate in electoral politics. The MVR set its sites on the presidential elections of late 1998. Chávez and the MVR arrived to this point via a path that bears little resemblance to the evolution of conventional political parties. Indeed, his résumé was one of anti-party politics and the MVR programme was clearly oriented towards exposing the fraudulent commitments of the parties that dominated the Venezuelan political establishment. In view of the preceding discussion, the MVR's successes should pose little surprise much less any paradox. It was precisely the anti-establishment politics of the MVR that constituted one of the principal reasons for its electoral success. The thorough discrediting of the country's dominant parties, increasing poverty, the weakening of the state's capacity to govern, and in general, the effects of neoliberalism all converged to facilitate the triumph of Chávez as the "anti-candidate" of the MVR. The candidacy of Chávez had managed to at once represent the negation of the establishment and an alternative for the country.

During the first year of his government, President Chávez concentrated his efforts on the re-organisation of political power. He won the referendum that approved the election of the National Constituent Assembly (ANC) with 92% of the votes in April of 1999. By July, the election of the members of this Assembly delivered a victory by a wide margin for those candidates loyal to Chávez under a grouping known as the Patriotic Pole.

In December of that same year, the new Constitution was promulgated, with the functions of the old Congress now being absorbed by the Assembly. This led to the formation of the new National Assembly and the Executive seat of power that reinforced its power over the armed forces, the economy, and society in general. In 2000, elections that were stipulated by the new Constitution were held and Chávez confirmed his majority in the National Assembly while at the same time winning the presidency once again under the new constitutional order. By this process, he achieved one of his principal objectives, i.e., the eradication of the decisive influence of the old elites in the heart of the institutional political establishment.

Despite the success that Chávez had in the Constituent Assembly for obtaining special powers in the state's administration of the economy, the results were less than impressive. This was largely due to the unfavourable international prices of petroleum prevailing at that moment. In 2000, in contrast, the economy initiated a recovery, with a 3.9% rate of growth. This trend continued in 2001, when the economy grew by another 2.9%. At the same time, the rate of urban unemployment also began to slightly decline, to 14.0% and to 13.4% respectively during those same years (ECLAC 2002). Poverty, both in general and among the very poorest, was also reduced while wages rose by 4% between 2000 and 2001. The government managed to bring inflation under control and to hold it at 12% in 2001 (ECLAC 2002, 2003).

In contrast, 2002 was completely different. Oil production that fell during the second half of 2001 continued to fall during the first half of 2002. The reduction in oil income aggravated the fiscal crisis. The reduction of earned foreign exchange led the government to relax control on hard currency exchange rates, allowing it to freely fluctuate against the dollar while dipping into convertible currency reserves. The US dollar rose 70% in 2002 against the Bolivar, making imports significantly more expensive. This in turn adversely affected production and local consumption. Inflation shot up to 31.2%, the gross domestic product fell by 9%, private sector real wages lost 10% and unemployment increased to 15.8%. Even though the trade balance remained favourable, capital outflows tripled. This rather negative economic evolution essentially continued during 2003 (ECLAC 2003).

The political conflict that developed over the early years of the Chávez Administration would seem to account in large measure for these developments. First, Chávez had to wrest control of the national petroleum enterprise (PDVSA) away from the established elites in order to assume management over national oil production surpluses. Then, it had to effectively impede the United States from coming to exercise greater influence over Venezuela's oil industry. In so doing, the state came to represent a threat to those strategic enterprises working outside the sphere of the unfolding economic transformation. At the same time, the state had to put limits on the advantages that had been previously offered to foreign capital by state enterprises. The state was simultaneously demanding to private employers that it grant greater concessions to labour, particularly in terms of wages. On top of all of this, the state was also threatening the power of landowners, both in urban centres (as a result of popular housing programs) as well as in rural areas (via agricultural activation projects that sought to put peasants back to work by allowing them to farm those lands that have been left idle).

It therefore came to nobody's surprise that the Bolivarian government was steadily generating powerful social and political forces in opposition to its programme of transformation. Demonstrations against the government were growing in frequency, magnitude and aggressiveness during the course of 2001. The approval of the "Enabling Laws" (*Leyes Habilitantes*) that permitted Chávez to implement the Bolivarian Programme on a nationwide basis indicated that the government was firmly resolved to carry out a process of social transformation. One concrete example of this was the distribution of 105,000 acres of untilled land to the National Agrarian Institute for its distribution to peasants (CIDOB 2002). Not only landowners but also employers in general saw actions such as these as attacks on their private property. So, the new legislation became a crucial state resource in the face of the increasing level of political opposition. As Cristina Xalma put it: "When Chávez sent the *Leyes Habilitantes* (. . .) for approval by the National Assembly the opposition brought the economy to a standstill and boycotted their entry into force: the approval of the first two laws was followed by an entrepreneurial strike which lasted four months and a two month halt in oil production" (Xalma 2004). These mobilisations would reach their climax with the *coup d'etat* against Chávez launched on April 11th, 2002.

The attempt to overthrow the Chávez government, even though it collapsed, nevertheless indicated that the social and political correlation of forces had changed. On the one hand, the internal cohesion on the part of the armed forces had been broken, with one sector within the military deciding to join the ranks of the opposition. Respect for democratically constituted legislation had been overrun by the demands being set forth by the business sector.

Once the constitutional order became restored, Chávez was urgently obligated to reorganise the command structure within the Venezuelan military.

On the other hand, a sector of middle strata that had previously supported
Chávez now withdrew their support and gravitated towards the opposition.
The devaluation of the Venezuelan currency was undoubtedly a contributing factor in this, particularly in the way it increased the prices of imported
consumer goods as well as the cost of travelling abroad. More generally, the
government, limited in its resources, had consistently concentrated its efforts
in a way that showed little favour for the middle strata (Wilpert 2002).

At the same time, the ideological impact of a powerful mass media almost
universally and relentlessly bent on the destabilisation of the government
had begun to take its toll. Just like in other countries operating in the neoliberal framework, those parties that had long since lost their capacity to design
proposals and having abandoned their direct contact with the population,
had sought refuge in the mass media where they tirelessly worked to frame
the national agenda for political discussion. Under the Chávez government,
this oppositional base in the privately owned media became a critical tool of
destabilisation in the context of all political parties having been discredited.
The media offered these political elements carte blanche to represent themselves as leaders of the patriotic opposition.[9] The media helped construct the
image that the opposition political parties were immersed in a struggle to
advance the interests of the middle sectors of the country. Finally, the opposition also felt emboldened by the support they received from the United
States, whose government appears to have been directly involved in the
attempted Coup of April 2002.[10]

For its part, the large strike led by the private sector indicated to what
point the economic interests of the business owners were being directly
expressed through their politics. Once the government managed to dislodge
their strike, they transformed the temporary suspension of business activity
into a political force. These actions did not signify renouncing their economic
interests but simply postponing them in order to recover their prior political

[9] According to Antonio Guillermo García, this was so much the case that Hugo
Chávez opted at one point to discuss with Gustavo Cisneros, owner of the television
station Venevisión, rather with the opposition political parties, the terms under which
the government and opposition would co-exist until the revocation referendum could
be held in August 2004. http://www.home.woldcom.ch/melopez/actualidad.html.
[10] See *Memoria* No. 160, June 2002, Mexico.

standing relative to the state. The fact that this led up to the attempt to over-throw Chávez also placed into sharp relief the extent to which the business sectors remained committed to democratic mechanisms of government. In the end, they were only interested in exclusive democracy, the type of polit-ical regime that keeps the poor excluded from any real participation. For the business sector, democracy meant allowing them to freely manage the eco-nomic surplus produced by working people and the rent that accrues to the nation by the export of natural resources. In short, they sought a democracy free of troublesome social consensus-making that might obligate them to share some of their riches with the exploited sectors. For that reason, they came to reject the Bolivarian government as a means of political regulation of social conflict. If it meant that they now had to renounce democracy in order to overthrow this government, they would not vacillate in so doing.

Hugo Chávez, for his part, has resisted the temptation to hardening his government, probably in order to prevent his efforts at democratisation from being derailed. On the contrary, he ultimately accepted that his continuation in power be submitted to a referendum, according to the rules of the new Bolivarian Constitution. He took the decision with the full knowledge that the correlation of forces had significantly deteriorated against him.

This revocation referendum showed that a new political reality was emerg-ing in the country. The population massively participated in the vote. In a country where voting is not obligatory, abstention went down to 27%. (In the year 2000 when Chávez was re-elected, the abstention was 44%.) Electoral democracy was eventually called upon and the results constituted an over-whelming spectacle and indisputable political force in legitimating the Chávez government. This force was one and the same that rejects the return to exclu-sive democracy so intensely desired by the opposition. In reality, what was being witnessed was a change in the form of liberal democracy.

The deal being offered by the Venezuelan state to the popular sectors had changed by genuinely taking their needs into account in national policy-making. This has been amply demonstrated by a wide range of measures that have worked to benefit popular interests. More than 116,000 families have been the beneficiaries of a redistribution of two million hectares of land. Almost a million children living in poor areas have received free education and more than a million illiterate citizens have received educational services from the national literacy programme. High school and university education has been significantly expanded. The population has won access to health

care, thanks to the installation of more than 10,000 new clinics in the neighbourhoods of the popular sectors.[11] The government has created 200,000 new
housing units as part of its programme to combat homelessness. Indigenous
peoples have seen their rights legally recognised, this as part of much larger
battle to confront racism. The financial credits offered to poor citizens have
tripled. In the final analysis, although progress in the areas of employment
have not been so evident, the Bolivarian government has been consistently
attacking in various ways the problems that most affect the popular sectors.
It has evidently become the case that the income being netted from the sale
of petroleum no longer solely benefits a tightly constituted oligarchy and
their clients.

The great majority of Venezuela's poor are seeing their immediate interests being effectively involved in the electoral realm. This new dynamic of
inclusion into the national *economic* agenda has been a clear component of
this new *political* inclusion. An inclusive democracy is clearly taking root in
the country. The struggle over the distribution of economic surplus, in this
case, the rents produced by petroleum, has become plainly revealed as a fundamental part of the struggle for this new democracy. Most clearly of all, this
economic inclusion constitutes a threat to the neoliberal political domination
over oil-rich Venezuela.

Conclusion: Whither Inclusive Democracy in Venezuela?

In the year 2004, Chávez won the referendum designed to oust him by a
greater percentage than that which he obtained in 2000 when elected under
the terms of the Bolivarian Constitution. The economy also experienced
a vigorous recovery in 2004, with economic growth reaching around 18%,
and a growing participation of non-petroleum activity. Inflation which had
peaked at 27% began to come back under control by the end of the year at
around 19%.

Two factors have to be taken into consideration in order to critically evaluate the political situation. First, the victory in the referendum, although
important, was not as convincing as it should have been. The fact that the
opposition under the leadership of the oligarchy could garner 40% of the

---

[11] This programme is referred to as the "*Misión Barrio Adentro.*"

vote is disquieting. Second, the ability of certain sectors of the oligarchy to make a serious analysis of the national reality and to then integrate this into their discourse in addressing the central problems of the moment must be recognised. They had adequately perceived the need to modify their political approach. In order to capture popular support, they had to come closer to the people, listen to them and address their needs. Their electoral disasters of the past were the result of a badly mistaken relationship which they had formed with the electorate.

So at least for a sector of the oligarchy, it was now clear that they had become erroneously displaced from the electoral struggle. In order to advance their interests, they would need to adapt their struggle to the terms of an inclusive democracy. This difficult context for the opposition consists of a transition from one liberal democratic scheme to another, and they find hope that the resistance to this transition may not disappear so easily. Indeed, we can see that this democratic transition systematically reproduces and reinforces resistance to the extent that class interests are affected.

At the international level, the arrival of Condoleezza Rice to the post of Secretary of State did anything but relax the tense relations between Caracas and Washington. As newly seated Secretary, she quickly clarified the position of the Bush Administration that "the government of Venezuela represents a negative force in the region" and that is necessary to demonstrate that "we are aware of the difficulties that [this government] is causing its neighbours" (Prensa Latina 2005). Statements like this have made it quite explicit that Washington sides with the right wing administration in Colombia which has steadily escalated the longstanding border-area problems with Venezuela.

On the domestic front, there continue to be open confrontations in Venezuela, particularly with respect to agrarian reform. Armed squads of thugs organised by the landowners have caused over a hundred murders of peasants who had benefited from reform measures taken by the government. So on the one hand, the oligarchy appears to be willing to accept the electoral challenge in a context where the popular sectors play a decisive role. On the other hand, they do not discard the option of resorting to violence.

For Chávez, the stability of his government cannot be taken for granted. Indeed, his administration continues to experience real threats. However, this stability is not likely to be achieved by slowing the overall pace of reforms. On the contrary, the operative slogan seems to be "advance and consolidate." This has been reaffirmed by the government's decision to pursue ten "strategic objectives" that encompass diverse social spheres of the Venezuelan nation. They can be summarised as follows:[12]

- Deepen the transformation of the economy. Special attention is to be placed on the diversification of production and its orientation towards the internal market. The aim is to reduce Venezuela's dependence upon petroleum, substitute imports, stimulate investment and employment, and guarantee the provision of goods and stability of real wage levels. In rural areas, these efforts will include greater redistribution of land, based on a plan to allow peasants access to lands which are chronically left uncultivated. In general, the government will organise its efforts around "development poles" or zones that already display a certain level of economic integration, or creating them where they are not presently found.
- Give institutional form to popular participation and raise it to a higher level. In this way, the limitations of the state can be overcome in the pursuit of the tasks set forth by the "Bolivarian Revolution." This will include Local Public Planning Councils and other forms of popular organisation in both rural and urban areas that can contribute to programme implementation. Participation in elections will seek to be strengthened through registration campaigns and encouraging citizen participation in the designation of candidates.
- Reinforcement of the popular inclinations of the armed forces, particularly in strengthening Bolivarian ideology and the incorporation of citizens in the tasks of national defence.
- Introduction of new legal norms that can help contain the abuses being committed by the mass media, including the opening of new spaces of media communication.
- Insistence on the importance of greater regional integration in Latin America as well as encouraging multilateral responses to challenges within the sphere of international relations.

Through the pursuit of these strategic objectives, Chávez hopes to consolidate the Bolivarian government in Venezuela. The content of most of these projects (especially agrarian reform), as well as his international policies (par-

---

[12] "Líneas Estratégicas de actuación para los próximos años", Speech of Hugo Chávez before the high ranking leaders of his party. November 12, 2004. Available in Spanish at: http://www.rebelion.org.

ticularly in those areas where he openly defies the United States) bode well for the continuation of a high degree of social conflict.

But Chávez is right in supposing that nothing is to be gained by abandoning the reforms of his most radical programmes. This can only ensure that the support of the popular sectors will wane, opening the floodgates to a correlation of forces that can capitalise upon the resulting isolation of the government. The air of certainty displayed by the government that it is helping to construct a better society remains impressive. The government continues to reason that only through greater revolutionary advances can the social and political forces be mobilised that are necessary to construct a new reality in Venezuela. Without doubt, the Chávez project is limited, but it continues to display the audacity and vision necessary for opening the door to greater possibilities.

Until now, the experience of the Bolivarian government has reflected the difficulties signified by a genuine democratisation of society in the context of neoliberal globalisation. Despite the increasing signs of exhaustion, neoliberalism has not ceded to defeat in the region. Chávez came to power in the context of an international crisis where the ideological force of neoliberalism has begun to wane, but where the scheme that will replace it has not yet been born.

In reality, the Bolivarian government has not put forward a project that can effectively achieve a negation of the structures of international domination, much less those of capitalism. Real political independence demands economic independence, that is, the capacity to internally produce progress and a material basis for sustainable development. While the Bolivarian programme displays no consistent proposal in this direction, the revolutionary experience nevertheless displays promising movement. It has definitely generated expectations that a new point of departure has been established for the definitive overthrow of neoliberalism in the region, opening the way to a more optimistic horizon for Latin America's poor.

Hugo Cores

Former Guerrillas in Power: Advances, Setbacks and Contradictions in the Uruguayan *Frente Amplio*

For over 135 years, Uruguayan politics was essentially a two party system. There had been other "small parties" including socialist parties, communist parties or those inspired by Christian groups but all of them garnered little electoral support. Within the two principal political parties that competed for power, however, there were factions within each that could be considered to a greater or lesser extent progressive, anti-imperialist, and/or committed to some kind of vision of social justice. For the most part, the working class vote tended to gravitate towards these progressive wings within the dominant parties.

The Twentieth Century history of the Uruguayan left would have been very distinct had pragmatism prevailed, an attitude that was later called the logic of *incidencia* by leaders of the Independent Batllist Faction (CBI – *Corriente Batllista Independiente*). Indeed, what sense did it make during the 1920s, 30s, 40s and 50s to be a socialist, communist, or Christian Democrat when if all taken together, they failed to reach even 10% of the vote?

When the "theorists" of the CBI spoke of the "logic of *incidencia*, they referred to the idea that voting and cultivating an accumulation of left forces within the traditional political parties was a viable strategy to have an organised impact upon the state apparatus, establishing positions of influence from within. The intent of the CBI itself to pursue such a strategy ultimately failed and disintegrated or became absorbed within the ranks of political support given to the Colorado Party of Sanguinetti.[1]

To remain outside of the traditional political parties, in contrast, meant that the opposition would be deprived of *incidencia*. Partisans of the CBI asserted that political groups that maintained such a posture were destined to remain activists purely of principle. This form of pragmatic reasoning ultimately managed to keep much of the left tied to the conservative political parties for decades and this posture remained influential right up until the elections of 1999. That was the year that Jorge Batlle of the Colorado Party beat Tabaré Vázquez, the latter being the candidate of the leftist *Frente Amplio*.

The *Frente Amplio* (Broad Front) as a Centre of the "Accumulation of Forces"

The 1960s was a time of change for the traditional parties. It had become increasing difficult for progressive forces to remain in the traditional parties as the space available to them was shrinking. Batllistas like Zelmar Michelini decided it was necessary to leave the Colorado Party and Enrique Erro had already left the National Party.[2] It was from out of these progressive tendencies in conjunction with the prior independent tendencies mentioned earlier that the *Frente Amplio* (FA) was formed. It was a conceived as a broad political front created to change the country's direction, to break with the IMF, to implement an agrarian reform, to free political prisoners, defend national industry and provide work for the nation. If we logically analyse that situation from the point of view "of the possible," keeping our eyes strictly limited by pragmatic electoral politics, we would have to say that the *Frente Amplio* with all of its formidable composition was a failure after its first bout of participation in national elections when it obtained just 18.8% of the vote. Indeed, the traditional parties together garnered the support of over 80% of Uruguayan voters.

Did this mean that the formation of the *Frente Amplio*, its programme and its style of politics was a mistake? That its principled attitude of resolute

---

[1] Julio María Sanguinetti of the Colorado Party was President of Uruguay from 1 March 1985 to 1 March 1990 and from 1 March 1995 to 1 March 2000.
[2] Both would later become important activists of the *Frente Amplio*.

rejection of the civic-military dictatorship was an error? That its denunciation of the repression, its solidarity with the disappeared and the political prisoners were all misplaced? Not one of these postulates responded to the vagaries of the "immediately possible" and certainly none of them were adopted with the idea that they would translate into an immediate triumph at the hour of the polls.

On the contrary, these principled and non-immediatist attitudes resulted in imprisonment, sanctions and martyrs. From a pragmatic point of view, it was definitely a bad deal. However, from the point of view of the accumulation of forces against despotic power and neoliberalism, it turned out to be an adequate path. From its very inception, the *Frente Amplio* was formed totally outside of the institutional apparatus. During those early years, the *Frente* knew how to develop political action with great ethical and emotional force. This today forms an important part of our political identity.

Political Assets in Support of Advances

Today, the *Frente Amplio* is in government and the nature of its struggle has changed as it faces the drama and day to day dilemmas of a conservative country. Now just as before, political action cannot be exclusively reduced to institutional practises. The rules of the game that the establishment sets through its legal order and archaic constitution remains one designed to conserve the established order rather than change it in a progressive sense.

As a political force, the *Frente Amplio* is endowed with experience and political reserves that constitute definite assets for contributing to the gestation of social changes and for overcoming the obstacles imposed by the old society of injustice, impunity and privileges. As a political force, it knows how to intelligently relate with the social organisations and operate alongside of them, how to win on the streets, collect the necessary signatures and go on well beyond popular consultations at the polls.

As León Duarte[3] would say, with our programme and political trajectory, we carry Uruguay in our hearts. In government and with political force, we must help social change to flourish by putting it into the streets, informing

---

[3] León Duarte was a leftist labour militant and one of the principal founders of the Party for People's Victory (PVP) when he was forced into exile to Argentina in 1975. A year later, he was kidnapped and disappeared by the security forces of the Argentine Dictatorship as part of the counterinsurgency campaign known as "Operation Condor."

the people and encouraging them to participate and getting them to take ownership of the process. In this way, they can improve our proposals with greater debate, democracy, participation and struggle.

The present day Uruguyan state is the historical product of the prior work of political parties, of the pressure from lobbies both within and outside of the country, of the efforts of trade unions, and very exceptionally, of the demands of its users. This background signifies that it contains elements of a distinct nature. In its most glorious hour, shaped and socialised by the early ideas of Batllism and certain currents of progressive nationalism, it culminated a chance convergence of social commitments among the diverse interests that led to its formation.

For a whole series of reasons too involved to enumerate here, it was not easy to liquidate that relatively successful form of state that was eventually formed out of Batllism. This was a complex blend of elements of nationalism and the demands of workers, all wrapped up in a high degree of corporativism and sustained by a thickly layered system of clientelism from which so many participating politicians had benefited. The fact is that this state, condemned to death by the liberal right, the IMF and the international financial institutions, survived and even in the height of its decadence managed to make proud a good part of its internal detractors who knew better.

The policies of cutting-back on democracy were coincident with the installation of economic neoliberalism and an imposition of anti-state, free market policies that were contrary to all forms of protection over national economic space. Democracy was incompatible with a system in complete submission to the schema developed by an evangelical wave of IMF policies thrust upon the entire region. Operating under a conception that the national economic goal was exclusively limited to complying with creditors, increasing exports and reducing the fiscal deficit, the existing system of social services deteriorated, real salaries were slashed, and the gap between rich and poor expanded. In the face of discontent and resistance provoked by such policies, the state declared "vacations" for democracy as it was cynically referred to during that period.

The application of the neoliberal model implied deep and lasting institutional restrictions. Indeed, the neoliberal recipe permits few witnesses and very few protagonists. Action by the authoritarian state ensured that the people were kept at a distance from all underlying debates. Popular participation was discouraged and any kind of political activity was proscribed if it sought to go beyond the limits set by conservative parties, the submissive press and the obedient bureaucracies. Political decision-making became centralised in Executive Power. The parliament, even before the 1973 Military Coup, was increasingly being deprived of its power.

This in turn deflated the political parties as mechanisms of democratic debate that could meaningfully impact upon state decision-making. This meant that the fewer people present to bear witness to decision-making, the better. The fewer intermediating mechanisms, the smoother was the functioning of power that aimed to impose a plan accurately termed a "conservative remodelling of the country."

Constitutional reforms made up part of that process, favouring the expansion of executive power at the expense of the legislative branch. There were endless state decrees and an increasingly common process of forming "enclaves" where political and administrative decisions were made. Everything tended to reinforce secrecy and the concentration of decision-making power. Absent was any kind of authentic interplay of competing ideas from the political parties, making for a generalised suppression of democratic representativeness within Uruguayan state rule.

Under the dictatorship, the ruling despots that seized the helm of the state apparatus and the public enterprises discarded any worries about winning votes. They ruled by fear and by way of a streamlined hierarchical structure. Supported by liberal politicians such as Végh Villegas,[4] they retook the initiative against the state begun in prior periods. But throughout the country, there was a growing democratic resistance. The "reactionary reform of the state" began to slow and by the 1980s when a "political process of transition" had become initiated towards return to civilian rule, the dismantlement was far from being completed.

The magazine *Búsqueda*[5] saw this with clarity, aided by the virtuous philanthropic vision of the banking community. It advised of the imprudence of initiating a process of political democratisation without having decisively eradicated the remains of paternalistic and corporativist nationalism that persisted in the state. In order to bring forward a plan for a total political opening,

---

[4] Végh Villegas served as Economics Minister and other high level posts during the military dictatorship and is associated with Uruguay's economic liberalisation.
[5] *Búsqueda* (Search) is a rightist news magazine published weekly and founded in 1971, with links to the Sanguinetti and Lacalle governments.

it insisted on the need to continue reforming the state apparatus so as to preclude the partisans of the old form of state from regaining their momentum.

And that is the way it was. From time to time, new peaks were felt in this longstanding pulse. The Lacalle government[6] retook liberal and privatising ideas that were already old in 1903 and pressed the accelerator to the floor. The popular organisations with the *Frente Amplio* at their head managed in 1992 to put the brakes on the Public Enterprises Law that sought to pave an open way to unlimited privatisation.

With the Sanguinetti presidency and above all with the presidency of Jorge Batlle, the pro-U.S. and privatisation project was put back on track. It generated resistance that was so intense and widespread that it fuelled the accumulation of political forces that would later manage to beat the traditional political parties in the referendum of December 2003, opening the way for an electoral victory of the left on October 31, 2004.

After almost fifty years of erosion and sabotage, the state that received the left into government continued being a "state in transition." It is the slow and corrosive result of a displacement towards "non-existence" or exclusive existence at the service of a few privileged economic groups. This is the same state apparatus in which our comrades are now working, attempting to apply a programme of systemic change. The historic task of the *Frente Amplio* has always seen itself as one of resistance and of reversal of the tendencices towards de-nationalisation, privatisation, and the retreat of the state from essential functions. In a word, it favours a sovereign national development strategy with social justice.

Inverting the Established Tendency: The Government of the *Frente Amplio* and its Commitment to Participation

In 2003, it would have been somewhat difficult to imagine that a *Frente Amplio* government along with its progressive allies would have produced an economic programme so well-received by the (very unqualified) authorities of the IMF, at least not without an intense and highly public process of negotiation. This was surprising. It was going to be difficult to think that we would abandon our opposition to the established economic model after so many

---

[6] Luis Alberto Lacalle of the National Party was President of Uruguay between 1990–1995.

years of struggle. The programme of the *Frente Amplio* did not limit itself merely to a commitment to increased social spending, the recovery of the country's productive model, greater redistribution of the national rent and combating social exclusion. Rather, it included as a central aspect what was called the "democratisation of society and the state," i.e., increasing political transparency and citizen participation in the formulation of public policies. That is to say, it brought forth the same posture put forward in the years when the *Frente Amplio* administered Montevideo beginning in 1990. It was during that time when Tabaré Vasquez and Mariano Arana developed the banner of participation and decentralisation. Both leaders of the *Frente* participated more than once in a dialogue with neighbours about issues related to the public budget. This period constituted a unique democratic experience and was something that had a lot to do with the electoral victories that have occurred since then.

In contrast, the Parliamentary discussions of the national budget now taking place have involved very few who actually participated in its elaboration. Now that the budgetary parameters have begun to publicly reveal themselves, discussion has shifted to confrontation in the Judicial Branch, with the FUCVAM,[7] and among distinct civil society associations where organised protest has begun to appear. To the delight of our adversaries, the government has complied with the IMF. But before broad sectors of the society, the cutbacks in public spending will result in especially contentious public debate. This discontent will have been reinforced by the expedited and technocratic treatment of those decisions taken. Such policies require far more open political dialogue with the larger society, including with the political forces participating in the governing front, and greater flexibility in their implementation.

To put forward the kinds of changes that constitute our reason for existing, the *Frente Amplio* will need to appeal to the active support of the citizenry. A tributary reform that favours the workers and the poorest social sectors will necessarily come down upon the rich sectors of speculative capital and high income earners off the national rent. This will require a process of open national debate similar to the experience when the popular referendum

---

[7] FUCVAM is a popular and broad based Uruguayan cooperative federation made up of hundreds of base cooperatives working around popular housing and urban development issues throughout the country. It was founded in 1970.

in defence of the public enterprises was carried out and won, or when the drive to privatise ANCAP, the state petroleum distribution company was beaten back.

Without political information and mobilisation, the democratic capacities of the citizenry begin to languish. The state from where governance is still exercised and might continue to be exercised for a good long time remains highly conditioned by the old practises that almost led to its definitive collapse. The control and cleaning up of its intermediate levels of authority cannot be indefinitely postponed. If in key areas, the state apparatus remains hostile, those who have an absolute majority in the Parliament must proceed to enact laws that are capable of removing the obstacles to participatory democratic governance.

There are, for example, pockets of resistance to the progressive and egalitarian transformations in health that are required in Uruguay. There remains some doubt that the majority of the population supports the government's plans to establish a national system of health insurance. What role can the *Frente Amplio* and its militants play in the dissemination of these proposals? What role must it assume in the organisation of the prospective users of such a plan? How can it act to ensure the defence of public health that today remains so intolerably inaccessible?

Openness to Public Opinion Strengthens Rather than Weakens

The majority decision by the *Frente Amplio* government (EP-NM) with respect to the participation of the Armed Forces in *Operación Unitas*[8] displayed serious errors and left behind unnecessary fractures. In fact, the way in which authorisation was solicited from the Parliament did not allow for a discussion that could have sat well with us. There is a wide diversity of opinions within the democratic organisms making up the *Frente Amplio*, including a very strong opposition to participation in *Operación Unitas.* Indeed, everything would seem to indicate that the issue was not discussed with adequate participation even within the various constituent political parties. Nor was

---

[8] Operation *Unitas* refers to annual joint military exercises conducted by the United States Southern Command in coordination with South American military forces that have been held since 1959.

sufficient margin allowed for a serious discussion in the Parliament. The fact is that having an absolute majority in both parliamentary houses does not exempt us from the obligation of hearing arguments regarding our proposals.

There is an expression in fashion these days that is repeatedly heard to the point of almost sounding ridiculous in this context: "The country should carry out a broad discussion about each and every problem." Meanwhile, things go on being resolved in their customary way, some in an effective manner and many of which reflect positions democratically agreed upon for a long time within the *Frente Amplio*. But in other cases, such as with Uruguay's participation in *Operación Unitas*, the decision involved a big turnaround on what has been our position for decades. It was a moment that even if a nationwide discussion was not going to be had, at least a discussion that touched upon the connotations of this decision would have if nothing else helped us to explain it to the Uruguayan people.

In allusion to this "expedient" style of abruptly and drastically resolving issues and deferring broader debate, some commentators have used the term "political realism." The idea is that "there may be some errors or backsliding along the way, but in general terms, things are going rather well." "Besides, the people agree with us as the opinion surveys indicate." But I do not think that this is realism. It is instead a recourse to pragmatism and the politics of the "possible," especially with an eye towards the elections of 2009. Meanwhile, the idea is to continue doing what can be done in accordance with people's prevailing mood. A different attitude is therefore put forth in other areas such as in the Ministries of Health, Labour, Social Security and Interior with respect to a law for humanising the prison system.

This pattern of reasoning in terms of "what is possible" does not take into account the reality that the political force of the *Frente Amplio* is a democratic factor that is fundamental as a generator of the state of opinion for a considerable sector of the population. In the conformation of political moods that are contrary to progressive transformation, there are factors in play that are controlled by others who do not share consensus with our programme.

The pragmatic pursuit of "the possible" is a conception that if applied goes against everything that the left in the country has struggled for, especially the *Frente Amplio* itself. Of course, what might provide bread today can result in hunger tomorrow. There has been considerable talk about discontent among the base elements of the *Frente Amplio*, of widespread defections and of a presumed divorce unfolding between the *Frente's* leadership and its militants.

Curiously, there are those who also speak in name of a supposed "post-modernity" in referring to militancy and ideological identification as arte-facts of the past and as something that a modern left should have thrown in the garbage a long time ago.

In any case, the culminating point of tension in this early phase rested in the Parliamentary debate for authorisation as requested by the Executive authority of participation in *Operación Unitas* by the Uruguayan Armed Forces. It was a traumatic process that put the left in a bad position. In fact, only the conduct displayed by Deputy Chifflet[9] represented the feelings of the major-ity of the ranks within the *Frente Amplio*.

One of the keys to a way out is that the government will have to accept critiques and seek to correct its positions and non-participatory style of work. For their part, the militants of the *Frente Amplio* will have to increase their activity in defence of the real achievements that this government has been accomplishing step-by-step while also generating others on their own.

What we cannot do is allow incomprehension and demobilisation to pre-vail. A large part of what must be done will require struggle at various lev-els. This means a struggle of ideas, increased popular mobilisation, the denunciation of privileges, and the demoralisation of those authoritarian remnants that survive within the state, among others. How can all of this be done if we do not remain united in the struggle?

It is essential to remain conscious of what is in play. One thing is the var-ious errors and internal ripples within our government and another is the advantageous positioning that the rightist forces wish to obtain from these circumstances. At stake here is the ability to deepen the real significance of a fundamental fact, namely, that the left came to power in the elections of October 2004 and this marks a transcendental shift in the country's history.

If assuming charge of the state apparatus is a hitherto unexplored and dis-orienting experience for the left, the fact of others being pushed far from it provokes desperation among those who were previously accustomed to occu-pying the spaces of privilege. Although for now this is something merely symbolic, it can eventually evolve into something far more dangerous.

---

[9] Guerrermo Chifflet of the Socialist Party of Uruguay broke ranks with the lead-ership of the *Frente Amplio* and voted against authorizing the President's request for participation in the U.S. led military exercises.

A Popular Programme and the Factors of Retreat

The realisation of the programme for change that was put forth by the left shares a close relationship with the deepening of democracy. We begin from the premise that the commitment for building another Uruguay, one of justice, welfare and freedom, is possible and that it is being put into practise. The fulfilment of this commitment to change brings with it the need to expand citizen participation in the treatment of issues of public interest. In the face of secrecy, communication must be strengthened. In place of the concentration of decision-making power in the executive branch, there must be greater openness in the representative levels of the Parliament, the Departmental Boards, the Local Boards, and the Neighbourhood Councils.

The broadening of new collective spaces for social participation with the presence of workers and citizens in the development of management is essential. It should take place in the public enterprises as is envisioned in the reforms being put forward in the health care sector, or with the participation of teachers in management of the institutions of public learning. This widening of popular participation implies effort and dedication. Democratising public decisions requires a dedication of more time and energy than does the style of decision-making that remains concentrated in the hands of executive state organs. Convincing takes more effort than ordering and it takes much more time than sending in the police to break up a local being occupied by strikers. Being on the left ultimately means convincing people.

The decisions adopted in socially embedded levels with the presence of cooperative organisations, civil society associations, neighbourhood groups, cultural organisations and others, demands the strength and resources of that which has been engendered and cultivated out of society's roots. Those decisions are born with the comprehension and support of the community, conscious of the foundations of the norms and decisions of the government.

A progressive government must not repeat the same patterns of imposition that characterised the neoliberal administrations. In order to overcome the resistance of conservative forces and the political and economic interests of North American imperialism, something which still finds considerable expression in the established economic powers, the mass media and in management, the logic of change demands that the left win over the greatest possible number of supporters for its popular transformational project.

There is a need to construct lines of communication that inform and clarify, that encourages interest in participating and contributes to organising it, and that demonstrates the reality, opinions and above all its context and its background. We intend to represent a national project that is distinct and antagonistic to that which we legitimately overthrew on October 31, 2004. The popular character of the programme that this government stands for is well-established. The search on the part of the administration in matters both large and small is for favourable solutions to the problems of the poorest, the workers and the excluded.

Some of these steps being taken are relatively small given the gravity of the situation such as the efforts that are being undertaken by way of the Emergency Plan. But they have a profound significance for they help demonstrate the fact that for the first time, a government recognises the seriousness of the existing misery and seeks to repair the weakest links of the chain. The rendering of the free student ticket in the greater metropolitan area has been an important achievement. What a struggle it has been for over 30 to 40 years for the student movement to win this!

Other acts having even greater importance include the convocation of the Wage Councils that represent hundreds of thousands of workers. Importantly, it also covers domestic workers now and for the first time. There are new unions, stronger associations, and more challenges for transmitting to new generations that which has been learned over a long period of years of struggle and sacrifice. In the same vein falls the decision to protect trade union rights and to prevent the dislodging of union locals when they are being occupied by workers in exercise of their right to strike. These policies still remain virtual in a certain sense but they are decisive steps in an important process of an organisational strengthening of the working class. Clearly, this is something quite central in a process of the accumulation of forces.

The organisation and struggle on the part of workers is a factor that tends to order the entirety of political affairs. That which organises is progressive while that which divides and demoralises is not. At the same time, there are elements of stagnation at various levels. The most transcendental have been the commitments assumed with the IMF that are being carefully complied with. The process of wagering on foreign private investment, defended as the "only path" to economic progress, threatens to abort any national productive project. The government may elicit praise from the galleries of neoliberalism but these are not our allies nor will they ever be. Rather, they are diplomatic representatives of the dominant interests that rule an ever more unjust world and who wield impositions ever more difficult to withstand by peripheral countries such as ours.

The gradualist line which aims to "not make waves" before the eyes of the defenders of the imperial order is a silhouette that might for a period have proved useful in dissolving "public alarm," the fear of radical change and the "imminence of chaos" in the event that the left would arrive to government. All of this was trumpeted by the right but it has not managed to deprive the government of its popular support.

A line of polemics now arises with all that is involved with developing and demanding greater participation of the base of the *Frente Amplio*. The base must above all demand the changes that are still to come. This government may be one of little and slow changes but it should leave no doubt that it will be a government of changes and one destined to reverse the legacy of selling out and impoverishment that earlier administrations have left behind.

Conclusion: Discord and Division are Luxuries that We Cannot Afford

A large part of the battles that are appearing on the horizon will require a change in the level of popular participation in everyday political decision-making and the overall public climate. In order to overcome the remains of the bureaucratic state, it will be necessary to have debate and to create an effervescent climate among the popular sectors that does not presently appear to exist. This is true, for example, in the implementation of a new health care model or in carrying out a tributary reform as a means of redistributing national income. All of this will require external and internal debates and given the certainty that resistance will have to be overcome, popular mobilisations will be necessary. There will have to be a struggle against the remaining pockets of managerial privilege that persist in the public enterprises. Laws will need to be created that can put an end to the dangerous remnants of the national security doctrine still present in the Armed Forces. There will have to be support for the factories that are already being managed by their own workers or that will be in the future.

For all of these battles of ideas and political polemics, greater information will be necessary in order to ensure a more organic life of the popular organisations and greater infusion of citizen participation in the debates. In this essay, I have alluded to the example of the health care programme that the government is formulating. In the national debate that is taking shape, who will carry greater weight? The professional groups that have enriched themselves by transforming medicine into a pedestrian business, or the million or more Uruguayans that lack any kind of medical attention?

To pose the question is to answer it. The very existence of a situation of injustice and inequality with regard to the enjoyment of an essential human right such as health care calls upon us members of the *Frente Amplio* to place ourselves at the side of those who will be redressed by the new health programme. Putting it another way, we have the obligation to cultivate a certain measure of independence from the way that government is conducted on a day to day basis. We must demand information and ensure debate from our own comrades, and we must insist on uniting forces in order to move forward in ensuring transformations towards greater justice and equality. There have been mistakes made and some of the family crystal has been broken but the world does not end there. It is only just beginning.

Part III: Contradictions of Domination and Resistance

The Cuban Revolution's first generation of Social Workers

James Petras and Henry Veltmeyer

Social Movements and the State: Political Power Dynamics in Latin America[1]

Introduction

Economic and social development requires changes in the structure of class relations and the configuration of political power. The question is how to bring about these changes. This question continues to bedevil social and political analysis, and politics, notwithstanding the plethora of sociological and political studies into, and decades of theorizing about, the political dynamics of class struggles and power relations in different contexts and conjunctures. Related questions that also remain unsettled include questions about the organisational form that social change should take and the politics involved. Change at what pace and in what direction? On the basis of what agency and strategy? Despite the many theoretical probes into these dynamics, such questions remain at issue in a series of theoretical and political debates on changes in class relations and political power. But what is clear is the dominant view that the road towards social change and the transformation of class structures is paved with political power. Also the central issue remains control of the state, the major repository of political power in

[1] This work appeared earlier in *Critical Sociology*, Volume 32, N° 1, 2006, pp. 83–104.

regards to both the allocation of society's productive resources and the coercive power with which to enforce its decisions and policies.

With particular reference to developments in Latin America it is possible to identify three basic modalities of *social change* and *political power*. One is electoral politics – the pursuit of political power on the basis of political parties, which, as Max Weber noted years ago, were formed for this purpose. Another involves the construction of social movements. Unlike political parties social movements are not organised to pursue power as such. Although they are clearly engaged in the struggle over state power this struggle is an inescapable consequence of their quest for social change and anti-systemic politics of mass mobilisation. A third way of "doing politics" (social change via political power) in the context of developments in the 1980s and 1990s) entails social action in the direction of local development. This form of politics seeks to bring about social change (and a process of economic and social development, i.e., improvements in the lives of the poor) not through a confrontation with the structure and agencies of political power but through the accumulation of social capital (the capacity of the poor to network and organise collectively) within the local spaces available within this structure. This concept of "social capital" is central to and defines the dominant approach towards social change in the mainstream of development theory and practice within the framework of the neoliberal model (Dasgupta and Serageldin 2000; Harris, 2001; Woolcock and Narayan 2000).[2]

While the electoral road to political power requires conformity to a game designed and played by members of "the political class," social movements generally take a confrontational approach towards change and pursue a strategy of mass mobilisation of the forces of resistance against the system and the political regime that supports it. In this context, structural and political dynamics are polarised between two fundamentally different approaches

---

[2] The World Bank, the Inter-American Bank and other such organisations involved in the process of "international cooperation for development, a project that can be traced back to the post Second World War geopolitical concern that countries might be tempted towards a socialist path of national development, have elaborated variations of an approach, a model of development based on the accumulation of "social capital." The literature on this approach towards social change and economic development is voluminous, most of it supportive. For a critical perspective on this model and the "social capital" approach towards development (micro-projects) and politics (local democracy and governance) see, inter alia, Harris (2001), McLean et al. (2002) and Schuller (2000).

towards social change and political power. The action dynamics of this political option – *reform or revolution* in the classical formulation, or, *local development versus social movements*, in our recontextualised formulation – are not new. With diverse permutations they can be traced out across Latin America. What perhaps *is* new are the dynamics of change associated with the advance of an alternative social or non-political approach – a "new way of doing politics" associated with the rise of grassroots, community forms of social organisation and local development. The dynamics of this approach is a central issue in political developments across Latin America today. The authors have come to this conclusion on the basis of a systematic comparative analysis of the relationship between the state and social movements in four countries: Argentina – Brazil, Bolivia and Ecuador (Petras and Veltmeyer 2005). A summary of considerations that led us to this conclusion is presented below.

The Capitalist State in Latin America

The neoliberal model is predicated on a minimalist state – withdrawal of the state from the process of economic and social development and its replacement with the "free market," a structure supposedly freed from the constraints of government regulation and other interferences in the normal workings of a system in its allocation of society's productive resources (to determine "who gets what," or, in the language of economics, securing an appropriate "return" to each factor of production). Conditions for this retreat of the state emerged in the early 1980s, following the first round of neoliberal policies linked to the region-wide external debt and fiscal crisis. The first neoliberal experiments were led by military regimes in the southern cone of South America (Chile, Argentina, Uruguay) under conditions of a "dirty war" against "subversives" (unionists, political activists, etc.).

A second round of neoliberal reforms, implemented under conditions of "redemocratisation" (the rule of law, constitutionally elected civilian regimes and the emergence and strengthening of "civil society" (a sphere of groups and associations between the family and the state). This round of "reforms" allowed for and induced the widespread transfer of property, productive resources and incomes from the working class and the mass of direct producers to an emerging capitalist class of investors and entrepreneurs. With the popular classes experiencing the brunt of the sweeping structural reforms associated with the "new economic model" (neoliberal free market capitalist development) and bearing most of its social costs (social inequalities, unemployment, low income, social exclusion and poverty), widespread discontent spawned several waves of protest movements directed against the system. The neoliberal policy regimes became ungovernable, generating pressures to move beyond the Washington consensus. The outcome was the construction of a new policy regime – a neoliberal programme of macroeconomic policies combined with a new anti-poverty social policy and the institutionality of a "new economic model" (Bulmer-Thomas, 1996).

Parts of this model, such as a policy of administrative decentralisation and a social policy that targets the poor for reduced public resources (a "new social investment fund"), were widely implemented in the 1990s. Other elements of this model, such as the municipalisation of development and a system of "democratic or local" governance based on the "participation" of civil society ("stakeholders" in the development process) were experimented with on a relatively limited basis, primarily in Bolivia (Palma Carbajal 1995; Ardaya 1995; BID 1996; Blair 1997; Booth 1996).

These experiments constituted a third round of neoliberal policies but yielded few positive results in terms of economic growth and social development. By the end of the decade (the 1990s) and into the new millennium economic growth rates across Latin America were far from "robust," a far cry from the prosperity and economic growth promised by the World Bank and the ideologies of neoliberal capitalist development. Indeed, ECLAC, a UN agency that over the years has led the search for an alternative to the (neo)liberal model, was compelled by the growing evidence of sluggish and negative growth rates and a propensity towards economic crisis (in the late 1990s, after two decades of neoliberal reforms) to project "a new decade lost to development." "Others erstwhile supportive of the new economic model were constrained to recognise the fundamental dysfunctionality of the neoliberal model and the need for fundamental reform of the reform process – and ultimately to move beyond the Washington Consensus" (Burki and Perry 1998; Stiglitz 2002).

As evidenced by the country case studies conducted by the authors, the neoliberal form of capitalist development is not only economically dysfunctional but profoundly exclusionary in social terms and politically unsustainable. A decade of state-led reforms to the model has not fundamentally changed the Washington Consensus on macroeconomic policy. Nor has it changed the character of capitalist development in the region. Two decades of neoliberal reforms have resulted in deepening social inequalities, the spread of poverty and conditions of social crisis and disorganisation. Even Carlos Slim, Mexico's major contribution to the Forbes billion dollar club, and one of the region's greatest beneficiaries of the neoliberal reform process, has joined the chorus of negative voices levelled against "new economic model," viewing it as not only dysfunctional in economic terms but inherently ungovernable. This conclusion, to which, as it happens, a number of economists at the World Bank and other international organisations involved in the development project, suspected all along, has fuelled a widespread search for "another form of development," a decentralised and participatory form of local development based on more sustainable forms of "democratic" or "good" *governance* (Blair 1997; Bowles and Gintis 1999; Dominguez and A. Lowenthal 1996; Goss 2001; World Bank, 1994). The result has been a veritable flood of proposals and alternative models for bringing about "development" on the basis of social capital, i.e., though the agency of "self-help" of community-based or grassroots organisations, with the assistance and support of partner institutions and "international cooperation" for development (Dasgupta and Serageldin 2000; Hooghe and Ditelin Stolle 2003; Woolcock and Narayan 2000).[3]

Social Movements versus the State

A decade of efforts to give the neoliberal reform process in Latin America a human face has failed. But what is needed is not simply a move "beyond the Washington Consensus" towards face-saving reforms of the model. A redesign of the structural adjustment programme is not the solution. What is needed is a social revolution that will change class relations, property relations and the class character of the state. We establish this conclusion in the form of several propositions elaborated as follows:

1. *Capitalism in its social and institutional forms is "the enemy," but in the current historical context the neoliberal state is the major locus of class struggle.*

State power is generally defined in terms of an "authoritative allocation of society's productive resources." But what sets the state apart from other

---

[3] Harris (2001) is one of few authors to provide a critical perspective on the World Bank's construction of this concept of "social capital." See also Veltmeyer (2002).

institutions is control over coercive power, or in the language of social science, its monopoly over the instruments of coercion and repression in its defined function of maintaining "political order." The state has a range of powers but, as demonstrated by our review of state-social movement dynamics (Petras and Veltmeyer, 2005), ultimately it is backed up by force. This fact has been well established in theory and the social movements are all too aware of it in practice. In each of the following cases – Lula in Brazil, Kirchner in Argentina, De Lozada and Mesa in Bolivia, and Gutiérrez in Ecuador – the coercive apparatus of the state has been systematically directed against the social movements. In this context state coercion has not been a matter of last resort, as viewed by so many analysts in the liberal tradition – a justifiable exercise of state power. Coercion or repression is part of an arsenal of weapons used by the political class to control the movements – to weaken them in their struggle for change in policy or social transformation. It is the range of powers that defines the relationship of the state to the social movements.

This proposition is confirmed by a review of the dynamics that surround the relationship between the state and the social movements in Argentina, Brazil, Bolivia and Ecuador (Petras and Veltmeyer, 2005). In the context of the political dynamics examined by the authors, the relationship of the state to social movements can be defined (and is structured) in terms of the following strategies:

(i) Setting up *parallel organisations* to class-based anti-systemic organisations, such as peasant organisations and unions, that have non-confrontational politics;[4]

(ii) *repression* of class-based organisations with an anti-systemic agenda under certain circumstances and where possible or necessary;[5]

---

[4] The creation of a parallel organisation typically involves staged elections for a new board of directors. Government agencies or the courts then award the organisation's legal identity (along with offices, bank accounts and other resources) to a favoured faction, whether it represents the membership.

[5] Governments in the region have frequently resorted to repression as a means of demobilising organisations with an anti-systemic agenda. At times, it has involved the full weight of the state's repressive apparatus as in the dirty war orchestrated by a coalition of armed forces and a series of authoritarian-bureaucratic or military regimes in the Southern Cone of South America against the labour movement in the 1970s. In other conjunctures, as in Ecuador in the mid-1980s, the instruments of state terror and repression were wielded against the working class by regimes that are formally democratic. In this conjuncture – and other such conjunctures in the 1980s in Bolivia, Venezuela and elsewhere, involving conditions of a brutal repression – radical oppo-

(iii)   a process of dialogue and negotiating with representatives of class-based organisations with the capacity to mobilise forces of opposition and resistance (FARC in Colombia, MST in Brazil, EZLN in Mexico);

(iv)   *Accommodating* the leadership to policies of economic, social and political reform, often with the mediation of NGOs;[6]

(v)   *pacifying* belligerent organisations on the basis of a reform agenda, a partnership approach and a populist politics of appeasement and clientelism;

(vi)   *strengthening organisations within civil society* that have a reformist orientation and a democratic agenda, and weakening organisations with an anti-systemic agenda, a confrontational direct-action approach in their politics;[7] and, when all else fails

(vii)   *incorporating* groups with an anti-systemic agenda into policy-making forums and institutions.

---

sition to the government's neoliberal agenda, led at the time by the labour movement, was disarticulated and demobilised, weakening and close to destroying working-class political organisations in the process (Editorial, *Boletin ICCI*, Vol. 1, No. 8, November 1999). As it happens, in the case of Ecuador, the repression and destruction of the labour movement's capacity to challenge the government's agenda coincided with the emergence and formation of CONAIE which, in the 1990s, would take over leadership of the popular struggle.

   [6] In the context of conditions found throughout the region in the 1990s, a marked development and trend was toward the disarticulation of class-based organisations and a demobilisation of the forces that they had accumulated and mobilised. The dynamics of this political demobilisation are not well studied or understood, and there are doubtless many factors involved. However, it is also doubtless the case that a combination of strategies pursued and implemented by governments in the region, and with the support of both outside or international organisations and NGOs within, was a critical factor in the widespread demobilisation of many social movements in the 1990s. This factor is clearly evident in the case of the *Alianza Democratica de Campesinos* (ADC), which in the post-civil war context of El Salvador emerged as the most representative and dynamic social movement of peasants organised around the issues of land redistribution and indebtedness. As a coalition of diverse peasant organisations, the ADC initially pushed its land reform agenda through a politics of direct action (land invasions, marches and so forth) but was soon constrained to operate within the framework of reforms established through the peace accords. Under these conditions, and with the active support of the *Frente Farabundo Marti de Liberación Nacional* (FMLN), transformed from a belligerent armed force into a left-wing political party, the struggle for cancellation of the land and bank debts was more or less resolved in political-legal terms (through legislation) in the interest of the beneficiaries of the first phase of the government's land reform programme. However, all direct and even indirect action on the land issue was definitively stalled by a politics of economic development projects funded by the World Bank and other donor agencies and executed through NGOs. On some dynamics of this process, see Veltmeyer (2005).

   [7] This strategy was pursued and implemented by all multilateral and bilateral development agencies in the 1990s.

2. *In the context of electoral politics mass parties are transformed into parties "of the system" – pro-business, beholden to the "Washington Consensus" on appropriate macroeconomic policy.*

The best case of this proposition can be found in the transformation of the Workers Party (PT) from a "party of the masses" into a "party of big business." This outcome is the result of the long term, large-scale structural changes *within* the party and in its relationship to the state. The decisive shift in this case, as in the case of developments in Bolivia related to the *Movimiento al Socialismo* (MAS), is from mass popular social struggles to electoral politics. In this evolution the PT became an "institutional party," embedded in all levels of the capitalist state, and attracting as a result a large number of petit bourgeois professionals (lawyers, professors, journalists), trade union bureaucrats, upwardly mobile ex-guerrilla, ex-revolutionaries recycled into the electoral arena. A process of substitutionism takes place. Here the electoral apparatus replaces the popular assemblies, elected officials displace the leaders of the social movements, and the institutional manoeuvres of the national political leaders in congress substitute for the direct action of the trade union and social movements.

The historical and empirical data demonstrate that elitist electoral leaders *embedded* in the institutional structures of the capitalist state end up competing with the other bourgeois parties over who can best administer the interest of the foreign and domestic, agrarian and financial elites. But the fundamental change in the shift of mass parties towards electoral and institutional politics is found in its class composition: it tends to become the party of ambitious *upwardly mobile* lower middle class professionals whose *social reference* is the capitalist class. Both political developments in Brazil and Bolivia provide evidence for this assertion. Behind these developments can be found a change in *class consciousness* that reflects a change in *material conditions* of the elected politicians. Under these conditions, depending on the capacity of these Leftist labour-oriented politicians to garner voting support among the working class, landless workers and urban *favelados* become bargaining chips to negotiate favours with big business.

The "new class" of electoral politicians tends to look *upward* and to their *future* ruling class colleagues, not *downward* and to their former working class comrades. A similar development seems to occur inside the trade union movement in its relationship to the state. In the case of Brazil under Lula, for example, upwardly mobile trade union officials look upward to becoming congressional candidates and ministers, or administrating pension funds rather than downward to organizing the unemployed, the urban poor in general strikes with the employed workers. The PT's transformation into a party of international capital was accompanied by the transformation of the major trade union confederation – the CUT – from an independent class-based union into more or less an appendage of the Ministry of Labour. The CUT in this context followed the PT along the path of "state institutionalisation" and "substitutionism" as the national leaders pre-empt the factory assemblies in making decisions and relocate activities from the streets to the offices of the Labour Ministry. Thus the parallel transformation of the PT and CUT avoided any rupture between them, a development that has not been followed in Bolivia. However, there are political forces in Bolivia that follow the Brazilian example.

The key theoretical point from this analysis is that the bourgeoisification of "working class" or "socialist" parties is not the inevitable consequence of globalisation. Rather it is the result of changing class ideology, the internal dynamics of party politics – changes that lead to institutional assimilation and, ultimately, subordination to the dominant sectors of the ruling class. This conclusion points to the profound limitation of electoral institutional politics as a vehicle for social transformation or even consequential reforms. Social transformation is far more likely to occur from the direct action of independent class based social political movements oriented toward transforming the institutional basis of bourgeois state power.

3. *Electoral politics is a trap designed to demobilise the forces of resistance and opposition*

This proposition is amply demonstrated by political developments in every country case that we have examined, and particularly in Bolivia, Brazil and Ecuador. In their efforts to advance the struggle for political power, many social movements seek a strategic or tactical alliance with electoral political parties, as with the MST and the PT, or, as with CONAIE in the case of Ecuador (*Pachakutik*) or MAS and MIP in the case of Bolivia. In this alliance, the social movements evolve and are transformed into a political instrument for the purpose of influencing regime policy within the system. As regards the outcome of this evolution the conclusion is clear. It is invariably at the expense of the popular movement, whose forces of resistance and opposition rather than being brought to bear against the power structure are dissipated and demobilised. *Pachakutik* in Ecuador provides a good exemplar of this development but to appreciate its theoretical and political significance we cannot do better than turn to Bolivia.

Our studies into ostensibly "progressive" regimes with links to the social movements and neoliberalism suggest that electoral regimes, no matter what their social base or ideological orientation, inevitably became integrated into, and subordinate to, the imperial system. The result is that social movements and their members are blocked from achieving even their minimum goals.

Take the case of Ecuador. The petroleum workers and CONAIE, through its electoral arm *Pachakuti*, in the conjuncture of political developments that followed the 2000 indigenous uprising, entered into an electoral alliance with Lucio Gutiérrez and his *Sociedad Patriotica*. Upon taking office, catapulted into power on the basis of this alliance, Gutierrez embraced a policy of privatisation of petroleum as well as the policies of the IMF, FTAA and Plan Colombia. Gutiérrez repressed the petroleum workers and turned the government's back on the indigenous movement (betrayed it, in the conception of CONAIE at its National congress in 2004). The result was a much weakened Petroleum Union, a discredited *Pachakutik*, and a seriously weakened and divided CONAIE.

In Bolivia, Evo Morales, the leader of the *cocaleros* and the Movement to Socialism (MAS), like so many electoral politicians and parties after some advances, turned to the right. In the wake of the October 2003 uprising, in which he was notably absent, Morales supported the pro-imperialist, neoliberal regime of Carlos Mesa, playing a major role in dividing and attacking any large-scale mobilisations in favour of nationalising petroleum. Our analysis of diverse electoral regimes suggests that this development is not in the least surprising. It is the built into electoral politics, the inevitable result of its dynamics. In the case of Evo Morales his politics is undoubtedly geared to his quest to win the 2005 Presidential election, a prospect that many analysts today see as increasingly unlikely given the mechanics of Bolivia's electoral politics (the need for a second round of voting should no candidate achieve over 50% in the first round).

Political developments in Brazil suggests that no matter the situation or electoral prospects once a popular movement turns towards electoral politics it is constrained to play by political rules that sustain the dominant model and, in the current context, the neoliberal agenda. The MST in this context has not suffered the same debacle as CONAIE, because only a few members

were in the government and it managed to retain a sufficient degree of autonomy so as to maintain the loyalty of its members. Also, unlike the *cocaleros*
in Bolivia, the MST is not dominated by a single electorally ambitious per-
sonality and is sufficiently grounded in class politics to avoid becoming a
tool of the bourgeois state. Nevertheless the MST's confidence in Lula and
ties with the "Left" of the PT has undermined its opposition to Lula's reactionary attack on pensions, minimum wage, the IMF pact and military support of US colonial occupation of Haiti. The danger here is that by continuing
to give "critical" support to a discredited regime the MST will suffer the same
discredit, a lesson that CONAIE has learnt all too well.

4. *Local development provides micro solutions to micro problems, designed as a*
   means of eluding a confrontation with the power structure and substantive social
   change

The best exemplars of this proposition are found in Bolivia and Ecuador. This
is in part because of the "indigenous factor" in the national politics of these
two countries. In both cases indigenous communities have demonstrated the
greatest capacity for mobilizing the forces of resistance and opposition, organising some of the most dynamic social movements in the region. For this reason the World Bank and the IDB targeted the indigenous communities and
the social movements based on them as the object of what amounts to an
anti-insurgency strategy: local development in the form of micro-projects of
poverty alleviation.

Given the established dysfunctionality of the neoliberal model, and the tendency of this model to undermine democracy and generate destabilising
forces of resistance in the form of social movements, the architects and
guardians of the "new world order" have turned towards "local development" (micro-projects) as *the* solution (to the neoconservative problem of
ungovernability). The World Bank in this context finances nongovernmental
organisations (NGOs) within the "third sector" of "civil society" as agents of
"local development" and "good governance" – to combat the emergence of
mass movements.

The first step in this strategy (Imparato 2003; Tussie 2000; World Bank 2004)
was to establish at the level of the state an appropriate institutional-admin-
istrative-legal framework. The next step was to enlist the services of the NGOs,
converting them into front-line agents of the "development project" (poverty
alleviation) and, in the process, into missionaries of micro-reform. The NGOs

provided the imperialist organisations cooperating in the development project entry into the local communities. The micro-reforms and NGOs promoted a pacific or "civil" (non-confrontational) form of politics, turning the rural poor away from the social movements into local self-help "projects" funded (and designed) from above and the outside. It also created local conditions for an adjustment to the discipline of globalisation and its governance requirements – to create local conditions of imperial governance. In this context Heloise Weber (2002: 146) could write of micro-finance and micro-credit as a "coherent set of tools that may facilitate as well as govern the globalisation agenda." From "the perspective of the architects of global development," she adds, "the micro-credit agenda (and thus, the 'poverty alleviation' strategy of the World Bank – 'Sustainable Banking with the Poor') . . . is conducive to facilitating policy changes at the local level according to the logic of globalisation . . . while at the same time advancing its potential to discipline locally in the global governance agenda" (Weber, 2002: 146). With reference to these developments we can well conclude that the official discourse on "civil society" is little more than an ideological mask for an imperialist agenda – to secure the political conditions for neoliberal capitalist development.

5. *Mass mobilisation is the revolutionary way to political power – and the only way towards social change*

Political developments in every country case examined by the authors confirm what has long been a truism in Marxist class analysis. At issue in the class struggle is political power in the form of the state. Each advance in this struggle has been associated with mobilisational politics while the recourse to electoral politics in each case has perpetuated the status quo.

In no Latin American country are the conditions of a revolutionary situation as well developed as in Bolivia. At the moment, at the time of this writing (June 2004), the swell and rising tide of revolutionary ferment has abated but this could very well be the calm before the storm to come, which is to say, Bolivia presents us with the possibility of a truly revolutionary movement with all of its trials and tribulations.

However, to advance the popular movement in a revolutionary direction certain conditions are required. First, the popular movement needs to coalesce around a powerful organisation of insurgent forces. In the case of Bolivia an organisation with the greatest potential in this regard is the COB, an organisation that has uniquely managed to both represent politically and advance the interests of both organised workers and indigenous peasants. A major source of COB's political potential is its organisational structure, a single structure of affiliation at the provincial, departmental (regional) and national level with a demonstrated capacity for bringing together and concentrating the collective action and mobilisations of diverse sectors of the popular movement.

Notwithstanding its historic failures and limitations, the COB in the current conjuncture has the potential of constituting a critical mass of insurgent forces and to mobilise them into a movement that could potentially not only bring down the Mesa government but also change the course of Bolivia's history. At issue here are three factors. One is the form of organisation. Another is leadership. A third critical factor is an appropriate and effective strategy and associated tactics, particularly as regards selected forms of struggle and political alliances. In this regard, the COB has to combine with other revolutionary forces, particularly those constituted by the *Aymara* indigenous proletariat of El Alto, organised by CTUCB and presently under the command of Felipe Quispe. A second requirement is that the working class, led by COB, needs to unite their struggle with the indigenous movement and the broader popular movement. MAS to some extent provides a political condition of such unity, COB less so in that it is precisely the division between different sectors of organised labour and the indigenous movement that has tended to and still divides COB, weakening its political responses to the government's macroeconomic policy. A third requirement for the Bolivian revolution is for the base organisations and insurgent forces in the popular movement to break away from the system of electoral politics. The conclusion is inescapable.

The prospect for these developments is difficult to gauge. Some observers see this as "not that difficult." Nevertheless they recognise the formidable obstacles in the significant number of union and movement leaders who dialogue with the government within the framework of a social pact. Other union leaders support the electoral path followed by MAS and the politics of a truce between movement and the government. Others see an even greater obstacle in the diversion of the indigenous communities at the base of the popular movement into a politics of local "autonomous" development and their adhesion to an electoral strategy, not only in regard to the projected takeover of municipal government by MAS but the 2005 presidential elections. In this context, MAS is an important repository of oppositional forces but these forces are tied into the system via electoral politics of incremental reform. Thus the social movement has to contend with not only the forces ranged behind the government but the demobilising approach of a powerful political movement on the Left.

The best if not only hope for the movement is for the rank and file to depose the leaders who are holding the movement back – to leave them behind. This might be possible, in the case of the neoliberal parties of the system bound to a capitalist path to development and neoliberalism. But for MAS this is not so easy, or even possible, unless as recently proposed by ex-MAS Senator Filomen Escóbar, in his battle with Morales, MAS is put under the control of a revitalised COB and thus subordinated to the broader popular movement as one of its major political instruments. But this scenario has various difficulties, not least of which is Evo Morales himself. Having chosen the electoral path towards power – the *toma municipal* in 2004 and the presidency in 2007 – he has not only abandoned the dynamics of mobilisation (the "revolutionary path" towards power, we might say) but any pretension of being a socialist let alone a revolutionary. He knows all too well that a commitment to play by the rules of electoral politics commits him to pursue a capitalist path towards national development should he, as he very well might, eventually be elevated to state power. This is one reason why he turned or swung to the right – to avoid any situation that might jeopardise the viability and survival of the institutions of the capitalist state.

As for Carlos Mesa it is abundantly clear that he is not the progressive reformer that some have made him out to be. Whether it is by ideological conviction, vulnerability to pressures from outside interests, ties to the dominant class, or simply political ambition, he and his regime has to be characterised as fundamentally neoliberal. Thus Mesa has not the slightest intention of negotiating the end of a neoliberal approach towards national policy, even if his government were able to ignore the inexorable pressures exerted by the World Bank, the IMF and the US, i.e., the imperial state. Mesa's predicament, as he himself prefers to see his situation, is how to balance these pressures, and the requirements of good government (with sound policies, etc.), against the conflicting pressures of the popular movement.

On this point, we conclude that the prospect for revolutionary transformation of the country's politics and economics is not distant. We can point towards the likelihood that the contradictions that besets the ruling class and existing regime will continue to generate revolutionary situations of one sort or another. The question is whether or not the revolutionary Left will be able to respond to the challenge provided by these situations. While this remains open-ended several things are clear. One is the critical issue of state power – capture of the greatest repository of political power. Another is that mass mobilisation of insurgent forces, rather than electoral politics – the revolutionary road to state power – is the only viable method and means by which the popular movement can by its own actions bring about substantive social change.

6. Social movements have failed to respond to the revolutionary challenge

Marx along time ago argued that the capitalism in its advance creates its own gravediggers – a working class aware of its exploitation, disposed to overthrow the system. However, he noted, this development requires a revolutionary situation, the conditions of which are objectively given and subjective – structural and political. In several countries we have examined, particularly Bolivia and Ecuador but also Argentina, these conditions have come together a number of times in diverse conjunctures: 19/20 December 2001 in Argentina, 8–19 October 2003 in Bolivia, and January 2000 in Ecuador.

To date in Brazil no such conjuncture has materialised. But at the same time, the presidential elections that brought Lula to state power did create the opportunity for a new regime to use this power to bring about a social transformation. But this would require a socialist regime and Lula's regime is anything but that. In fact, we conclude that a socialist regime cannot take state power this way. Electoral politics binds any party to the system, turning it towards neoliberalism – towards forces that govern the system. Thus, as in the other cases examined, the "moment" of state power as it were – and the "opportunity" of mobilising the forces of resistance against the system – was lost. In the case of Brazil, the reasons for this were predictable given Lula's politics and the class nature of his regime.

In Argentina the struggle for political power has taken a different form. What emerges from the extended and massive popular rebellion is that spontaneous uprising are not a substitute for an organised political movement. The social solidarity formed in the heat of the struggle was impressive but momentary. Little in the way of class solidarity reached beyond the barrio. The parties on the Left and local leaders did little to encourage mass class action beyond the limited boundaries of geography and their own organisation. Even within the organisations, the ideological leaders rose to the top not as expressions of a class-conscious organised base but because of their negotiating capacity in securing work plans or skill in organising. The sudden shifts in loyalties of many of the unemployed – not to speak of the impoverished lower middle class – reflect the limitations of class politics in Argentina. The *piquetero* leaders rode the wave of mass discontent and lived with the illusions of St. Petersburg, October 1917 failing to recognise that there were no worker soviets with class-conscious workers. The crowds came and many left when minimum concessions came in the form of work plans, small increases and promises of more and better jobs.

As in the other countries examined, the domestication of the unemployed workers movement is located in a number of regime strategies. Kirchner in this connection engaged in numerous face-to-face discussions with popular leaders, making sure that the best work plans would go to those who collaborate with the government while making minimal offers to those who remained intransigent. In this context he struck an independent posture in relation to the most outrageous IMF demands while making concessions on key reactionary structural changes imposed by his predecessors. *Lacking an overall strategy and conception of an alternative socialist society*, the majority of the *piquetero* movement was manipulated into accepting micro-economic changes to ameliorate the worst effects of poverty and unemployment, without changing the structure of ownership, income and economic power of bankers, agro-exporters or energy monopolies. The resulting political situation, played out with diverse permutations across Latin America was a variation on the all too dominant theme of local development and reform – and a politics of negotiation and conciliation.

The problem with this style of politics is that the question of *state power* is eluded. In the specific context of Argentina it was simply a declaratory text raised by sectarian leftist groups who proceeded to undermine the organisational context in which challenge for state power would be meaningful. In this they were aided and abetted by a small but vocal sect of ideologues who made a virtue of the political limitations of some of the unemployed by preaching a doctrine of "anti-power" or "no power" – an obtuse mélange of misunderstandings of politics, economics and social power. The emergent leaders of the piquetero movement, engaged in valiant efforts in raising mass awareness of the virtue of extra-parliamentary action, of the vices of the political class, were unable to create an alternate base of institutional power for unifying local movements into a force that could confront state power.

What is clearly lacking in this and other situations is a unified *political organisation* (party, movement or combination of both) with roots in the popular neighbourhoods, capable of creating representative organs that promote *class consciousness* and point toward taking state power. As massive and sustained as the initial rebellious period (December 2001-July 2002) was no effective mass political party or movement emerged. Instead a multiplicity of localised groups with different agendas soon fell to quarrelling over an elusive "hegemony" – driving millions of possible supporters toward local face-to-face groups that lacked a political perspective. Under these circumstances the forces of opposition and resistance were dissipated and the wave of revolutionary ferment receded.

Viewing these issues retrospectively leads us to the conclusion that is entirely consistent with the evaluation made by many activists within the movement: that it is a political mistake to seek state power from within the system – to turn towards electoral constitutional politics and join the government. This much is obvious. Assessments of the state-movement dynamic in other contexts have produced the same conclusion. The problem is that this conclusion does not get us too far.

Mobilising the forces of opposition and resistance against the system is part of the solution – in fact a large part, given the limits and pitfalls of electoral politics. This is clear enough. Indigenous leaders, like Humberto Cholanga of Ecuador, on the basis of struggles within the social movement have embraced a class perspective on the "indigenous question." But another part of the solution is to create conditions that will facilitate the birth of a new revolutionary political party oriented toward state power. We can be certain that the process will be fraught with difficulties and will require the leadership of conscious political cadres. A close look at the experiences of the four countries briefly discussed earlier provides answers to the limitations of social movements and electoral politics.

7. *Socialism on the horizon – the agenda of the social movements*

The socialisation of the means of production and the egalitarian distribution of goods and services has been implicit and explicit among the rank and file of the mass social movements. The ritual declarations by the leaders of these movements of the vague slogan "Another world is possible" has failed to define a political direction and economic strategy which links popular needs with fundamental economic structural changes. Faced with the growth of large-scale agro-export enterprises, "agrarian reform" can only be consummated through collective ownership and production – as the MST has recently acknowledged. The return of the financial elite in Argentina demonstrates that "regulation" is incapable of directing capital toward large-scale, long-term investment in employment-creating economic activity. Only through a publicly owned banking system oriented by a regime based in the unemployed and employed workers, can employees and professionals design and implement financial policies which would develop the internal markets. Our study (Petras and Veltmeyer 2005) demonstrates that "national" bourgeoisie, including those producing for the local market, have been addicted to directing their profits to overseas accounts, recycling their earnings into the financial sector and/or intensifying exploitation of their workforce, instead of expanding employment, reinvesting in the home market and technical innovations. The conclusion is that sustained and comprehensive industrial growth on a national scale requires public ownership under the control of employed and underemployed workers and professionals. The crisis of electoral elite politics – riddled with corruption, beholden to foreign creditors, immersed in the politics of privatisations – can only be resolved by a transition to democratic collectivism, which prioritises political control from below, internal investment over debt payments, and recovers the strategic sectors of the economy.

There is a growing popular dissatisfaction with the endless social forums, vacuous declarations and ritualistic self-congratulations that have become a substitute for organising mass struggle based on a clear and expressive socialist programme.

Throughout our five years of field work in the four countries involving direct contact with hundreds of unemployed and employed workers, in the formal and informal labour market, among downwardly mobile public employees and under-employed professionals, among Indian leaders and activists, we have found a much clearer option for a socialist transformation and rupture with the electoral political class than among the professional Social Forum attendees who still live in the Babel Tower of diversity and dispersion of ambiguous formulas, rather than collective class organisation.

Conclusion

Historians of development theory have written of a counterrevolution in development theory and practice traced back to the exhaustion of the Keynesian model of state-led economic development and the appearance of a "new economic model" based on the neoclassical doctrine of free world market as a fundamental engine of economic growth as well as the most efficient mechanism for allocating productive resources across the system, essentially replacing governments in this role. Other historians have identified a paradigmatic shift traced back to a "theoretical impasse" brought about by a structuralist approach towards social analysis and a political project to create a form of society characterised by a fundamental equality in social relations and equity in access to, and distribution of, the world's wealth. As in Marx's day these intellectual developments "appeared" and analysed by many as a war of ideas, a struggle by different ideas to realise themselves. However, as Marx understood so well in a different context this conflict in the world of ideas reflected conditions of a class struggle in the real world, namely actions of working peoples across the world to improve their lot through a process of social change. The 1970s saw a new conjuncture in this struggle: a counter-offensive launched by capitalists and their ideologues and state representatives against the working classes, seeking to arrest and reverse the gains achieved over two decades of economic, social and political development. The New Economic Model of neoliberal policy reforms was one major intellectual, and ideological, response, a major weapon in the class war unleashed against the popular classes. Another such response took the form of a sustained effort to disarm the popular movement, to disarticulate its organisational structure and class politics, to turn the popular movement away from its struggle for social change and state power – for control over the major repository of political power. The aim here was to construct a new modality for achieving social change based on a new way of doing politics, namely to take the path of "anti- or non-power;" to rely on social rather than political action in bringing about social change without a confrontation of the power structure; to seek change – and improvements within the local spaces available within this structure; to partner with other agencies in the project of local development – to empower the poor to act in their own lives, participate actively on their own development and the good governance agenda, without challenging the larger structure of economic and political power.

The conclusion that we draw from an analysis of this modality of social change and the political dynamics of the development project in Latin America is inescapable. The only way forward for the working classes and the popular movement is political power: to abandon the development project and engage the class struggle – to directly confront the holders of this power and to contest power in every arena open to it. However, as in earlier political conjunctures there are two roads to state power, both fraught with pitfalls: the road of electoral politics and a revolutionary politics of mass mobilisation. Perhaps Evo Morales, the leader of MAS and erstwhile leader of the cocaleros, the coca-producing indigenous peasants of Chapare, best exemplifies the dilemma (and the difficulties in pursuing both paths at the same time). Morales' decision to take the electoral road to state power (to bet on his chances of wining the 2007 presidential elections) was largely responsible for defusing the revolutionary situation created by insurrectionary politics of the popular movement in October 2003. Carlos Mesa would never have come to power without the support of Morales in that context (he did not play a major role in this insurrectionary politics – in the bloody street protests that forced Gonzalo Sánchez to resign and seek exile in the US) and the weak Mesa government would never have survived without support for Mesa's call for a referendum on the explosive gas issue or his continuing support. As Eduardo Gamarra (*The Herald*, January 15, 2005:5A) noted: "The length of Mesa's tenure [in office and power] is largely due to Evo's supportive role." At the same time Morales himself continues to be pressured from the Left of the popular movement, compelled to respond to its more radical politics. For example, Morales continues to insist that he wants to win power only through the ballot box[8] but in January 2005 was constrained by the politics of the radical Left to publicly demand that Mesa resign and call an early election unless he agreed to roll back recent gasoline price increases. At issue for Morales was how to maintain his position in the popular movement while finding himself standing on the sidelines of the class struggle during anti-government strikes that shut down the cities of El Alto and Santa Cruz. The radical Left in this context is rejecting elections as a means of achieving state power but Morales is hanging tough on the line of electoral politics while at the same time being forced to respond to the radical politics of the revolutionary Left. Alvaro García, a university professor who is a part of this Left but at times serves as an advisor to Morales (he has severed

---

[8] Various analysts are of the opinion that Evo Morales' electoral democratic approach towards politics has been influenced by his November 2003 meeting with Brazilian PT President Luiz Inácio (Lula) da Silva, who lost three bids or the presidency before winning in 2002. Needless to say, Lula told Evo to be patient, learn from his defeats to represent all Bolivians, even the economic elite [the dominant and ruling class]. As Lula put it: "you cannot be limited to being an indigenous leader or a coca leader." He did not have to add that electoral politics is the only way to achieve state power.

ties to most of the radical Left), in this political context observes that "[w]hen the radicals powerful he moves towards them." The point is, he adds, Evo "fears that he will lose his base of support to the more radical elements." And well he might.

The response of Morales to radical politics tends to be tactical rather than strategic. It ties into a general conclusion that we have drawn from our analysis of diverse class struggles and the politics of social change. The inescapable conclusion is that a radical politics of mass mobilisation is an indispensable condition for advancing the struggle for social change – to bring about a new world of social justice and real development based on popular power (control of working peoples of the state). In practice it is probably necessary to combine both electoral and mass revolutionary politics. But a mobilised people is the sine qua non of revolutionary change – and revolutionary change is the only way out.

James D. Cockcroft

Imperialism, State and Social Movements
in Latin America[1]

The principal leaders of the United States have on
various occasions tried to explain what neoliberal
globalisation is. For example, the highest ranking
U.S. trade representative once said that "Globalisation
is the United States." Concerning Latin America
and Canada, former Secretary of State Colin Powell
declared at one point: "our objective is to guarantee
that the control of U.S. companies extends from the
Arctic to Antarctica and that free access reigns for
our products, services, technologies and capital, without any kind of obstacle throughout the entire hemisphere." His successor, Condoleezza Rice, once said
while still serving as National Security Advisor that
"We want to change the Iraqis' minds."

In other words, globalisation is imperialism. The
FTAA (Free Trade Area of the Americas) is an annexation of Latin America and the role of the U.S. state
in all of this is evident. The idea that the state
has lost its reason for existence due to neoliberal

[1] The essay is an expanded version of a keynote presentation given at the Inter-
national Conference "The Nation in Latin America: From its Invention to Neoliberal
Globalisation" held at the end of May, 2004 at the Institute of Historical Research,
Universidad Michoacana de San Nicolás de Hidalgo and the Colegio de Estudios
Latinoamericanos (CELA), Faculty of Sciences and Politics, National Autonomous
University of Mexico (UNAM). It appeared in *Critical Sociology*, Volume 32, N° 1, 2006,
pp. 67–81 and a version electronically published in Spanish is available at Inprecor
América Latina. See: http://www.inprecor.org.br/inprecor/index.php?option=
content&task=view&id=69&Itemid=68.

globalisation and the privatisation of economic public sectors is an idea which is indemonstrable and lacking of any theoretical or realistic content.[2]

The classical authors on imperialism, such as the anti-Marxist Hobson and Marxists Luxemburg and Lenin, have defined imperialism as the necessary expansion for capitalism during its stage of domination by monopoly capital. Presently, the United States controls much more than half of the major banks and corporations in the world and constitutes the planet's principal imperialist power. In order to extend and guarantee the control of big capital, "endless" military expansion and wars are necessary. As Thomas Friedman, a politically liberal journalist from the *New York Times* suggested, the invisible hand of the market would never work without the "iron fist" of the U.S. military ensuring that the world remains safe for Silicone Valley technologies (Friedman 2000:464).

By reflecting and promoting the interests of monopoly capital, the U.S. government implements a militarisation of the world that threatens preventive military attacks upon sixty nations under the pretext of "the war against terrorism." This militarisation serves to ensure and increase control over natural resources, the expansion of big financial and industrial capital, and the best possible conditions for U.S. trade and investments.

For that reason, Washington has established more than 700 military bases in 132 countries, including almost all of Latin America, where it has also suffered various defeats in recent years. In Puerto Rico, the mass rejection on the part of the Puerto Rican people put an end to the use of the Island of Vieques as a military free fire zone for constant live ammunition military exercises. In 2001, more than 15,000 Latin American military personnel were trained by the U.S. government in the re-named facilities formerly known as the "School of Americas," well-known for its training of military dictatorships during the "dirty wars" that raged throughout the region.

---

[2] As Ellen Meiksins Wood (2004) states in her article "El imperio capitalista y el Estado nación: ¿Un nuevo imperialismo norteamericano?" *Revista Viento Sur*. June 12, 2004: "This imperial power depends not only on its own domestic state but on the global system of multiple states. This signifies that every one of those states is an arena of struggle and a potential counter-force. It is not necessary to say that the struggles in the heart of global imperialism are an important target for oppositional forces and for international solidarity. But every state upon which global power depends is an important target for oppositional forces and international solidarity. Protests against the summits of the World Trade Organisation or the G-8 can without doubt change the political climate. But in the end, they do not substitute for politically organised opposition to the power of capital organised in national states." See: http://www.vientosur.info/articulosweb/textos/index.php?x=246.

Likewise, there have been a lot of new U.S.-training programmes for the police forces of Latin America. Plan Puebla-Panama, Plan Colombia and more recent initiatives for the integration of the Andean region, presented as plans for "economic integration and sustainable development," constitute in reality the military wing of the FTAA, a form of recolonisation of Latin America. Various U.S. companies, for example, Coca Cola and Drummond Co., Inc. (a mining company in Birmingham, Alabama), speak publicly about the use of armed forces and paramilitaries in Colombia for repressing strikes and assassinating trade unionists, all in an attempt to maintain low levels of production costs. In many Andean Countries, bio-terrorist campaigns have been waged against peasants involved in the cultivation of coca and other crops.

Meanwhile, Monsanto and six other companies that globally dominate agribusiness and biotechnology are commercialising trans-genetic products and easily obtaining new patents under the rules of the World Trade Organisation (WTO). In this way, they seize control of all agricultural seeding products and put an end to the food sovereignty of entire countries, with disastrous consequences for the environment and human health. Working alongside of them are a handful of pharmaceutical companies that are exploiting the rights granted under "commercial intellectual property patents" and recognised by the WTO, in order to ransack flora and fauna in what is now most commonly referred to as "bio-piracy." This includes the pillaging of the beneficial scientific knowledge that has been culturally accumulated in over 500 years of tradition by indigenous peoples.

As part of its national security strategy, Washington worked on the possibility of eventually aiming biological arms or a virus that is toxic to certain specific genotypes, for example Arabs, Blacks, or any other group deemed to be a threat. It is no coincidence that the U.S. government denied permission to international inspectors investigating the possible existence of bio-chemical weapons on its own territory. Such arms are expressly prohibited by international treaties signed at the end of the 1970s.

Even worse, a classified document that found its way to the press in October 2002, prepared for the "Defence Science Board" for Secretary of Defence Donald Rumsfeld, revealed a Pentagon plan for use of a new, "Proactive, Preemptive, Operations Group (P2OG)" for carrying out violent and secretive missions with the goal of "encouraging reactions" among terrorist groups. The idea is to provoke attacks and create the pretext for war and other acts in "defence of national security." Much has been said about the possibility of a self-generated provocation so as to justify new wars, possibly involving

Iran, Syria or Cuba. Moreover, the U.S. government has declared on various occasions its intent to use nuclear arms if it were to "become necessary."[3]

The criminal U.S. state is the only national state that has been convicted by the International Court of Justice at The Hague, Netherlands, for having committed international terrorism (in 1986 against Nicaragua). Washington for its part has vetoed a UN Security Council Resolution calling on governments to observe international laws. In this context, one can appreciate why the Organisation of American States voted the U.S. off of its Human Rights Commission in 2003. All of this happened *before* the discovery of the torture and criminal abuses committed at the Abú Ghraib Prison in Baghdad. According to the *New Zealand Herald* (May 17, 2004), there are more than ten thousand prisoners being held in secret U.S. prisons based in various countries and it is not known how many hundreds have been tortured to death.

For decades, imperialism has conducted comprehensive programmes of torture, disappearances, and assassinations, harkening back to "Operation Condor." It is a practise that has been documented for a long time in U.S. prisons as well, notably against political prisoners. One has to feel for U.S. citizens whose President can now decide to label them "enemy combatants" and proceed to detain them indefinitely without any rights. Numerous "suspected terrorists" detained in various part of the world constitute the new "disappeared" of the 21st Century. Bush himself informed the U.S. Congress that for three thousand of these suspects, in his words, "Let's put it this way: they are no longer a problem for the United States."

It is important to note that U.S. imperialism has a highly political character. The largest corporations and banks are well integrated with the state and the two main political parties. The state, in its search for political hegemony, is heavily immersed in political and economic institutions such as the UN and the IMF (International Monetary Fund), World Bank, and the Inter-American Development Bank. For that reason, and not only to grab control of petroleum, the Clinton and Bush Administrations both prepared an eventual war against Iraq. It is a means to affirm its military, economic and political hegemony over imperialist rivals in Europe and Japan. In the words of an official document that circulated by internet around mid-September, 2002,

---

[3] Among other sources, see Chris Floyd, "Global Eye – Into the Dark", Page XXIV, November 1, 2002; Prensa Latina, "Expansión nuclear de EEUU," *Red Eco Alternativo Boletín Informativo*, May 3, 2004, VI(38). http://www.redeco.netfirms.com/.

"The goal of the National Security Strategy of the United States of America is global and infinite in scope, designed to establish complete spectrum rule through the use of preventive war."[4]

The "United States Space Command Vision for 2020" distributed to the media in June, 2002, mentions space-age plans for U.S. military interventions. In the region, this can be envisioned for Colombia, Venezuela, Ecuador, Panama and Peru, the so-called "failed states" whose "viability" will depend upon U.S. "assistance." This is a doctrine that one supposes can be applied to any country as it was applied in Haiti in 2004.

Today, the planet's economy is based on relatively little production, due to the crisis of over-production. There is an ever greater level of financial speculation, drug and sex trafficking, money laundering and arms sales inter-twined with ongoing regional wars. Gold and silver that ruled in the 16th Century had been replaced by narcotic substances and increasingly the sale of women and children, commodities which in contrast to narcotics can be sold more than once. Many economists estimate that the profits from the trafficking of women are now greater than the narcotics trade. While many unknown cases of women being traded in slavery continue to come to light, so too is the homicidal violence being carried out against women. The case of Ciudad Juárez, Mexico stands as a telling example.

With so much financial speculation taking place alongside of the global expansion and centralisation of banks and insurance companies, one can now speak of a dominant bourgeoisie based on rent earnings. But the industrial and mercantile bourgeoisie continue on as strong powers and influential voices, conducting systematic wage enslavement alongside of the rent-based bourgeoisie. All of these fractions of the bourgeoisies are united in the ideology of market fundamentalism within neoliberal globalisation.[5]

In spite of everything, imperialism is nevertheless weak and in crisis. The alter-globalisation movement has made considerable advances. Many people have become aware that the emperor has no clothes beneath the new mantle of globalisation. When the 21st Century began, the world had already

---

[4] See the source at http://www.whitehouse.gov/nsc/nssall.html.
[5] This reality does not contradict the existing tendency of some fractions of the bourgeoisie in the "developing world" to unite, on occasion, against the more powerful bourgeoisies of the "industrialised, developed world" in certain international negotiations with respect to the terms of trade, conditions for foreign investment, etc. See Claudio Katz (2004).

entered into an economic recession with some national economies becoming "Argentina-ised." Imperialist disasters were unfolding in the wars of Afghanistan, Iraq and on a smaller scale in Colombia, the Philippines and Palestine. The Atlantic Alliance almost collapsed under the weight of a massive global movement in opposition to the Iraq war. All of these events must be seen as related to the stagnation of the U.S. economy. This condition forms part of a long descending economic phase that began in 1973 and which continues, despite a tentative recovery in the rate of profit during the 1990s.

Strong militarily, U.S. imperialism is economically and politically weak. This is why it wages its infinite policy of warfare, mistakenly believing it can win against weaker nations such as Afghanistan and Iraq. The human costs have resulted in an anti-war movement in the United States that has involved military families as major actors. Various generals have expressed their concern that U.S. forces are too far extended to effectively resist potential counter-attacks.

The United States has begun to expose itself to the risk that Japanese, Chinese, Arab and other investors in U.S. bonds and financial markets will shift their holdings towards other countries. With the scandals of Enron, AOL Time Warner, Andersen, Halliburton (best known for its direct links to Vice-President Dick Cheney) and other gigantic companies, coupled with a monumental fiscal deficit, the U.S. economy has found itself in a situation where its weakening dollar can lose monetary dominance and thus its control over other economies. Even before the war in Iraq, many oil-producing countries joined Europe in pressuring for a new scheme of pricing and trade of oil based on Euros rather than U.S. Dollars.

It is not surprising that the U.S. ruling class has begun to fracture, with disagreements from within both political parties, the Armed Forces and even the same White House. These divisions are not related to the ultimate goal of global domination, but over which strategies and tactics should be pursued in order to best ensure this domination. Unilateralism or multilateralism? Should torture become legalised? Is there a need for more mercenaries, private armies and sub-contractors? Should the Geneva Conventions be followed? (Bush's legal advisor described some of the clauses in these Conventions as "curious and obsolete." Should the U.S. continue with the IMF, World Bank and WTO, or modify them, or do away with them?

The Challenge of Latin American Social Movements

Although in the long term, it is China that will probably constitute the principal challenge to the United States, a present-day challenge consists of the new wave of social movements and electoral radicalisation occurring in Latin America which Washington so fondly regards as its "backyard." I wish to call attention to seven points that are most frequently under-estimated in the region's resurgent challenge to imperialism:

(1) The role of indigenous peoples, most notably in Bolivia, Peru, Ecuador, Guatemala and Mexico, but also to a surprising extent in countries with smaller indigenous communities such as Chile and Argentina. Indigenous peoples in the Americas widely recognise that imperialism forms part of more than 500 years of genocidal subjugation. In mounting a popular resistance, indigenous peoples are highly conscious of certain fundamental realities that are derived from the continuity in imperialism, such as the use of kidnapping, disappearances and torture; ecological destruction; and the creation and perpetuation of an unpayable foreign debt as a tool for dominating entire nations. There is an instinctive understanding that U.S. imperialism has its roots in the British Empire and stands as an inheritance of the overthrow of the Spanish Empire.

(2) The role of women and the poor in the upsurge of resistance and its leadership can be seen in cases such as the Zapatista movement of Mexico. It is likewise displayed in Argentina by the Mothers of the Plaza de Mayo and in the "street picketers" and workers protests, including in the self-managed factories that were established when workers moved into abandoned factories during the economic crisis and resumed production on their own. These actors figure prominently among the impoverished Venezuelan masses and the Bolivarian circles who in the face of a U.S. supported destabilisation plan, rose up in defence of their elected president and the new Bolivarian constitution. Other examples include the working women, vendors and housewives of Bolivia who have organised their community defence committees for a block by block struggle. They were evident among the thousands of Nicaraguans who joined a massive march in April, 2004 and who continue to mobilise. In these uprisings, there is a marked advance of women's consciousness and this has been picked up by new feminist analyses and in economic research on impoverishment and its role in the accumulation of capital. It demonstrates the urgent necessity of incorporating a theory of patriarchy and conceptualising the triple-exploitation of women in any serious analysis

of imperialism and the development of social movements.[6] It could well be that if the popular struggles eventually manage to bring down imperialism, people will be able to look back and reconceptualise it as something that was not only the last stage of capitalism but also the last stage of patriarchy, genocide, racism and mass poverty.

(3) The role of the mass media as political actors is readily manifest throughout the region. It can be seen in the attempts of right-wing, Mafioso and pro-imperialist forces to provoke incidents and overthrow progressive governments as in the case of Venezuela and Cuba. The illegal act of provocation involving the U.S. government's launching of an aerial C-130 platform for the transmission of Radio and TV Martí is another striking example. The media further plays an important role in the criminalisation of social movements. In news reporting, the words "acts of violence" are repeatedly invoked, without any reference to state provocateurs, to describe the peaceful protests of the anti-globalisation movement during events such as the WTO Summit in Cancun and the FTAA meeting in Miami in 2003. The latter helped force the U.S. government to accept the notion of a "Flexible FTAA". Similar results occurred at the 2004 meeting of the European Community and Latin American Nations in Guadalajara.

(4) The role of youth. They were well-represented in the streets of Argentina during the mass protests of 2001 in the form of student strikes, in the movement against the continuing impunity of military and political officials involved in the past dirty war and in present-day repression, in movements demanding the rights of gays, lesbians and transsexuals, and in the clamour for "another world is possible."

(5) The role of peasants and trade unionists, in spite of the new and extremely violent waves of repression directed against them. In many countries, such as Mexico for example, the peasantry has become in large part a new proletariat that operates as a cheap, flexible and migrant labour force. At the same time, however, a process of transformation of peasant workers back into classical peasants has begun, forcing them back to rural land parcels in order to cultivate the minimum foodstuffs necessary for their survival. Be it in the movements of coca cultivators in the Andean Countries or the Movement of Landless Workers (MST) of Brazil, the rural regions and the urban outskirts

---

[6] For a synthesis, see James D. Cockcroft (1998; and 2001: 274–289).

of Latin America have generally come to constitute an extremely intense zone of class-warfare.

In the case of trade union struggles, workers have developed new forms of struggle against the owners and corrupt union leaders who collaborate with the workers' class enemy. Independent or alternative labour confederations have been formed, such as the Authentic Workers Front (FAT) and the National Union of Workers (UNT) in Mexico, and the new workers confederation in Venezuela. There has been a greater internationalisation of their battles, including struggles in the Mexican and Central America *maquiladora* plants and the Coca Cola plants of Guatemala and Colombia.

Another exemplary case is the strike of 625 workers affiliated with the independent National Revolutionary Union of Workers (SNRTE) at the Hulera Euzkadi Company, owned by the German transnational Continental Tire in El Salto, Jalisco, Mexico. In February 2004, the union won official recognition after a strike that lasted over two years. Its leaders had travelled to Germany in order to rally more international support. Many unions also participate in the large anti-globalisation demonstrations like those that took place in Cancun and Miami in 2002, Guadalajara in 2004, or in the World Social Forum (WSF) that attracts more than 100 thousand participants of the anti-globalisation movement to its annual meetings.[7]

(6) The role of fundamentalisms is another important aspect. This is not limited only to the terrorist fundamentalism of some Muslim groups or the kind of Christian terrorist fundamentalism organised in the White House that has been practiced by imperialism for decades, better known as "state terrorism." Even more significant is the market fundamentalism of neoliberal globalisation, something that underlies all fundamentalisms in their contemporary stages. This fundamentalism tortures millions of people daily. Each year, over 36 million people die from hunger while half of the world's children

---

[7] Concerning the peasantry and trade unions in Mexico, see Chaps. 6, 7 & 8 in Cockcroft (2001) and "Los obreros mexicanos de Euzkadi – Una huelga ejemplar", *Rebelión*, February 28, 2004 [http://www.rebelion.org/sociales/040228cockcroft.htm]. The UNT of Venezuela makes it clear in its declaration of principles that it is an: "autonomous, democratic, internationalist, class-based, independent, unitary (representative of the entire working class) movement organisation that stands for solidarity and equality for men and women and which struggles for the transformation of capitalist society into a self-managed society in a new model of anti-capitalist and autonomous development that emancipates human beings from class exploitation, oppression, discrimination and exclusion. See: http://www.aporrea.org/dameverbo.php?docid=17087.

suffer from malnutrition. The pauperisation and mass exclusion of people are two principal methods used by capitalist owners for the accumulation of their wealth in this era of neoliberal globalisation. Market fundamentalism helps to increase state terrorism through its effort to control the conditions of production and distribution of wealth while repressing resistance movements.[8]

(7) Finally, the growing recognition among Latin American peoples regarding the necessity to form alliances in their struggles and to internationalise them merits further attention. Examples of the new internationalism include the World March of Women[9] that incorporates Latin American women who have proposed regional level actions through 2005 and beyond. They participate in the Continental Campaign against the FTAA, sponsored by the Continental Social Alliance; the MST in Brazil that forms part of the *Via Campesina*, a network of peasant movements that spans 87 countries; the campaign for the demilitarisation of Latin America that begin in Chiapas in 2003 and which already had links with the international campaign to close U.S. military bases worldwide; and the World Social Forum (WSF) whose annual general assembly of anti-globalisation/alter-globalisation activists brought together thousands from around the world to Porto Alegre, Brazil and in 2004 to Mumbai, India (Cockcroft 2004).

At the onset of the new century, Latin American social movements achieved a series of sensational victories. The people of Cochabamba, Bolivia won their "water war" against the U.S. transnational Bechtel. On a grander scale, a popular uprising led by indigenous peoples in protest against Occidental Petroleum and the complicit Ecuadorian government resulted in bringing down the president. The Argentine uprising of 2001 brought down three consecutive presidents. The next year, Brazil witnessed the immense electoral victory of Lula da Silva and the Brazilian Workers Party (PT). Talk soon began to spread in Washington about a new "axis of evil" – Brazil, Venezuela and Cuba – as well as the possible need to create an "economic protectorate" in Argentina.

The U.S. state without further delay began to intensify a mobilisation of forces, including the Pentagon, CIA, the DEA, Coast Guard, Southern Command and the new Northern Command that unites armed forces of Mexico, Canada and the United States under U.S. command. The move was to implement a sophisticated, co-ordinated and well armed policy of intervention using the

---

[8] See David Harvey (2003); Wood (2004); Cockcroft (2001:171–290).
[9] Visit: www.marchemondiale.org.

most modern technologies for war and espionage. Nevertheless, the social movements just seemed to multiply.

In 2002, the homeless and indigenous women of CONAMURI along with thousands of other Paraguayans, cut off 17 major routes and marched on the Congress, forcing abandonment of two proposed anti-terrorist and privatisation laws. In southern Peru, a popular coalition forced the suspension of a planned privatisation of electricity. In Bolivia, the indigenous leader Evo Morales and his organisation "Movement towards Socialism" (MAS) won a plurality of votes in the presidential elections, although he was deprived of the Presidency that time around through electoral proceedings designed to perpetuate elite rule. The anti-neoliberal programme of MAS supports the re-nationalisation of privatised industries, including those of petroleum and gas. They also call for a new agrarian reform and the convocation of a Constitutional Assembly that is freely elected.

In the following year, a series of electoral victories against rightist candidates took place. In Argentina, Kirchner beat Menem and proceeded to defy the demands of the IMF. In Paraguay, Nicanor Duarte Frutos who strongly favoured MERCOSUR won the presidency. In Colombia, the right wing government of Álvaro Uribe lost an important referendum designed to expand its powers, and many mayoral races, including the city of Bogotá, were captured by the centre-left alliance of the *Polo Democrático*.

The Bolivian insurrection of October 2003 in the "gas war," something foreseeable after the police strike in the preceding February, brought down President Gonzalo Sánchez de Lozada who was an unabashed lackey of the U.S. Embassy. In Uruguay, the voters rejected by popular referendum a law that permitted the state petroleum company to form a partnership with foreign capital, paving the way for the leftist "Broad Front" coalition to expand its terrain and eventually capture the presidency in 2005.

Even in Chile, where Pinochet-style repression has been modified and modernised, there have been new protests against the informal alliance between the "socialist" led party alliance in government and the extreme right. This has included transportation strikes, hunger strikes by political prisoners and parents of the disappeared, and demonstrations by youth in the form of "Memory Brigades." Their actions frequently included demonstrations in front of the homes, clubs and offices of military and civilian authorities responsible for atrocities during the dirty wars, demanding an end to impunity.

What is in play throughout Latin America is nothing less than the sovereignty of all countries and the control over their natural resources, including oil and other energy sources, abundant cheap labour, biodiversity, sources of clean water, schools, hospitals, housing, transportation, social security, pensions, and other public sector institutions, along with banks, industries, and the continuation of social movements. The popular movements are protesting the privatisation of nature, the commodification of life, and the pillage that neoliberal globalisation imposed by imperialism signifies for them, together with the illegitimate foreign debts that are in many cases impossible to ever repay as in the case of Argentina, Haiti, and most of Central America.

In the case of Mexico, millionaire thieves and foreign interests are together trying to use the rightist government of Vicente Fox to privatise everything, including the public education system. They seek their justification in the foreign debt and work tirelessly to reform the national constitution which to date remains one of the most progressive in the world. Their goal is to end the human right to a job with a dignified salary and to impose more taxes on foodstuffs, medicines, books, and loans. Nevertheless, it can be seen that since 1994 when the Zapatistas staged an uprising in Chiapas, Mexican social movements have strongly resisted the capitulationism of Fox and his PRI predecessors. Examples of this include the campaign by the Mexican Electricians Union (SME) against the privatisation of electricity, and the movement of the peasant cooperatives of San Salvador Atenco who in 2002 beat back the plans of the Fox Administration to construct a new international airport on their collectively farmed lands.

According to various sources, including the World Bank and the International Labour Organisation (ILO), Latin American poverty is increasing. More than half of the population lacks decent work and 70% of the region's population works in the informal sector. One out of four inhabitants on the planet lacks access to safe drinking water, including 80 million Latin Americans. Foreign direct investments in Latin America and the Caribbean have decreased during 2000–2003, while the outflow of convertible foreign exchange in the form of profits being remitted to transnational corporations in their countries of origin has increased. In short, the economic genocide of neoliberal globalisation continues albeit more precariously to plunder the region.

For that reason, there is a new popular resurgence and an intensification of class struggle throughout all of Latin America. There are also strong countertendencies, including attempts to destabilise centre-left governments; counterrevolutionary plots and mobilisations; massive and selective repression; an accelerating violence against women, gays and transsexuals, ethnic minorities and progressive associations; and grave threats against the sovereignty of rebellious countries like Venezuela and Cuba.

The greatest social movement in Latin America is that of the Cuban people who continue to resist intense waves of U.S. aggression. In May, 2004, more than 10% of the Cuban population filled the streets of Havana to denounce the latest counter-revolutionary plans of Washington for a "regime change" on the island, the only space in the region liberated from its rule.

The social and political system of Cuba to date constitutes the most completely formed alternative to the imperialist order of exploitation, ecological degradation and exclusion imposed by globalisation. The Cuban state is the only one in the world that has resisted the aggressive U.S. doctrine of permanent and preventive war, both before and after the invasion of Iraq. It has successfully combated U.S. state terrorism for decades. Regrettably, five young Cubans are imprisoned in the United States under false charges while the terrorists that they had infiltrated and monitored fully enjoy their freedom and even appear with Bush II and other public officials that treat them like heroes. The five Cubans gave information to the U.S. FBI that helped avoid 170 terrorist attacks. At the same time, it is possible that there are immense oil deposits in the Cuban part of the Gulf of Mexico. This has caused the Bush Administration to intensify its campaign for "regime change" against the Cuban people, creating a significant danger for all of "Our America" as it was referred to by Jose Martí.[10]

Yes, There Are Alternatives

The defenders of capitalism like to say that "there is no other real alternative." But on the contrary, there are indeed alternatives, quite a few of them.

The participants in the World Social Forum and in their regional forums (like the First Social Forum of the Americas held in Quito in July 2004) regularly consider various alternatives that are both creative and realistic. They do this in a climate of mutual tolerance for different ideas and a desire to

---

[10] See the website of "The Cuban Five" [www.freethefive.org]; Saxe-Fernández (2004). According to a well documented study carried out by Frank Martin, "The anti-Cuba obsession has been so great that the Office of Foreign Assets Control has since 1990 opened 93 investigations related to terrorism while during the same period, initiated 10,683 with respect to violations of the Cuban Embargo" *La Jiribilla*, May 21, 2004.

learn about other cultures and individuals. It is also the case that the first two international meetings of pre-eminent intellectual activists "in defence of humanity," held in Mexico City, 2003 and Caracas, 2004, created a diverse, cultural space where respect for different national identities prevailed. In those gatherings, a tremendous intellectual energy was mobilised in rejecting the dominant neoliberal ideological paradigm along with the privatisation and monopolisation of knowledge that is imposed in banal and consumerist oriented media and institutions.[11]

During the inauguration of the first meeting in defence of humanity, a young Mexican intellectual and internationalist, Raquel Gutiérrez Aguilar, who was formerly a political prisoner in Bolivia, affirmed that the best source of alternatives for resolving the world's problems could be found in "the common sense of dissidence." That common sense says that if today's globalisation is imperialism, i.e., the expansion of monopoly capital, then the only solution to the problems created by globalisation is the socialisation of those large enterprises and its operations in Latin America and the rest of the world. In order to achieve this, it will logically be necessary to form organised, well-conceived, anti-capitalist alternatives that are revolutionary and pluralistic, participatory and democratic. She also noted that this means constructing internationalist alliances.

An alternative that frequently arises is that of the so-called "Third Way" that was established in the "Consensus of Buenos Aires." With its origins in the strategic alliance between Brazil and Argentina, this alternative sought to slow and avert a final agreement on the FTAA under the conditions imposed by the United States. The Consensus of Buenos Aires seeks to formulate an alternative political project to neoliberal model, a kind of "neoliberalism with a human face" in what obviously stands out as a contradiction in terms.

Another popular alternative is that of "sustainable growth," a kind of more socially responsible and ecologically sensitive path to capitalist economic development. This attempted alternative, just like the "Third Way," is not possible within the capitalist system because the goal of capitalist enterprises remained eternally fixated on profit maximisation, thus leaving scarce room for considering the possible consequences that their actions pose for the environment.

---

[11] See http://www.defensahumanidad.org/.

Yet another popular alternative in Brazil is the famous "participatory budget" model introduced in Porto Alegre and other cities. It is a good example of democratic participation "from below." But this local alternative does not go very far if the entire country lacks the funds to create an adequate budget for fighting hunger and other serious problems.

Hugo Chávez, the President of Venezuela, supports a "Bolivarian alliance" in order to commercially and politically unify Latin American states. This idea is very useful as a way of rejecting imperialist interventionism in the Region's economic affairs. But an even better and more immediately possible option would be an international accord between various states, proclaiming that the foreign debt is impossible to pay. This kind of rupture with finance capital would leave a considerable amount of funds disposable for national states and create space for a fairer economic system.

Many people call this alternative a kind of "internationalist socialism" but it would not operate well without mass participation "from below," a solidly democratic organisation, and the political will adequately mobilised to defend it, as they say in Cuba, "to the death!" For the survival of humanity and the planet, this practical alternative must be discussed more seriously in the meetings of the alter-globalisation forces and intellectuals of the Americas and the world at large. In the final analysis, it is an alternative that can be readily incorporated into many other emerging alternatives.

Richard A. Dello Buono

The Changing Face of Latin America's Political Parties[1]

Political parties all across the Latin American political spectrum find themselves in crisis. A lot has been
written about corruption in the traditional parties,
the syndrome of charismatic and anti-establishment,
anti-candidates who have entered politics outside of
the traditional parties, the fiscal crisis of the Latin
American states, among other factors that have weakened the parties that once had a lock on political
power in their respective countries. A critical perspective, however, requires that we postulate these
and other similar kinds of observations not as causes
but rather as effects of more systemic (and in some
cases, counter-systemic) dynamics that have become
prevalent in the region. If we wish to reaffirm the
necessity of contextualising such phenomena in the
framework of structural and conjunctural tendencies
of the changing political economy in the Western
hemisphere, it would seem inevitable that we move
towards linking those dynamics to a more general,
overarching tendency towards crisis in the model of
neoliberal capitalism.

Following this line of reasoning, I had argued at
the onset of the decade (Dello Buono, 2002a; 2002b)

---

[1] This chapter is a revised and expanded version of a paper presented at the
International Scientific Seminar "La crisis del neoliberalismo y los futuros derroteros
en América Latina" at the Universidad Autónoma de Zacatecas, Mexico in February,
2003.

that a macro-conceptualisation of the changing panorama of the Latin American political parties should be contemplated by taking into account the following conditioning factors:

- A party's socio-historical construction and traditional base of support
- Structural changes in the regional economy associated with increasing globalisation
- U.S. hegemony and interventionism throughout the region
- Extra-constitutional involvement of national military forces in politics
- Regional networks of narcotics trafficking
- The paradigmatic crisis of the post-war left.

Five years later after making these arguments, it would seem apparent that many things have changed. Nevertheless, I will argue in the present essay that with little modification, the factors listed above continue in diverse combinations being principle factors that condition the development of national contexts. These factors delimit many of the principal dilemmas that states in practically all parts of the region of Latin America and the Caribbean continue to face, thus defining the political and ideological context in which political parties struggle to reproduce their self-definition and in some cases their very survival. This is especially relevant in so far as parties form their conceptions about the field of possible alternatives in the face of the neoliberal debacle. In the final analysis, what is changing in Latin America today is principally the magnitude of the accumulating crisis of neoliberalism and it is precisely that which I want to reflect upon in the present work.

The Socio-Historical Construction of Latin American Political Parties

To speak of political parties, it seems logical to take as ones starting point the particular history of each in a given country. Political parties always develop in a macro-context that is fundamentally national. Beginning here, it is possible to establish a set of social factors that delimit political party formation and their institutional development. As is well established in the field of critical sociology, the class struggle framework has offered the most convincing analytical approach for characterising the dynamics and constant movement of this social context. From a dialectical point of view, it is possible to analyse the basic contradictions that determine class conflicts as well as the dynamic tensions within social classes, be it the ruling class or among the subordinated classes.

While political parties struggle in various arenas of social mobilisation, including most typically, albeit not exclusively, in the electoral arena, various studies over recent decades have shown how structural class contradictions are key to understanding their relative triumphs and sometimes crushing defeats.[2] More recently, studies in this tradition have focused on the importance of "new social actors" such as the organised women's movement, race and ethnicity-based organisations, indigenous and subordinated nationalities, informal sector and self-employed workers, excluded and homeless peoples, environmental groups, and so on, all in the changing developmental context where the political panorama reflects new situations emerging out of the social contradictions of increasing globalisation.

Obviously, the dynamics of the political parties never manage to reflect the complex totality of the contradictions of a developing society, but rather by nature constitute only a partial reflection of this set of social dynamics. In every concrete case, the changing historical circumstances results in changes in the political tendencies that figure prominently in the composition, decomposition and recomposition of political parties.

It is moreover undeniable that some historical periods, such as the era of the military governments, drastically altered the development of political parties, above all those which carried the banner of populist reformism. Clearly, foreign interventionism in the Cold War context was also instrumental in bringing down the reformist regimes while the radical and often fractious left movements of the 1960s and 1970s helped fuel the violent response of the most reactionary forces of the continent, solidly backed by Washington. The repressive internal wars that were directed by the region's military forces at uprooting and eradicating those leftist forces which managed to establish a popular base served in the final analysis delimited the political space of almost all political parties.

In some cases, equally or even more devastating to political party development was the use of intimidation by ultra-radical political movements of both a leftist sort as in the paradigmatic case of the Peruvian Shining Path as well as the rightwing, fascist variety such as the Tontons Macoutes in Haiti.

---

[2] Among the masters of this line of thought are the French Structural Marxists Althusser, Poulantzas, Therborn, et al.

In the 1990s, the peace negotiations did not decisively eliminate this problem in countries like Guatemala where the ex-paramilitary patrols or "ex-PAC" continue to exercise pervasive violence against a wide range of political opponents while the government flirts with recognising its legitimacy. Something similar continues in Colombia where the persistent failure of a peace process to take hold has coincided with a systematic and violent state and paramilitary repression. In both cases, the development of most political parties has suffered. In Peru where there was also no type of negotiation in the armed conflicts but simply violent repression to eradicate all forms of leftist expression, the Fujimori Dictatorship following its auto-coup of 1992 utilised diverse authoritarian means in order to continue weakening all surviving political parties right up to the day that Fujimori fled the country amidst a massive political corruption scandal.

In general terms, the crisis of accumulation that resulted following the inward-oriented, structuralist strategies of development during the 1980s coincided with the intensification of globalising processes that rapidly transformed the previously established nature of the region's development patterns. The rise of neoliberalism as the new recipe bequeathed from the North imposed a deregulation of economies, the transnationalisation of the regional economic flows, and the creation of new illicit industries. The corruption that had emerged out of the logic of economies regulated by a strong state became quickly replaced by an even more spectacular corruption of the "shrunken state," with new forms of foreign intervention that soon coalesced into a kind of hegemonic regional integration.

Precisely when the need for an alternative development model was most acute, the collapse of the Soviet Union and "actually-existing" socialist countries of the East occurred, provoking a profound and generalised disorientation among the left on a global scale. The Cold War ended abruptly but the pattern of the regional militarization would linger indefinitely, leaving the armed forces as a strong political actor in many of the region's countries. With the consolidation of the war against illegal narcotics, a war that would be soon consolidated further as a war against terrorism, the pretext was created for reinforcing an expanding U.S. interventionism both in the military field as well as in the political field. All of these tendencies continue to constitute up to the present day some of the principal conditioning factors of the regional political panorama.

Globalisation and Neoliberalism in Crisis

The political and economic pattern that has dominated Latin America and the Caribbean for well over two decades has been that of neoliberalism. A systemic expansionary process of globalising capitalism has with few exceptions in the region managed to impose a series of complex changes in national policymaking. The experience of trade liberalisation and the opening of national economies across the hemisphere was an early manifestation of the neoliberal transition. The cumulative result of these policies was quite significant for political parties, with the traditional parties being confronted with intense opposition to neoliberal reforms while on the other hand, space was created for the formation of new political parties and party formations as an expression of the emergent social movements in a changing political landscape.

The impact of neoliberal measures was felt particularly strongly in those countries that had cultivated a political culture revolving around a "strong state." In those cases, the effect of globalisation was to seriously affect the prospects of political parties groomed in that tradition and heavily conditioned their prospects for survival under a painful process of redefining their political orientation. Why was this the case?

As is well known, the phenomenon of globalisation is characterised by the restructuration of the system of production worldwide, fuelled by the accelerated intensification in the use of new technologies. These technological developments have produced changes no only in productivity but also in the rules of the economic game. The advance of capitalist globalisation becomes associated with rapid growth in direct international investments, greater market share on the part of transnational companies, a growth of direct investments in services, increasingly higher volume of business transactions taking place intra-firm, and an accelerated concentration of international capital through increased trans-border acquisitions.[3] The resulting economic restructuration is made up of globalised commodity chains that result in new social configurations. The old division of labour breaks down, the nature of the state changes, and the relations between the traditional industrial social classes become transformed on account of the creation of interconnected production platforms.[4]

---

[3] See José Bell Lara in *Globalisation and the Cuban Revolution,* Havana, Cuba: Editorial Jose Marti.

[4] See Watson, Hilbourne, *The Caribbean in the Global Political Economy.* Boulder and London: Lynne Rienner Publishers, Inc., 1994.

It now quite evident that neoliberal globalisation from its very onset was characterised by a highly unequal development. With the understanding that underdeveloped countries are ever more conditioned by the manner in which they are incorporated into the global chains of production, the general consensus of the era was that regional integration could offer certain specific benefits in adjusting to the process. The integration processes that developed, however, were themselves so highly asymmetrical as to do little more than prepare the way for ever more hegemonic control from the North.

What is absolutely certain over the period in which the neoliberal model was imposed is that industries which took great effort to construct over a period of many decades were forced out of business, resulting in the disappearance of many jobs formerly based in this sector. The growth of unemployment in a region aggravated already high poverty rates, provoking a sharp rise in economic migration. These characteristics helped generate intense social conflicts in receiving countries and led to a wave of new anti-immigrant policies. The contraction of manufacturing resulted in a shift back towards emphasising the primary goods sector while reeling economies witnessed an explosive growth in informal sector activities, particularly in urban areas, as the victims of this restructuration attempted to compensate and obtain a survival income. The desperate flight to the cities by former agricultural producers left unemployed by cheap food imports quickly overtaxed the capacity of urban centres to provide essential social services. All of these dynamics generated intense discontent and demands on the state and figured in the growing social demands being made upon political parties.

The effects of neoliberalism in the region brought with it various social changes that affected the popular bases upon which many political parties were based. While social problems steadily multiplied, neoliberal regimes demanded the privatisation of public services, the substitution of inefficient state apparatuses with "no state" or "less state," all of which is to say that neoliberal state conduct made it impossible to sustain minimally necessary levels of social spending.[5] In the end, reforms championed by the neoliberal state under the guise of adjustment to the new global dynamics showed themselves to be little more than "de-nationalising agendas."

---

[5] On this issue, a highly recommended work by the Peruvian economist Oscar Ugarteche is *The False Dilemma: Opportunity or Threat?*, Zed Books, 2000.

Among the resulting consequences of the neoliberal model were high unemployment rates and the construction of a permanent threat of extinction for trade unions through the implementation of ever more flexible labour regimes. The privatisation and financial transnationalisation of primary commodity production intensified the de-nationalisation of the economic rents that were so strategic in the past, from the oil of Mexico to the bauxite of Jamaica. This transformation and crippling of the social spending base of states across the region dovetailed with the flash growth of poverty and social exclusion, leading to a crisis of legitimacy among various types of political party regimes in power across the region. In addition to the intense pressures it put upon governing parties, this process also dealt severe blows to traditional parties whose electoral strength was based in the representation and defence of the interests of one or another of the sectors most affected by increasing globalisation.

For its part, the Bush Administration worked systemically in this area, placing great emphasis upon the utilisation of its foreign policy as a weapon to enforce ever greater economic liberalisation via free trade agreements such as the FTAA and a whole generation of sub-regional and bilateral FTA's that were to follow. Each new agreement was a building bloc in a new regional trade order bent on ensuring transnational access to new markets such as in basic services, this thanks to a systematic deregulation and privatisation in these areas. The FTA agreements likewise served to enforce legal recognition of intellectual property rights, maintain secure access to raw materials goods for the United States under permanently favourable terms of exchange, and progressively degrading any capacity for economic regulation on the part of *other* national states in the region. This general framework put forward a broad geo-policy evidently linked to the persistent preoccupations of Washington about the supply of petroleum, its Achilles heel that was to become so overtly determinant over U.S. foreign policy in the opening years of the 21st Century. By 2003, Mexico figured as the second largest provider of crude petroleum to the U.S., with Venezuela in 4th place, Colombian in 10th and Ecuador in 12th place (U.S. Department of Energy, 2004).

On the other hand, the growing opposition on the part of those social sectors most harmed in the region continued to evolve in accordance with these changing conditions. Latin American resistance, born in the context of the social fragmentation and ideological hegemony characteristic of neoliberalism in its opening phase, began to present undeniable signs of development and consolidation by the halfway point of the 21st Century's first decade. A sustained presence of multisectoral social movements began to make their presence felt during this period with their protests directed in large measure towards the regional and bilateral FTA's. In this context, anti-FTA sentiments emerged as an important focal point in unifying mass protests. While popular sectors mounted their struggles against the neoliberal model, there was an insistent imposition of hegemonic formulas of integration throughout Latin America and the Caribbean. The broadening and deepening of this logic represented a "NAFTA-isation of integration processes, something that posed as the essence of regional integration in the course of free trade negotiations.

The examples of social resistance in the region and their impact in the political sphere are numerous. In Panama, negotiations for a bilateral TLC with the United States were met with demonstrations that brought together popular agrarian organisations, students and public sector workers, with roots in the popular resistance against the privatising reforms of the nation's social security system. The political result of this could be observed in 2005 when the party of President Mireya Mosoco was electorally crushed and deposed by the opposition led by her nemesis, Martín Torrijos of the PRD. Once in power, however, Torrijos opted for a basic continuity in Moscoso's platform, actively seeking the selection of Panama as the regional headquarters of the FTAA, supporting the FTA with the United States, and insisting on the necessity to reform the social security system. The ensuing protests put a rapid end to the new administration's honeymoon with the popular sectors, with intense demonstrations mounted under the multisectoral umbrella organisation known as FRENADESSO. These protests were violently repressed under Torrijos' orders during May 2005 including the brief closure of the University of Panama where student opposition was especially intense. Torrijos managed to gain legislative approval of the reform on June 1, 2005 but under the shadow of large protests in the capital and a high political cost that the ruling party has had to face since that time.

The muiltsectoral movements of Colombia, Ecuador and Peru also demonstrated their strength in a similar manner. In Peru, there was a significant growth in the cola growers movement beginning in 2004, joining their voices in the national movement against the ruling party in a manner similar to the more advanced situation in Bolivia. The Toledo administration was persistently dogged by strikes and protests, with a civic action spearheaded by the CGT Trade Union Federation in mid-July of 2004 that gained significant support throughout the country. In Ecuador, a more paradigmatic case could be observed when the government of Lucio Gutiérrez, steadily weakened by the unceasing protest actions of the popular sectors, culminated in indigenous uprisings led by the indigenous people's confederation CONAIE, the President's former allies who originally helped propel into power. When Gutiérrez decided to abandon his political base and pass decisively into a neoliberal and pro-U.S. camp, he faced a popular response in April of 2005 that was impossible to contain. In humiliating fashion, Gutiérrez was forced to flee into exile, initially in Brazil and then into hiding in Peru. In the Andean countries, the protests against neoliberalism have taken the form of ensuring through direct action the right to throw elected officials out of office when their rule becomes decidedly anti-popular.

Although some partial accords have been reached by the protest actions, largely symbolic in nature, there has also been a notable tendency towards an increase in the use of repressive measures. Perhaps the greatest illustrative case in this regard has been the Uribe Administration in Colombia. Acting in concert with Washington and bolstered by massive U.S. military support, Uribe has installed a "war neoliberalism" in Colombia, utilising all means including military (under his so-called "Patriotic Plan"), legal (implementing an "Anti-terrorist Statute") and police actions, including mass arrests. This was the violent package required to impose neoliberalism in a country with a long history of popular resistance. With U.S. troops actively involved in counterinsurgency combat, there has been a notable militarization of border regions as well. In October 2004, the Bush Administration gained congressional administration for doubling the troop presence in and increasing the number of civilian mercenary advisors contracted by the Pentagon.

The symphony of sectorial mobilisations, civic and opposition party-led groups, and anti-establishment movements has once again become an undeniable part of the political panorama in Latin America. It is a scenario of active resistance across the region that constitutes the "really existing globalisation," something which has exhibited tendencies towards an eventual ungovernability of neoliberalism. The social forces in struggle against the neoliberal debacle and its partner schemes of hegemonic integration constitutes the nucleus of an incipient integration "from below" whose partisans find themselves ever more obliged to collaborate in networks of diverse elements in order to consolidate their objectives. But if economic globalisation constitutes a large part of the current context in which Latin American political parties develop their political platforms, it is also important to draw into relief the persistent and intensifying set of external pressures that accompany these tendencies and have conditioned the political context of parties in an equally notable way.

Interventionist Policies and Regional Hegemony

It is essential to recognise that U.S. policies in the region have played an important and largely underestimated role in the development (and decomposition) of many of Latin America's political parties. In the 1980s, above all in the Caribbean Basin, the militarisation that was pursued by the Reagan and Bush (father) Administrations resulted in a direct troop in conjunction with a systematic deployment of intelligence forces and military aid. In that context, control over maritime routes also became designated as high priorities. The Caribbean islands contain various natural resources seen as strategically important by Washington such as petroleum, bauxite, gold, nickel, and other minerals. Under the banner of anticommunism, the Reagan Administration never hesitated to violate the sovereignty of countries in the region in order to further strategic and long-term U.S. interests.

Around the time of the invasion of Panama, the Bush (father) Administration ideologically consolidated post-Cold War U.S. policy under the ideological framework of progressive liberalisation of the market, perversely identified with "democratisation" and the "war against illegal drug trafficking. This remained dominant up until September 11, 2001 when the "War against Terrorism" was instituted as the dominant legitimating element for intensifying the most aggressive aspects of U.S. imperial interventionism.

If it is important to recognise that Washington has wielded dominant influence as a regional power, it is equally essential to remember that its punitive policies enjoy only a relative degree of success. In other words, interventionist policies generally demonstrate their limitations in accordance with parameters that are created by the accumulated "blowback" (Fine, 2006) of preceding interventionism and conditioned by the evolving macro-ideological and political context. One of the ways this becomes empirically discernable is through analysis of the extent to which ruling or oppositional political parties show a willingness to collaborate with foreign interventionism, either openly in its platforms or by other means including passive inaction or clandestine actions.

U.S. foreign policy under the so-called Bush Doctrine (Bush Jr.) unfolded under a newfound unilateralism and arrogance characterised by a pronounced irreverence for international law and the regional and international conventions that served Washington's interests so well in the past. Its open endorsement of "regime change" and explicit preference for "preventive interventions" has been the object of protest around the globe. Through hyper-militarisation and agreements designed to impose a hegemonic integration, Washington has sought to alleviate the precarious nature of neoliberal regimes in the short term while establishing a longer term framework of "inevitable interventions" that can manage to criminalise the forces of popular opposition.

The manifestations of this type of aggressive shift in imperial conduct through a regional recalibration of the economic and military order became placed in evidence during the period following the 2003 invasion of Iraq. Virtually all of the governments of the region were subjected to a new wave of pressure to accept its role as Washington's backyard. Various U.S. military aid recipients were threatened with a cut-off if they would not guarantee immunity to U.S. citizens before any International Criminal Tribunals. This kind of pressure to demand impunity for U.S. military personnel coincided with a period when the international mass media was filled with images of prison torture practised by U.S. military forces in Iraq and with allegations of the same surfacing in Afghanistan, Guantánamo and various third countries. The inevitable result was to fuel critical reactions on the part of social movements throughout a region that has been eternally accused by Washington to be human rights violators whenever a government responds to popular interests.

Just weeks before the war in Iraq commenced, demonstrations were occurring throughout the hemisphere. At the moment of the March invasion, Washington publicly maintained that it had the support of 49 countries in a so-called "coalition of the willing" that included Colombia, Costa Rica, Dominican Republic, El Salvador, Honduras, Nicaragua and Panama. Protests continued across the region against the invasion and subsequent military occupation, with many focusing on the sending of troops and cooperating personnel on the part of Honduras, El Salvador, Nicaragua and the Dominican Republic, countries that initially sent more than 300 of its people to Iraq in support of the occupation forces.

Indeed, only the governments of Cuba, Venezuela, México and the majority of the CARICOM countries manifested their complete disagreement with the invasion of Iraq while Central American and Panama along with the Dominican Republic provided the strongest positions of support for Washington. The alliance of the governments of Great Britain and Spain with the United States, in spite of the large popular opposition that existed in both countries, resounded in the region as the two principal ex-colonial powers. Given the fact that neoliberal globalisation and the imposition of hegemonic schemes of integration generates permanent conflicts in those areas where South-South relations collide with the interests of the North, the geopolitical climate produced by the U.S. military intervention in Iraq favoured the agglutination of popular opposition in Latin America against the Bush Doctrine. This in turn substantially elevated the pressures upon the region's political parties who needed to declare themselves as either "with Washington or against them."

The Extra-Constitutional Involvement of Armed Forces

The extra-constitutional involvement of the region's military establishments has its roots in a long history of the class exercise of power by national elites, reinforced by decades of foreign interventionism by countries of the North. During World War II, the United Sates sponsored a military coordination that attempted to consolidate the region in the event that war were to expand towards the region. The *Acta de Chapultepec* signed in Mexico City in 1945 established that any act of aggression in the region would result with a concerted response on the part of the entire hemisphere. In 1947, Inter-American Treaty of Reciprocal Assistance (Rio Treaty) established an even more closely integrated strategy of hemispheric defence as a result of Washington's preoccupation with an eventual confrontation with the former Soviet Union. With this plan in place, the United States had established the military framework for regional security under its hegemony.

With the rise of the populist government of Jacobo Arbenz Guzmán as part of the continuation of the October 1944 Revolution in Guatemala, the threat of a leftist radicalisation that would follow through on the clamour for transforming the elite structures in the region was interpreted in Washington through a Cold War lens. When Arbenz accepted the minority participation of the Guatemalan Communist Party in his administration as part of democratisation of Guatemalan politics, the oligarchy of that country collaborated with the U.S. Central Intelligence Agency to orchestrate the regime's overthrow in 1954 together with all of the reforms enacted since 1944. The history of Guatemala's political parties since then has been inseparable from the role of the nation's armed forces operating in defence of the reactionary class interests of the nation's oligarchy.

The success of the Guatemalan counter-revolution reinforced the Washington's emphasis upon its strategic collaboration with the region's military establishments in a broad campaign against insurgent movements and political oppositional fronts deemed receptive to Soviet penetration. Just as the Cuban Revolution of 1959 was a spark for revolutionary movements throughout the region, the failed mercenary invasion in 1961 at the Bay of Pigs, modelled precisely on the Guatemalan counter-revolution of 1954, marked the qualitative expansion of the U.S. counter-insurgency campaign throughout the region. The military commands of the region were shaped to accept their role as the guardians of the established order in the face of the insurgent left's growth. While military forces were trained in all kinds of repression, the public emphasis was placed on defence of the nation against the "weaknesses of liberal democracy" under the raging conditions of the Cold War.

This evolving national security doctrine conditioned the development of political parties across the entire region. The paradigm took shape with the military coup in Brazil in 1964 against the populist reform government of João Goulart. With the 1966 military seizure of power in Argentina, the pattern was established that would be replicated in other countries, such as in Chile and Uruguay in 1973 and once again in Argentina in 1976. From Central America down to the Southern Cone, the region's military establishments backed by their Northern sponsors would never hesitate to intervene in the process of "restoring order" in the face of the "political chaos" that popular demands represented.

The wave of military dictatorships that resulted all across the continent accorded the armed forces of each country with a permanent role in the political sphere. This process generally favoured the centralisation of executive power via the systematic weakening of parliaments that were periodically repressed by emergency decrees. The dictatorships managed national economies without any type of political representation while the reorganisation of the judicial realm permitted substitution of civil courts with military tribunals that were better suited to repress all forms of political opposition, thereby instituting strong restrictions on civil rights and the possibilities for political expression.

While it clearly evident that all of these processes conspired to transform the panorama of possibilities pertaining to political parties during the dictatorships, it is also the case that this perverse political framework survived the era of military governments. Virtually every transition to civil democracy was supervised and regulated to a significant degree by the military, serving to perpetuate the means by which military figures could continue on as major political actors.

The mythology that the political influence of military forces had been reduced in the neoliberal era is in complete contradiction with reality. The longstanding impunity of Pinochet in Chile and Rios Mont in Guatemala, the blanket amnesties of Argentina, the coup dramas of Ecuador, and the complete ease in which Fujimori and Montesinos were able to escape Peru in 2000 are just a few examples of the political orchestration conducted by regional armed forces. The persistent expression of paramilitary activity in various countries, always in close alliance with their respective military establishments, also provides testimony of the social control wielded over civil societies. While the nightmarish scenario in Colombia provides perhaps the most striking example of this, it can also be observed in a country like Brazil where the *União Democratica Ruralista* (UDR) acts on behalf of traditional landowner's interests to exerts its violent resistance land reform thanks to their strong ties to the country's armed forces (See Dello Buono, 2001).

Clearly, the failure of the military coup mounted against Hugo Chavez in Venezuela in 2002 and the fissures in impunity that have appeared among the most heinous cases of genocidal military actors in recent years in Argentina, Chile, Guatemala and other cases testify to the fact that extra-constitutional influence of the region's military establishments ultimately have social parameters. The precise location of these parameters itself becomes a polemical issue for debate among the political parties. In the case of Colombia, the war against "narco-guerrillas" has provided a smokescreen for justifying a massive expansion of the armed forces establishment, likewise facilitating the use of paramilitary organisations in a dirty war against any expression of popular forces in the country. Taking into account that way in which illegal drug trafficking has complicated the political panorama of not only Colombia but in countries all across the continent, above all in the Andean countries and the Caribbean Basin, it merits a brief, dedicated discussion of its overall impact.

Illegal Drug Trafficking and the Anti-Narcotics Security State

The issue of illegal narcotics climbed up the list of foreign policy priorities in the 1990s and has figured prominently there ever since. Production, consumption, trafficking and money laundering make up the four principal components of the issue, although there direct links as well to arms trafficking and corruption. From the onset of the so-called "war against drugs," there was a notable contradiction in the way that Washington pressured states to take a strong role in combating these elements through prohibition, crop eradication and especially financial regulations on the one hand while arguing for a minimalist state on the other.

The fact is that neoliberalism spawned the most favourable conditions imaginable for illegal narcotics trafficking and money laundering through the reduction of the state presence in national economies. Indeed, the illegal narcotics industry is one of the most globalised commodity chains ever created, its particular legal status notwithstanding. There is no question that the legal and illegal markets of the region are intimately interconnected and in some cases such as Colombia, narcotics capital has constituted an important driving force in the development of its macro-economy. It is highly probable that the pressures of globalisation generate a strong stimulus for economies throughout the region to involve themselves in narcotics trafficking at various levels.

Just as liberalisation of banking policies facilitates money laundering, the collapse of traditional crops makes it difficult to avoid rural involvement with the lucrative earnings associated with coca and other illicit crops. When the magnitude of profits and their associated interests are taken into account, including its linkages with arms and other finance, it is easier to explain the high levels of violence and the increasing participation of political elites as protectors and partners in crime. The resulting corruption is capable of altering the balance of power in practically any country in the region.

Andean and Caribbean Basin countries have undoubtedly been those most affected by the corruption and massive impact of this industry which includes widespread practises of intimidation, repression and control over political figures. With the exception of Cuba, it is difficult to find a country in these sub-regions where the substantial infiltration of illegal narcotics earnings has not been a major electoral campaign issue. Amidst this so-called "Colombianisation" of the region, it is increasingly difficult to determine which aspect of this globalised phenomenon is more problematic: the direct effects of the illegal drug business or the "anti-narcotics security state" designed to combat it.[6]

What is clear is that the anti-narcotics security state just like the national security state during the Cold War represents a convergence of foreign hegemonic power with various fractions of the region's ruling classes. The anti-narcotics agenda has been assimilated in the foreign agendas of almost the entire hemisphere. It has been presented in the agenda of the Summits of the Americas, the Association of Caribbean States, and so on. It is logical that the forced adoption of policies designed by foreign countries can substantially alter the political panorama of a peripheral nation and this imposition is perhaps the most pronounced example to be found today. To all of this must be added the effect caused by anti-narcotics policing which had produced a displacement of traditional routes originally established in the Caribbean towards Central America and Mexico.

Since the 1990s, Washington has employed the mechanism of "certification" of cooperation with U.S. anti-narcotics operations as a punitive instrument aimed at those countries who fail to adequately collaborate. Forced cooperation in interdiction and extradition has a great influence on new ties of North-South cooperation in the military sphere and impact negatively upon important national policies as in the case of the collapse of the peace talks in Colombia. The denial of certification to Colombia in 1996 during the Samper Administration had important implications for the stability of his government and later proved to be a key factor in his party's defeat in the presidential elections. The expansion of Plan Colombia under both the Clinton and Bush (Jr) Administrations that evolved into the "Andean Initiative" was in the reality the recycled logic of an earlier initiative first sponsored by the Bush (father) Administration during the 1989–1992 period. Its impact upon Colombian party politics is undeniable and managed to completely transform the destinies of the two main political parties of Colombia, giving rise to the pro-U.S. political grouping that eventually assumed power with the candidacy of Alvaro Uribe. In other countries, similar effects have resulted

---

[6] For an excellent discussion, see Jorge Rodríguez Beruff, "De la 'narcodemocracia' y el Leviatán antidrogas: fuerzas de seguridad, Estado pospopulista y nuevas formas de autoritarismo en el Caribe", in Wilfredo Lozano (ed.), Cambio político en el Caribe: Escenarios de la posguerra fría – Cuba, Haití y República Dominicana, Caracas: Nueva Sociedad and FLACSO-Programa Dominican Republic, 1998, pp. 183–207.

from anti-narcotics interventionism, beginning with the invasion of Panama and arrest of Manuel Noriega to the collapse of various Caribbean notables.

In the case of Bolivia, years of social conflict linked to state anti-narcotics policies shook the country. Bolivian coca producers strengthened their organisation and energetically opposed crop fumigations imposed from abroad. The eventual political consequences has become evident with the emergence of Evo Morales at the head of the Movement towards Socialism (MAS) which build a broad social base out of the coca producers movement in opposing repression against coca cultivators and denouncing the lackey stance of the pro-U.S., elite dominated political establishment. Morales made a strong showing in the 2002 elections, becoming an important oppositional political actor who later proved victorious in the 2006 presidential elections. His victory has placed the issue of blind compliance with Washington on crop eradication measures on the regional agenda.

The electoral victory of Evo Morales was an important point of political reference for all leftist parties in the region. Yet, the left cannot generally claim to have escaped the larger crisis that has come to affect all Latin American political parties. On the contrary, the left has experienced a deep and persistent crisis that in itself constitutes an additional factor in explaining the broader crisis of all the region's parties.

The Post-Cold War Crisis of the Latin American Left

While it is not the purpose of this work to summarise the causes of the crisis of the Latin American left, there are some excellent studies that delve into this issue and have offered some basic elements for our discussion.[7] It can briefly be argued that during the Cold War, leftist political parties and movement organisations ideologically shared pro-Moscow or Maoist platforms, with a smaller Trotskyst presence that was centred mostly in Argentina and Peru. The armed movements of the left most notably gained force in Cuba, Venezuela, Colombia, Bolivia, Guatemala, El Salvador and Nicaragua. The influence of figures such as Che Guevara was strong in the 1960s, proposing the possibility of an armed victory of popular forces over the established armies in an arena of popular guerrilla war.

---

[7] For example, see Marta Harnecker, *The Left at the Threshold of the XXI Century: Making the Impossible Possible*, LINKS no. 16: September to December, 2000, published in Spanish by Editorial de Ciencias Sociales (1999) , Havana, Cuba.

The defeat of the armed campaigns in which Che and Camilo Torres participated along with the electoral triumph of Salvador Allende in Chile, among other factors, generated a shift in emphasis on the part of substantial portion of the left in the early 1970s towards a strategy of forming class alliances in order to win electoral victory. The Chilean military coup in 1973 quickly took the wind out of the sails of this euphoria, convincingly demonstrating that the region's ruling classes in collaboration with imperialism was not going to easily permit the possibility of real structural change by peaceful means. With the left, the reaction was to turn once more to a new proliferation of armed clandestine resistance movements in Uruguay, Argentina and other countries where the conflicts soon shifted towards urban centres. This included the Montoneros and the Revolutionary People's Army of Argentina, the Tupamaros in Uruguay, the M-19 in Colombia, the Alfaro Vive in Ecuador, and the MRTA and Shining Path insurgencies in Peru.

In spite of the tremendous repression unleashed to eradicate the region's armed movements, the decade of the 1970s ended with the Sandinista (FSLN) Revolution in Nicaragua and the New Jewel Movement's (NJM) Revolution in Grenada. With the transformation of the FSLN and NJM into political parties in power, and significant advances of the popular movements being registered in El Salvador and Guatemala, the 1980s initiated a period of intense U.S. intervention in the region. Washington turned to eliminate everything it perceived as Soviet penetration in the region. The collapse of the revolutionary movement in Grenada following a period of destabilisation and consolidated with a military invasion and occupation of the island marked the commencement of military intervention in the Caribbean Basin. Washington moved to militarise the entirety of Central America, managing to detain the steady advances of the Salvadoran and Guatemalan insurgencies while bogging down Nicaragua into a costly counterrevolutionary war. After ten years of intervention, the Sandinista government was defeated electorally, increasing the isolation and effectively surrounding the Salvadoran and Guatemalan popular forces. The earlier collapse of the Grenadian revolution had an equally negative impact in the Anglo-Caribbean, above all in countries like Jamaica.

By the early 1990s, the collapse of the Soviet Bloc and the resulting economic crisis that subsequently affected Cuba all served to weaken the left's ideological points of reference. In Central America, this served to further increase the pressure on the revolutionary left in Central America to move towards peace talks. Negotiations eventually gathered momentum leading

El Salvador and later Guatemala into a negotiated settlement and disarmament. Former armed movements were now becoming electoral political parties, including the FMLN of El Salvador, the URNG of Guatemala, M-19 in Colombia and others, seeking a reinsertion into the national political landscape as an alternative to kind of military defeat experience by the Shining Path and the MRTA in Peru. More recently, the Zapatista (EZLN) movement has moved in that direction, seeking to join a trend towards electoral advances by parties such as the *Frente Amplio* of Uruguay and the *Polo Democrático Alternativo* of Colombia, providing a new line up of leftist political party formations.

Conclusion

The panorama of Latin America's political parties, marked by the internal conflicts and external interventions of preceding decades, continues to shift in the wake of the structural transformation and social movements associated with the crisis of neoliberalism. Many of the armed movements of the left have become converted into electoral parties, reformulating its ideological consensus in meetings such as the Sao Paulo Forum and exploring the most adequate kind of linkage to force with the new social movements that have risen in opposition to political and social exclusion. Some such as the FSLN discuss the reformulation of their platforms in an attempt to reconcile the new conditions in the electoral field produced by globalisation and neoliberal restructuration. Their various electoral defeats at the hands of the political establishment has proven that winning with such a strategy will not be easy.

Nevertheless, this hope in the electoral area has its explanation. Globalisation and neoliberal reforms in conjunction with the imposition of hegemonic regional integration schemes have imposed changes on the dominant political parties in which their self-transformation effectively undermines their traditional bases of electoral support. In Venezuela, the popular response to the abrupt turn to the right and neoliberalism on the part of Carlos Andrés Pérez helped to accelerate a near total loss of support of the established political parties. This in turn prepared the electoral rise to power of Hugo Chavez and the Bolivarian Revolution that has shaken the entire region.

In Mexico, the historic fall from power of the PRI, the traditional ruling party was also produced by the contradictions in the model of transition to a neoliberal platform which the PRI was forced to assume. The decomposition of Mexican corporativism made the fall of the PRI inevitable. Among those that abandoned the PRI included those who formed the PRD, with Cuauhtémoc Cárdenas, ex-presidential candidate and leader of the PRD, declaring at one point his resolute opposition to neoliberalism, condemning it as an assault upon the popular sectors. The PRD has since grown to be a major political force in Mexican politics.

Each of these important changes in the region show roots in some of the conditioning factors discussed in this chapter. In Peru, the decomposition of the Fujimori Dictatorship in the throes of massive corruption and subsequently, the free fall in popularity of the Toledo Administration helped pave the way for the likely political return of the APRA party under the leadership of Alan Garcia in 2006. It also produced an ascent of the anti-establishment candidacy of Ollanta Humala. Despite Garcia's narrow victory in the Presidential runoff, he is destined to be greeted by a strong opposition in the Congress where forces loyal to Humala handily won a plurality.

We have seen that the U.S. anti-drug policies have also exerted considerable pressures upon the Andean and Caribbean Basin countries, with Plan Colombia serving as the prototype of intervention in the region. The importance of the armed forces in the region, something that casts a shadow over the political panorama of countries such as Chile and Guatemala continues to be an issue that demarcates among political parties and elevates the importance of electoral defeats of figures such as Rios Mont while increasing the significance of electoral victories of candidacies such as Bachelet in Chile. Both cases illustrate a persistent social polarisation that has its origins in the military dictatorships and patterns of repression that popular forces have lived in the recent past. Finally, the fall in disgrace of those figures most associated with the neoliberal transition demonstrates the limits of the anti-popular regimes and their political parties, be they traditional parties such as the PRI and the Pro-Menem faction of Peronism in Argentina, more recent party formations such as those of Fujimori in Peru or Moscoso in Panama, or even those that initially were propelled into power with the strong support of social movements such as Gutierrez in Ecuador.

The precise role of the popular movements and new forms of resistance that have appeared in recent years continues to be an issue for further investigation. In Bolivia, Colombia and Peru, a strong wave of peasant resistance has arisen around the organising initially conducted by coca cultivators. This movement has achieved its maximum expression in Bolivia with the electoral victory of Evo Morales, symbolising a triumphant articulation of class-based demands with the rights of Andean peoples to cultivate coca, preserve their indigenous way of life and transform their popular organisations into a political party capable of electoral victory.

In the South, the Landless People's Movement (MST) in Brazil has been the prototype of a the new generation of social movements dedicated to organising the demands for socioeconomic rights. Their actions have achieved a favourable balance of support in public opinion and have strengthened political opposition to neoliberal policies, something that initially favoured the electoral victory of President Lula of the Brazilian Workers Party (PT) and which has subsequently generated pressure upon his administration for more radical change.

In Panama, the heterogeneous grouping of social movements FRENADESSO has mobilised workers, students, and various progressive sectors in campaigns of direct action in defence of social security and in favour of national development based on social justice. Its mass mobilisation forced the Torrijos government to suspend parts of the social security reform that it imposed. More broadly, however, it demonstrated the lack of an adequate response on the part of the established political parties to the demands being made by the popular sectors in the throes of neoliberal crisis.

The complex relationships between new political actors and political parties remains an important area of investigation. This includes the role of the NGOs which have become increasingly important actors in the Latin American political landscape. In almost all of the region, activists of leftist political parties and organisations eventually became inserted in NGO projects. Many of these activists have had to assume the task of directly confronting the impact caused by the abrupt reduction in state services resulting from neoliberalism. In some case, they have helped form the nucleus of political opposition when the possibility of directly organising political party opposition has been too difficult. NGO's have been active in issues such as the environment, indigenous and displaced populations, women's rights, rights of ethnic and racial minorities, the elderly and children, among other discriminated sectors. In this sense, it is impossible to ignore their relations with political parties.

Nor can the importance of trade union movements be ignored in the panorama of political parties. The 1990s witnessed strong mobilisations on the part of miners in Chile and Bolivia, rural workers organisations in Paraguay and Brazil, and public sector employees in practically the entire region, being particularly active in the struggles against privatisation. Public sector works have confirmed their status as an important social actor and one that is pivotal in the new correlation of social forces in opposition to neoliberalism.

In addition, new points of convergence between the organised expressions of popular resistance can been seen, for example, between the academic sector and regional networks, between trade unions and agrarian organisations, between indigenous organisations and ecological groups, and so on. It would seem ever clearer that only an alliance of organised movements of the popular sectors together with the multi-class organisations of indigenous peoples, the women's movement, threatened segments of the small private sector and students would be capable of breathing life into a broad political project alternative to neoliberalism. Globalisation has intensified the basic contradictions of neoliberal capitalism in Latin America, something well illustrated by the crisis in hegemonic regional integration that has become bogged down in intense popular opposition. The desires of the regional superpower notwithstanding, the real process of regional integration will have to be analysed with respect to the cumulative dynamics of resistance that neoliberal globalisation has itself created.

Although an overall assessment of the recent electoral advances of the left and centre-left is still the subject of controversy, the victories of Lula in Brazil, Tabaré Vasquez in Uruguay, Chavez in Venezuela, Kirchner in Argentina, and Bachelet in Chile have demonstrated that the alignment of ruling political parties can change as a result of the changing configuration of factors such as those discussed in this study. Capitalist globalisation has produced new forms of popular resistance in opposition to neoliberalism on the part of the most exploited and excluded sectors of the region. In part, the parties of the left and the centre-left have begun to capitalise upon those contradictions of the period.

As analysts such as Petras and Veltmeyer (2006) have argued, these advances can be more apparent than real. If they are correct, these ruling parties will almost certainly lead towards accommodation with the neoliberal establishment, contributing to a loss of credibility on the part of the left and increased popular disaffection with electoral politics. The most populist among them will continue to experience serious challenges that will oblige them to seek a self-transformation that is compatible with advanced neoliberalism, thus favouring the disintegration of their political bases. The discussion of neoliberal globalisation in this paper suggested the strong limitations which the present structural conjuncture places upon ruling political parties. Although few on the left will rush to the conclusion suggested above by Petras and Veltmeyer, the mounting evidence from the political evolution of diverse political currents in power such as those of Panama's Torrijos, Brazil's Lula, Uruguay's Vasquez, Argentina's Kirchner, Peru's Garcia and Chile's Bachelet will inevitably force us back to the examining table.

A happier conclusion rests in the possibility of a broad regional opposition to neoliberalism that can continue accumulating forces, permitting the construction of a counter-hegemonic bloc and favouring the cultivation of an alternative model of development and popular integration for Latin America. While it is a more desirable scenario, the evidence of its definitive emergence still remains scant. Among all of these contradictory dynamics, the crisis of the region's political parties is in good measure a reflection of the structural and multidimensional impact of neoliberalism. To that extent, political parties remain an indispensable arena of struggle, among others, in the social transformation of the region.

Wim Dierckxsens

Social Movements and the Capitalist Crisis: Towards a Latin American Alternative

Introduction: A Social Movement Born Amidst the Neoliberal Crisis

The world social movement for an alterative to neoliberalism, that is, the so called "alterworld movement" was born and is developing amidst the internal contradictions of global capital locked in a struggle for world domination. The neoliberal model does not reinforce the economic growth of the world economy, but rather the dividing up of the world market on behalf of transnational capital. Investments therefore do not fuel growth but rather the repartition of the existing market by way of mergers, acquisitions, privatisations, and the substitution of local and national markets by other transnationals. The kind of transnational capital growth that occurs through capturing already existing markets takes place at the expense of the growth of the market as a whole. The Washington Consensus favoured the partitioning of the world market on behalf of transnational capital and the finance capital that is tied to it.

This unfolding process has been costly for the countries of the South. Beginning with the decade of the 1990s, it also proved costly for the ex-Soviet Bloc. With the fall of that Bloc, it seemed that there was no longer any alternative to neoliberalism. With much fanfare, ruling elites at the beginning of the 1990s celebrated the "End of History." It was proclaimed that there was no longer any other utopia but the sole and total option of neoliberalism for all time. During the first half of the 1990s, there was no broad social movement beyond particular and localised movements. In sum, it was a period of little hope.

Towards the end of the 1990s, however, the panorama began to change. The world market was basically distributed among the principal transnational enterprises. Since then, a redistribution of the market in favour of some transnationals was taking place ever more exclusively at the cost of others. In those circumstances, the Washington Consensus began to come to an end, i.e., neoliberalism began to confront itself as transnational and finance capital.

The ensuing dispute among big capital for the redistribution of the existing market began to become increasingly evident by the end of the 1990s. The first confrontation of interests among the principal superpowers took place in 1997. The Asian crisis and the management of same by the IMF and World Bank was carried out to the benefit of the United States. Huntington, perceiving that there was insufficient room in the world for the West and the East, put forward his thesis (See Huntington 1994; 1997) concerning the inevitable nature of the clash of civilisations. In a world where all of the existing worlds cannot fit, the West according to Huntington would have more rights than the East in order to defend its place.

In 1998, a new confrontation of interests developed among the Western powers themselves. In a Paris meeting of the OECD (made up of 28 highly industrialised countries) around the so-called Multilateral Investment Agreement (MIA), conflict surfaced among the Western powers. In 1999 during the World Trade Organisation (WTO) meeting in Seattle, the disagreements between powers over dividing up the world market among transnationals was once again evident. In short, the neoliberal model was now spawning increasingly more direct conflicts on an increasingly more frequent basis between big centres of capital and their national agents. This conflict of private interests became translated more and more visibly into an economic war between the various nation-states that represent transnational and finance capital.

Towards the end of the 1990s, the free reign of the market that was dogmatically predicated upon neoliberal ideology was showing in practice a face that was manifestly contradictory. The free market is based on a notion that "others" must follow, i.e., a normative rule of conduct that all must respect except of course the transnationals themselves. Governments have to respect and protect the interests of the transnationals if they are weaker than the competition. However, for the weakest of the lot, the free play of the market must rule without mercy, even if it annihilates everything in sight.

Every product or service in the globalised world must be transformed into a commodity and the entire world needed to open its borders to the big transnationals so that they could avail themselves of the surrounding markets. This opening was valid for the entire world, so long as it did not come to negatively affect the transnationals themselves. The countries of the South in general and Latin America in particular where their own transnationals practically do not exist, were inexorably pushed to open up its economic borders.

With the world market opening up, national products became substituted by transnational products. By this time, the replacement of national goods could be evidenced in any supermarket in the hemisphere. Public services became progressively privatised by transnational companies. Private investments had their way with a market based on products or services already established by previous public development. These were investments that did not contribute to further growth but rather the cornering of existing markets. The same occurred in the private sectors by way of mergers and acquisition of existing companies. All of these investments into repartition were making no contribution to absolute economic growth.

Finance capital cast its lot with these investments since the profits were fabulous and secure. In the meantime, it abandoned investment in national production. This policy encouraged the concentration of markets and earnings into ever fewer hands. Almost all of international trade became transnational in nature, with an increasing percentage being made up of intra-firm transactions of these same transnational companies.

As the transnationals appropriate more and more of the South's market, there is ever less remaining to divide up. The repartitioning of the global market tends to decelerate, bringing a fall in profits along with it. With all of the prior emphasis on existing markets rather than an expansion of productive investments, accumulation based on economic growth also begins to decelerate. The rate of growth for the transnationals, under such conditions, now relies almost exclusively upon greater aggressiveness in this same non-productive game of competition for existing markets.

Concretely, a greater opening of markets among the same capitalist powers gradually became necessary. This kind of economic opening, however, tends to affect the interest of the transnationals themselves in one or another bloc and in one or another sector. Transnational capital, nevertheless, does not tolerate anything that "its government" does which may go against its strategic interests. The confrontation between countries of the North over the mutual opening of its own markets is a logical consequence. In the multilateral forums, such disputes between the governments of the principal capitalist powers have come to dominate discussion.

The protection of the market of the North in benefit of the transnationals emerged as an issue of high visibility and it obviously contrasts with the deregulation that has been imposed upon the South. This contradictory policy nonetheless subverts the general neoliberal creed.

The conflicts in multilateral forums (WTO, MIA) constituted a political set of brakes on the deepening of the politics of deregulation. Since then, a political environment in favour of national sovereignty has developed which is beneficial for the transnationals based in the principal capitalist countries. This position contrasts with the deregulation that was applied in the periphery without any regard for their development interests. The capitalist powers prioritise sovereignty at the expense of deregulation of the market in their own territories when greater economic opening places their strategic interests at risk. At the same time, these powers impose with all of their force the policies of deregulation beyond their borders when such practise reinforces the interests of their transnationals. The resulting contradiction in neoliberalism's own doctrine becomes visible for the entire world to see and it comes to a head in the discord that continues to break out within the multilateral forums. It is precisely this visible contradiction that opened up the political space for social movements that question the neoliberal model.

The "alterglobalisation movement" was born on all continents at practically the same time. In the mainstream mass media, there was a considerable hurry to discredit the anti-globalisation movement. During the final years of the Twentieth Century, demonstrations took place all across the world against the multilateral institutions (IMF, World Bank, WTO) that were responsible for policies of methodical extermination in the South. Atrocious policies of structural adjustment had been applied without any concern for the periphery. The outbreak of social struggles was therefore an expression of a worldwide questioning of the policies pursued by the multilateral institutions. Activists now took direct aim at the neoliberal policies being put forward by the main capitalist powers in the G-7 forum. The persistence of this cycle of protests together with their worldwide scope points not only to a crisis of legitimacy for the targeted institutions but suggests the rise of a global social movement in opposition to neoliberalism.

The simultaneous combination of protectionist policies alongside of an insistence on the free reign of the market acquires special significance for the half of the world's population that subsists on agriculture. In 1995, the volume of public agricultural spending (subsidies) increased to US$286 billion according to the WTO. At least 90% of this spending took place in the Triad that includes the United States and Canada; European Community; and Japan. The agricultural priorities on the WTO agenda have been selected in such a way so as to serve the objective of the opening of the markets of the South to the huge and subsidised agricultural surplus of the North which must be exported.

As the WTO maintained following the Doha Conference in November of 2001, agriculture will be integrated into the set of general rules of competition, assimilating agricultural goods within the category of "trade commodities." The consequences of this policy will be catastrophic for the half of humanity that depends upon agriculture under a gigantic world stage of technological inequality. No industrial development, not even in China despite its extremely dynamic economic situation, can possibly absorb even a third of this displaced population. Worse yet, the unfolding of this "authentic neoliberalism" with or without export subsidies of the North, will be catastrophic for peasants in the South. This is where the necessity to maintain peasant agriculture in the 21st Century originates, something that is for example well-acknowledged by China (See Samir Amin, 2004: 269–272).

In the WTO summit of 2003 in Cancún, it became clear that the United States and the European Union were not willing to offer any substantial lowering of its high subsidy levels. This was so even while they intransigently argued that the countries of the South must unconditionally open their markets to Northern Agribusiness. The intolerance of the main capitalist powers was evident: either the world agrees to negotiate under their conditions or there will be no negotiations.

It should come as no surprise that China, India and Brazil together were leading the "Group of 21" in representation of almost one-half of the world's population, this given that their countries would greatly suffer from the exclusion of peasants. The domestic struggle of the peasantry in these countries acquires an especially massive character (such as the Landless Peoples Movement in Brazil) and if the proposed accords were to come into force, the situation would be uncontrollable. The interaction between these social movements and the governments of the South, has acquired greater objective space ever since the failed summit in Seattle.

The protectionist and intransigent attitude of the main powers with respect to agriculture in Cancun was the very argument that ensured the collapse of the talks. The multilateral negotiations around agricultural liberalisation were soundly rejected by the countries of the South. Ever since this defeat, the WTO can no longer claim to represent a viable instrument for the main capitalist powers. In order to impose its will upon the rest of the world, these powers must now rely upon new strategies.

The Specific Context of the Social Struggle in Latin America

Since the end of the past century, the multilateral accords aimed at partitioning the world have repeatedly failed. With that, the battle for the global market has acquired a visible and geographical expression. This fact is manifested with the reaffirmation and accelerated expansion of different economic blocs. This is not to say that the blocs didn't exist earlier. Beginning with the final years of the 1990s, however, the policy of annexation kicked into high gear.

Europe over a period of more than forty years had gradually advanced towards a European Union in order to be economically equipped to compete with the United States. Since the end of the 1990s, the European Union opted for a rapid annexation of the Eastern European countries rather than internally consolidating itself. At the same time, the United States has worked on an accelerated regional project to create a macro-area that can permit it to confront the mega competition of the European Union. Following the commencement of the North American Free Trade Agreement in 1994 and the collapse towards the end of the 1990s of the multilateral WTO accords, the United States accelerated its project to annex Latin America by way of the FTAA. This included adoption of the so-called "fast track" approach, i.e., submitting to Congressional approval that which was agreed to by the respective governments, without any option for modifying the agreement.

Since then, the world has become more visibly divided than before into economic blocs with different areas of strategic interest. The big powers of these economic blocs seek exclusive trade and investment rights over the annexed markets. In this way, some obtain exclusive rights while others do not. Upon the formation of these blocs, the main powers confront each other in a global market war. Within the bloc, the transnationals impose the principles of total free market rule in favour of their interests such as the case of the FTAA. To be annexed as a country or a region implies having ones markets forced opened. This offers secure spaces for foreign investment that can guarantee North American-based transnational capital a total freedom of movement and complete protection in the face of any possible limitation, condition or loss of profitability. Economic blocs become transformed into mega markets for a few transnationals to defend themselves against their main competitors and to take complete territorial control. Through the FTAA, the United States sought unrestricted access not only to Latin American markets but to the continent's natural resources as could be seen in the Québec summit of 2001 (See Tablada and Dierckxsens, 2005: 274–276).

All of the multilateral policies of structural adjustment focused upon lifting the protections accumulated in the countries of the South. Economic integration under the neoliberal conception signified a total opening of the Latin American region to trade and investment of the transnationals, all in the name of greater efficiency. By incorporation into an economic bloc, annexation was to signify an opening up to the North American transnationals. The formation of a bloc is seen as an exclusionary and protectionist policy in exclusive benefit to a few North American transnationals at the cost of others (European, Japanese, etc.) and at the cost of the population that lives in the annexed countries.

The formation of economic blocs under the initiative of the capitalist superpowers of the North under their own protectionist policy offered a new opportunity to the countries of the South to create their own economic blocs. The same policy of creating economic blocs reopened the possibility of a return to protectionism in the South. It was in this context that the MERCOSUR bloc was formed (Argentina, Brazil, Paraguay and Uruguay) and indeed, one increasingly hears of the possibility of a South-South bloc (South Africa, Brazil, China, India, etc.).

In the February 2004 Cancún meeting of trade ministers of 34 countries in the framework of the FTAA, the issue of agricultural subsidies in the United States was once again the point of contention that led to the failure of the talks. The MERCOSUR representatives demanded the elimination of agricultural subsidies and of supports for production in the United States as a necessary pre-condition for reaching any agreement on opening their countries to North American agribusiness. Once again, it predictably showed that with the United States, it was necessary to negotiate as they wanted or there would be no negotiations at all. After the WTO had stalled, the FTAA likewise came to a dead end.

In this protectionist context, the popular struggle for the defence of food security gained currency all across the continent. Every failed set of negotiations of multilateral or regional treaties signified a victory for the popular movement. These achievements fuelled the movement and put the protagonists of free market trade on the defensive. The *Coordinadora Latinoamericana de Organizaciones del Campo* (CLOC) and *Vía Campesina* have fought a hard struggle for the defence of local and regional markets with the aim of guaranteeing just prices for agricultural products. The Landless People's Movement (MST) of Brazil, *Vía Campesina* and the *CLOC* struggle for greater access to land and a more just distribution. They also struggle to detain and avoid privatisations, the issuance of patents to genetically modified materials, and in general to defend the interests of peasants and indigenous peoples. Thanks to the failed multilateral negotiations, foodstuffs are no longer considered just another commodity and the food production system is not being treated strictly in accordance with the logic of the market (See Rafael Alegría, 2003: 15–18).

Characteristics of National Social Movements

To the extent that the FTAA has faltered, the United States has searched for an alterative means to consolidate its regional bloc, namely, the proliferation of Free Trade Agreements (FTA's). The policy is to advance via the conclusion of bilateral agreements with countries such as Chile (2004), Colombia, Ecuador, Peru, and Bolivia, along with a free trade agreement with Central America and the Dominican Republic. In January of 2002, the Bush Administration proposed to the OAS the opening of negotiations with the Central American countries. At the beginning of the century, the White House had argued that a Free Trade Agreement with Central America was still not viable due to the small size of their economies. It was considered at that time that the FTAA was the most adequate mechanism for the region. However, the difficulties encountered by the United States during the various negotiating rounds and the subsequently critical vision that more and more governments adopted forced Washington to change its approach, but not its logic.

The opposition to the Free Trade Agreements first expressed by the action of the Zapatistas in Mexico back in 1994 became considerably broadened across the continent with the opposition to the FTAA. Innumerable resistances were generated, forming a broad alliance which has included social movements in Latin America, Canada and the United States.

Peasant and Indigenous Peoples' Movements

Social protest against the Free Trade Agreements (FTAs) intensified an already existing struggle in each country against the policies of structural adjustment. Neoliberal policies in general and the FTAs in particular are characterised by a veritable agrarian counter-reform and a new concentration of land that is expressed through the rise of agribusiness. In Paraguay, Argentina and to a lesser extent in Brazil (due to legal limitations until relatively recently), the area cultivated by genetically modified crops (that demands the use of high impact herbicides) grew at accelerated rhythms over recent years and have deepened the processes of land concentration while causing irreversible ecological damage. This policy brings with it a sometimes brutal elimination of production by small peasants and indigenous communities. In the face of the massive exclusion of peasants and indigenous peoples, there exist scant possibilities for inclusion with a neoliberal framework.

In this context, a war emerged against trans-genetic crops and on behalf of life and sovereignty. The struggle was particularly illustrative in Paraguay with blockaded highways and land occupations. In this so-called "Crop War" at the beginning of 2004, a dynamic process unfolded that included land occupations and demands for the redistribution of land that involved a broad alliance of social organisations. This resulted in the National Front for the Struggle for Life and Sovereignty (FNLSV) that promotes an anti-neoliberal development programme. The FNLSV's mobilisations placed enormous pressure on the government. The government's failure to abide by the agreements reached with Front led to a series of open confrontations, culminating in a national civic strike. In this manner, the social movement transcended its sectoral grievances and acquired a political character demanding an alternative systemic model (See Seoane and Taddei, 2005:2–3).

One threat is the development of agribusiness while another equally lethal one is the overly wide opening to agricultural products from the United States. The relentless importation of agricultural and livestock products under

the existing free trade agreements accelerates the destruction of national production and regional markets of the small and medium-sized producers.
These treaties leave them to fend for themselves in an unviable situation of
competition as can be seen in the Mexican experience. Agricultural and livestock subsidies in the United States are concentrated in products such as corn,
sugar, rice and dairy products, precisely those products which are fundamental for feeding countries and for which national producers retain a certain level of competitiveness.

Washington was adamant in showing its unwillingness to compromise on
its policies, particularly in the regulations contained in the CAFTA framework. The result was the destruction of the regional agricultural base, food
security and national sovereignty along with a larger external debt. It is the
height of absurdity that Mexico, a corn based culture, is now importing subsidised, transgenetic corn from the United States. An equally ridiculous situation can be found in the potato-producing Andean Countries that stand to
increase their importation of genetically-altered U.S. potatoes, just as Central
America has increased its importation of transgenetic rice, a traditional food
crop consumed by the region. With the threat of its massive exclusion without any possibility of reinsertion, there are no alternatives offered to the ruined
peasants under this total market system. The struggle for land and agrarian
reform appears not as a goal as such but rather as a struggle for life.

In Brazil, this struggle takes on a special significance on account of the
numbers of people involved and its political dimension. The Brazilian Landless
Peoples Movement (MST) is the most important social movement in Latin
America. The political project that the MST is developing transcends the mere
desire of individuals to obtain land. Rather, MST activities revolve around a
broader and more ambitious project of creating a democratic society based
on solidarity, equality, and greater ecological consciousness. The internal
organisation of the movement adheres to principles of participatory democracy, thus situating it in a similar kind of current as the Zapatistas of Mexico,
within a framework of a new orientation that contrasts with the tradition of
centralism, bureaucratism, and vanguard-ism (See Amin and Houtart, 2003:
130–131).

In view of a neoliberal environment that is ever more aggressive, the social
and economic rights of landless peasants and indigenous communities become
reduced to almost nothing. The indigenous communities are at risk of losing
the right to their own survival. They offer little benefit to big capital and their

link to the market is so weak that their exclusion tends to be massive and definitive. There is practically no possibility that they can be reinserted into the market economy. To not be linked to the market today and having no future prospect for such a linkage tomorrow, the population is superfluous to the present system. Indeed, to the extent that they occupy certain territories desired for their lands and natural resources, they become transformed into an obstacle to the transnationals that must be eradicated. For their part, the social mobilisations of the indigenous peoples do not solely revolve around the demand for land. Rather, they increasingly exhibit the character of territorial defence and of struggle for another possible world where the indigenous peoples' way of life has a safe and secure place.

It has become a common practise that the intervention of military and paramilitary forces is deployed to "clean up" territories of interest to the transnationals through the implementation of mega projects. This can be very clearly seen in Colombia, Bolivia, Paraguay and Peru. With the implementation of radically neoliberal policies in the agricultural sector, there is little hope for the large majority of landless peasants much less the indigenous communities. The only possibility for survival rests upon a collective resistance against neoliberal policies as can be readily observed not only in Mexico but also in Ecuador, Peru, Paraguay and Bolivia. It is not strange that the central demand of the indigenous communities is for a world where multiple worlds, including indigenous ones, can co-exist. This has become the common scenario of nearly all of the indigenous communities of Latin America. The coordinated struggle of such communities has not only appeared at the national level but also across borders. On the national level, worthy of mention is the National Confederation of Indigenous Nationalities of Ecuador (CONAIE – *Confederación de Nacionalidades Indígenas de Ecuador*) and the FSLNV of Paraguay. Beyond that has emerged the notion of the pluri-national state that can channel the representation of various indigenous nationalities at an even broader level (See Amin and Houtart, 2003: 137; 2004: 144).

Workers Movements and Organisations of the Excluded

Social and economic rights are derived from the link that an individual has with the labour market. An urban worker is generally less replaceable and has greater work stability than rural workers. A skilled labourer has even greater stability than an unskilled one, with more stable salaries and a greater probability of having some form of insurance. Professionals have, as a general rule, greater opportunities for work and more job security, stability and higher income than do skilled workers. Professionals are the least replaceable and most expensive to employ since they enjoy greater social protection. Men tend to have greater work opportunities and options than do women. In this regard, whites have advantages over other ethnic groups and the workers of the core countries have far greater opportunities than their counterparts in the periphery.

Having greater work opportunities signifies being less replaceable or less disposable, which in turn translates into greater economic security. The less replaceable the work force is, the higher cost it implies, thus improving its level of social protection. Economic and social rights, in other words, depends on the position of the individual in the labour market and the particular evolution of that market. If the opportunities for work in the labour market increase, i.e., greater inclusion, the replacement capacity of the labour force shrinks and labour stability increases. With that, social and economic rights of the workers become enhanced. This scenario corresponds with Keynesian policies. If the labour market, in contrast, actually contracts as is the case with neoliberal policies, there is greater exclusion and lost of labour stability. In that context, no matter how much workers struggle, they are ever more replaceable and even disposable and thus remain at risk of losing their social and economic rights.

With neoliberal policies in place, the opportunities for work diminish as investments become oriented towards non-productive sectors of finance and speculation. Instead of investing in productive branches that would expand the economy as a whole, investments flow towards acquisitions and the privatisation of already existing enterprises. The massive substitution of local or national products by those of the transnationals, once tariffs are dismantled, has signified a huge loss of opportunities for work that cannot be compensated for by the new kinds of poorly compensated work being created such as openings in *maquiladora* plants. All of this implies a permanent, general decline in opportunities for work. The rates of unemployment and underemployment increase without pause and immigration creates an escape valve for the massive lack of work. Given the restrictions and selectivity of immigration, this cannot hope to compensate for the lost opportunities for those affected.

Neoliberalism in Latin America made the replacement of the labour force ever easier, making the labour market more flexible and dragging down the economic and social rights of workers along with it. The evolution of wages tends to always remain behind inflation, with the proportion of people earning close to the poverty line increasing, the length of the work day extending, and the prevailing low level of wages leading to a greater reliance on underpaid child and female labourers. In other words, there is general decline in social and economic rights for workers and this has been observed all across Latin America.

In this context of seemingly permanent reverses for workers, trade unionism remains on the defensive with respect to workers rights. Their struggle in the neoliberal environment is a struggle to avoid even greater losses of their social and economic rights. In this period, trade unionism is no longer the most dynamic social organisation but on the contrary tends to lag behind in the social struggle for an alternative, experiencing one reversal after another. Amidst the threat of its massive exclusion and with the ever-present prospects of their corrupt leadership selling them out, the working class can find no alternative within the existing trade union system. It is in this setting where new movements of the excluded were born, such as the "picketers' movement." Although this phenomenon is best known in Argentina and Uruguay, it is also present in other countries and has the greatest potential in those countries where the urban working class was relatively numerous but has become massively threatened by exclusion.

The picketers' movement as it arose in Argentina and Uruguay represented the vital necessity for the working masses (not exclusively the unemployed) to struggle against exclusion and unemployment, ironically demanding the "right to be exploited." Under an extreme form of neoliberalism as existed in the case of Argentina after 1995, unemployment and labour instability generated an enormous economic and social insecurity. The abandonment of the unemployed on the part of the trade union bureaucracy in conjunction with the persecution of trade union workers on the part of the owners all worked to further increase this sensation of insecurity. It is the midst of this generalized insecurity and feeling of abandonment and persecution that the excluded peoples' movements grew in strength. Their growth constitutes a brake on the attempt of the bourgeoisie to disarticulate the working class on account of widespread unemployment. The picketers' movement has managed to mobilise hundreds of thousands of workers threatened by the social exclusion generated by the system.

This tendency has revolutionised the internal life of the trade unions and spawned a new generation of popular leaders among the workers. The street blockades, pickets and larger trade union struggles of recent years have been developed practically in opposition to the formal union leadership and indeed outside of the framework of the trade unions so pervasively dominated by a corrupted bureaucracy. It is a movement evolving from street and highway blockades towards larger scale actions and the planning of general strikes. It has gone well beyond the scope of an unemployed people's movement and has actively incorporated sectors of the urban industrial workers in self-managed factories, creating economic alternatives based on social solidarity. Indeed, the picketers' movement has managed to develop an international projection.

The shift of the struggle of organised workers from the factories to the spaces of the community has had spin-offs in Latin America within this general context of an exhausted trade union movement. The social struggles against the first wave of privatisation in the region, beginning in the early 1990s, was characterised by a trade union resistance. As workers, they were the most visibly and directly affected, such that with every new merger or privatisation, workers were being constantly thrown out into the ranks of the unemployed. Following the first wave of privatisations, when the accumulated experience of increased utility bills, water and electricity above all, were found to be accompanied by poor service (cuts in water, black outs) or with a total cut-off of service in more marginalised areas where service provision was considered to be unprofitable. Under these conditions, the entire citizenry became affected in its most basic living conditions and not just the working class. The social struggle that emerged from this situation is less narrow and exclusive in scope than the trade union struggle.

Over the most recent years, the social struggle against privatisation subsequently shifted from the factories to the communities. With this, the struggle moved from the circuit of the valorisation of capital to the space of the reproduction and care of social life itself. Within this space, leadership is no longer the sole dominion of the male, adult worker. Rather, the new actors that rise to this occasion based on the participation of whole communities include a strong presence of women, youth, peasants and indigenous peoples. In other words, the most permanently excluded sectors of the system, those who can no longer find ways of reproducing their lives, are now part of the search for an alternative. In this context of a more inclusive struggle, there is room for all those currents seeking the reproduction of social life in the face of the systemic pressures that surround them.

Some examples of this we can mention would include the historic struggle for water in Cochabamba, Bolivia; the struggles of Paraguay, Ecuador,

Peru, Dominican Republic, Costa Rica, and Bolivia with regard to electricity services; and of the course the extremely important case of the "Natural Gas War" in Bolivia. These types of struggles assume a marked radicalisation in the forms of contention by way of urban uprising, prolonged blockades of highways that cut off key commercial routes, and the occupation of factories. With these kinds of conflicts unfolding throughout Latin America, there is a political and social convergence of a broad kind in a struggle for sovereignty and dignity, opposition to Free Trade Agreements, and rejection of the privatisation of essential services such as water, electricity, and energy resources such as petroleum and gas.

During some of the above-mentioned mobilisations, Latin American presidents have been forced out of office. In showing these leaders to be defending the narrow interests opposed to the common good, the societal sectors in revolt have once again issued popular demands for change. With this form of struggle unfolding, a new modality has appeared for seizing power in an unprecedented opportunity to transform people into historical subjects. These struggles demonstrate a permanent community organisation that sooner or later is obliged to seek power on behalf of the common good of the community.

All of this represents, however, a significant shift from the classic "taking of power" by a revolutionary vanguard. Centralised power defines the common good for the larger society but fails to incorporate its participation and structural incorporation into popular governance. The definition of the public good by a vanguard that asserts the interests of the masses but fails to accord them a structural role for carrying it out leaves them as an "enlightened vanguard" but without the vast majority incorporated into its project.

The eventual approval of the Free Trade Agreements (FTAs) foreshadows that the social struggle will not stop here, but instead become radicalised in more and more countries. The logic of the FTA's rests in the annexation of Latin American over a gradual series of steps, but with ever greater aggressiveness and intolerance to its opposition. In this way, the United States hopes that through a series of FTAs in Central America and the Andean region, the remaining countries of the Southern Cone will experience isolation, thereby forcing them, above all Brazil, to sign a treaty in the long run. Threats of aggression and corruption are part of this annexation process. In this context, the smallest countries practically have no other alternative but to sign the treaties. For the larger Southern Cone countries such as Brazil, however, this is not so readily the case.

The World Social Struggle against Global War

In the battle of dividing up the world market, a growing part of it has been absorbed by the transnationals at the expense of national and local markets, above all in the periphery. The participation of the 200 largest enterprises in the World Gross Product (WGP) went from 17% in 1965 to more than 35% towards the end of the 1990s, i.e., doubling their share of world production in a twenty-five year period (Beinstein, 1999:60). This concentration of income, nevertheless, places limits on the very same economic dynamics through the reduction of global demand, something that occurs when the richest sectors of the global population consume a smaller percentage of their income than do the poorest sectors. With that, the world economic dynamics tend toward recession. However, as the highest income earning quintile consumes almost exclusively transnational products while the lowest earning quintiles tend to consume more local products, the concentration of income, for a time, tends to benefit the transnationals due to the effective demand for their production.

Amidst the growing misery of the majority and a decline in the rate of economic growth, the demand for transnational goods produced by big capital grows. During the 1980s and above all in the 1990s, the principal stock markets unceasingly rose precisely during a period where immiseration was become ever more widespread. To bet on the transnational companies appeared to be an almost certain profit and ever greater sums were invested with ever greater risk credit. These investments were not expanding the productive base but simply inflating the prices for stock actions without any base in the expansion of real wealth. The stocks tended to rise at a geometric rate at the same time that the real base of the economy was growing at an ever slower pace. The result was a growing mass of virtual money without any backing in the real economy.

With the concentration of wealth falling in ever fewer hands and with speculation ever more generalised, the growth in the world economy lost its rhythm of growth. The rate of growth of the world economy went from 5.3% at the beginning of the 1970s to 3.1% during the 1980s, arriving to barely a 1% growth rate by the end of the 1990s (Beinstein, 1999: 115). The opening of the new millennium threatened a world recession and by the end of 2001, the core countries had all entered simultaneously into recessionary territory. With contracting economic growth, the effective demand for transnational products was in decline, putting transnational profits at risk. As a result, the trend for stocks tended to fall and the stock market entered into a crisis. Between April of 2000 and Sept. 10, 2001, stock values had fallen by a world average of 31%. In the month following the September 11 attacks of 2001, stocks fell barely a few more points. The events of September 11 were therefore not responsible for the stock crisis of that period (Tablada and Dierckxsens, 2004:167–168).

This fact notwithstanding, the September 11 2001 attacks were frequently cited as the cause of bad economic results. The resulting war against terrorism in essence embodied the unfolding strategy of a deepening division of the world market. It was a geopolitical game of exclusion that is no longer based on the free play of the market but rather upon mechanisms of force. If there is no room for all of the capitalists in this world, some (Western ones, particularly the United States) considered that they have more rights to this world than others (such as Eastern ones, particularly Islamic countries). To legitimate the politics of exclusion upon the basis of a supposed terrorist threat of Islamic peoples to the West, with an ideological justification that there are civilisations and fundamentalist religions that are dangerous and ultimately inferior, not only makes the process of exclusion visible but implies the next step from exclusion to methodical elimination. The result is that the geopolitics of exclusion not only becomes radicalised but also ever more transparent. This in turn fuels an accelerating breakdown in legitimacy.

The official posture of the war on terrorism that considers that "those who are not with us are allies of terrorism" leaves no space for an inclusive alternative. The aggression of the United States in response to those designated as terrorist enemies accomplished nothing more than to escalate the spiral of terrorism. This "official terrorism" spawned more terrorism on the part of those being attacked, resulting in a vicious circle of terror. The result is a world where nobody feels safe, not even in the centres of power. Amidst this terror, sooner or later and with a lot of pain, the consciousness was born of the necessity and practical option of creating another possible world. From the throws of pain, an ethic of solidarity was born. It is not entirely clear how much pain had to be endured throughout the world in order to give birth to this new ethical solidarity, but inevitably it arose. Solidarity with the "other," without concern for nationality, race, culture, gender, or religion ends up being the necessary premise for ones salvation as a nation, race or gender.

Helping to foment this new consciousness is precisely the role of the social movements whose culmination at the world level became expressed in the

World Social Forum, born in January 2001 as a response to the World Economic Forum in Davos, Switzerland. In Davos, the global elite met as it had done annually since 1971 in sketching global economic policy in the interests of the most powerful elements of the world. In 1999, when the fissures of neoliberalism could begin to be foreshadowed, the first popular response arose during the same days as the Davos Forum. The "Other Davos" protests took place with the participation of hundreds of members of popular organisations and intellectual critics from all continents. It was there that the initiative was taken to create the World Social Forum (WSF).

The first WSF took place in January 2001 in Porto Alegre, Brazil with a participation of 20,000 people. In January 2002, just several months after the September 11 attacks, the number of participants rose to 50,000. In 2003, during the preparatory phase of the U.S. invasion of Iraq, participation in the WSF surpassed 100,000 and by 2005, it now involved over 150,000 people.

The utopia of the WSF is related to a vision of emancipatory democracy. In the words of Boaventura de Souza Santos (2004: 222–223), emancipatory democracy is a process of transforming the relations of power into relations of shared authority. Taking into account that the relations of power exhibited by those that the WSF are confronting are multiple, the processes of radical democratisation must also be multiple. Given that this is the distinctive utopian element of the WSF, it is not a coincidence that the issue of internal democracy is increasingly a central topic of discussion. The overall credibility of the WSF in its struggle for democracy in society depends upon the credibility of its internal democracy. The initial phase of the WSF corresponded to the principal forums in Porto Alegre, followed by a process where other forums were held at the continental, regional, and national levels as well as thematic forums.

The evolution of its activities demanded that a new organisational structure be formed. The challenge consisted in changing the organisational structure in accordance with the demands of this new phase, taking into account the need to deepen its democratic framework. One way was to transfer the WSF nucleus from the global event to the national, regional and thematic levels. In that way, the WSF could streamline some of its present centralism. This path, however, would not in itself resolve the essential issue of democratic representativeness.

The other means is by constructing democracy internally from the bottom upwards. Upon the base of the local and thematic forums, representative structures at different levels can form structures of the global organisation and representatives could be elected directly by local members (See Michael Albert in, Boaventura de Souza Santos; 2004: 224–225).

The Disconnection from Globalisation: A Requisite for Another Possible World

The world hegemonic power of the United States is sustained upon two pillars: the dollar as an international currency and the Pentagon. The social struggle for an alternative presupposes the disconnection from the process of globalisation. This disconnection as proposed, for example, in the Bolivarian Alternative for Latin America (ALBA) has clear prospects in the context of a crisis of hegemony. The crisis in U.S. hegemony is in sight and we want to be able to visualise it.

The ALBA initiative is a response to the FTAA and seeks to develop a political, social and economic project from within Latin America for Latin Americans, i.e., a project of disconnection from the process of U.S. economic annexationism and the loss of sovereignty. The ALBA proposal emphasises agricultural sovereignty and considers agriculture as a way of life with its corresponding cultural worldview. This provides a sharp contrast with the view of agriculture as simply another commodity such as the extension of patents over products which are essential for life itself. Beyond integrating Latin America for Latin Americans, ALBA seeks to create a multipolar world with a greater presence of the countries of the South.

The United States possesses the monetary reserve and currency of world exchange on account of its economic might of the past. Today, that country lives on the rent that this position of economic hegemony has left it. This position is being undermined, however, by the non-productive and parasitic character of an economy rooted in a rent-based character. To the extent that the economic power of an empire declines, the history of humanity shows us that its ultimate resource is to resort to the use of force. The United States today has a vastly superior military capacity to that of the rest of the world and instead of growing smaller the gap tends to become ever larger. Increased military spending based in an economic foundation in decline cannot continue to be sustained indefinitely as the dramatic collapse of the Soviet Bloc demonstrated some years ago.

In possession of the world currency, the United States could sustain its military spending for a time on pure credit. However, a county that lives increasingly on credit depends ever more upon the wealth of others and progressively will find it difficult to impose its criteria over its creditors, i.e., it loses its hegemony. In losing its economic hegemony, the imperial power tends to resort to force, and eventually moves against its creditors. A hegemony based on a war economy but sustained by the pure credit of its enemies has no future and invariable leads to its collapse.

The world recession that was first announced with the stock market crisis of 2000 and 2001 was attenuated by economic interventions and a general lowering of interest rates. In the world as a whole and above all in the United States, a generalised lowering of interest rates beginning in 2001 up until June, 2004 was observable. The idea was to maintain the effective demand for transnational products.

The end result was a wave of speculation in commodities markets and a substantial increase in personal consumption. The United States with 5% of the world's population presently consumes 30% of the World Global Product. The private debt of U.S. households reaches a sum equivalent to that country's GDP. The accumulated public and private debt of the United States for 2004 amounted to US$38 billion, i.e., nearly the equivalent of the World Gross Product (See Frank, 2006).

By virtue of its control over the world monetary supply, the United States can indebt itself more than any other nation by transferring the debt abroad in its own money by virtue of control over the emission of this global currency. If emission of the currency at uncontrolled levels were to take place, other countries across the world would suffer a severe inflationary process that they in turn cannot transfer abroad. By its possession of the international monetary reserves, the United States receives guaranteed credits from almost all of the countries of the world that deposit their international reserves in U.S. dollars. The public and private debt at the world level amounted in 2001 to US$60 billion, or more than 150% of the Global Gross Product. While the United States accounts for half of the world's public and private debt, the foreign debt of the South and the ex-Soviet Block combined does not reach 5% of the world total debt. The external debt of the entire periphery does not represent more than 10% of the public and private debt of the United States alone. Its debt in 2001 was calculated to be US$29 billion but the magnitude of the debt at the world level and in the U.S. in particular, has been accentuated in the years since then. Between 2001–2004, the combined private and public debt of the United States increased by 9 million, or 30% (See Toussaint, 2004: 149–150).

With U.S. hegemony based on its two pillars, it becomes strategic for Washington to preserve the dollar as the privileged currency of reserves, something that was instituted at the end of World War II, and its currency as the international standard, something that it acquired thanks to the petroleum market beginning in the crisis years of the 1970s. Until November of 2000, it maintained both of those privileges. In that year, Iraq changed its international reserves from Dollars to Euros and negotiated petroleum priced in Euros rather than dollars. Iran also followed this policy in December of 2002 and there existed the possibility that other OPEC countries were going to follow suit, placing the dollar at risk of a free fall. In this context, the United States initiated its "preventive war" against Iraq so as to intimidate the entire world from substituting dollars with Euros, leading to its eventual status as the principal reserve currency.

War does not finance itself. Somebody always has to pay for it. If it is not financed with domestic taxation, there is no other alternative than to transfer its costs abroad. Washington hoped to transfer its war costs to third nation parties as it did during the 1991 Gulf War. Besides direct contributions from its allies, the United States hoped to raise funds by way of increased prices of petroleum and thus to reap direct donations while sharing the extraordinary income from a temporary increase in petroleum prices with its Arab oil producing allies.

With the invasion of Iraq in 2003, the United States did not manage to transfer the costs of its war for a variety of reasons. In the first place, there was too much opposition to the war among the majority of its European allies for them to collaborate in the financing of the war. Second, the war proved not to be short-lived and evolved into a quagmire, leading the costs to skyrocket far in excess of what was previously imagined. Washington had no other alternative than to finance a significant portion of the war with an increased public debt. Half of that public debt is being financed abroad, with half of that amount by Asian countries. The other half of the debt is being financed internally, and of that, almost half by funds from social security that is being threatened by bankruptcy (See Frank, 2006).

The increasing U.S. public debt compromises the dollar as the international reserve currency. Since the end of 2000 up to the end of 2004, the Euro increased its share by 45% as a currency of reserve and raised its value relative to the dollar by 65%, or in other words, the dollar has fallen by 40% relative to the Euro. As the dollar depreciates, the international reserves of countries lose their value and above all from those countries that possess international reserves in dollars such as China. The constant increase of China's international reserves in dollars allows large Chinese exporters to increase the supply of Chinese products in the U.S. market.

The U.S. commercial trade deficit with China has steadily increased and China, instead of repatriating the dollars, augments its dollars reserves in order to avoid a contraction of demand. This policy can delay the free fall of the dollar but eventually implies an even more precipitous decline in the form of a monetary time bomb. The United States, together with Japan presently maintains China under the threat of war in order to avoid that it changes its Dollars for Euros. In this way, Washington can postpone the dollar's free fall but cannot permanently prevent it.

Since the end of the Cold War in 1991, and particularly under the G.W. Bush Administration, the United States has been doing everything possible to promote the rearming of Japan in the scenario of an eventual confrontation of that country with China. This conflict between two of its economic rivals could be caused by Washington but it could also ultimately result in Washington's downfall. During the Cold War, Japan was forced to maintain a policy of disarmament as a consequence of its military defeat in the Second World War. Following the Cold War, the Japanese government began to resume military spending under U.S. pressure, implanting a plan of rearmament. The United States required this as part of the new scenario to transfer some of the costs of its military industrial complex. The Japanese arms race has contributed to its present public debt of US$ 7 billion, comparable to that of the United States, but with the difference that it has a far smaller population (Johnson and Dispatch, 2005).

China is the country that for over two decades has grown at an average rate of 9.5% and which saves half of its domestic product. Chinese investments are basically concentrated in the productive sphere, ensuring the growth of the economy as a whole. Chinese defence spending is relatively modest and China is a net exporter of arms. In this manner, defence spending does not impede the growth of its economy. Chinese investments in the civil economy reflect a strong sustained growth fuelled by enormous domestic savings. The investments of the U.S., the European Union and Japan, in contrast, is more oriented towards a redistributive practise of mergers, purchases, privatisations, speculation, etc., as well as greater defence spending.

Western investments not only are non-productive in nature but tend to increase the concentration of existing wealth while committing income and future wealth to military spending at the expense of growing the civil economy. This in turn fuels an ever larger debt. China is being transformed into a gigantic workshop of the civil economy of the entire world, while the "West" is mortgaging its future, buying more and more of China's civil products. All of this signifies an eventual loss of hegemony in the "West", a fact that at the same time intensifies the existing rivalries. Any eventual conflict between Japan and China that involves the United States either directly or indirectly can be confronted by China with a massive sale of dollars that would in turn imply a total crisis of that currency.

The eruption of that conflict is not necessary, however, to the unfolding of a global crisis. Western accumulation based on its parasitic concentration of wealth is finite and it tends towards a global recession. We are in the preliminary stages of a global economic depression of proportions not previously seen in human history. In this regard, the situation involving a disconnection from the globalisation process is not only an opportunity but a necessity. The international crisis will become manifested in a collapse of global demand and consequently global trade. A collapse of global trade signifies the bankruptcy of many transnationals and the sharp fall of the stock markets in the entire world. An abrupt fall in international trade not only brings forth opportunities for a resurgence of local markets, indeed it becomes imposed as an absolute necessity in the face of the drastic contraction of imported transnational products.

The gigantic international debt is unpayable and this fact will lead us sooner or later into a general crisis of international banking. The impact will be so strong as to disarticulate the world economy. The result of this disarticulation is the opportunity and necessity of orienting the economy beginning with what can be locally and nationally resolved amidst the structural contraction of the international economy. In this setting, violent confrontations may increase but the "everybody save themselves" situation will escape nobody, not even the imperial power.

The birth of ethical solidarity in these cataclysmic circumstances will prove to be not only an opportunity but an absolute necessity. The search for the common good is at the same time both possible and necessary in order to orient the economy towards life itself. Anticipating this situation and developing the adequate consciousness to build off of it is part of the task of the left.

Conclusion: The Place of Latin America in the Struggle for a Multipolar World

In the face of the eminent crisis of U.S. hegemony, the multipolar reconstruction of the world is not only an objective strategy but also an emerging reality. The expansion of relations between the European Union, Russia, and China in confronting Washington is evident. The European Union, above all France, together with Russia and China share a common vision of a multipolar world that must replace the current uni-polar one. There is increasing evidence of these multipolar relations and China occupies a central place in the struggle. China has not only begun to displace the United States as the principal actor in the Organisation of Pacific Asian Cooperation (APEC), but is also displacing Japan in the area of petroleum investments.

Indeed, China is emerging as the principal commercial partner of some of the largest Latin American economies. China and Brazil signed an important set of commercial agreements in November 2004. In December, China signed additional agreements with Argentina, Venezuela, Bolivia, Chile and Cuba. Venezuela has accorded broad access of the Chinese to its vast petroleum reserves. The commercial and investment agreements between Venezuela, Brazil and Colombia, and the central strategic role played by Cuba in these negotiations, was a setback for Washington. China and India reached an agreement in April 2005 with the explicit intention of transforming the present world order based on their might of possessing more than a third of the world's population. All of this reinforces the view that the United States is increasingly less able to impose its will around the world. In other words, its hegemony is crisis (See Johnson and Dispatch, 2005; Luis Bilbao, 2005:4–5).

All of the preceding generates a certain amount of anxiety worldwide that the United States when faced with its decline will turn to war as a final resort. This could effectively be possible by a generalised broadening of existing international conflicts on various fronts, fuelled by the same market that has generated armed conflicts for decades. Nonetheless, there are several reasons that weigh in favour of doubting the likelihood of this scenario or at least of its success. An invasion of Iran following the debacle in Iraq is probably now less likely, although it is possible that a selective bombing could take place.

The U.S. objective would be to take greater control over the region's oil supply but the adverse results for Washington would not take long to unfold.

Any further increase in the price of oil in the United States would be a clear sign that a recession or depression cannot be far behind. If Iran were bombed, the United States would be alone in the conflict. Not even Great Britain would support them in that conflict. A U.S. incursion into Iran could have consequences far more immediate than those in the case of Iraq. Iran's forces are armed with Russian missiles that have the capacity to close the strategic Straights of Harmuz for weeks or even months. With that, the petroleum traffic of the entire Persian Gulf would come to a standstill which would put the price of oil somewhere in the clouds while the dollar goes into a free fall. In other words, an armed conflict with Iran could accelerate the collapse of the U.S. economy and provoke a major crisis in the global economy.

From the perspective of an international conflict scenario, the primordial interest of the United States would be to assure its petroleum supply. In an internationalised conflict, the petroleum of the Persian Gulf would provide no firm guarantee. For this reason, interest in Venezuela's petroleum grows with each passing day. Without assured access to petroleum, the U.S. would eventually lose any major international conflict in a short time. Nevertheless, at the same moment that Washington attempted to exert renewed pressure upon various South American capitals to isolate President Hugo Chávez, to reinstate the dynamic of the FTAA through bilateral treaties, and to impede the consolidation of the South American Community of Nations, the "strategic alliance" signed by Brazil and Argentina on February 14 2005 produced exactly the opposite result. A foreseeable conflict in Venezuela could eventually truncate the consolidation of any neo-developmentalist policy of the Brazilian government. Venezuela is a key country for its petroleum reserves and would lead to a destabilisation of all of South America, capable of putting in check even the Brazilian Government.

A U.S. war with Venezuela would signify the large scale deployment of U.S. troops into the entire region. The Amazonian region, a strategic objective of Plan Colombia, would become a major theatre of military operations. For this reason, not only President Lula but the large Brazilian private sectors and the armed forces have good reasons to support the strategic alliance. Indeed, this agreement helped to begin to change the position of Colombia with regard to Venezuela. Instead of deepening the conflict with Venezuela to the exclusive benefit of Washington, there is a growing process of regional realignment revolving around a hemispheric geopolitical axis (See Luis Bilbao, 2005: 4–5). This change will greatly complicate any eventual U.S. intervention in Venezuela.

A final question remains: Where is all of this heading? No war is necessary to witness the unfolding of a world recession. It is a question of time before the world economic crisis arrives, with higher U.S. interest rates implying a meltdown of finance capital as we have shown in a previous publication (See Dierckxsens, 2004). The widening of the global war can only further deepen the crisis while it cannot avoid it. The crisis will be deeper and more immediate than that which resulted from the crisis of real socialism, implying not only the collapse of neoliberalism but of capitalism itself as we have discussed in other works (See Dierckxsens, 2003). It was not long ago that another world seemed possible without knowing how or what. It will not be long now before this other world will be not only possible but urgently necessary.

Andre Gunder Frank[1]

Meet Uncle Sam – Without Clothes – Parading Around China and the World[2]

Introducing Uncle Sam – Without Clothes

Uncle Sam has just reneged and defaulted on up to
40 percent of its trillions of dollars in foreign debt,
and nobody has said a word except for a line in *The
Economist*. In plain English, that means that Uncle
Sam runs a global confidence racket with his self-
made currency based on the confidence that he has
elicited and received from others around the world.
It also means that he is a dead-beat in that he does
not honour and return the money he has received.
How much of a dollar stake we lost depends on how
much we, the creditors, originally paid for it. He let,
or rather through his deliberate political economic
policies, drove his currency down by over 40 percent from one Euro at US$.80 at its highest to now
US$1.35 against the Euro in January 2005, and sim-
ilarly against Yen, Yuan and other currencies. And
the US dollar is still declining, indeed apt to plum-
met altogether.

There was also a spate of competitive devaluations
in the 1930s, and it was called the "Beggar Thy
Neighbour Policy" of shifting the costs for the neigh-
bour/s to bear. True, with the decline of the US dollar, so too has the real value decreased that foreigners

---

[1] The author died in April, 2005. A memoriam is included at the end of this work.
[2] This work appeared in *Critical Sociology*, Volume 32, N° 1, 2006, pp. 17–44.

pay to service their debt to Uncle Sam. That works only if they can themselves earn a profit from an increase in value of other currencies against the US dollar. Otherwise, foreigners earn and pay in the same devalued US dollar, plus a loss from devaluation between the time they received US dollars and had to repay it to Uncle Sam. China and other East Asians do earn in and have pegged their currencies to the US dollar, so they have already lost a substantial portion of their world's by far largest US dollar stake. And they, like all others, will also lose the rest.

Uncle Sam's debt to the rest of the world already amounts to over one third of his annual national domestic production and it is still growing. That already makes his debt economically and politically unrepayable, even if he wanted to, which he obviously does not. Uncle Sam's domestic debt, e.g. by consumers on credit cards and mortgages, is almost 100 percent of GDP and consumption, including that from China. Uncle Sam's federal debt is now US$ 7.5 trillion, of which all but US$1 trillion was built up in the last three decades, the last US$ 2 trillion in the last eight years, and the last US$1 trillion in the last two years. Alas, that costs over US$ 330 billion in interest, compared to US$15 billion spent on NASA.

The "Who Me, Worry?" Congress recently raised the debt ceiling to US$8.2 trillion. To help us visualise, only US$1 trillion in tightly packed US$1,000 dollar bills would match a building 40 stories high, so the US$ 7.5 trillion would be 300 stories or about three times the height of the Empire State Building. Nearly half of that is owed to foreigners. All Uncle Sam's debt, including private household debt of about US$10 trillion, plus corporate and financial debt, with their options, derivatives and the like, plus state and local government debt comes to an unimaginable US$ 37 trillion. So to help you visualise, imagine 1,480 Empire State buildings high and nearly four times Uncle Sam's national domestic production.

Uncle Sam's issue last year of a mere record high US$140 billion in high-yielding junk bonds must seem puny, even if they are so called because they are [only!] the first to be defaulted, after or along with consumer and mortgage debt and business belly ups. Only some of that debt and its coming default can be managed domestically, but with dangerous limitations for Uncle Sam, still to be noted below. That is only one reason I want you to meet Uncle Sam, the dead-beat confidence man, who may remind you of the Meet Joe Black movie. For as we get to know Uncle Sam better below, we will find that he is also a Shylock and a corrupt one at that.

Uncle Sam's Cold War Proxy for the North-West vs. South War

Before we go on, let's first translate this jumble of numbers into plain English. It was already done back in 1948 by George Keenan, otherwise known as "Mr. X," the architect of Uncle Sam's Containment Policy:

> We have about half the world's wealth . . . but only 5 percent of its population. . . . In this situation . . . our real job in the coming years is to devise a pattern of relationships which permit us to maintain this position of disparity. . . . To do so we have to dispense with all sentimentality and daydreaming, . . . concentrate everywhere on our immediate national objectives . . . [and] deal in straight power concepts. The less we are hampered by idealistic slogans, the better.[3]

Of course, that statement was for Uncle Sam's private internal consumption only. For the rest of the world, including most "Uncle Sammies," "idealistic slogans" will do better, so long as they don't hamper us, of course. For they manifest the world's grandest ever "Ponzi Scheme Confidence Racket" run around the world by Uncle Sam. How else "to maintain this disparity"? Naked power helps, but it is not enough. All the more so, given that since the time that Mr. X wrote, the already then terribly unfair world distribution of income has become about 3 times more unequal. For today, just consider this simple index: 265 million Uncle Sammies consume more oil, 22 percent of the world's total, than over three billion Asians, who all put together get 20 percent – and want more, especially the Chinese. Of course, Uncle Sam also accounts for a similar proportionate share of the Good Earth. To help him do it, he relies heavily on the Pentagon, which to boot is itself probably the biggest and least observed single polluter of all.

This observation also displays continuity with that other wall, the one that fell in Berlin in 1989. It shows that Mr. X's Cold War containment was not only or even primarily against the Russians, but also a containment of the other 95 percent of the world and especially of the vast poor majority who suffers most from the observed disparity. Indeed, he suggests that the East-West Cold War, that he was instrumental in starting as Uncle Sam's ambassador in Moscow, was largely a proxy for the North- and especially Uncle Sam-South real war over that half, or both halves, of the world's wealth. So

---

[3] See George Keenan 1948 United States Department of State Policy Planning Study No. 23, Washington, DC.

that should leave us less surprised at the failure of the mistakenly anticipated "Peace Dividend" to materialise after that little wall fell down in 1989. The other, or the real, war continues and only takes other forms or rather labels, for "human rights," "democracy," the "free market" and "free trade," "freedom" in general, indeed even "'civilisation," all of the last several of which are echoes of the "white man's burden" from the 19th century.

Just add a few new "againsts," first "narco terrorism" by Bush Daddy vs. Noriega, and now just undefined "terrorism" by Son of Bush vs. anybody and everybody "who is not with us." I forgot "weapons of mass destruction," the ones of which Uncle Sam has and uses the most of, oh, and the weapons of mass deception that Uncle Sam uses like nobody's business. That is of course a *sine qua non* of any Confidence Racket and he runs the world's grandest ever, as we will observe *ad nauseum* below.

Uncle Sam Lives Holy Off the Fat of the World's Land and from Chinese Work

Uncle Sam is the world's most privileged for having the exclusive right to print the world's reserve currency at will at a cost of nothing but the paper and ink it is printed on. By so doing, he can also export to foreigners the inflation that his irresponsible printing of home currency generates. For there are already at least three times as many dollars floating around the world as there are in Uncle Sam's home. Additionally, his is also the only "foreign" debt that is mostly denominated in his own currency. Most foreigners' debt is also denominated in the same currency, but they have to buy dollars from Uncle Sam with their own currency and real goods.

So Uncle Sam simply pays the Chinese and others essentially with those dollars that have no real worth beyond its paper and ink. So especially China gives away for nothing at all to Uncle Sam, hundreds of billions of dollars worth of real goods produced at home and consumed by rich Uncle Sam. Then, China turns around and trades these same Uncle Sam paper dollar bills in for other Uncle Sam paper currency called Treasury Certificate bonds, which are even more worthless, except that they pay a percent of interest. For as we already noted, they will never be able to be cashed in and redeemed in full or even in part, and anyway they have lost much of their value to Uncle Sam already. In an earlier essay, I argued that Uncle Sam's power rested on just two pillars, the paper currency and the Pentagon. Each supports the other, but the vulnerability of each is also an Achilles heel that threatens the viability of the other. Since then, Afghanistan and Iraq have shown that much of the confidence in the Pentagon was misplaced. That has in turn helped reduce confidence and value in the dollar, which has in turn reduced Uncle Sam's ability to use that currency to finance his Pentagon's foreign adventures.[4] Additionally we must also realise that Uncle Sam's numbers above and below are all literally relative. So far the relations – in particular with China – still favour Uncle Sam, but they also help to maintain an image that is deceptive. Consider the following:

> "... a US\$ 2 toy leaving a Uncle Sam-owned factory in China is a US\$ 3 shipment arriving at San Diego. By the time a Uncle Sam consumer buys it for US\$10 at Wal-Mart, the Uncle Sam economy registers US\$10 in final sales, less US\$3 import cost, for a US\$7 addition to the Uncle Sam gross domestic product (GDP)."[5]

Moreover, ever-clever Uncle Sam has arranged matters so as to earn nine percent from his economic and financial holdings abroad, while foreigners earn only three percent real return on theirs, and only one percent on their Treasury Certificates, invested in Uncle Sam's God's Country. Note that this difference of six percent is already double what Uncle Sam pays out, and his total nine percent take is triple the three percent he gives back. Therefore, although the reciprocal foreign holdings by each other with Uncle Sam and abroad are now about equal, Uncle Sam is still the big net interest/ed winner, just like any Shylock, but there is no other who ever did so grand a business.

But Uncle Sam also earns quite well, thank you, from other holdings abroad, e.g. from service payments by mostly poor foreign debtors. The sums involved are not peanuts. For from his direct investments in foreign property alone, Uncle Sam's profits now equal 50 percent, and including his receipts from other holdings abroad, now are a full 100 percent, of Uncle Sam's profits derived from all of his own domestic activities combined! These foreign receipts add more than four percent to Uncle Sam's national domestic product. That helps nicely to compensate for the failure of domestic profits to as

---

[4] See my 2004 essay "Coup d'Etat and Paper Tiger in Washington, Fiery Dragon in the Pacific," which also conjures up the productive growth of China http://rrojas databank.info/agfrank/new_world_order.html#coup.

[5] See: http://archives.econ.utah.edu/archives/a-list/2004w07/msg00083.htm. The original said "US" in place of "Uncle Sam."

of yet recover even to their 1972 level. That is because Uncle Sam has failed to make enough real good investments at home to boost productivity and profits thereon. That extra profit from foreigners also compensates for much of Uncle Sam's still rising trade deficit of US$ 600+ billion a year from excess home consumption over what he himself produces. That has resulted in the trillions amount of his foreign debt, just around three according to him. But Uncle Sam is playing his cards close and is understandably reluctant to make any official revelation of how high [more than the Empire State building in US$ 1000 bills?] his foreign debt really is. Nonetheless, we may rest assured that his gross foreign debt is by far the world's largest and remains so, even as net foreign debt if we deduct foreigners' debts to him.

The productivity hype of Clinton's "new economy" of the 1990s was limited to computers and IT, and even that proved to be a sham when the dot com bubble burst. Also, not only the apparent increase in "profits" but also that of "productivity" was being boosted by shop-floor, office and sales floor worker speed-up and/or longer work-times at the bottom. WAL-MART obliges its non-union [it won't permit any] workers on threat of dismissal to "clock-out" and then return to work at no pay. At the top, productivity and profits were boosted by "creative accounting" hype by Enron, Worldcom, Arthur Anderson and others of their likes who engaged in now well-known shams.

Uncle Sam Cannot Save Himself: He Is Hooked on Consumption and Other Drugs

Why any and all this?, we may well ask. The simple answer is that Uncle Sam, who is increasingly hooked on consumption, not to mention harder drugs, saves no more than 0.2 percent of his own income. The Fed's guru and "now you see him-now you don't" Dr. of financial and media magic, Alan Greenspan, recently observed that this is so because the richest 20 percent of Uncle Sammies who are the only ones who do save, have reduced their savings to just two percent. Yet, even these measly savings (other and poorer countries save and even invest 20, 30, and even 40 percent of their income) are more than counterbalanced by the six percent deficit spending of the Uncle Sam government, which does so largely on their behalf. That is what brings the average between the two together to 0.2 percent. So Uncle Sam has a US$ 400+ billion reported budget deficit, which is really US$ 600+

billion if we count, as we should, the US$ 200+ billion that Uncle Sam "borrows" from the temporary surplus in his own Federal Social Security fund that he is also bankrupting. But never mind, Uncle Sam President Bush just promised to privatise much of that and let people buy their own old age "security" in the ever more insecure stock market.

Rich Uncle Sam and primarily his highest off the hog earners and consumers as well as of course the Big Uncle in Washington himself, manages to live off the fat of the rest of the world's land. Apart from printing the world's money, Uncle Sam also does so with his "twin deficits," first his US$ 600+ billion budget deficit and the above-mentioned related US$ 600+ billion trade deficit. With these, Uncle Sam absorbs the savings of others who themselves are – often much – lower on the hog, particularly their central banks that place much of their reserves in US currency and thus in the hands of Uncle Sam in Washington and some also in home currency. Their private investors send dollars to or buy dollarised assets on Wall Street, all with the confidence that they are putting their wealth in the world's most safe Uncle Sam haven [that of course is part of the above mentioned confidence racket]. From the central banks alone, we are looking at yearly sums of over US$100 billion from Europe, over US$100 billion from poor China, US$140 billion from super-saver Japan, and an amount of many tens of billions from many others around the world. That also includes, of course, the investors and banks from the poor Third World.

How Uncle Sam Creates and Collects Third World Debt

In addition, Uncle Sam also obliges the Third World states to act as collection agencies or even as Repo Goons, where the goons are sent out to repossess the Godfather's property by any means that deliver. Only in this case, it is not even that, for he is taking new possession since the original debt has long since been paid off. The states raise taxes and fees from the population but lower social spending on education and health at home so as to divert funds to pay the debt abroad. They also borrow in turn from private capital at home at high interest rates that the state pays to the rich lenders, but out of taxes collected from the poor. That way, income is "recycled" from poor to rich at home as well as from these poor via the foreign debt to the even richer abroad. These literally forced savings of the poor are then sent to Uncle Sam in the form of "service" on the monetary debt that is "owed" to him.

ɔn is the name of the game in the Third World as elsewhere, debt! Only the debt was socialised after it had been incurred ate business. Only the state had enough power to squeeze the bulk of back payments out of the hides of its poor and middle-class people and transfer them as "invisible service payments" to Uncle Sam. When Mexicans were told to tighten their belt still further, they answered that we can't because we already ate it yesterday. Only Argentina and for a while Russia declared an effective moratorium on debt "service" and did so only after political economic policies, imposed by Uncle Sam's advisers and his IMF strong arm, had destroyed their entire societies like never before, despite being during "peacetime." Uncle Sam's Treasury Secretary and his IMF hand-maiden blithely continue to strut around the world insisting that the Third – and ex-Second, now also Third World of course continue to service their foreign debts, especially to him. No matter that with interest rates multiplied several times over by Uncle Sam himself after the Fed's Paul Volker's coup in October 1979, most have already paid off their original borrowings three to five times over. For to pay at the interest rates that Volker boosted to 20 percent, they had to borrow still more at higher rates until their outstanding foreign debt doubled and tripled. And so did their domestic debt from which part of the foreign payments were raised as was particularly the case in Brazil. All that, while Uncle Sam himself is blithely defaulting on his own foreign debt, as he had already done several times before in the 19th century.

Speaking of that, it may be well to recall at least two pieces of advice from that era. Lord Cromer, who administered Egypt for then dominant British imperial interests, was sad that his most important instrument for doing so was Egypt's debts to Britain. These had just multiplied when Egypt was obliged to sell its Suez Canal shares to Britain in order to pay off earlier debts. British Prime Minister Disraeli explained and justified his purchase of the canal on the grounds that it would strengthen British Imperial interests. Today, that is called "debt-for-equity swaps," which is one of Uncle Sam's latter day favourite policies to use the debt to acquire profitable and/or strategically important real resources, as was the Canal that served as the short cut to the jewel of the British Empire in India.

Another piece of practical advice came from the premier military strate-gist Clausewitz. "Make the lands you conquer pay for their own conquest and administration." That is of course exactly what Britain did in India through the infamous "Home Charges" remitted to London in payment for Britain administering India. Even the British themselves recognised this as "tribute" that was responsible for much of "the Drain" from India to Britain. How much more efficient yet to let foreign countries' own states administer themselves (Britain called it "Indirect Rule," but by rules set and imposed by the Uncle Sam run IMF, and so then effect a drain of debt service anyway. It seems the British also set a 19th century precedent with "independent" states. It has since been called the "imperialism of free trade." As long as the rules work, fine. When they don't, a bit of gun-boat diplomacy can help and Uncle Sam already learned to use that early in the 20th century. When even that was not enough, the next option is to invade, and if necessary to occupy – and then to rely on the Clausewitz rule to make the victims pay for their own occupation. We shall note several recent instances thereof and pay special attention to the ongoing example in Iraq.

While writing this essay, I received the following e-mail:

Confessions of an Economic Hit Man: How the U.S. Uses Globalisation to Cheat Poor Countries Out of Trillions. We speak with John Perkins, a former respected member of the international banking community. In his book Confessions of an Economic Hit Man he describes how as a highly paid professional, he helped the U.S. cheat poor countries around the globe out of trillions of dollars by lending them more money than they could possibly repay and then take over their economies.

JOHN PERKINS: Basically what we were trained to do and what our job is to do is to build up the American empire. To bring – to create situations where as many resources as possible flow into this country, to our corporations, and our government, and in fact we've been very successful. We've built the largest empire in the history of the world, primarily through economic manipulation, through cheating, through fraud, through seducing people into our way of life, through the economic hit men. I was very much a part of that. I was initially recruited while I was in business school back in the late sixties by the National Security Agency, the nation's largest and least understood spy organisation, and then [it] send[s] us to work for private consulting companies, engineering firms, construction companies, so that if we were caught, there would be no connection with the government . . .

I became its chief economist. I ended up having fifty people working for me. But my real job was deal-making. It was giving loans to other countries, huge loans, much bigger than they could possibly repay. One of the conditions of the loan-let's say a $1 billion to a country like Indonesia or Ecuador-and this country would then have to give ninety percent of that loan back to a U.S. company, or U.S. companies, a Halliburton or a Bechtel. A country today like Ecuador owes over fifty percent of its national budget just to pay down its debt. And it really can't do it. So, we literally have them over a barrel. So, when we want more oil, we go to Ecuador and say, "Look, you're not able to repay your debts, therefore give your oil companies your Amazon rain forest, which are filled with oil." And today we're going in and destroying Amazonian rain forests, forcing Ecuador to give them to us because they've accumulated all this debt. [We work] very, very closely with the World Bank. The World Bank provides most of the money that's used by economic hit men, it and the IMF.[6]

Uncle Sam Consumes and Controls Oil

Last but not least, oil producers also put their savings in Uncle Sam. With the "shock" of oil that restored its real price after its dollar valuation had fallen in 1973, ever clever Henry Kissinger made a deal with the world's largest oil exporter in Saudi Arabia that it would continue to price oil in dollars, and these earnings would be deposited in Uncle Sam, partly compensated by military hardware in return. That deal was de facto extended to all of OPEC and it still stands, except that before the war against Iraq, it suddenly opted out by switching to pricing its oil in Euros, and Iran threatened do so as well. North Korea has no oil but trades entirely in Euros. That constitutes the triple "rogue states axis of evil." Today Venezuela is a major oil supplier to Uncle Sam and also supplies some at preferential rates as non-dollar trade swaps to other poor countries like Cuba. So Uncle Sam sponsored and financed military commandos from its Plan Colombia next door, promoted an illegal coup, and when that failed, a legal referendum in his attempt at yet another "regime change" there as well; and now along with Brazil all three are being baptised as yet another "axis of evil."

I later discovered that the good [hit] man Mr. Perkins was in Saudi Arabia too:

---

[6] See: http://www.democracynow.org/article.pl?sid=04/11/09/1526251.

Yes, it was a fascinating time. I remember well . . . the Treasury Department hired me and a few other economic hit men. We went to Saudi Arabia . . . and we worked out this deal whereby the Royal House of Saud agreed to send most of their petro-dollars back to the United States and invest them in U.S. government securities. The Treasury Department would use the interest from these securities to hire U.S. companies to build Saudi Arabia-new cities, new infrastructure-which we've done. And the House of Saud would agree to maintain the price of oil within acceptable limits to us, which they've done all of these years, and we would agree to keep the House of Saud in power as long as they did this, which we've done, which is one of the reasons we went to war with Iraq in the first place. And in Iraq we tried to implement the same policy that was so successful in Saudi Arabia, but Saddam Hussein didn't buy. When the economic hit men fail in this scenario, the next step is what we call the jackals. Jackals are CIA-sanctioned people that come in and try to foment a coup or revolution. If that doesn't work, they perform assassinations. Or try to. In the case of Iraq, they weren't able to get through to Saddam Hussein. His bodyguards were too good. He had doubles. They couldn't get through to him. So the third line of defence, if the economic hit men and the jackals fail, is our young men and women, who are sent in to die and kill, which is what we've obviously done in Iraq.[7]

The World's Grandest Ever Ponzi Scheme Confidence Racket

To return to the main issue, all of the above are part and parcel of the world's biggest ever Ponzi scheme confidence racket. Like all other ones, its most essential characteristic is that it can only continue to pay off in dollars and be maintained at the top as long as it continues to receive new dollars at the bottom, voluntarily through confidence if possible and by force if not. Of course, the Clausewitz and Cromer formulas result in the poorest paying the most, since they are also the most defenceless, so that the ones sitting on/above them, pass as much of the cost and pain down to them.

But what if and when confidence runs out, and the money no longer comes? Things are already getting shakier at the Uncle Sam house. The declining money reduces the necessary money inflows. In early 2005, only US$ 48 billion was flowing in per monthly against outflows of US$ 55 billion. So Uncle

---

[7] See: http://www.democracynow.org/article.pl?sid=04/11/09/1526251.

Sam's Dr. Greenspan needs to raise interest rates to maintain Uncle Sam as attractive for foreign money he needs to fill the trade gap. As a quid pro quo for being reappointed by President Bush, he promised to do that only after the election. That time has now arrived, but doing so threatens to collapse the housing bubble that was built on low interest and mortgage – and re-mortgage- rates. It is in their house values that most of Uncle Sammies have their savings if any. They and this imaginary wealth-effect supported over-consumption and a household debt nearly as high as national domestic production. Volker's high interest rate successor at the Fed, Greenspan, lowered interest rates almost to zero, which made borrowing and mortgages, i.e., debt – cheap and plentiful. That increased the demand for consumer goods and houses. The former are cheap from China, but the latter drives up the price and "value" of houses, which has encouraged upgrading to still more expensive ones, increased "collateral," and still more borrowing, and still more consumption. So did capital flight from East Asia after its 1997 financial crisis. It fled to Uncle Sam's safe haven, both to Washington into Treasury Certificates and to New Work into Wall Street equities. At the same time, Uncle Sam benefited from the crisis by buying devalued East Asian currencies and using them to buy up East Asian real resources, and banks in Korea at bargain basement reduced prices. That is what generated the big bull market of rising stock prices and again apparent greater wealth, which also supported more consumption. Since then, the stock market has already crashed again.

When the housing market also crashes with Dr. Greenspan's present and future increase in interest rates, and therefore mortgage costs, a collapse of the housing price bubble would not only drastically undercut house prices. It would also have a falling domino effect on the owners' enormous second and third re-mortgages, consumer credit card and other debt, their consumption, corporate debt and profit and investment. In fact, these factors would be enough to also plunge Uncle Sam into deep recession, if not depression, and another Big Bear deflation on stock and de facto on other prices, thereby rendering debt service even more onerous. If the dollar declines, even domestic money price inflation is de facto deflationary against other currencies, something that Russians and Latin Americans discovered to their peril as we will observe shortly. Still lower real Uncle Sam investment would reduce its industrial productivity and competitiveness even more – probably to a degree lower than can compensated by further devaluing the currency and making its exports cheaper as is the confident hope of many, probably including the good Dr.

Until now, the apparent inflation of prices abroad in roubles and pesos and their consequent devaluations have been a de facto deflation in terms of the dollar world currency. Uncle Sam then printed dollars to buy up at fire-sale, bargain money prices the natural resources in Russia (whose economy was then run on US$100 bills) and companies and even banks, as in South Korea. True, now Dr. Greenspan and Uncle Sam are trying again to get other central banks also to raise their interest rates and plunge their own people into even deeper depression. But even if he can, thereby also cancelling out the relative attractiveness of his own interest rate hike, how could that save Uncle Sam himself?

So far beyond Osama bin Laden, Al Quaeda and all terrorists put together, the greatest real world threat to Uncle Sam is that this money does not keep coming in. For instance, foreign central banks and private investors (it is said that "overseas Chinese" have a tidy trillion dollars) could any day decide to place more of their money elsewhere than in the declining dollar and abandon poor ol' Uncle Sam to his destiny. China could double its per capita income very quickly if it made real investments at home instead of financial ones with Uncle Sam. Indeed Henry G. K. Liu writes, albeit a bit unrealistically, that "if the US$ 430 of Chinese exports were consumed domestically at their final market price, US$ 2.15 trillion would be added to China's 2003 GDP of US$1 trillion, tripling it."[8]

Dump Uncle Sam Dollars for Euros and East Asian Community Currencies?

Central banks, European and others can now put their reserves Euros or even soon to be revalued Chinese Yuan. Not so far down the road, there may be an East Asian currency, e.g. a basket first of ASEAN + 3 (China, Japan, Korea) – and then + 4 (India). While India's total exports in the past five years rose by 73 percent, those to ASEAN rose double that rate and six-fold to China. India has become an ASEAN summit partner and its Prime Minister has declared that India wants ever closer relations with ASEAN. Its ambitions

[8] See: http://archives.econ.utah.edu/archives/a-list/2004w07.

stretch still further to an extended community from India to Japan.[9] It is no coincidence that during the 1997 crisis of East Asian currency, followed by a full economic crisis, Uncle Sam strong-armed Japan not to start a proposed East Asian currency fund that would have prevented at least the worst of the economic crisis. But now, the indeed Uncle Sam friend in need China is already taking steps toward such an arrangement, only on a much grander financial and now also economic scale.

I remember reading a report recently in the Economist[10] on the summit meeting of Asean+3 in Malaysia. Its Prime Minister announced that this summit should lay the groundwork for an East Asian Community (EAC) that "should build a free-trade area, co-operate on finance, and sign a security pact that would transform East Asia into a cohesive economic block . . . In fact, some of these schemes are already in motion. China, as the region's preeminent economic and military power, will doubtless dominate and host the second East Asia Summit." The report goes on to recall that in 1990, Uncle Sam shot down a previous initiative for fear of losing influence in the region. Now the report is entitled "Yankee stay home."

So what if already long before that comes to pass, oil exporters simply cease to price their commodity in an ever devaluing dollar and instead make a mint by switching to the rising Euro and/or to a basket of East Asian currencies? In one stroke, that would vastly diminish the world demand for and price of the dollar by obliging anyone who wants to buy oil to instead purchase and increase the demand price of the Euro or Yen/Yuan (in place of the dollar). That would help crash the dollar and tumble Uncle Sam in one fell swoop, as foreign and even domestic owners of dollars would also sell off as many of them as fast as they could while other countries' central banks would switch their reserves out of dollars in the no longer safe haven Uncle Sam. That would in turn drive the dollar down even more, and of course halt any more dollar inflow to Uncle Sam by the foreigners who have been financing Uncle Sam's consumption spree. Since selling oil for a falling dollar instead of a rising Euro is evidently bad business, the world's largest exporters in Russia and OPEC have been considering doing exactly that. In the meantime, they have raised the dollar price of oil so that in Euro terms,

[9] See: *Economic and Political Weekly*, Mumbai, Dec. 4, 2004:5189.
[10] See *The Economist*, Dec. 11–17 2004:50.

it has remained about stable since 2000. So far, many oil exporters and others still place their surplus dollars with Uncle Sam, even though he now offers an ever less attractive and less safe haven, although Russia is now buying more Euros with some of its dollars.

As many countries' central banks have begun to put ever more of their reserves into the Euro and currencies other than Uncle Sam's dollars, now even the best friend indeed, the Central Bank of China, the greatest friend of Uncle Sam in need, has begun to buy some Euros. China itself has also begun to use some of its dollars – as long as they are still accepted by them – to buy real goods from other Asians and thousands of tons of iron ore and steel from Brazil, etc. The Brazilian President recently took a huge business delegation to China while the Chinese president just went to Argentina. They are going after African oil and South African minerals too.

Uncle Sam's Own Economy Is Really a Hollow Doughnut

All Ponzi schemes build a financial pyramid. Many who pay into them also live in a financial world themselves. Others need to derive their in-payment through earnings from production in the real world. In today's world of financial transactions that each day surpass one hundred fold all payments for real goods and services put together, the financial ones overshadow the real ones behind their brilliance. To over-simplify a very complex matter into more intelligible lay wo/man's language, options, derivatives, swaps and other recent financial instruments have been ever further compounding already compounded interest on the real properties in which their stake and debts are based, which has contributed to the spectacular growth of this financial world. Nonetheless, the financial pyramid that we see in all its splendour and brilliance, especially in its centre at Uncle Sam's home, still sits on top of a real world producer-merchant-consumer base, even if the financial one also provides credit for these real world transactions.

Now what if we look at the world as a doughnut, analogous to so many cities in Uncle Sam's rust belt. The centre is derelict and hollowed out since production and consumption has long since moved to the surrounding suburbs. In mo-town Detroit, the windows of the main department store Hudson's have been boarded up for years, even as Detroit has built an expensive "Renaissance Centre" to re-gentrify the city centre. This is a process that has supposedly "succeeded" in some other cities. Derelict General Motors Flint gives us Michael Moore, who featured it in "Roger and Me" and "Fahrenheit 9–11." So how about if look at the entire world in doughnut terms, with the whole of Uncle Sam in the empty hole in the middle that produces almost nothing it can sell abroad. The main exceptions are agricultural goods and military hardware that are heavily subsidised by the Uncle Sam government from its taxpayers and its paper printing press. Even still, Uncle Sam runs a US$ 600+ billion budget deficit.

The big difference in this Uncle Sam doughnut is that both the budget and the US$ 600+ billion trade deficit are financed by foreigners, as we have already seen. Uncle Sam would exclude most of them as persons, but gladly receives the real goods they produce. As world consumer of last resort, as already suggested, Uncle Sam performs this important function in the present-day global political-economic division of labour. Everybody else produces and needs to export while Uncle Sam consumes and needs to import.

The crash of the dollar would (will?) crumble this entire world-embracing political-economic doughnut and throw hundreds of millions of people, not to mention an untold quantity of dollar owners, into turmoil with unforeseen and perhaps unforeseeable consequences. Many people, high and low on the world totem pole, have a big stake in avoiding that, even if it requires continuing to blow the empty Uncle Sam up like a balloon. Or to refer to a well know simile, to continue to pretend that the Emperor with no Clothes is dressed up, and to send him some clothing to boot. That still includes China, for which a financial show down with Uncle Sam would be a blessing in disguise. That would oblige China to change political economic course. Instead of giving its goods away for free to Uncle Sam, it would have to turn production and consumption inward to its poor interior and to the near outward in East Asia, all of which it could and should be doing already. While China has recently begun to do the latter, it has not yet seriously contemplated the former.

So what will happen to the rich on top of the Uncle Sam Ponzi scheme, when the confidence of poorer central banks and oil exporters in the middle runs out, and the more destitute of the world's poor, confident or not, can no longer make their in-payments at the bottom? The Uncle Sam Ponzi Scheme Confidence Racket would – or will? – come crashing down, like all other such schemes before, only this time with a world-wide bang. It would cut the world's present Uncle Sam consumer demand of last resort down to real/istic world size and hurt many exporters and producers elsewhere in the world.

In fact, it may involve a wholesale reorganisation of the world political economy presently run by Uncle Sam.

The Uncle Sam Paper Dollar Tiger Poses a Mad Geo-Political Catch 22

Of course, crashing the dollar would also wipe out altogether in one fell swoop, i.e., by default, the debt of Uncle Sam. It would also simultaneously make all foreigners and rich Americans lose the whole of their dollar asset shirt. They are still desperately trying to save as much of it as possible by not going for the crash, that is, for broke. They are trying to protect the remainder of their dollar investment shirt by keeping their dollar sustaining pump going. The whole business of maintaining the Uncle Sam Ponzi Scheme poses the world's biggest and craziest Catch-22 since MAD, and it is just about as mad.

This is all the more reason why it must be resolved. But the way out of the mad Catch 22 need not be a soft landing. It can be a hard one indeed. This dissolution of the Uncle Sam Ponzi Scheme will be costly and the greatest costs will as usual be dumped most probably on the poorest that are least able to bear these costs and conveniently the least able to protect themselves from being forced to do so. The historically necessary transition out from under the Uncle Sam run doughnut world could bring the entire world into the deepest depression ever. Only East Asia is in a relatively good position to save itself from being pulled – or pushed – down to the bottom, and even then, they will also pay a high cost for this transition – toward itself!

However, the world is facing an even MADer global geo-political and military Catch 22. It remains the great unknown and it is perhaps unknowable. How would [will?] Uncle Sam react as a Paper Money Tiger that is wounded by a crash of the Ponzi Scheme Confidence Racket from which he and millions of un-knowing Uncle Sammies have lived the good life? To compensate for less bread and civil rights but more "patriotic acts" at home, a more chauvinist Uncle Sam can provide a World War III circus abroad. A crash of the dollar will pull the financial rug out from under and discourage his foreign victims from continuing to pay for new Pentagon adventures abroad. But some more wars may still be possible with the weapons he would still have and some more military Keynesian government deficit spending at home, including for the new "small nukes" he is preparing for the occasion.

That could well be the horrible cost to the world of his current policies to "defend Freedom and Civilisation." The Super Catch 22 is that almost nobody other than Osama bin Laden wants to run that risk.

Yet, such a transition would [will?] not be historically new. Recall how much the transition to Uncle Sam cost: a 30 Year War from 1914 to 1945 with the intervening second Great Depression in a century that cost 100 million lives lost to war, more than in all previous world history combined, not to mention the literally hundreds of millions who suffered and died from unnecessary starvation and disease. Or the previous transition to the British Major Bull cost the Napoleonic Wars, the Great Depression of 1873–95, colonialism and semi-colonialism, to name a few, and their human costs. The latter coincided with the most pronounced El Niño climatic changes in two centuries, which ravaged Indians, Chinese, and many others with famines. But these were in turn magnified by the Imperial Colonial powers who used the situation in their own interests, e.g. increased export of wheat from India especially during years of famine.

The parallels with today, including even again taking advantage a century later of renewed and stronger El Niños, are too horrifying and guilt generating for practically anybody to suggest. They include Uncle Sam's IMF imposed "structural adjustment" that obliges Mexican peasants to have already eaten the belt that the IMF wants them to tighten still further. Three million dead and still counting in Rwanda and Burundi, and then some in neighbouring Congo, came after the IMF imposed strictures and the cancellation of the Coffee Agreement, primarily by Uncle Sam, that had sustained prices for these producers. And now – not since the CIA murder of Lumumba and the elevation of Kosavubu in Katanga in 1961, indeed since the King of Belgium's private reserve of the Congo in the 19th century, have we seen something like the scramble for and production and sale there of gold for Uncle Sam's Fort Knox, and even titanium so that we can communicate by mobile cell phones and diamonds for ever, and so on. Uncle Sam also took advantage of yet another strong El Niño event that ravaged South East Asia, and especially Indonesia, simultaneously with the post-1997 financial crisis that Uncle Sam deliberately parlayed into an economic depression. It was so great that it swept out of office President Suharto whom Uncle Sam himself had installed thirty years earlier with his CIA coup against the popular father of Indonesian independence, Sukarno. That had cost at least half a million and estimated close to one million lives that Suhartu took directly, not to mention the poverty generated by the infamous "Berkeley Mafia" that he installed to run the Indonesian economy into the ground. The parallels with the past also include environmental degradation and the shift of ecological damage from the rich who generate it to the poor Third World who bears its greatest burden. And of course we should not forget World War III that Daddy Bush began against Iraq in 1991.[11]

Yet there are also others in the world who do not (yet?) feel all that caught up in the Catch 22. In a well-calculated manner just before the 2004 Uncle Sam election, one such voice said so out loudly in a video broadcast to the world. It seems to have been the least publicly noted by its principal addressee, Uncle Sam, who should have been the most interested party. None other than bin Laden himself announced that he is "going to bankrupt Uncle Sam!" In view of the deliberate Uncle Sam blindness to the shakiness of his real world foundation abroad, so massive a collapse abroad may not be more difficult to arrange than toppling its Twin Towers symbol at home.

The Pentagon Is the World's Largest Planned Economy

Meantime back on the farm, as the saying goes in Texas, what does Uncle Sam himself so blithely do with the world's hard earned savings and money? His consumers still over-consume it without 99.9 percent of them ever knowing what they are doing, especially since hardly anyone tells them so. Uncle Sam's government uses much if not all of its increase of hundreds of billions of dollars for the Pentagon. That money is not spent to pay its poor professional soldiers who come mostly from small town rural America and took the only job they could get, and even less is spent on its hapless reservists. They told Rumsfeld in Kuwait that he does not even provide them with sufficient and safe equipment. Rummy replied, "I am an old man, I just got up, and I need time to get my thoughts together."

But at home in the Pentagon, Rummy faces no such problem. There he knows very well what he is doing, privatising the war in Iraq just as at home. The Military-Industrial Complex against which General Eisenhower warned in his 1958 parting Presidential address is alive and kicking, "now more than ever" under the stewardship of "Vice" President Cheney and his De[a]f

---

[11] See my "Third World War" at http://rrojasdatabank.info/agfrank/gulf_war.html.

Secretary Rumsfeld. With their jobs disastrously well done, both were kept on for a second term as was Paul Wolfowitz "of Arabia" who with Douglas Feith is one of the duo at the Pentagon that went to Israel. Regarding the latter, the German *Der Spiegel* quoted Tommy Franks in 2004, the commander of the Iraq invasion, as calling him "the greatest total idiot that there is on God's Earth, with whom I have to battle almost every day."[12]

Between 1994 and mid-2003, Uncle Sam's Pentagon signed over 3,000 contracts valued at more than US$ 300 billion with 12 Uncle Sam private military companies out of the 35 active players estimated by the *New York Times*, others of which are small and offer only mercenary services. More than 2,700 of those contracts were given to just two companies, Kellogg Brown & Root (KBR), a subsidiary of Cheney's Halliburton, and to Booz Allen Hamilton.[13] In Iraq these private military companies now have as many mercenaries as Uncle Sam and UK troops combined. That is of course still "small potatoes," since the bulk of Pentagon money is Uncle Sam-ed to buy expensive weapons systems from the only four major Uncle Sam "Defence" contractors and the likes of Vice-President Cheney's Halliburton. Uncle Sam then uses these arms unilaterally to twist others arms by armed threat and blackmail, and if that is not enough, to invade the world that provided the money in the first place. After all, Uncle Sam has to do what it must to keep the money coming in.

To Carry the "White Man's Burden" to Defend his "Civilisation"

Uncle Sam unilateralism is not just about going it alone as is so often mistakenly supposed. Yes, it is also to proclaim fighting for "Freedom" (whose we may ask?) and "saving civilisation" as Uncle Sam President Bush and his even more eloquent UK mouth piece Tony Blair proclaim every day. The best way to "save" civilisation was by simply abolishing in a day its most precious gift, the entire body of international law, so as to keep the peace which the West had taken centuries to develop, although admittedly having done so in its own imperial interests. Still, it was the best and only international law we had, and at the very least better than nothing at all. Now the only law of the West that remains is indeed "The law of the West," that spaghetti

---

[12] See: *Der Spiegel*, Dec. 20, 2004:33.
[13] See: Centre for Public Integrity's International Consortium of Investigative Journalists, note by Mafruza Khan, Aug. 16, 2003.

western vigilante law of posses that, with or without a conniving judge, take the "law" into their own hands in forming their lynching parties. They go after whom and where and when they please. Alas, now in the real world, the self-appointed posses operate "out of area" on a much grander scale than any fictional spaghetti western film could ever have imagined.

That also means disembowelling and paralysing the institution that was established to guard the peace, the United Nations, except when Uncle Sam calls on them after its own wars to pick up the pieces he has shattered in places like ex-Yugoslavia, Afghanistan and now Iraq. In so doing, he also means to dupe, threaten, cajole and blackmail all others – friends and foes alike – to do his bidding on every issue, big and small. He has trained a whole civilian army of officials to do that. Uncle Sam "unilaterally" throws his apparent weight around in all other international institutions that deal with endeavours from agriculture and aviation to zoology. But Uncle Sam extorts real unilateral favours for himself in the process and even more so through his bilateral relations. That is why the World Trade Organisation (WTO) was dead on arrival. Indeed Uncle Sam now prefers to orchestrate his bilateral relations unilaterally, as he increasingly isolates himself internationally. That way, he can exercise even more military, political and economic bargaining power over any one of his victims than he any longer can over all or even many of them via international institutions.

Uncle Sam's Proud March From The Halls Of Montezuma To The Shores Of Tripoli – On To Panama, Twice To Iraq, Afghanistan . . .

When that bargaining is not enough, or even if it could be, Uncle Sam simply attacks when he feels the need and invades little Grenada (population: 300,000); Nicaragua (with the help of arch-enemy Iran); Panama (7,000 civilians killed in one night to capture one man only, Daddy Bush's one-time friend and ally Noriega); Iraq in 1991 (that was even a money making venture as Uncle Sam extorted more dollars from his allies to pay for the war than it actually cost him!) But Iraq was contaminated by Uncle Sam's depleted uranium, which has multiplied birth defects there – and which caused the infamous "Gulf War syndrome" among his own and British troops, which Uncle Sam still refuses to acknowledge. The less said about Somalia the better. Yugoslavia was attacked in part to make an example out of what can happen when a state is weak enough and, yet in abject defiance of Uncle Sam and his IMF, maintains some significant state ownership of means of production and still provides social welfare state protection to the population. That is like Belarus today, where Uncle Sam also tried to get "regime change" but found that military action is more difficult on the border of Russia, unless it is in accord as in the case of Afghanistan or at least bought off. Moreover, Yugoslavia only gave up in 1999 after Russia withdrew its support from it, mostly because Uncle Sam successfully used political economic blackmail and partly bought it off in Berlin.

Then poor Afghanistan became a targeted victim, again with the help of Iran and Russia. That is after Uncle Sam created and sponsored the Taliban government that eradicated opium. But the "liberated" Afghanistan now grows opium again even more that before the Taliban eradicated it. Opium now accounts for one third of Afghanistan's GDP according to its President who was installed by Uncle Sam. At the same time, Uncle Sam is launching a renewed military offensive against Taliban but there is hardly any mention of bin Laden. And now innocent Iraq, already a former Uncle Sam target and now a victim again. Who is next, Iran? Syria? Not Libya since it is now obediently making oil deals with Uncle Sam. Not North Korea that made nukes to protect itself against precisely that.

I have neglected to mention two additional perhaps possible alternatives prior to invasion. One is of course sponsoring, organising, or even making a military or otherwise coup d' etat of which the CIA has a proud record: Iran in 1953; Guatemala in 1954; Congo in 1960; Vietnam in 1961; Brazil in 1964; Guyana in 1964; Indonesia in 1964–65; Dominican Republic in 1965; Ghana in 1966; Greece in 1967; Cambodia in 1970; Chile in 1973; Argentina in 1976; Bolivia again and again; Fiji in 1987; Nicaragua in 1990 by way of "election" under threat of continuing the Contras war; Haiti again and again – against the ex-puppet who Uncle Sam put there in the first place, just to name a few of the better known cases. Another alternative is better known and attempted several times against Fidel Castro in Cuba, using explosive cigars and other imaginative CIA "dirty tricks," all of which have been notably unsuccessful. So too was the bombing of Cornel Ghadafi's tent home that only killed his daughter. But our friend Mr. Perkins relates a successful CIA attempt:

> The Japanese wanted to finance and construct a sea-level canal in Panama.
> [Omar] Torrijos talked to them about this which very much upset Bechtel
> Corporation, whose president was George Schultz and senior council was
> Casper Weinberger. When Carter was thrown out (and that's an interesting

story-how that actually happened after he lost the election, and Reagan came in, making Schultz Secretary of State (from Bechtel Corporation) and Weinberger (likewise from Bechtel) to be Secretary of Defence, they were extremely angry at Torrijos and tried to get him to renegotiate the Canal Treaty and not to talk to the Japanese. He adamantly refused. He was a very principled man. He had his problem, but he was a very principled man. He was an amazing man, Torrijos. And so, he died in a fiery airplane crash, which was connected to a tape recorder with explosives in it, which – I was there. I had been working with him. I knew that we economic hit men had failed. I knew that the jackals were closing in on him, and the next thing, his plane exploded with a tape recorder with a bomb in it. There's no question in my mind that it was CIA sanctioned, and many Latin American investigators have come to the same conclusion. Of course, we never heard about that in our country.)[14]

Simple inspection also reveals that being too good a political friend or tool of Uncle Sam can also be just about the riskiest, foolish thing any statesman can do for it can easily spell his political or physical death sentence after Uncle Sam stabs him in the back. A successor of Torrijos, as we noted, is now sitting in an Uncle Sam jail after loyally serving and smiling in a photo with (father) George Bush. But the line is long and goes all the way around the world starting in the 1950s and 1960s with Rhee in Korea, Diem in Vietnam, Trujillo in the Dominican Republic, Somoza in Nicaragua, virtually everybody in Haiti from Papa and Baby Doc to Father Aristide installed by Clinton and removed by Bush. There was the Shah of Iran – put there after the 1953 CIA coup against Mossadeq after he had nationalised Iran's oil industry. Apparently, he was let go when his usefulness faded, as was Mobutu after three decades in Zaire, Saddam Hussein in Iraq, and Yugoslavia's Milosevic, the necessary and reliable implementer of the Uncle Sam Dayton agreement in Bosnia. Of course we need to mention the Taliban – Uncle Sam himself formed and put it in charge of Afghanistan, not to mention one Osama bin Laden – he also served Uncle Sam there.

A simple inspection of the facts on the ground also reveals that, if the above "lines of defence" fail and Uncle Sam goes to war, except for little Grenada, not a single one of these or other Uncle Sam wars was ever won by his

---

[14] See: http://www.democracynow.org/article.pl?sid=04/11/09/1526251.

military force, except for the Pacific campaign against Japan. World War II was won in Europe at Stalingrad in 1943 by Russian troops. The Korean War was and remains a stalemate. The War against Vietnam was lost. The War against Yugoslavia was "won" only when the Russians withdrew their support, and then all but seven Yugoslav tanks and all of its planes left Kosovo unharmed. Only the Yugoslav civilian infrastructure had been bombed to smithereens and its wider Balkan landscape polluted for eons by Uncle Sam's renewed use of depleted uranium. The War against Afghanistan is being lost and so is the War against Iraq, despite the reported use of depleted uranium there as well, along with napalm as in Vietnam and even chemical gas.

Uncle Sam's Geo-Political Muslims and Oil "Middle Eastern" Plan from Casablanca to Jakarta

Nonetheless, Uncle Sam has plenty other geo-political economic military plans in motion. For starters, he has already built 800 military bases around the world and especially in the oil rich "heartland" of Zbigniew Brzezinski's global "Chessboard" and to surround China. The Pentagon is said to be redeploying 60 percent of its submarine fleet to the Western Pacific. All that is for future military use but also for political influence in the present. Apart from that, Uncle Sam President Bush has a new "Plan for the Middle East" which now stretches from Morocco beyond Pakistan – to Muslim Indonesia? Just what this plan involves is not yet clear, but civil society is already paving the way as well: Yale University Press already lists Pakistan among its "Middle Eastern" Studies, and Swissair has a paper placemat that places Karachi, Delhi and Mumbai on its "Middle Eastern" destinations. What is clear is that Israel is to remain Uncle Sam's political and military stalking horse in the region that it has always been. Never mind whether Republicans or Democrats rule in Washington, Israel's hunting dog-like role for Uncle Sam in its oil rich area of operation remains stable and does the security Israel in turn enjoys from Uncle Sam's international diplomatic, political and military protection. Without Uncle Sam's direct economic and military support, Israel could not exist. Its assigned and self-appointed regional reach may expand even further. Meanwhile, Bush himself went to Africa, especially West Africa to look at its oil prospects.

In the Americas, Uncle Sam's "Plan Colombia" (another oil supplier) has been extended to the whole Andean region (Ecuador also exports oil). He has yet another plan for the Amazon (maybe some oil is to be found there and in the meantime he built a huge base there, allegedly for NASA which is not unknown to engage in military ventures), with help from the World Bank, to "take care of" the world's largest underground deposit of sweet water under Iguaçu Falls, where Brazil, Argentina and Paraguay all meet. He is already training 40,000 Latin American military personnel on Uncle Sam bases at home, of which he has another half dozen beyond his shores as well.

All this is a giant global military political economic foundation on which to maintain Uncle Sam's financial Ponzi Scheme Confidence Racket. It is cheap at twice the price for those that end up with the dollars as long as he can pay for it all with the self-made paper dollars that so far also maintains the global Ponzi business. To be honest, it's not only for the dollars. After all, those are only useful if you can actually buy something with it, especially the oil that keeps the foundation running.

Not only does Uncle Sam have to buy ever more oil, today with self-printed currency, but perhaps tomorrow with Euros or Yuan. He also has to try to make sure to have his hand on every spigot so he can control who else can, and especially who can *not* buy it. So that is why we now find him attempting to exert political and financial monetary control of the oil spigots, wherever he still can, and for establishing a military presence in Central Asia, or Uncle Sam-ing military power to go in like to Iraq. That is both to use it as a lever of control and/or to warn its neighbours what may happen to them if they fail to continue to play along with Uncle Sam. Fortunately for him, most of East Asia and especially China also seems to be obliged to buy foreign oil, even if tomorrow perhaps no longer with dollars but with Yuan/Yen. On the other hand, it is sad but true that the world's biggest seller of oil is Russia whose spigots remain beyond Uncle Sam control. But how could Uncle Sam continue to pay for and maintain all these bold Uncle Sam ventures in Defence of Freedom with that self made paper currency – if nobody accepts it any more? And why should anybody?

Uncle Sam's Grand Cause for Iraq: US$30 Billion to Halliburton, et al.

The *Financial Times*[15] offers some additional tip of the iceberg examples of Uncle Sam's Defence of Freedom in Iraq. Though poor Iraq sits on top of the

---

[15] See: *Financial Times*, Dec. 10, 2004.

world's largest still unexploited pool of ever more precious oil, it remains in the background or only at the bottom of the *Financial Times* story that barely mentions it and, like the present essay, focuses instead on related dollars and Uncle Sam. In two different reports, it relates how three helicopters flew 14 tons of US$ 100 dollar bills in to the Kurds, who long since have been an Uncle Sam Fifth Column in the area. The money, much of the US$1.8 billion Uncle Sam pay-off to the Kurds, was part of Iraq's earnings in the UN "oil-for-food" fund. Initially, of course, the bills were simply the product of the same Uncle Sam self-printing press for which Iraq had exported real oil. It did not come from the US$18 billion that Uncle Sam's Congress appropriated for the "reconstruction" of Iraq. As a *Financial Times* graph clearly shows, no more than US$ 388 million – or 2.15 percent – of that Uncle Sam money had yet been spent, and only US$ 5 billion of it had even been budgeted by Uncle Sam in Iraq by the time Uncle Sam pro-consul Brenner went home with a job well done.[16] No, Uncle Sam had in its wisdom thought it best to have spent US$13 billion of the US$ 20 billion of Iraqi funds. That was 65 percent of the Iraqi money compared to the still only two percent of the nearly equivalent amount of original Uncle Sam money. By the time the new Iraqi government took over some tasks from Uncle Sam who put them there, they discovered that a full US$ 20 billion of their funds had been spent, US$ 11 billion from the sales of oil. How come? – we may ask. So simple is the answer of the "responsible" finance officer, Uncle Sam Admiral Oliver, "I know we spent some money from [the Iraqi] fund. It was purely the matter that we'd run out of Uncle Sam money" – of which there was only another US$17.5+ billion unspent. We might wonder whether the good General was schooled in Clausewitz on war or just happened to discover his good advice about making the conquered victim pay for his own military occupation, in this case by Uncle Sam.

The Iraqi representative on the funding disbursement and oversight committee attended only one of its 43 meetings. But why bother when most expenditures were authorised without any meeting at all? So although Uncle Sam funds were budgeted for all sorts of projects, they were nonetheless paid out of Iraqi funds. Of these, many disbursements were even made without any contract whatsoever as in one case involving a mere US$1.4 billion. Most others occurred without any multiple bids, competitive or otherwise. The

---

[16] The citations from the *Financial Times* The numbers cited from the *Financial Times* were from December 10 and 15, 2004.

Uncle Sam funds, on the other hand, remained virtually unspent in Iraq. Maybe Admiral Oliver had "run out of Uncle Sam money" in Iraq because it remained with Uncle Sam at home in Washington. If disbursed at all, it simply changed hands and remained in bank accounts right there. After all, that is much more efficient than it would be to send it back and forth, and a bit of it might not even make it back. Moreover, it has also long since been standard operating practise for the bulk of the dollars that Uncle Sam lends or even "gives" "to" and "for" all Third World countries, just to leave it at home where it belongs and would return to anyway. This notwithstanding, Uncle Sam's Congress appropriated another US$ 30 billion in early 2005 in order to "prepare for transition to elections."

All that being the case, it would of course be altogether undesirable for Iraqi, let alone Uncle Sam's, funds to be squandered on any Iraqi service of old foreign debt to others. So it was only logical to strong-arm "allies" who can't help already losing Uncle Sam debt to them, also to forgive the Iraqi debt. That is, as we may recall from above, while Uncle Sam still insists that the rest of the Third World must continue servicing their debts to him! God forbid that any re-payment of Iraqi debt should go instead to those un-Godly Russians, traitorous Frenchmen or even to the Chinese best friend indeed, who most invested in Iraq, a dastardly thing to do in the first place, when Uncle Sam has much more worthy causes for the Iraqi money.

Just what are these grander worthy Uncle Sam causes? The largest single payment of US$1.4 billion was of course to Vice President Cheney's Halliburton. Yet, we now know that at the same time that this company was cheating even his generous Uncle Sam benefactor out of hundreds of millions more dollars on the side, buying petrol for $X in Kuwait and selling it in Iraq for 5–10 times more, and other sly frauds. Altogether, Halliburton got Iraq contracts for a cool US$10 billion plus change. Cheney also has an interest in UNO-CAL that has long wanted to build an oil pipe line from Central Asia to the Indian Ocean through Afghanistan, first with the help of Taliban whom Uncle Sam had put in charge there for precisely that purpose and then invited to Texas for talks while they still seemed to be doing their assigned job. Indeed, they also visited the purely Afghanistan-focused "academic research" outfit at the University of Nebraska in Omaha. But alas, the Taliban was not up to their assigned task of keeping order for the construction of the pipe line and so they had to go. Now Uncle Sam and UNOCAL will instead use the good offices of the new Afghan President and Uncle Sam Ambassador in Kabul, both of whom just "happen" to be former(?) UNOCAL people.

Uncle Sam's "Medal of Freedom" for Brenner, Franks & Tenet: A Job Well Done in Robbing Iraq for the Benefit of Cheney, et al.

Without the shadow of a doubt, most of the other abundant Iraqi and so far sparse Uncle Sam dollars spent in Iraq went to other Uncle Sam cronies, with some crumbs off the table for the UK, corporations and even to private and military individuals who have their fingers in the till. Alas, we will never know who they all are, since according to Uncle Sam's Inspector-General: "I was, candidly, not interested in having army auditors because I thought we had to slide into the Iraqi system as quickly as possible." Since I am both non and anti-military, I have not myself read Clausewitz. So I do not know what, if any, good advice he gives about relying on corruption as the first principle in cutting and dividing up the conquered pie.

All of the above "speculation" of mine was written before the UN International Advisory and Monitoring Board for Development in Iraq (IAMBDI) issued a report on its findings about the Uncle Sam stewardship. Before I end with a comment on the Report, we should keep in mind that the *Financial Times* has diplomatically observed that "the UN has been reluctant to take Uncle Sam to task publicly over its spending of Iraqi funds." The *Financial Times* quotes directly from the Report: "There were control weaknesses, inadequate accounting systems, uneven application of agreed-upon contracting procedures and inadequate record keeping." The *International Herald Tribune* also makes its own summary of the same report: "There had been widespread irregularities, including financial mismanagement, a failure to cut smuggling [outward of oil and other Iraqi physical property; nobody knows at what price and to whose benefit] and over dependence on no-bid contracts."[17] The *Financial Times*, for its part, offers a bit more of specifics from the Report: "Of particular concern were contracts for sometimes billions of dollars that were awarded to Uncle Sam companies such as Halliburton from Iraqi funds without competitive tender." So when Uncle Sam President Bush gave Uncle Sam's highest civilian award, The Medal of Freedom, to L. Paul Bremer III, the Uncle Sam civilian pro-consul who oversaw it all, to General Tommy Franks, who led the invasion that made it all possible in the first place, and to George Tenet, the Director of the CIA that provided all the bogus Uncle Sam information to "legitimatise" the whole enterprise to begin with

---

[17] See: The *International Herald Tribune,* December 15.

and who has since been discredited and forced to resign, the three were all smiles with Bush who was smiling too. After all, it was due recognition for a job well done in their service to "Freedom."

Conclusion: Uncle George W. Sam Says Its Only Right for Our Boys to Lay Their Lives On the Line to Protect Halliburton's Freedom to Rob Iraq

We may rest assured that others who had their hands in the till and trough were among those whom, we may recall, the Fed's Dr. Greenspan labelled as the upper 20 percent of Uncle Sam's income earners. They are the most privileged over-consumers, who are totally (ir)responsible for Uncle Sam's under-saving, he said, and also for the growing trade deficit about which the Dr. so bitterly complained about in Berlin. If we examine the Uncle Sam income distribution a bit further, we may well learn that among this 20 percent, the lion's share of this money like most of that from the Pentagon, ends up in the pockets of the upper 2 percent most super-privileged, so they can over-consume still more of the fat of the earth.

Who would deny that this is surely a worthy cause for the protection of freedom at any price? That includes President Bush's (in)famous invitation to the Iraqis to "let them come on" against Uncle Sam. It is difficult to understand the President when he encourages the Iraqis "to come" at him when they are already at home in Iraq and it is Uncle Sam who sent his troops there. But maybe Falluja explains what President Bush had in mind about the Iraqis "coming" on against Uncle Sam. As Uncle Sam's President Bush himself told the world, it is only right that "we" exclude other countries from the trough and till in Iraq. He explained that when the Iraqis accepted his invitation, it was "our boys who put their lives on the line." I wish the personification of Uncle Sam had also explained for what and for whom.[18]

---

[18] All illustrative figures, unless otherwise indicated, were derived from Gerard Dumenil & Dominique Levy, 2004, *Review of International Political Economy* 11:4 (Oct.):657–676. The author is thankful to Gerard Dumenil and Dominique Levy in Paris, to Jeffrey Sommers in Riga, William Engdahl in Frankfurt and Mark Weisbrot in Washington for their useful and much used comments. Barry Gills in Newcastle insisted that I refer only to Uncle Sam and proposed the world division of labour between Uncle Sam consumers and producers everywhere else. He also referred me to Clausewitz. Readers will be most grateful to Arlene Hohnstock for having rendered all of this tale readable. Of course none of them have any responsibility for the doughnut shaped use I have made of them.

Andre Gunder Frank

In Memory of Andre Gunder Frank
1929–2005

On Saturday, 23 April 2005, André Gunder Frank
passed away, a victim of the cancer he had struggled against for over a decade. With his death, the
social sciences lost one of its most acute and prolific
analysts. Hundreds of articles and dozens of books
are testimony to this fact.

Frank was an innovative thinker and a much discussed author. His intellectual trajectory was filled
with great successes and also some errors, the latter
if you take his word for it. Many academic figures
have alluded to the power of his ideas which so
invariably provoked others to respond. His theoretical production included more than 1000 publications in thirty languages, including 49 books, 169
book chapters or contributions to 145 books, and
hundreds of essays and smaller articles that have
appeared in academic journals and periodicals. The
impressive fertility of his thought, the tremendous
diversity of issues he analysed, and his only recent
silence, all make it rather difficult to evaluate the
whole of his intellectual contributions.

André Gunder Frank was born in Berlin, Germany
on 24 February 1929. At the age of four, he and his
family were exiled to Switzerland as Hitler rose to
power. In 1941, he arrived to the United States where
he completed his high school and university studies,
remaining in that country until 1961. His academic
training culminated in 1957 with a thesis on Soviet
agriculture at the University of Chicago. Imagine

Frank in the cradle of the Chicago Boys, that infamous gang of genocidal economists responsible for scorching Latin America and devising recipes of death and misery at the hands of international financial agencies. Frank's thinking hurdled the ideologues that supervised his academic training and he soon came to the conclusion, as mentioned in his intellectual autobiography, that the determinant factors of economic development are really social in nature. Social change was consequently the key to all social and economic development.

In 1962, Frank travelled to Latin America as an associate professor at the University of Brasilia. Subsequently, he taught at the National Autonomous University of Mexico (UNAM) and between 1967–73, conducted research at the Centre for Socio-economic Studies (CESO) at the University of Chile. His contact with Latin America brought him a high level of personal and intellectual commitment that lasted the rest of his life. He, like his father, had irreversibly opted for the political left.

Frank's study *Capitalism and Underdevelopment in Latin America* is a classic work in the critical sociology of Latin America. His conception of the "development of underdevelopment" today has more relevance than ever, since the realities of the continent show it all too clearly. Generations of Latin Americans were influenced by his thought. His contributions to dependency theory were decisive ones. Frank, moreover, was one of the creators of world systems theory, although in our judgement, there is a clear continuity between both theoretical paradigms. Indeed, it is possible to talk of a dependency-world systems perspective for analysing the problems of development and the structures of underdevelopment.

One of his last books, *ReORIENT: Global Economy in the Asian Age* was a no-holds barred, frontal assault against Euro-centrism and Occidentalism. This work was read widely, especially in Europe and Asia, uncorking a sharp polemic that yielded diverse critiques of the book, even from Frank himself![1] In dispute were the possible future scenarios of global hegemony, including the position of China. Frank identified China as the former centre of the global economy, temporarily displaced by the Industrial Revolution, and now emergent full circle in recovering its former hegemony. Clearly, all of the ensuing debates were of the type that only history can one day decisively resolve.

---

[1] See http://www.rrojasdatabank.org/agfrank/reorient.html.

Anybody who knew Frank could appreciate his perpetual sense of humour. In his "Personal is Political Autobiography," he wrote the following about how earlier practical life experience helped shape his intellectual attitude:

... During summer vacations in college and for many years after that, I held down all sorts of jobs until I was fired from most of them – always for the same reason: insubordination. These jobs included building pre-fab houses in the Washington DC suburbs, digging ditches and laying the concrete sidewalk from the north-west corner of the campus of the University of Michigan campus to its library. I was therefore able to tell my son that I had once made a 'concrete' contribution to his welfare there as a graduate student. In Washington State, I worked in a saw mill and then as a logger, as well as again digging ditches and 'gandy-dancing,' that is laying railroad track. In Michigan, I built automobiles at Willow Run in a plant which had been built during World War II to manufacture B-17 bombers. In New Orleans, I tended 32 spools in a row of twine to spin them for the International Harvester Corporation. There, I also worked as a private eye as well as of course in the French Quarter tourist industry as a waiter on Bourbon Street, a picture painter in Jackson Square, and in the Mardi Gras parade walking around dressed as a huge paper-mache Old Grand Dad whisky bottle, on which people knocked asking for samples that I was unable to supply.

Alas, I had no "aptitude" for any of these: I had taken an employment aptitude test at the Louisiana State Employment Commission, which showed that, as they duly informed me, I had aptitude for NOTHING and especially NO INTELLECTUAL aptitude. Therefore, they said, I should try my hand as an automobile mechanic ... In Chicago, I loaded freight cars at night, and in the daytime I was supposed to placate the irate customers of a furniture store whose sales personnel made their sales by promising delivery dates that were impossible to meet. Since I sided more with their innocent customer victims, the sales people had me fired. [2]

In a certain sense, Frank lived his entire life in exile. In childhood, he was exiled from Germany by the ascent of Nazism; from the United States, he was professionally exiled because his ideas did not jive with the establishment in which he was trained; in Latin America, he was exiled by the installation of military dictatorships; only to once again be exiled after returning

---

[2] See http://www.rrojasdatabank.org/agfrank/personal.html.

to Germany on account of the vagaries of academic politics. This led him to pursue academic posts in diverse parts of the world. The historical records will show that during his career, Frank carried out teaching and research activities in nine universities in Canada and the United States, three in Latin America, five in Europe. He conducted numerous seminars and conferences in all corners of the globe. It was only during the Clinton era that he could bring himself to return briefly to reside in the United States.

Frank was also a man who had the good fortune to share life with extraordinary companions such as Marta Fuentes, his first wife, with whom he lived with for over 30 years. Marta was a seasoned intellectual and acknowledged first reader and mediator for all of his works. Frank attested that she was a pillar of companionship and support in his personal life until her death from cancer in 1993. With Marta, they had two children, Pablo and Miguel. In 1999, Frank met Alison Candela, the person who was to continuously breathe life into Frank as he eventually endured a total of four major operations. The two were married in 2003 and she was on the frontline right up to the final moment of his life, helping him confront his illness. Frank's last days were spent in Luxembourg.

The ideological hegemony of neoliberalism has long sought to counter the critical currents of thought spawned in the 1960s with its vacuous, "market utopia" imagery. It hoped to convince entire generations of scholars that an "end of history" was imminent and the reign of intellectual giants like Frank was coming to an end. But our commonsensical way of thinking about dependency and underdevelopment is far too permeated with the influence of his work. The explosion of new scholarship in historical and global studies will continue to come up against his immense theoretical legacy. As the battle cry "another world is possible" sounds ever louder throughout Latin America, the enemy will long be haunted by the accusing voice of André Gunder Frank.

José Bell Lara and Richard A. Dello Buono

About the Contributors

José Bell Lara is a Cuban sociologist and Professor at the University of Havana. As a senior researcher in the FLACSO-Cuba Program, he has conducted various studies concerning development, social change and social policies in Cuba and Latin America. He has lectured extensively in Latin America, Europe and North America over a period of decades and has been a visiting professor at universities in Chile, Canada, Panama, and Mexico. Among his numerous published articles and books are *Globalisation and the Cuban Revolution* and the anthology *Cuba in the 1990s*. He is co-editor of *Cuba in the 21st Century: Realities and Perspectives* (with Richard Dello Buono).

James D. Cockcroft is an award-winning author and a life-long human rights activist. Presently a SUNY Internet professor, he served as Vicepresident of the Benito Juárez Tribunal that heard charges of U.S. state terrorism against Cuba in April 2005 in Mexico City. Author of 35 books on Latin America, Mexico, human rights, development and technology, labour migration, multiculturalism, the Middle East, and public policy, he is also a poet, a three-time Fulbright Scholar, and an honorary editor of *Latin American Perspectives*. His recent books include: *Latin America: History, Politics, and U.S. Policy; Mexico's Hope: An Encounter with Politics and History; Salvador Allende: Chile's Voice of Democracy;* and *Latino Visions: Contemporary Chicano, Puerto Rican, and Cuban American Artists*. A Canadian immigrant, he is a member of the Coalition *Venezuela Nous Sommes Avec Toi* and of the International Coordinating Committee in Defence of Humanity. His bilingual blog is <www.jamescockcroft.com>.

Hugo Cores is an Uruguayan political leader and professor of 20th Century Latin American History. He is a former deputy and vice-president of the *Convención Nacional de Trabajadores*, virtually the only trade union organisation that existed in Uruguay during the repressive era of the 1960s–70s. He has authored various books concerning the history of the workers and revolutionary movement in Uruguay during the 1950s through the mid-1970s. Imprisoned for a time in Uruguay and later in Argentina, he was forced into temporary exile to France and later Brazil. Cores is presently the Secretary General of the *Partido por la Victoria del Pueblo* that forms part of the ruling Uruguayan *Frente Amplio*.

Ximena de la Barra is a Spanish social scientist who was born in Chile and professionally trained as an architect. She was part of the Chilean socialist experiment of the early 1970s and was appointed delegate to UNCTAD III on behalf of the Salvador Allende government. After the 1973 military coup, she actively opposed the military dictatorship until forced into exile to Spain where she acquired dual citizenship. For a time, she lived in New York and was visiting professor at Columbia University in the fields of urban and social policy planning. For the last 15 years, de la Barra has worked in the United Nations, first at UN Habitat and most recently at UNICEF, serving in high-level positions including Country Representative, Regional Advisor for Public Policy for Latin America, and Senior Global Advisor. She has written on a wide range of urban and development issues.

RICHARD A. DELLO BUONO is a U.S. sociologist born in Philadelphia, PA. He taught sociology and international studies for 18 years at Dominican University before resigning his tenure in 2005 to take up residence abroad. His research areas include comparative social problems and Latin American/Caribbean Studies. He has been a visiting professor at the University of Havana, National University of Colombia, Autonomous University of Zacatecas and a Fulbright Professor at the University of Panama. He is a recent Vice-president and current Global Division Chair of the Society for the Study of Social Problems (SSSP). He also collaborates with Project Counselling Service and AUNA-Cuba, two non-governmental organisations working for genuine regional integration in Latin America. He is author and co-editor of *Social Problems, Law and Society* (with A. Kathryn Stout and William J. Chambliss) and *Cuba in the 21st Century: Realities and Perspectives* (with Jose Bell Lara).

WIM DIERCKXSENS is a Dutch economist and researcher who has been working in Latin America since 1971. He is currently based at the Ecumenical Department of Research (DEI) in San José, Costa Rica where he coordinates the research of the World Alternatives Forum (FMA). Dierckxsens is author of numerous books and articles including *From Neoliberalism to Post-Capitalism* (2000) and *El ocaso del capitalismo y la utopía reencontrada* (2002).

VICTOR M. FIGUEROA is a Chilean sociologist dedicated to studying the political and economic problems of Latin America. He was trained at the Institute of Sociology at the Universidad de Concepción in Chile where he also developed his leftist militancy in that country. At the moment of the Coup that overthrew the popular government of Salvador Allende, he was Regional Secretary of the MAPU in Concepción as well as member of the Central Committee of that party. After a year of working in the resistance against the Pinochet Dictatorship, he was forced into exile to England where he became active in Chilean solidarity work while also completing his graduate studies. Since 1982, he has been on the graduate teaching and research faculty at the Autonomous University of Zacatecas in Mexico where he is Director of the Doctoral Program in Political Science. He is author of numerous publications including the book *Reinterpretando el subdesarrollo*.

ANDRÉ GUNDER FRANK was born in Berlin and is one of the founders of the "Dependency perspective" that rose to prominence in the 1960s within the sociology of development. Trained as an economist at the University of Chicago, he completed his dissertation on Soviet Agriculture in 1957. Over his long career, Frank published over a thousand scholarly works on diverse topics concerning the economic, social and political history and contemporary development of the world system, the industrially developed countries, and the Third World including Latin America. In his more recent work, he focused his attention on the analysis of crisis in the world economy and global world history. [Frank died in April, 2005.]

MARCO A. GANDÁSEGUI, JR. is a Panamanian sociologist trained in Chile and the US. He presently teaches at the University of Panama and is a research associate at the Centro de Estudios Latinoamericanos "Justo Arosemena" (CELA) in Panama City. In addition, he is editor of the Panamanian journal *Tareas* and regularly publishes work concerning political and social issues. Gandásegui is author of several books including *El Canal de Panamá en el Siglo XXI* and *Las clases sociales en Panamá*. He currently chairs a regional working group dedicated to the study of the "Crisis of US Hegemony," sponsored by the Latin American Council of Social Sciences (CLACSO).

DELIA LUISA LÓPEZ is a Cuban economist, senior researcher in the FLACSO-Cuba programme, and professor at the University of Havana where she has served as President of the Cátedra Ernesto Che Guevara since 1995. She has lectured widely about the social and political problems of Latin America, including at various universities in Mexico, Spain and Venezuela. She was also a recent visiting professor at the Dalhousie University Institute of Development Studies in Nova Scotia, Canada. Her publications include "Crisis económica, ajuste y democracia en Cuba," "Guía para el estudio del sistema político cubano," "Cuba: Underdevelopment, Socialism and Strategies of Development", "Che Guevara: una economía para la transición socialista," and "Apuntes sobre el concepto hombre nuevo."

JAMES PETRAS is Professor Emeritus in Sociology at Binghamton University, New York. He is widely regarded as one of the left's most astute and critical observers of current global and Latin American affairs. A prolific author of numerous works on global development, imperialism, and Latin American revolutionary movements, Petras is one of the most cited scholar-activists ever. His essays and articles have appeared in *Monthly Review, New Left Review, Le Monde Diplomatique* and on various progressive websites. His books include *The Left Strikes Back: Class Conflict in Latin America in the Age of Neoliberalism* and *Globaloney*. He is also co-author, with Henry Veltmeyer, of *The Dynamics of Social Change in Latin America; Unmasking Globalisation;* and *System in Crisis*.

EMIR SADER is a Brazilian political scientist and a former President of the Latin American Sociological Association (ALAS). In 1968, he went to Paris where he collaborated with Nicos Poulantzas. Upon his return to Brazil, he was forced underground by the military dictatorship and later into exile for 13 years where he lived in Chile, Argentina, Italy and Cuba. He has taught in various universities, including the University of Sao Paulo, University of Chile, University of Paris VIII – Vincennes and the University of Oxford. Presently he directs the Public Policy Laboratory at the State University of Rio de Janeiro (UERJ) and is a member of the Executive Committee of CLACSO. He has authored more than forty books in the field of social sciences, including *A vingança da história* (2004) and *Cuba: um socialismo em construção* (2002).

DARÍO SALINAS FIGUEREDO is Professor and researcher in the Graduate Program in Social Sciences at the Ibero-American University of México. He also serves as member of the CONACYT National System of Researchers as a specialist in Latin American Studies.

HENRY VELTMEYER is Professor of Development Studies/Sociology at the Universidad Autónoma de Zacatecas (Mexico) and Saint Mary's University in Halifax, NS (Canada). He currently serves as Editor-in-Chief of the prestigious *Canadian Journal of International Development* and is a researcher for the United Nations Research Institute for Social Development (UNRISD). An internationally recognised expert on political and social processes in Latin America, he has published numerous scholarly articles and award winning books in these areas, including *Globalization and Antiglobalization: Dynamics of Change in the New World Order* and *The Labyrinth of Latin American Development*. He is also co-author of *Transcending Neoliberalism: Community-Based Development in Latin America* with Anthony O'Malley; and *Empire with Imperialism: The Globalizing Dynamics of Neoliberal Capitalism* with James Petras and Luciano Vasapollo.

CARLOS M. VILAS, an Argentine political scientist, is Graduate Studies Professor at the Universidad Nacional de Lanús, Argentina. His book on the Sandinista Revolution in Nicaragua won the "Casa de las Americas Award" in 1984 and is widely cited as a seminal resource on the subject. An expert on processes of social and political change, his academic research covers a broad range of related issues such as public policies, everyday forms of social violence, and the impact of transnational actors and organisations upon political institutions and processes. He has published extensively in scholarly journals in Latin America and the Caribbean, United States, Europe and the

Pacific. During the 1980s and 1990s, he was a frequent visiting scholar at prestigious U.S. academic institutions such as Columbia University, Duke University and the University of Florida, Gainesville. At year's end in 2004, the political magazine *Le Nouvelle Observateur* in Paris recognised Dr. Vilas as one of the world's "most distinguished international contemporary thinkers."

References

Aguilar Carmín, Héctor. 1998. "La transición mexicana." In *Síntesis*, N° 6, Madrid, Sep-Dec.

Ahumada Beltrán, Consuelo. 1996. "La encrucijada latinoamericana y el modelo neo-liberal". Ponencia presentada al IV Taller Internacional Agenda Latinoamericana del siglo XXI, FLACSO-Cuba, La Habana.

Alegría, Rafael. 2003. "El ALCA y los campesinos", in CLACSO, *Observatorio Social de América Latina*, January. Buenos Aires, Argentina.

Alí, Tariq. 2004. "Por qué ganó Chávez?" [Why did Chávez win?], *La Jornada*, Mexico, August 17, 2004.

Altimir, Oscar and Luis Beccaria. 1998. "Efectos de los cambios macroeconómicos y de las reformas sobre la pobreza urbana en Argentina." Pp. 115–172 in E. Ganuza, L. Taylor and S. Morley (eds.), *Política macroeconómica y pobreza en América Latina y el Caribe*. Madrid: PNUD/Mundi-Prensa.

Altimir, Oscar, Luis Beccaria Martín Gonzalez Rozada. 2002. "La distribución del ingreso en Argentina, 1974–2000." *Revista de la CEPAL* 78 (Dec.): 55–85.

Amin, S. 1989. "Apuntes sobre el concepto de desconexión". *Revista Homines*, vol. 13, no. 2; and vol. 14, no. 1, 1990, San Juan, Puerto Rico.

Amin, Samir and Houtart, François. 2003. *Mundialización de las resistencias Estado de las luchas 2002*. Editorial Desde Abajo, Bogotá, Colombia.

Amin, Samir and Houtart, François. 2004. "Mundialización de las resistencias Estado de las luchas 2004", Editorial Ruth Casa Editorial, Panamá.

Anderson, Perry. 1996. "Balance del neoliberalismo. Lecciones para la izquierda", en: Viento del Sur, N° 6, México.

Anderson, Perry. 2002. "Antinomies of Gramsci", in "Electives Affinities" Boitempo, São Paulo.

Andreas, Petre. 1995. "Free Market Reform and Drug Market Prohibition: U.S. Policies at Cross-purposes in Latin America", *Third World Quarterly*, Vol. 16, Núm. 1, 1995, pp. 75–87.

Ardaya, R. 1996. *La construcción municipal de Bolivia*. La Paz: Strategies for International Development.

Arocena, R. 1994. *Ciencia, tecnología y sociedad*. Centro Editor de América Latina, Buenos Aires.

Bambirra, V. 1973. *Capitalismo dependiente latinoamericano*. Editorial Prensa Latino-americana, Santiago de Chile.

Banco Interamericano de Desarrollo (BID). 2000. *Informe 2000. Progreso económico y social en América Latina*, Washington.

Banco Mundial. 2003. *Desigualdad en América Latina y el Caribe: ¿ruptura con la histo-ria?* Estudios del Banco Mundial sobre América Latina y el Caribe.

Basualdo, Eduardo and Matías Sulfas. 2000. "Fuga de capitales y endeudamiento externo en la Argentina." *Realidad Económica* 173:76–103.

Beinstein, Jorge. 1999. *La crisis de la economía global*. Editorial Corregidor, Buenos Aires, Argentina.

Bell Lara, José. 1968. "Tres notas sobre el subdesarrollo". *El Mundo del Domingo*, Havana, June 30.

Bell Lara, José. 1995. "Los cambios mundiales y las perspectivas de Cuba", ponencia presentada en Washington, DC, en la reunión anual de la Asociación de Sociólogos Americanos, 18 de agosto.

Bell Lara, José. 1999. *Cambios mundiales y perspectivas de la Revolución Cubana*, La Habana: Editorial de Ciencias Sociales.

Bell Lara, José, López, Delia Luisa and Espinosa, Eugenio. 1993. *La Nueva América Latina*. Ediciones FLACSO-SODEPAZ, Madrid.

BID – Banco Interamericano de Desarrollo. 1996. *Modernización del estado y fortalecimiento de la sociedad civil*. Washington DC: Banco Interamericano de Desarrollo.

Bilbao, Luis. 2005. "Alianza estratégica Brasil-Venezuela", in *Le Monde Diplomatique*, March.

Blair, H. 1997. *Democratic Local Governance in Bolivia*. CDIE Impact Evaluation, No. 3. Washington DC: USAID.

Boaventura de Souza Santos. 2004. "El Forum Global Social: hacia una anti-globalización hegemónica", in Amin, Samir and Houtart, François, 2004, *Mundialización de las resistencias Estado de las luchas 2004*, Editorial Ruth Casa Editorial, Panamá.

Bonasso, Miguel. 2002. *El palacio y la calle. Crónicas de insurgentes y conspiradores*. Buenos Aires: Planeta.

Booth, David. 1996. *Popular Participation, Democracy, the State in Rural Bolivia*. Department of Anthropology, Stockholm University. La Paz.

Borón, Atilio. 1999. "América Latina: crisis sin fin o el fin de la crisis", en Francisco López Segrera y Daniel Filmus (coord.), *América Latina 2020: Escenarios, alternativas, estrategias*. Buenos Aires: FLACSO-Argentina and Temas Grupo Editorial SRL, 2000 (May), págs. 381–397.

Bossio, Juan Carlos. 2002. "Normas del Trabajo y Comercio Internacional, una Discusión Recurrente" [A Recurring Discussion on the Norms of Work and International Trade]. *Capítulos, Comercio y Desarrollo* (66), SELA, Carácas, Venezuela.

Bowles, Samuel, and Herbert Gintis. 1999. "'Social Capital' and Community Governance." University of Massachusetts, Amherst. <www-unix.oit.umass.edu/~bowles/papers/Socap>.

Bulmer-Thomas, Victor. 1986. *The New Economic Model in Latin America and its Impact on Income Distribution and Power*. New York: St. Martin's Press.

Burki, S. and G. Perry. 1998. *Más allá del consenso de Washington: la hora de la reforma institucional*. Washington DC: World Bank.

Cadermartori, José. 2004. *La globalización cuestionada*. Santiago, Chile: Editorial Universidad de Santiago, Chile.

Cafiero, Mario and Javier Llorens. 2002. *La Argentina robada. El corralito, los bancos y el vaciamiento del sistema financiero argentino*. Buenos Aires: Ediciones Macchi.

Camarasa, Jorge. 2002. *Días de furia. Historia oculta de la Argentina desde la caída de De la Rúa hasta la asunción de Duhalde*. Buenos Aires: Sudamericana.

Camejo, Yrayma. 2002. "Estado y mercado en el Proyecto Nacional-popular Bolivariano." *Revista Venezolana de Economía y Ciencias Sociales*, 8(3), Sept.–Dec.

Castells, Manuel. 1997. *La era de la información*. vol. 1. Alianza Editorial, Madrid.

Cavarozzi, Marcelo and Esperanza Casullo. 2003. "Los partidos políticos en América Latina hoy: ¿consolidación o crisis?" In Cavarozzi, Marcelo y Juan Abal Medina (h), compiladores, *El asedio a la política*, Konrad Adenauer Stiffung/HomoSapiens Ediciones, Buenos Aires, Argentina.

Centre for Global Development and Foreign Policy. 2003. *Ranking the Rich*. Centre for Global Development and Foreign Policy, Washington D.C.

CEPAL. 2002a. *Anuario Estadísticos de América Latina*, Naciones Unidas, Santiago de Chile.

CEPAL. 2002b. *Balance Preliminar de las Economías de América Latina y El Caribe*, Naciones Unidas, Santiago de Chile.

CEPAL. 2004. *Desarrollo productivo en economías abiertas*, Naciones Unidas, LC/G-2234–ses.30/3 www.cepal.cl

Chao, M. L. 1998. "Los servicios informáticos en Cuba". *Análisis de Coyuntura*, Year 2, no. 6, Havana, June.

Chossudovsky, Michel. 2004. "La desestabilización de Haití." In *Perfil La Jornada*, March 6, Mexico.

CIDOB Foundation. 2002. "Sucesión de contestaciones y auge de la oposición." *Biografia de Hugo Rafael Chávez Frías*. Barcelona, Spain. http://www.cidob.org/bios/castel lano/lideres/c-063.htm.

CITMA. 1998. *Balance de trabajo*. Havana, Cuba.

Cockcroft, James D. 1998. "Gendered Class Analysis: Internationalizing, Feminizing, and Latinizing Labour's Struggle in the Americas." *Latin American Perspectives* 26(6): 42–46.

Cockcroft, James D. 2001. *La Esperanza de México*. Mexico: Siglo Veintiuno Editores.

Cockcroft, James D. 2004. "El Foro Social Mundial 2004: nuevos avances, viejos problemas." *Rebelión*, February [www.rebelión.org].

Dabat, A. 1994. "Globalización mundial y alternativa de desarrollo". *Nueva Sociedad*, no. 130, Caracas.

Dasgupta, Partha and Ismail Serageldin, eds. 2000. *Social Capital: A Multifaceted Perspective*. Washington DC: World Bank.

De la Barra, Ximena. 1997. "Do Poor Urban Children Matter?" *The Urban Age* 5(1). World Bank, Washington D.C., 1997.

De la Barra, Ximena. 2002. "Metas Internacionales de Desarrollo Social y la Cooperación al Desarrollo." *Comercio y desarrollo* 66 (Sept.-Dec), SELA.

De la Garza T., Enrique. 2005. "Del concepto ampliado de trabajo al sujeto laboral ampliado," in *Sindicatos y Nuevos Movimientos Sociales en América Latina*, Buenos Aires: CLACSO, p. 9.

Dello Buono, Richard. 2001. "Uncivil Movements: The Armed Right Wing and Democracy in Latin America" (Leigh A. Payne), review in *Contemporary Sociology*, Vol. 30, No. 3 (May), pp. 278–279.

Dello Buono, Richard. 2002a. "Las crisis sociales y el cambiante panorama de los partidos políticos," *Tareas* # 111, Ciudad de Panamá, República de Panamá.

Dello Buono, Richard. 2002b. "Por qué la crisis de los partidos políticos latinoamericanos?, *Cuadernos de Nuestra América*, Vol. 15, Núm. 30, págs. 31–54.

Dierckxsens, Wim. 1994. "Globalización: límites de crecimiento e historicidad de las transnacionales" *Pasos*, no. 4, San José.

Dierckxsens, Wim. 2003. *El ocaso del capitalismo y la utopía reencontrada*, Ed. Desde Abajo, Bogotá)

Dierckxsens, Wim. 2004. *Fin de la era del dólar, fin de la hegemonía de EEUU: necesidad de otro orden económico*, PASOS, November–December, DEI.

Dominguez, J. and A. Lowenthal, eds. 1996. *Constructing Democratic Governance.* Baltimore: John Hopkins University Press.

Dos Santos, Theotonio. 1980. *Imperialismo y dependencia.* Ediciones ERA, México.

Dowbor, Ladislau. 1998. *A Reproducao Social*, Editora Vozes, Petrópolis, Brazil.

ECLAC (CEPAL). 2001a. *Notas de la CEPAL*, Santiago de Chile, March.

ECLAC (CEPAL). 2001b. *Notas de la CEPAL*, Santiago de Chile, September.

ECLAC (CEPAL). 2004a. *Panorama Social de América Latina 2004*, Santiago de Chile, November.

ECLAC (CEPAL). 2004b. *Una década de desarrollo social en América Latina. 1990–1999*, Santiago de Chile, August.

ECLAC. 2002. *Anuario estadístico de América Latina y el Caribe 2002.* http://www.eclac.org.

ECLAC. 2003. *Panorama Social de América Latina y el Caribe 2002–2003*, Santiago, Chile, August 2003.

ECLAC. 2005. *The Millennium Development Goals: A Latin American Perspective.*

ECLAC, IPEA, and UNDP. *2002 Meeting the Millennium Poverty Reduction Targets in Latin America and the Caribbean.* United Nations, Santiago de Chile.

ECLAC/OIJ. 2004. *La Juventud Iberoamericana: Tendencias y Urgencias*, United Nations, Santiago de Chile, October.

ECLAC/UNICEF. 2002. *La Pobreza en América Latina y el Caribe aun tiene Nombre de Infancia.* Mexico: UNICEF.

ECLAC/UNICEF/SECIB. 2001. *Construyendo Equidad desde la Infancia y la Adolescencia en Ibero América*, Santiago de Chile, September.

ECLAC/UNICEF/SECIB. 2003. *Las Necesidades de Inversión en la Infancia para Alcanzar las Metas de la Agenda del Plan de Acción Iberoamericano.* Panama: Sept.

Escolar, Marcelo, et al. 2002. "Últimas imágenes antes del naufragio: las elecciones del 2001 en la Argentina." *Desarrollo Económico* 165:25–44.

Everlenin Pérez, O. 1999. *La inversión extranjera en Cuba.* Havana.

Ferrer, Aldo. 1993. "Nuevos paradigmas tecnológicos y desarrollo sostenible: perspectiva latinoamericana". *Comercio Exterior*, vol. 43, no. 9, September, México.

Ferrer, Aldo. 2000. "La globalización y el futuro de América Latina: ¿qué nos enseña la historia?", in Francisco López Segrera and Daniel Filmus (coord.), *América Latina 2020: Escenarios, alternativas, estrategias.* Buenos Aires: FLACSO-Argentina y Temas Grupo Editorial SRL, 2000, págs. 351–364.

FIDE (Fundación de Investigaciones Para El Desarrollo). 2000. "Los roles de la deuda externa en la Convertibilidad." *Coyuntura y Desarrollo* 258:11–15.

Figueras, M. A. 1992. "La producción de bienes de capital en Cuba: retos y opciones". *Comercio Exterior*, vol. 42, no. 12, December.

Figueras, M. A. 1994. *La estructura económica de Cuba*. Editorial de Ciencias Sociales, Havana, Cuba.

Figueroa S., Victor M. 2002. *América Latina: El nuevo patrón de colonialismo industrial*, Unidad de Postgrado en Ciencia Política. Universidad Autónoma de Zacatecas.

Fine, Gary. 2006. "The Chaining of Social Problems: Solutions and Unintended Consequences in the Age of Betrayal," *Social Problems*, Vol. 53, No. 1, Pages 3–17.

Finkel, L. 1995. *La organización social del trabajo*. Madrid: Pirámides.

Flickling, David. 2004. "World Bank Condemns Defence Spending" *The Guardian, February 14*, United Kingdom.

Fradkin, Raúl O. 2002. *Cosecharás tu siembra. Notas sobre la rebelión popular argentina de diciembre de 2001*. Buenos Aires: Prometeo libros.

Frank, Andre Gunder. 1970. "Lumpemburguesía: lumpemdesarrollo". *Referencias*, vol. 2, no. 2, Havana, Cuba.

Frank, Andre Gunder. 2006. "Meet Uncle Sam – Without Clothes – Parading Around China and the World," Critical Sociology 32(1):17–44.

Friedman, Thomas. 2000. *The Lexus and the Olive Tree: Understanding Globalization*. New York: Anchor Books.

Gallo, Daniel. 2002. "Se mantiene alto el piso de las protestas." *La Nación*, October 15.

Gamarra, Eduardo A. 1998. "Transiciones perversas y patrones del narcotráfico en Cuba, República Dominicana y Haití", en Wilfredo Lozano (ed), *Cambio político en el Caribe: Escenarios de la posguerra fría – Cuba, Haití y República Dominicana*, Caracas: Nueva Sociedad y FLACSO-Programa República Dominicana, págs. 183–207.

Ganuza, Enrique, Ricardo Paes de Barros, Lance Taylor and Rob Vos (eds.). 2001. *Liberalización, desigualdad y pobreza: América Latina y el Caribe en los 90*. Buenos Aires: EUDEBA/PNUD/CEPAL.

García Canclini, Néstor. 1999. *La globalización imaginada*. Editorial Piados, Buenos Aires.

García, Carmen. 1993. "Integración académica y nuevo valor del conocimiento". *Nueva Sociedad*, No. 126, July–August.

García, E. 1998. "El sistema de ciencia e innovación tecnológica en Cuba: conceptos, antecedentes y perspectivas". *Análisis de Coyuntura*, Year 2, no. 7, July.

Gil, Melchor and J. Fernández. 1998. "Evolución internacional del comercio electrónico y la situación actual de Cuba". *Análisis de Coyuntura*, Year 2, No. 6, June.

Gilly, Adolfo. 2004. "Un sujeto político no identificado." In *Le Monde Diplomatique*, Edición chilena, 42 (June).

González Casanova, Pablo. 2001. *Sobre la explotación*. In *Tareas* No. 8, Panama.

Gorostiaga, Xabier. 1991. "América Latina frente a los desafíos globales". *Cuadernos de Nuestra América*, Vol. VIII, No. 17.

Goss, Sue. 2001. *Making Local Governance Work: Networks, Relationships and the Management of Change*. New York: Palgrave.

Grant, James. 1999. *Children in Jeopardy*, UNICEF, New York.

Grupo Académico Binacional. 1999. "Venezuela a finales del siglo XX", *Análisis Político*, Bogotá.

Hardy, Clarisa. 2004. *Equidad y protección social. Desafíos de políticas sociales en América Latina*. Ediciones LOM, Santiago de Chile.

Harnecker, Marta. 2000. *The Left at the Threshold of the XXI Century: Making the Impossible Possible*, LINKS no. 16: September to December, 2000, also published in Spanish by Editorial de Ciencias Sociales (1999), Havana, Cuba.

Harris, John. 2001. *Depoliticising Development: The World Bank and Social Capital*. New Delhi: Left Word Books.

Harvey, David. 2003. "El *'nuevo imperialismo': sobre reajustes espacios-temporales y acumulación mediante desposesión."* *Revista Viento Sur*, December 13. [http://www.vientosur.info/articulosweb/textos/index.php?x=196].

Hintze, Jorge. 2003. *América Latina la Región del Mundo con Peor Relación Pobreza – Desigualdad*, Group of Analysis for Development, July.

Holloway, John. 2002. *Cambiar el mundo sin tomar el poder*. Buenos Aires: Editor Andrés Alfredo Méndez.

Hooghe, Marc and Ditelin Stolle, eds. 2003. *Generating Social Capital: Civil Society and Institutions in Comparative Perspective*. NY: Palgrave.

Howard, Leslie. 1997. "Thinking Globally, Acting Locally: The Strategies of Subnational and Transnational Actors in Mexico and Canada", paper presented at the LASA Meetings in Guadalajara, México, April 17, 1997.

Huntington, Samuel. 1996. *The Clash of Civilization and the Remaking of the World Order*, Simon and Schuster, New York, USA.

IATP. 2005. *WTO Agreement on Agriculture: A Decade of Dumping*. Institute for Agriculture and Trade Policy, February.

IDB. 2000. "Inequality, Exclusion and Poverty in Latin America and the Caribbean," IDB document presented at the Guadalajara EUROLAC Conference.

Iglesias, E. 1997. "El desafío de la criminalidad urbana en El Salvador," *Proceso*, 17(753), April 16, San Salvador.

ILO. 2003. *Invertir en Todos los Niños, Estudio Económico de los Costos y Beneficios de Erradicar el Trabajo Infantil [Investing in All Children: An Economic Study of the Costs and Benefits of Eradicating Child Labour]*. Geneva: International Labour Organisation.

ILO. 2005. *Facts on Child Labour*. www.ilo.org.communication.

ILO. 2006. *Trabajo Decente en las Américas: una Agenda Hemisférica. 2006–2015*.

Imparato, Ivo. 2003. *Slum Upgrading and Participation: Lessons from Latin America*. Washington DC: World Bank.

INDEC (Instituto de Estadísticas y Censos). 2001. *Encuesta permanente de Hogares*, Oct.

Izumi, Julia. 2002. "Mendoza, entre las provincias con menos protestas." *Los Andes*, Sept. 18.

Johnson, Chalmers and Dispatch, Tom. 2005. "La realidad china", in www.zmag.org.

Karoly, Lynn A. et al. 1998. *Investing in our Children*. Santa Monica, CA: The Rand Corporation.

Katz, Claudio. 2004. "Burguesías imaginarias y existentes" *Enfoques Alternativos* 21 (February). Buenos Aires, published in *Correspondencia de Prensa* 242, February 8, 2004. [germain@chasque.net].

Kay, C. 2001. "Estructuralismo y teoría de la dependencia en el periodo neoliberal: una perspectiva latinoamericana." In *Tareas* No. 8 Panama.

Lage, C. 1999. "Intervención en el balance anual del Ministerio de Inversiones Extranjeras de Cuba (MINVEV)". *Granma*, 16 de marzo.

Latinobarómetro. 2003. *Informe-Resumen. La democracia y la economía.* Santiago de Chile.

Latinobarómetro. 2004. *Informe-Resumen. Una década de mediciones.* Corporación Latino-barómetro, Santiago de Chile.

Lechner, Norbert. 1992. "El debate sobre Estado y mercado." In *Revista Nueva Sociedad,* 121, Caracas, Venezuela.

Lechner, Norbert. 1995. *Cultura política y gobernabilidad democrática.* Instituto Federal Electoral, México.

Lechner, Norbert. 2002. *Las sombras del mañana. La dimensión subjetiva de la política.* Colección Escafandra, LOM Ediciones, Santiago de Chile.

Lerda, Juan Carlos. 1996. "Globalización y pérdida de autonomía de las autoridades fiscales, bancarias y monetarias", in *Revista de la CEPAL,* Abril, pp. 63–75.

Lewis, Stephen. 1997. "Forward." in Santosh Mehrotra and Richard Jolly, *Development with a Human Face: Experiences in Social Achievement and Economic Growth.* Oxford: Clarenden Press and New York: University Press.

Mcpherson, C. B. 1982. *La democracia liberal y su época.* Madrid: Alianza Editorial.

Majoli, Marina. 1999. *Ciencia, tecnología y desarrollo social,* Programa FLACSO-Cuba, La Habana.

Marini, R. M. 1996. "La integración, un proyecto supranacional solidario". *Política y Cultura,* año 1, no. 2, México.

Marquez, María Victoria. 2002. "Marcada tendencia hacia la baja en la protesta social." *Infobae,* Sept. 23.

Marx, Carlos. 1959. *El capital.* 3 Vol. Fondo de Cultura Económica, México.

McLean, Scott et al., eds. 2002. *Social Capital: Critical Perspectives on Community and "Bowling Alone."* New York University Press.

Medina, F. 2001. La pobreza en América Latina: desafío para el siglo XXI. In *Comercio Exterior,* 51(10), October.

Mehrotra, Santosh and Richard Jolly, (eds.). 1997. *Development with a Human Face: Experiences in Social Achievement and Economic Growth.* Oxford: Clarenden Press and New York: Oxford University Press.

Minujín, Alberto and Delamonica, Enrique. 2001. *Mind the Gap!* Chap. 3, in Harnessing Globalization for Children, ed. Andrea Cornia, Working Document, UNICEF, Innocenti Centre, Florence, Italy.

Molina, Emiro. 2004. UNICEF Working Paper, Simon Bolivar University.

Moulian, Tomás. 1999. *El consume me consume.* Libros del ciudadano, LOM Ediciones, Santiago de Chile.

Nararro, Ernesto. 2005. "Ley de Tierras vs oligarquía del campo." Rebelion, January 15 (www.rebelion.org) (http://www.rebelion.org/noticia.php?id=100055).

Noriega, Roger. 2004. Report of the U.S. Under-secretary of State for Latin America. Washington D.C., June 6.

O'Donnell, Guillermo. 2004. "Notas sobre el estado de la democracia en América Latina." *Informe sobre la democracia en América Latina,* New York: United Nations Development Programme, pp. 11–82. (http://www.democracia.undp.org).

OECD. 2004. "OECD Conference of April 2004." *IPS*, May 4.

Olivé, A. 1998. "La información en el desarrollo nacional: desafios y alternativas para las economías emergentes". *Análisis de Coyuntura*, año 2, no. 3.

Oman, C. H. 1994. "Globalización, la nueva competencia", in Moneta y Quenan (comp.): *América Latina: Globalización y regionalismo*. Ed. Corregidor, Buenos Aires.

Osorio, Jaime. 1997. *Despolitización de la ciudadanía y gobernabilidad*, División de Ciencias Sociales y Humanidades, UAM-X, México.

Osorio, Jaime. 2004. *Crítica de la economía vulgar. Reproducción del capital dependencia*. Universidad Autónoma de Zacatecas/Miguel Ángel Porrúa, México.

Oxfam International. 2002. *Cambiar Las Reglas [Changing the Rules]*. Barcelona: Intermón Oxfam.

Palma Carbajal, Eduardo. 1995. "Decentralisation and Democracy: The New Latin American Municipality," *CEPAL Review* 55, April.

Panebianco, Angelo. 1990. *Modelos de partido*. Madrid: Alianza Editorial.

Pardo R., Rafael. 1999. Nueva seguridad para América Latina, Bogotá: FESCOL y CEREC.

Partido de los Trabajadores de Brazil (PT). 1979. "Carta de Principios". In *Resoluciones de Encuentros y Congresos. 1979–1998*. Brazil.

Partido de los Trabajadores de Brazil (PT). 1980. "Programa. Reunión Nacional de Fundación del Partido de los Trabajadores". In *Resoluciones de Encuentros y Congresos. 1979–1998*. Brazil.

Paulani, Leda. 2003. "Brazil delivery: razões, contradições e limites da politica econômica nos primeiros seis meses do governo Lula ", in *A economia politica da mudança – Os desafios e os equivocos dos inicios do governo Lula*- João Antonio de Paula (editor) – Autêntica Publisher – Belo Horizon, Brazil.

Pelicani, L. 1992. "La guerra cultural entre Oriente y Occidente". In *Nueva Sociedad* No. 119, Caracas, May-June.

Petras, James. 1997. "Latin America: The Resurgence of the Left", *New Left Review*, London.

Petras, James and Henry Veltmeyer. 2005. *Social Movements and the State*. London: Pluto Press.

Petras, James and Henry Veltmeyer. 2006. "Social Movements and the State: Political Power Dynamics in Latin America", *Critical Sociology*, Vól. 32 (1): 82–104.

PNUD. 1992. Proyecto Regional para la superación de la pobreza. Magnitud y evolución de la pobreza en América Latina. *Comercio Exterior*, 42(4), Mexico, April.

Prensa Latina. 2005. "Condoleeza Rice amenaza a Venezuela con posibles sanciones." *Prensa Latina*, January 21. http://www.rebelion.org/noticia.php?id=10281.

Quijano, Aníbal. 2004. "El laberinto de América Latina: ¿hay otras salidas?" In *Revista Venezolana de Economía y Ciencias Sociales*, 10(1), Caracas, Venezuela.

Ramírez, M. A. 1999. "El comercio electrónico ¿una revolución en marcha?" *Comercio Exterior*, vol. 49, no. 10, México.

Reilly, Charles. 1989. *The Democratisation of Development: Partnership at the Grassroots*. Arlington: Inter-American Foundation Annual Report.

Reynolds, Clark W., Francisco E. Thoumi and Reinhart Wettmann. 1995. *Regionalismo abierto en los Andes: Implicaciones para la integración en un período de ajuste estructural en el hemisferio*, Bogotá, Colombia.

Rodríguez Beruff, Jorge. 1997. "De la 'narcodemocracia' y el Leviatán antidrogas: fuerzas de seguridad, Estado pospopulista y nuevas formas de autoritarismo en el Caribe", in Wilfredo Lozano (ed.), *Cambio Político en el Caribe: Escenarios de la Posguerra Fría – Cuba, Haití y República Dominicana*, Caracas; Nueva Sociedad y FLACSO-Programa República Dominicana, 1998, págs. 183–207.

Rojas Aravena, Francisco. 1993. "America Latina: El difícil camino de la concertación y la integración", *Nueva Sociedad* N° 125: 60–69.

Rostow, Walter. 1967. *La economía del despegue*. Alianza Editorial, Madrid, Spain.

Sachs, Jeffrey. 2005. *Millennium Project, Investing in Development: A Practical Plan for Reaching the Millennium Goals*. New York.

Salinas, Darío. 2002. "Gobernabilidad en la globalización. Concepciones y procesos políticos en América Latina." In *Revista Venezolana de Economía y Ciencias Sociales*, 8(3), Caracas, Venezuela.

Salinas, Darío and Tetelboin, Carolina. 2005. "Las condiciones de la política social en América Latina." In *Revista Papeles de Población* 44, Centro de Investigación y Estudios Avanzados de la Población de la Universidad del Estado de México, México.

SAPRIN. 2001. "Las políticas de ajuste estructural, En las raíces de La crisis económica y la pobreza" [Structural Adjustment Policies: At the Roots of Poverty and the Economic Crisis]. *Informe SAPRIN*. Washington, DC: SAPRIN Secretariat.

Saxe Fernández, John. 1994. "México ¿Globalización o inserción neocolonial?", en: Problemas del desarrollo, vol. XXV; N° 961, Jan.–Mar., pp. 27–35.

Saxe-Fernández, John. 2004. "Cuba y los Hoyos de Dona", *La Jornada*, April 1.

Schorr, Martín. 2000. "La industria manufacturera argentina en los noventa: crisis ocupacional, caída salarial e inequidad distributiva." *Realidad Económica* 175:48–52.

Schuller, Tom et al., eds. 2000. *Social Capital: Critical Perspectives*.Oxford University Press.

Schvarzer, Jorge. 1998. *Implantación de un modelo económico. La experiencia argentina entre 1975 y 2000*. Buenos Aires: A-Z Editora.

Seoane, José. 2003. *Movimientos sociales y conflicto en América Latina*. OSAL/CLACSO, Buenos Aires.

Seoane, José and Taddei, Emilio. 2005. "Movimientos sociales, democracia y gobernabilidad neoliberal en América Latina" in www.rebelion.org.

Sontag, H. 1994. "Las vicisitudes del desarrollo." In *Revista Internacional de Ciencias Sociales* No. 140, Paris, July.

Stallings, Barbara and Jürgen Seller. 2001. "El empleo en América Latina, base fundamental de la política social." *Revista de la CEPAL*, No. 75, Dec. United Nations, Santiago de Chile.

Stiglitz, J. 2002. *Globalisation and its Discontents*. New York: Norton Press.

Stocker, Karen, Howard Witzkin, and Cecilia Iriart. 1999. "The Exportation of Managed Care to Latin America." *New England Journal of Medicine* (340:14). Boston: Massachusetts Medical Society.

Svampa, Maristella and Sebastián Pereyra. 2003. *Entre la ruta y el barrio. La experiencia de las organizaciones piqueteras*. Buenos Aires: Editorial Biblos.

Tablada, Carlos and Dierckxsens, Wim. 2005. *Guerra global, resistencia mundial y alternativas*. Editorial Nuestra América, Buenos Aires, Argentina

Taccetti, Victorio. 1977. *Constelación Sur: América Latina frente a la globalización*, Buenos Aires: Fondo de Cultura Económica.

Toffler, Alvin. 1982. *La tercera ola*. Plaza & Janes Editores, Barcelona.

Torres Rivas, Edelberto. 1998. "La gobernabilidad democrática y los partidos políticos en América Latina", in Corina Perelli, Soma Picado and Daniel Zovalto (comps.) *Partidos y clase política en América Latina en los 90*, pp. 295–309.

Toussaint, Eric. 2004. "La bolsa o la vida", Editorial CLACSO, Buenos Aires, Argentina.

Trueba, G. 1993. *Cuba: una potencia caribeña en transición*. (Ponencia presentada en el seminario El socialismo cubano hoy). Programa FLACSO-Cuba, La Habana,

Tussie, Diana, ed. 2000. *Luces y sonmbras de una nueva relación: el Banco Interamericano de Desarrollo, el Banco Mundial y la sociedad civil*. Buenos Aires: Temas Grupo Editorial.

Ugarteche, Oscar. 1997. El falso dilema: América Latina en la economía global. Caracas: Editorial Nueva Sociedad, Fundación Friedrich Ebert en Lima, Perú.

UNDP. 1998. *Human Development Report 1998*. Madrid: Ediciones Mundi-Prensa.

UNDP. 2003. *Human Development Report 2003*. Madrid: Mundi-Prensa.

UNDP. 2004. *La democracia en América Latina: Hacia una democracia de ciudadanas y ciudadanos*. Buenos Aires, Argentina: Aguilar, Altea, Taurus, Alfaguara, S.A.

UNDP. 2005. *Human Development Report 2005*. Madrid: Mundi-Prensa.

UNICEF. 2000. *The Voice of Children and Adolescents in Latin America and the Caribbean*. Panama: UNICEF-TACRO.

UNICEF. 2001. "Harnessing Globalization for Children." *UNICEF Working Paper*. Florence, Italy: Innocenti Research Centre.

UNICEF. 2006. *The State of the World´s Children 2005*.

United Nations. 2000. *The Millennium Declaration*. New York: United Nations.

United Nations. 2000b. *United Nations, Implementation of the Copenhagen Action Programme*, Geneva.

United Nations. 2003. *Application of the Millennium Declaration of the United Nations, Secretary General's Report*, A/58/323, September.

United Nations. 2004. *Application of the Millennium Declaration, Secretary General's Report*, A/59/282, August.

United Nations. 2005. *Review of Advances on the 1995 Social Development Summit*, UN Social Development Commission, February.

United Nations. 2005b. *The Millennium Development Goals Report*, Wolfensohn, James.

United States Department of Energy. 2004. *Energy Information Administration/Petroleum Supply Monthly*, Washington, D.C., February.

Vaca, Ángel and Horacio Cao. 2001. "¿Es la solución un ajuste en la Administración Pública Nacional?" *Realidad Económica* 180:33–39.

Valenzuela, J. 1997. "Cinco dimensiones del modelo neoliberal." In *Política y Cultura* No. 8, Mexico (Spring).

Veltmeyer, Henry. 2002. "Social Exclusion and Rural Development in Latin America." *Canadian Journal of Latin American and Caribbean Studies*, Vol. 27, No. 54.

Veltmeyer, Henry. 2005. "Civil Society and Social Movements: The Dynamics of Inter-Sectoral Alliances and Urban-Rural Linkages in Latin America." *UNRISD Programme Paper* No. 10, October.

Vilas, Carlos M. (Coord.). 1995. *Estado y políticas sociales después del ajuste*. Universidad Nacional Autónoma de México- Nueva Sociedad. Caracas 1995.

Vilas, Carlos M. 1999. "El Estado en la Globalización." Unpublished Manuscript.

Vilas, Carlos M. 2001a. "Crisis y reforma de la política: ¿de qué política?." *Máscara/s* 2 (August): 37–49.

Vilas, Carlos M. 2001b *"Como con bronca y junando . . .* Las elecciones del 14 de octubre 2001." *Realidad Económica* 183:6–15.

Wallerstein, Immanuel. 2000. "Which Globalization", Paper presented at the American Sociological Association, August 11, 2000, Washington, D.C.

Watson, Hilbourne (ed.). 1994. *The Caribbean in the Global Political Economy*. Boulder y Londres: Lynne Rienner Publishers, Inc.

Weber, Heloise. 2002. "Global Governance and Poverty Reduction: the Case of Microcredit." In Rorden Wilkinson and Steve Hughes (eds.), *Global Governance: Critical Perspectives*. London and New York: Routledge, pp. 132–151.

Wilpert, Gregory. 2002. "¿Por qué la clase media venezolana (en su mayoría) se opone a Chávez?", *Rebelión*, October 30.

WOLA. 1993. *¿Peligro inminente? Las FF.AA. de Estados Unidos y la guerra contra las drogas*, Bogotá: Tercer Mundo Editores.

Wood, Ellen Meiksins. 2004. "El imperio capitalista y el Estado nación: ¿Un nuevo imperialismo norteamericano?" *Revista Viento Sur* (June).

Woolcock M. and D. Narayan. 2000. "Social Capital: Implications for Development Theory, Research and Policy." *The World Bank Research Observer* 15(2) August.

World Bank. 1990. *Informe sobre el desarrollo mundial*, Washington, D.C.

World Bank. 1991. *Informe sobre el desarrollo mundial*, Washington, D.C.

World Bank. 1994. *Governance. The World Bank Experience*. Washington D.C.: World Bank.

World Bank. 2000. *Report on Poverty*. International Reconstruction Bank, Washington D.C.

World Bank. 2004. *Implementation Completion Report [SCL-45360] to the Republic of Peru, Indigenous and Afro-Peruvian Peoples Development Project*. World Bank, Report 30700, Dec. 8.

World Bank. 2004b. Report to the World Bank Development Committee and the International Monetary Fund, April.

World Bank News Service. 2005. Interview with James Wolfensohn, World Bank President. *Berliner Zeitung*, February 10.

Xalma, Cristina. 2004. "Hugo Chávez y Venezuela: ¿Por qué tanta controversia?" Barcelona, Spain: Indymedia (www.indymedia.org). http://barcelona.indymedia. org/newswire/display/79351/index.php.

Yanes, Hernán. 1997. "Gobernabilidad y militares en América Latina". *Revista de Ciencias Sociales*, La Habana, Cuba.

Index